Popular Movements and
Secret Societies in China
1840-1950

Contributors

Lucien Bianco	Ella S. Laffey
Lilia Borokh	Charlton M. Lewis
Jean Chesneaux	John Lust
C. A. Curwen	Mark Mancall
Lev Deliusin	Boris Novikov
Guillaume Dunstheimer	Guy Puyraimond
Winston Hsieh	Roman Slawinski
Georges Jidkoff	Frederic Wakeman, Jr.

Popular Movements and Secret Societies in China 1840-1950

Edited by Jean Chesneaux

Stanford University Press, Stanford, California   1972

Stanford University Press
Stanford, California
© 1972 by the Board of Trustees of the
Leland Stanford Junior University
Printed in the United States of America
ISBN 0-8047-0790-1
LC 70-153816

Publisher's Note

The French version of this book, *Mouvements populaires et sociétés secrètes en Chine aux XIXe et XXe siècles* (Paris: Maspero, 1970), included the following papers that unfortunately could not be included in translation in this edition:

Feiling Davis, "Le Rôle économique et sociale des sociétés secrètes"
Sybille van der Sprenkel, "Les Sociétés secrètes et le droit chinois"
Vassili Iliouchetchkine, "Les Sociétés secrètes et les sectes hérétiques en Chine au milieu du XIXe siècle"
Joseph Fass, "L'Insurrection du Xiaodaohui à Shanghai (1853–1855)"
Nicolai Tchekanov, "La Plate-forme idéologique du Niandang"
W. J. F. Jenner, "Les Nian et le Laoniuhui: les rebelles et leurs adversaires dans la tradition populaire"
Wang Tianjiang, "L'Organisation et l'activité des sociétés secrètes vers 1850–1890"
Feiling Davis, "Modes de recrutement et composition sociale des Triades avant 1911"
Tadao Sakai, "Le Hongbang (Bande rouge) au XIXe et XXe siècles"

Winston Hsieh's paper on the Triads in the Waichow region was completed too late to be included in the Maspero edition and appears here for the first time in any language.

Seven of the fifteen papers in this volume were originally written in English. The rest, originally written in various languages, were translated either from the original or from the French of the Maspero edition by M. Chesneaux and his associates in Paris. Many have been substantially revised by their authors, and most have benefited from the editorial attentions of Muriel Bell and Autumn Stanley.

Philip W. J. Ho of Oregon State University Library offered indispensable assistance in editing, especially with Chinese-language problems in the text and reference matter, and prepared the index. Mr. Ho, formerly a research associate at the Far Eastern and Russian Institute, University of Washington, is working on a study of the social and political implications of Chinese secret societies.

Contents

Preface

This volume of papers is an outcome of the sessions on modern Chinese secret societies that were held in July 1965 within the framework of the Seventeenth Congress of Chinese Studies. The collection consists of papers read at the Congress and revised by the authors, together with contributions from scholars who joined the project at a later date.

Problems of the secret societies have, in addition, been discussed at my Paris seminars of 1964–65 and 1968–69 held at the Ecole des Hautes Etudes in which a number of visiting foreign scholars participated. Further discussions also took place when a session on Chinese secret societies was organized at the International Congress of Orientalists held at Ann Arbor in 1967.

The present book does not encompass all these exchanges of views, nor is it a fully rounded collective work, for it did not prove feasible to bring together all the people involved at the various stages of the discussions referred to above. (One author, having delivered his manuscript more punctually than the others, and possibly inexperienced personally in the trials of such editing work, got impatient and withdrew his manuscript in order to publish it separately; others were more civilized.) Rather it is a combination of individual pieces, and its introductory chapter is no more than a provisional attempt to review the contributions that were actually made available.

The names of the secret societies mentioned in the various chapters correspond throughout to the Wade-Giles system of transliteration and are translated only at the point of original mention in each chapter. However, an exception was made for a number of very common terms—Boxers, White Lotus, Triads, Black Flags, and some others—which are used in place of their Chinese equivalents—I-ho T'uan, Pai-lien Chiao, San-ho Hui, Hei-ch'i Chün, etc. All these names are listed in Glossary 1, together with the Chinese characters and their tentative translations. This list of some 250 names presents an interesting picture of the cultural horizon of the secret societies in terms of colors, animals, moral values, etc.

In Glossary 2 are listed those persons mentioned in either edition of the volume whose activities have been directly linked to the secret societies, with Chinese characters for their names. In fact, this glossary forms a modest embryonic *Who's Who* of these "non-eminent Chinese of the Ch'ing period." Glossary 3 is a collection of various terms related to the life of the secret societies: slogans, titles, ranks, customs. The Chinese characters for these terms are also given. The characters for other Chinese names and terms appearing throughout the volume have not been given as they are for the most part commonly known. They can be traced through the notes by those interested.

A systematic bibliography of all the books and articles on secret societies that came to our notice while working on the project is included, and a list of the Chinese and Japanese authors of those (with the characters for their names) makes up Glossary 4. The bibliography, though systematic, is not comprehensive. Most of the Japanese titles were kindly supplied by Professor M. Banno of Tokyo University, whereas many of the European and Russian ones were discovered by Mr. Sheriden Dillon during research for his M.A. degree at Columbia University. Mr. Dillon's list was combined with that prepared for the French edition of this book. No attempt has been made to separate the "sources" and the "secondary" works. These conventional categories of historical research are more and more considered to be irrelevant: even a "source" is the implicit reflection of a definite viewpoint influenced by time, culture, generation, and class. In this sense, no historical material is really "primary." Moreover, such a distinction is especially doubtful with regard to the Chinese secret societies, for many accounts that are formally of the character of secondary works are at the same time firsthand testimonies.

Chinese and Western sources mentioned in the notes but not specifically related to the secret societies (annals, press reports, etc.) have not been included in the bibliography, nor have characters been given for such material.

In Glossaries 1 and 3 an attempt has been made not only to present the Chinese characters for the names of the secret societies mentioned by the various contributors and the terms they cite but also to suggest tentative translations of these names and terms. There are, of course, a number of risks involved in approximation and the possibility of some errors. For each customary term—to say nothing of formulae that could be described as anti-establishment—carries with it a whole range of allusions, echoes, and ambiguous associations.

These effects of *connivence* (to use the apt term coined by the French school of political lexicology) are far too rich and complex to be conveyed in a so-called "translation." This is something that has been played down by those prophets of the technological revolution in the social sciences when they prepare their computer programs for an "automatic" translation. Transferring any such system of allusions, of *connivence*, from one language into another with its own set of allusions and connotations is always fraught with perils and runs the risk of mutilating the original context. This is especially the case when the socio-linguistic system under consideration belongs to the "little tradition" (R. Redfield's term), the tradition of the dissenting and persecuted groups of society. Thus today the language of the Black Panthers is far more difficult to convey in French translation than the language of Harvard. And the same is true of the language of the Chinese secret societies.

A further linguistic consideration, more technical, arises from the common use of homophones in Chinese. The secret societies were able to play on this feature: *hung* could refer to the first Ming emperor, to the color red, or to the ideas of utopian abundance. The adherents of the Hung Pang probably did not list or even separate these various notions.

Synonyms or partial synonyms were also sometimes used to stand for each other in a way that makes literal translations useless and useful translations unlikely. The term *hai-pi* is a good example. Literally (and nonsensically) translated, it means "ocean hide" (*peau de la mer*). But the ocean is a symbol of expansiveness and *pi* in its meaning of "hide" or "skin" is synonymous with *ko*. *Ko*, however, in turn can mean "reform" or "revolution," especially when used with *ming*. If *pi* were taken to refer to *ko* in this latter sense, *hai-pi* enabled those who used it to talk of "universal revolution" without seeming to do so.

Thanks are due to all those who contributed to the gradual realization of this project: Mrs. Feiling Davis, Messrs. Curwen, Lust, Cartier, Chang Fu-jui, and Ruhlmann, and, above all, my research assistant Annie Nguyen Nguyet-Ho. Fresh assistance came when it was necessary to translate into English those articles not originally written in that language. Without the help of American scholars visiting Paris, notably Jef Kaplow, Christine White, Don Layman, Richard Bernstein, Steve Headley, and Sheriden Dillon, this English version would not have been ready for publication.

It goes without saying that the present collection of research papers by no means represents the final word on Chinese secret societies. To some, the contributions may not correspond to conventional notions of scholarship, for the very reason that conventional standards in this field are based on the study and use of gentry material, on gentry history, on gentry concern for technicalities. We decided, however, to explore the "other side of the river."

J.C.

Popular Movements and
Secret Societies in China
1840-1950

Secret Societies in China's Historical Evolution

JEAN CHESNEAUX

*The "mirror of history" and its other side—The idea of a secret society—*Chiao-men *and* hui-t'ang—*The secret societies and the great rebellions of the nineteenth century—The expansion of the secret societies in 1860–90—The Black Flags and the Boxers— Secret societies and the Republican revolution—The contemporary evolution of the secret societies' social base—Relationships with the Communist Party and the Kuomintang—The Sino-Japanese War and the Communists' accession to power—The secret societies in Chinese history—The legacy of the secret societies*

For over a decade now, historians have been turning away from the respectable company of the establishment—bishops and merchants, bureaucrats and aristocrats—in favor of the study of popular movements, their struggle for power, and their uncertain dreams. Among recent explorations of this "second side" of history we have had books devoted to peasant struggles during the Fronde, to messianic religions among colonial peoples, to the extremist sects of the Middle Ages, to the English Levellers, to the Luddites and other "primitive rebels" of the beginning of the industrial era, and to modern Brazilian millenarian movements.[1]

In China, this inversion of perspective is particularly important. As Etienne Balazs has observed, classical Chinese history, on which the works of Western sinologists depended until very recently, was the history "of mandarins, written by mandarins, for a public of mandarins." In the classical Chinese language, a historical treatise is a mirror (*chien*) wherein the ruling class views itself; we have the same image in the medieval Latin *speculum*. It is time now to look from the other side of the mirror. The study of secret societies and the uncultivated and despised commoners who formed and joined them will, we hope, contribute to a history of China that goes beyond the narrow history of the "elite" (still a favorite category of a certain historical-sociological school, particularly in the United States). Ella Laffey's paper in this volume shows to what point the limits of human misery could be stretched in South China in the mid-nineteenth century. Millions of men knew that misery, and their story is every bit as important to modern Chinese history as the pomp and rituals of Li Hung-chang and Wong T'ung-ho.

A particularly rewarding term to focus on in our reversal of social perspective is *fei*, "bandit," whose etymology is instructive: it derives from a negative particle of classical Chinese. *Fei* were people whose social existence the literati, the cultivated, quite simply denied. Since they were beyond the reach of society's norms, they should and must be destroyed. But destroying them was not always possible, and they were accordingly given the negative label *fei*, whether *chiao-fei* (religiously inspired bandits), *hui-fei* (secret society bandits), *fu-fei* (turbaned bandits), *ko-fei* (bandits with lances), *hung-fei* ("red bandits"), *Hung-fei* (Ming restorationist bandits), *ni-fei* ("righteous bandits" or "rebels"), *t'u-fei* (local bandits), *hsiao-fei* ("night-bird bandits," i.e. salt smugglers), or *yen-fei* (opium bandits, or, with a different *yen*, salt bandits). Chinese and Western historians long considered these men unworthy of anything more than a disdainful mention.[2]

Chinese secret societies were an essential component of the "antisociety" evoked by these terms. Throughout Chinese history they constituted an opposition force whose dissent was better organized, more coherent, and better sustained than that of the bandits, the vagabonds, and the dissident literati, with all of whom they had close links. In this volume we are concerned with their role in the historical evolution of modern China, from shortly before the Opium Wars until shortly after the Liberation of 1949.

The origins of the secret societies go back far beyond the Opium Wars: to the end of the Ming for the Triad Society, and all the way back to the Sung for the Pai-lien Chiao (White Lotus Sect), if not indeed to the struggles of Liu Pang and his sworn brothers against the authoritarian Ch'in dynasty in the third century B.C., or to the Yellow Turbans at the end of the Han.[3] Secret societies played a large role in the overthrow of the Mongol dynasty in the fourteenth century and in the fall of the Ming in the seventeenth. They remained active under the Manchu dynasty, particularly in the late eighteenth century and the early nineteenth. During the century that followed the Opium Wars, their form, ideology, general activity, and social base followed the old, familiar pattern, the same essentially Chinese tradition. To study them only from the Opium Wars on, then, is to emphasize historical environment more than inner history.

The Ko-lao Hui (Elder Brothers Society) of Honan and Szechwan beginning in the 1880's, the Hung Hu-tzu (Red Beards) of Manchuria, the Boxers of Shantung, the Hung-ch'iang Hui (Red Spears) of Honan in 1925, were like the secret societies of classical China in all essential ways but one: they lived in a China threatened by the appetites of the Great Powers and racked domestically by new social and political forces, a China that had entered the modern era through a whole series of violent crises, political and ideological, social and economic. Our object in this book is to examine the role of secret societies in these crises, in the great rebellions following the Opium Wars, the break-up of the late nineteenth century and the quasi-cancerous growth of urban centers like Shanghai, the Revolution of 1911, the agrarian crisis of the 1920's and 1930's and the Communist-Kuomintang conflict of those years, the Sino-Japanese War of 1937–45. In short, if we may borrow a term from the new math, the history of secret societies in the nineteenth and twentieth centuries is here considered not as a subset of the history of secret societies since antiquity, but as a subset of the general history of China during the nineteenth century.

What exactly is meant by the term secret society? It does not apply to all groups forced into clandestine activities, for example to such clandestine political parties as the T'ung-meng Hui in 1905–10 and the Chinese Communist Party in the 1920's. Rather, it designates associations whose policies are characterized by a particular kind of religious, political, and social dissent from the established order. Applied to such organizations as the White Lotus Sect and the Triad Society, the term may seem artificial, imposed from outside on the Chinese reality. And indeed such present-day terms for secret society as *mi-mi hsieh-hui* and *mi-mi she-hui* are neologisms, literal translations of the Western term "secret society" used from the mid-nineteenth century on by such men as Schlegel, Gützlaff, and Wylie[4] in describing these Chinese groups as analogous to the Freemasons, the Carbonari, Sainte-Vehme, and the like. The Chinese language at that time had no accepted term for secret society. The modern term *pi-mi she-hui* was apparently introduced by the Japanese. Of two authors writing in the same period about the cooperation between the Republicans and the secret societies around 1910, the Japanese, Hirayama Amane, spoke of *pi-mi she-hui*, whereas the Chinese, T'ao Ch'eng-chang, retained the traditional distinction between *chiao-men* and *hui-t'ang*.

Some Chinese authors still rely on this distinction, among them T'ao Ch'eng-chang, Hsiao I-shan, and Wang T'ien-chiang. They see the *chiao-men* ("sects") as more concerned with religion or superstition and more closely associated with the poor peasantry, the *hui-t'ang* ("lodges") as more politicized and (some suggest) more closely associated with *déclassé* rural and urban elements.* The sects they see as characteristic of North China, the lodges as characteristic of South China, including the Yangtze basin. This traditional distinction has its uses if it is not applied too rigidly, for example to such intermediary cases as the Hung-ch'iang Hui and the Hung Hu-tzu in the north. At bottom, however, the sects and the lodges are variant forms of a single well-defined sociological category: organizations whose relation to the old regime was one of total hostility. The Ch'ing code was equally severe on the *chiao-men* and the *hui-t'ang*.[5]

There are various kinds of materials for the study of secret societies. As might be expected, internal documents are rare; for example, we have almost nothing on the Nien. Two of our contributors, Boris Novikov and Ella Laffey, have nevertheless drawn on direct documentation in studying, respectively, the ideology of the Triad Society and the youth of Liu Yung-fu. More often, however, our materials come from the other camp, that of the mandarin authorities; and papers like Frederic Wakeman's make valuable use of such materials. Still other documents come from foreigners residing in China, notably missionaries. In the nineteenth century, Catholic and Protestant missionaries alike regarded the heterodox world of the secret societies as more receptive to evangelization than the orthodox Confucian world.[6] Missionary journals like the *Chinese Recorder* are full of articles on secret societies.

That the documentation is rare, or (more accurately) scattered, is not, however, the chief reason for the lack of research on Chinese secret societies by Western sinologists. That reason lies rather in their overriding concern with the Confucian establishment, of which they were in a sense unconscious heirs as a result of the mandarin image imposed on China by the Jesuits. This lack of interest in the secret societies has been reinforced by the reluctance of the Chinese themselves to explore the subject. Thus Mao Tse-tung's appeal to the Ko-lao Hui is not included in the official collection of his works published in Peking, and Chiang Kai-shek's membership in the Ch'ing Pang (Green Gang) is a taboo subject on Taiwan.

In 1840 secret societies were active throughout much of China. Their seditious activity was a leading factor in the deepening dynas-

---

* The classical term is *hui-t'ang*, in which *t'ang* designates the lodge, the basic cell of certain of these societies. Starting early in the twentieth century, there was a tendency to substitute the term *hui-tang*, in which *tang* is the modern term for political party, derived from the traditional term for court clique.

tic crisis of the time, which expressed itself in such things as the bad condition of China's canals and dikes and the extreme negligence of administrators at all levels. According to a contemporary observer, Alexander Wylie, secret societies were the only possible form of opposition to China's authoritarian regime, the only political recourse for persons opposed to the empire's policies.[7] Since the late eighteenth century, secret societies had organized frequent revolts: the White Lotus Sect in 1796 in the north; the T'ien-li Chiao (Sect of the Celestial Order) in 1813, an uprising that almost succeeded in capturing the Imperial Palace in Peking; the Triad Society in Kwangsi in 1820, 1832, and 1836, and on Taiwan in 1826 and 1832.

It is generally agreed that in the mid-nineteenth century China's secret societies were organized in two large systems.[8] The northern or White Lotus system included the Pa-kua Chiao (Eight Trigrams Sect), the T'ien-li Chiao, the Tsai-li Chiao (Observance Sect), the Chai Chiao (Abstinence Sect), and the I-ho Ch'üan (Fists of Harmony and Justice; Boxers), then of little importance. The southern or Triad system included the T'ien-ti Hui (Heaven and Earth Society), the San-ho Hui (Triad Society; literally Three Harmonies Society), and the San-tien Hui (Three Dots Society),* and also the Ch'ing Pang (Ch'ing Band, later called the Green Gang), the Hung Pang (Hung Band, later called the Red Gang),† and the *chiang-hu hui* (associations of river and lake pirates), the predecessors of the Ko-lao Hui. Though very different from each other and only loosely related in any formal way, these various groups shared a common set of traditions and a common ideological predisposition.

This complex of tradition and ideology was at the same time religious, political, and social.[9] Secret societies were strongly impregnated with a Taoist sense of individual salvation, or rejecting the conventions of society; among other things, they observed (*tsai-li*) certain rules of sexual and alimentary abstinence. Nourished by Buddhist millenarianism, they awaited the coming of Maitreya and the new cosmic era (*kalpa*).[10] Politically they represented a kind of ethno-

---

* Some writers maintain that T'ien-ti Hui, San-ho Hui, and San-tien Hui are merely different names for the same society; others see them as standing for three distinct societies. (See Wakeman's paper below, p. 31.) In fact, it is plausible that the relations between the three terms should have remained vague, among other things as a protection against the police. The confusion on this point can perhaps be seen as an indication of the intrinsically decentralized character of the Triad lodges.

† Some secret societies were given to writing their name with different characters having the same pronunciation: thus the proper names Ch'ing and Hung became *ch'ing* (green) and *hung* (red).

centric proto-nationalism dating back to the Yüan, if not to the Sung, and vigorously expressed since the eighteenth century by the slogan *fan-Ch'ing fu-Ming* ("Overthrow the Ch'ing and restore the Ming").[11] Their social aspirations were manifested in the mutual-aid character of their organization, their lively sense of group solidarity, and their utopian egalitarianism. Inspired by the novel *Shui-hu chuan* (Water Margin), with its idealized "justice-bearing brigands" (*jen-hsia*), they called for "striking the rich and aiding the poor" (*ta-fu chi-p'in*). In the 1850's German Lutheran missionaries in China, shaken by the revolutionary wave of 1848 in Europe, went so far as to espy in this egalitarianism a dangerous ramification of the "international Communist conspiracy."[12]

Because of these characteristics, secret societies found themselves completely outside the legal order. The Ch'ing authorities repressed their activities with great severity; they were condemned as immoral (*yin*), perverse (*yao*), and heterodox (*hsieh*). What the state found most intolerable was that these rebel groups were not founded on the acceptance of the natural condition of man, as were the family, the clan, the village, and the guild, but on voluntary initiative and individual choice. They were in effect surrogate kinship groups, offering their outcast and rebellious members the services commonly furnished to the orthodox by their kinsmen.

The great popular rebellions that shook China in the mid-nineteenth century—notably those of the Taiping, the Muslims, the Miao, and the Nien—should be distinguished from the secret societies, except perhaps for the Nien, which are an intermediate case. But both were drawn from the same social classes, responded to the same pressures, and flourished in the same context of dynastic crisis.[13] Both consisted largely of poor peasants and rural outcasts; both took their inspiration from the same tradition. Indeed, the theme of "Great Peace" (*t'ai-p'ing*) invoked by the "long-haired rebels" of 1850 had been invoked seventeen centuries earlier by the Yellow Turbans at the end of the Han.[14]

Far from being swallowed up by the better-structured and more widespread popular rebellions, the secret societies actually intensified their activities, as we learn from the paper by V. Iliushechkin in the French edition of this volume. Indeed, Iliushechkin concludes that the forces mobilized by the secret societies during the period of the great rebellions surpassed in number those directly mobilized by the rebels. In Kwangtung in 1850, for example, it was officially reported that all the military and the yamen runners were members of the Triad Society. Attacks by secret society bands on merchant convoys were frequent, and government buildings in hsien capitals were raided. Afraid to arouse the anger of the *hui-t'ang*, the authorities did not dare try arrested persons in accordance with the articles of the Ch'ing code relating to secret societies, preferring the less severe charge of simple thievery.[15]

The revolt of the Red Turbans in Canton in 1851 and that of the Hsiao-tao Hui (Small Knives) in Shanghai in 1853[16] illustrate the positive reaction of the southern secret societies to the initial successes of the Taiping movement. Still another expression of the dynamism of secret societies in this crisis of imperial power was the appearance of new groups, such as the Chin-ch'ien Hui (Golden Coin Society). Founded in 1858 by a village restaurant owner, a boxer, and a blacksmith, all of them right out of the *Shui-hu chuan*, and rapidly swelled by malcontents of various sorts, this society ended by merging with the Taiping when they entered Chekiang.[17] This is not an isolated case; the Nien, among others, greatly profited from their military collaboration with the Taiping. There were instances of ideological contamination as well, among them the apparent spread of the Taiping religion among the Small Knives after their victory at Shanghai.[18]

The period of the great peasant rebellions was thus at the same time a period of flourishing secret society activity. The intermediate case of the Nien shows the close relationship of the two phenomena. In many of their characteristics—notably ideology, organization, ritual, and style of predatory activity—the Nien were very like a secret society. But in their size and the sustained character of their movement they were even more like the Taiping.[19]

The last third of the nineteenth century saw a decided slackening of popular movements and peasant uprisings. After the great wave of rebellions receded, the revolutionary ferment began that would end in the fall of the empire in 1911. In that interim period the secret societies played a key role, that of a "withdrawal structure" (*structure de repli*) for the political and social forces opposed to the dynasty and the imperial system.* Indeed, far from weakening or falling

---

* Many of the survivors of the Taiping movement, or their sons, were active secret society members in the last decades of the century; a good example is the Black Flags of Kwangsi, discussed in Ella Laffey's paper in this volume. As late as 1902 a young relative of the Taipings' leader, Hung Hsiu-ch'üan, was implicated

apart, China's secret societies expanded their activities in response
to the new pressures of modernization. The paradox is only apparent: that of a modernizing Old Regime whose very modernization
gave new life to its most archaic historical forces.

To understand this phenomenon, we must examine the delicate
question of the social base of the secret societies. According to the
most recent studies, secret society membership had two components.
One was poor peasants. The other was marginal and destitute elements of the towns and villages: porters, coolies, vagabonds, peddlers, itinerant artisans, boatmen, smugglers, patent medicine sales-
men, geomancers, bone-setters, itinerant herb doctors, wandering
monks.[20] All these types were closely linked to the peasantry without themselves being engaged in agriculture; freer in their movements than peasants tied to the land, they served as liaison agents
and transmitters of rumors. Or so one imagines, for in fact, owing to
the concentration of historians on the respectable elements of society, the sociology of the Chinese underworld in the late nineteenth
century is almost unknown to us.

Clearly, however, the last third of the nineteenth century saw a
decided increase in the number of marginal and displaced persons,
and a concomitant rise in the influence of secret societies. Four main
circumstances swelled the numbers of those who were ejected from
the accepted Confucian orders (literati, peasants, workers, and merchants): the migration of peasants to areas devastated by the Taiping
Rebellion, the progress of urbanization, the spread of steamboat
transportation, and the discharging of soldiers from the armies raised
to fight the Taiping and other rebels.

The war against the Taiping left large areas of Hunan, Kiangsi,
and Chekiang underpopulated, and these areas were subsequently
occupied by peasants from neighboring regions.[21] The newcomers
were commonly the poorest class of peasants; many had been only
marginally integrated into their original villages and clans, and most
were poorly received by the remaining inhabitants of the areas to
which they migrated. Understandably, they turned to the secret societies for welcome and support.* Things were even worse for the
peasants who emigrated to such rapidly growing cities as Shanghai

---

in a Triad plot to restore the Ming dynasty in Canton. (See Ch'ai Te-keng et al.,
comps., *Hsin-hai ko-ming* (The Revolution of 1911; Shanghai, 1957), 1: 315–21.)

* This phenomenon is comparable to the rise of the Hoa Hao sect in the late
1940's in reclaimed areas of western Cochin China, where the traditional village
structures were less solid than in other regions of South Vietnam.

to become workers in China's first factories and arsenals, and above all coolies, porters, vagabonds, and day workers of all kinds. Their moral and social isolation aggravated by language difficulties, these workers sought support in *pang-hui,* mutual-aid groups linked to the secret societies.[22]

The advent of the steamboat completely transformed the conditions of coastal trade in Kwangtung, Fukien, Chekiang, and Kiangsu, and of inland shipping along the Yangtze and its tributaries, not to mention the Grand Canal, which it soon rendered obsolete. Hundreds of thousands of sailors and boatmen were thrown out of work and turned to smuggling and piracy.[23] They were joined in these pursuits by vast numbers of discharged soldiers, estimated at nearly a million, many of them without resources and hundreds of miles from home.[24] Both the unemployed boatmen and the discharged soldiers were readily recruited by secret societies.

The cumulative effect of these factors was most evident along the lower and middle Yangtze. It is no accident that this region was the stronghold of the Ko-lao Hui, by far the most influential of the big secret societies in the decades before the revolution.[25] Nor was the Ko-lao Hui, which originated in an association of river and lake pirates, the only significant new secret society formed in this period. In Chekiang, for example, we find the following new societies by the end of the century: the Chung-nan Hui (Extreme South Society), the Shuang-lung Hui (Double Dragon Society), the Fu-hu Hui (Crouching Tiger Society), the Lung-hua Hui (Dragon Flower Society), and the Pai-pu Hui (White Cloth Society).[26]

During this interim period, secret societies were not as given to dramatic action as they had been during the great rebellions of 1850–70 and as they would be again in 1905–10; but their activity, however muted, was incessant, omnipresent, and too widely dispersed to be effectively suppressed.[27] Some of their activities were seemingly trivial: in 1876, for example, members of the White Lotus Sect in Nanking and Shanghai openly defied the authorities by pasting mysterious red-paper silhouettes on walls and distributing talismans of white cloth.[28] Others were more serious: in 1891, for example, chiefs of the Tsai-li Chiao adopted princely titles and launched a large-scale military uprising that required a large force of the regular army to put it down.[29] Liu K'un-i, governor-general of the Liang Kiang (lower Yangtze), declared in 1893 that secret societies were "a hidden disease in all the provinces."[30]

With the increased foreign pressure on China in the late nineteenth century, the traditional proto-nationalism of the secret societies, which until then had taken the Manchus as the enemy, turned against the West. Its new targets were Catholic and Protestant missions and the forces of economic modernization. The Boxers, for example, were not only a traditional secret society in the religious sense, given to amulets, mediums, and the crude millenarian belief that the natural calamities of 1897–98 heralded a cosmic cataclysm, but also a fundamentally anti-foreign organization that attacked Christian missions as a symbol of the foreign penetration of rural China. The fact that several leading Boxers were former boatmen from the Grand Canal may help to account for the movement's Luddite aspects, notably its attacks on telegraph stations and railroads.[31]

Though the Boxer Rebellion is often seen as an isolated episode, or a particular "catastrophe" for China,[32] it was in fact but one episode of many. At the time of the Franco-Chinese war of 1884–85, the Triad Society organized a great strike in the Hong Kong drydocks that succeeded in barring the use of those facilities to damaged French warships.[33] The anti-French manifestos published in the same period by Liu Yung-fu's Black Flags, who were fighting the French in Tonkin, show the same streak of popular nationalism,[34] as do the anti-foreign and anti-missionary riots of 1891 in the middle Yangtze region, which were apparently the work of the Ko-lao Hui.[35] Similar proto-nationalist sentiments led the Hung Hu-tzu in Manchuria to oppose Russian penetration of that region in 1895–1900. Their Luddite attack on the Russian railroad in northern Manchuria, which anticipated the similar attacks of the Boxers, required a veritable military expedition, led by four generals, to suppress.[36]

With the Revolution of 1911, the secret societies again entered the mainstream of China's political and social evolution. Although official Republican historiography has been generally silent on their role in the revolution, recent materials—notably the memoirs of Republican veterans published in mainland China[37]—demonstrate the importance of this role. Not only did the secret societies cooperate with the Republicans in political and military matters,[38] but there was considerable social and ideological interaction as well.[39] Indeed, the secret societies and the classes they drew on for their members showed a remarkable dynamism in the years culminating in the revolution.[40]

All in all, the Ch'ing dynasty was brought down by a process more like the classical process of dynastic change than is sometimes imagined.[41] To be sure, new kinds of forces were at work, and some of them played a key role in influencing a small but important part of the population.[42] But also at work was the recurring pressure of the secret societies, with their tradition of peasant agitation, anti-Manchu proto-nationalism, and utopian egalitarianism. In 1911, as John Lust makes clear in his paper, all the dark, disquieting world of the Chinese "primitive rebels"—of the *lü-lin* (forest brigands), the *yu-min* (peasants without village or clan ties), the *t'u-fei* (rural bandits)—once again intervened in Chinese history to destroy the established power.

The fall of the dynasty in 1911 owed at least as much to the traditional form of "withdrawal of the mandate" (*ko ming*) as to the influence of modern social classes favorable to a "revolution" (*ko-ming*). The originality of the revolution, its uniqueness, comes precisely from the conjunction of these two historical forces. The same fundamental ambiguity, be it noted, is found in the political regime that grew out of the revolution: on the one hand Sun Yat-sen and the Republic, on the other hand Yüan Shih-k'ai, the warlords, and the many others for whom the revolution amounted to no more than the beginning of a new dynastic cycle founded on the same social relations, a change not in substance but in form.

With the overthrow of the Manchu dynasty, the secret societies' main political mission was accomplished. Sun Yat-sen himself celebrated this accomplishment by organizing in Nanking, at the tomb of the first Ming emperor, a political and religious ceremony designating the Republic as the heir and continuator of the *fan-Ch'ing fu-Ming* movement.[43] Henceforth, the political function of the secret societies would be taken over by other organizations: by the Chinese Communist Party, with its subsidiary groups, its trade unions, its peasant associations; by the Kuomintang, with its mass organizations.

In nonpolitical matters, however, the secret societies remained very active indeed. Not only did such leading secret societies as the Ko-lao Hui and the Green and Red Gangs go on flourishing, but new societies of the same type continued to be formed. Essentially, the secret societies of the Republican era performed one or more of three kinds of functions for their members.

The first function was social and economic. Secret societies continued to organize and represent the interests of the lower elements of society in regions where the influence of modern parties and unions had not yet been felt. Thus the coolies who worked in France during World War I founded the Chin-lan Chiao (Golden Orchid Sect), which was primarily a mutual-aid association but had religious trappings of a secret society type.[44] And it was the Green Gang that organized the carpenters' strike of 1918 in Shanghai; the strikers assembled in a Taoist temple, where they drank *ch'i-hsin chiu* (wine that unites hearts).[45] In the industrial world secret societies were soon replaced as organizers by genuine unions; in the rural world they retained this role until and even after World War II.

The second function was essentially military. China's agrarian crisis, already serious in 1911, worsened with every passing year. Rents rose, the rural artisan class found itself increasingly superfluous, more and more land was concentrated in the hands of landlords.[46] One response of these pressures was the peasant insurrection led by the bandit "White Wolf" in the northwest in 1912–14 with support from the Ko-lao Hui.[47] Another was the peasant uprising in Hupeh in 1920–22, which raised the familiar slogans of *t'ai-p'ing* and *t'ien-kuo* (a heavenly kingdom). From the rebels' headquarters on the Szechwan-Hupeh border, their chief, the self-proclaimed "Jade Emperor" (*yü-huang ta-ti*), published edicts against merchants, militarists, and missionaries; his men called themselves "supernatural soldiers" (*shen-ping*), endowed with complete invulnerability.[48] In Szechwan in 1924, the peasant adherents of the Shun-t'ien Chiao (Fidelity to Heaven Sect) and the Lien-ho T'uan (Community Group) also thought themselves immune against bullets.[49] Interest in the military capacities of the Hung-ch'iang Hui (Red Spear Society) was expressed at the highest level of the Communist movement, by the Executive Committee of the Communist International.[50] In the 1930's, secret societies continued to be intimately involved with local peasant "self-defense" movements, especially in central China and the interior.[51]

Other secret societies, notably the Green Gang, turned to crime pure and simple, in the style of the Sicilian or especially the American Mafia. This kind of activity, which had always been a component of secret society behavior, became especially prevalent in great port cities like Shanghai and Hong Kong, whose vast floating population constituted an inexhaustible source of recruits and whose concentration of wealth made them particularly attractive to organized crime.

The third function was spiritual. Unlike the Ko-lao Hui and the Green Gang, old organizations with prestigious pasts, the secret societies that emphasized spiritual or religious appeals tended to be comparatively recent in origin. Among them were the Hsien-t'ien Ta-tao (Great Way of Former Heaven), whose teachings go back to the nineteenth century; the I-kuan Tao (Way of Basic Unity), founded in 1920 or thereabouts; and the Ta-t'ung Hui (Society of the Great Harmony).[52] To relieve the growing distress of the urban middle and lower classes these sects offered esoteric explanations and predictions. Their members commonly believed that the end of the world was near, or that an imminent cosmic catastrophe would inaugurate a new cyclic era.

Such beliefs were a natural response to natural and man-made disasters seemingly beyond people's capacity to comprehend or control. Thus the famine in North China in 1920–21 seems to have led to the forming of the I-kuan Tao, and the ravages of the Sino-Japanese War after 1937 (especially in the regions of North China occupied by the Japanese Army) are known to have caused widespread pessimism and despair among the sects. Some, notably the I-kuan Tao, were driven to collaborate with the enemy; others took refuge in a strict vegetarianism. Both reactions express the same flight from the hard realities of the time.

Throughout all these vicissitudes, however, the secret societies retained a real influence among the masses. They continued to represent a potential political force even though they had ceased to have a political position. Neither the Communists nor the Kuomintang could ignore them. Indeed, the Communists, whose initial commitment to modernism and the May Fourth spirit left no room for accommodation with the secret societies, little by little changed their attitude as the peasantry came to assume greater importance in their strategy.

The name of Mao Tse-tung is directly associated with this change. As early as 1925, Mao included a course on secret societies in the curriculum of the Peasant Movement Training Institute in Canton, which he directed for the Kuomintang.[53] His 1926 analysis of China's social classes contained the first systematic attempt by a Chinese Marxist to characterize the class basis of the secret societies; emphasizing the importance of outcasts in their membership, he also made a point of their revolutionary capacities.[54] In the same period, Mao's mentor Li Ta-chao published an interesting Marxist essay on the prospects of cooperation between the Red Spears and the peasant associations.[55] It is not surprising, then, that such high-ranking Chinese Communists as Chu Teh, Ho Lung, and Liu Chih-tan were secret society members;[56] they are also very naturally associated with the party's peasant strategy. A less significant case is that of the Communist cadre Li Ch'i-han, who in 1921 joined the Green Gang in

Shanghai as a way of acquainting himself with the world of the urban worker.[57]

By the 1930's the Communists knew that the Ko-lao Hui in particular was to be taken seriously as a potential political force. In 1936, at a meeting concerned with work among the masses, P'eng Te-huai urged that the party work closely with the Ko-lao Hui and other secret societies with a view to making them active allies rather than mere passive supporters of the party's anti-Japanese position.[58] Even more spectacular was the appeal addressed in July 1936 to the Ko-lao Hui by Mao in the name of the Central Committee, in which he proposed an actual "united front" against the Japanese.[59]

The Kuomintang for its part, especially after its break with the Communists and the labor movement, was also forced to rely on the secret societies for support. Several Kuomintang leaders were directly affiliated with secret societies, whether as a result of contacts going back to the Republican revolution or from complicity in the shady finances of Shanghai.[60] The Green Gang was particularly useful to the Kuomintang in the spring of 1927, when its leaders, Tu Yüeh-sheng and Huang Chin-jung, provided indispensable support in the disarming and the subsequent bloody suppression of the workers' militia in Shanghai.[61] In the following years the Green Gang continued to serve as the Kuomintang's agent in controlling the Shanghai proletariat; many of the city's labor bosses and the leaders of its new labor unions were Green Gang members.[62] In exchange, the Kuomintang authorities tolerated the shoddy traffic in opium, firearms, prostitution, and gambling on which the society's colossal fortunes were founded.

As one manifestation of this alliance, Tu Yüeh-sheng, chief of the Green Gang and a municipal councilor of the French Concession, was honored around 1930 in the official publications of the Kuomintang as a "philanthropist" and a "statesman."[63] Clearly, more is involved here than perfunctory cooperation between a "modern" political force and a "traditional" group of doubtful character. However archaic the organization of the Green Gang may have remained, and however disreputable its activities in the eyes of the "honorable" bourgeois of the Kuomintang, those activities clearly belong to the capitalist development of Shanghai in the twentieth century. The question accordingly arises of the place occupied by Tu and similar gangsters in the class structure of the Kuomintang.

During the Sino-Japanese War, the secret societies generally kept their options open, as they had during the period of direct confrontation between the Kuomintang and the Communists. They were ready to serve either side if they were sufficiently well paid; some were even ready to support the Nanking puppets.[64] Others, however, worked with the Communist-led anti-Japanese guerrillas in occupied territory.[65] A manual written for the cadres of the Communist New Fourth Army in 1941 described the Red Spears and the Ta-tao Hui (Big Knife Society) as peasant self-defense organizations whose concern was to resist both Japanese exactions and the depredations of Chinese bandits: "Politically, they are neutral, and they are led, for the most part, by rich peasants. . . . The strongest force in these groups is a kind of superstition, and as a result their conservatism is particularly intense. . . . Do not insult their religious beliefs and superstitions, but respect their creeds and leaders."[66]

In the southwestern zones held by the Kuomintang, the secret societies were even more influential. Szechwan was a traditional bastion of the Ko-lao Hui, not only among the lower orders but among the gentry and in the business world.[67] The Ko-lao Hui continued to run various more or less legal rackets, while at the same time serving as a kind of mutual-aid society for the masses.[68] The Kuomintang's cadres in Chungking, however, remained linked for the most part to the Green Gang and other Shanghai components of the Triad Society.[69] Thus Szechwan in the early 1940's saw a tacit struggle for influence between the Ko-lao Hui, which was better established locally, and the Shanghai secret societies, whose supporters in Szechwan were more influential. According to an oral tradition reported by Han Suyin, the Kuomintang's secret service made use of the Triad Society in staging the New Fourth Army Incident of 1941, an attack on Communist troops reminiscent of the coup of April 1927.[70]

With the advent of the People's Republic began a new chapter, no doubt the last, in the modern history of Chinese secret societies. To a people's government, such associations represented not only a political threat (many being closely associated with the Kuomintang and thus potentially subversive), but a hostile social force, especially among urban fringe elements and the relatively wealthy, and a conflicting ideology. In fact, the apolitical and more or less mystical character of movements like the I-kuan Tao and the Hsien-t'ien Ta-tao was seen as a potential obstacle to the rallying of public opinion behind the new regime. That there were grounds for this view is clear from an incident of 1954, when the Hsien-t'ien Ta-tao seized the occasion of a catastrophic flood of the Yangtze to announce the imminent end of the world.[71]

Indeed, secret societies, now officially called *hui-tao-men*,[72] were frequently mentioned in the reports of General Lo Jui-ch'ing, the new regime's head of public security, where they were classed with bandits, "rural bullies," and reactionary politicians as resolute adversaries of the People's Republic. In 1956, Lo noted that their activity had been most intense in 1950–51 and 1954–55.[73] Immediately after the Liberation, the government had set out to destroy the I-kuan Tao and other sects as part of the "movement to eliminate counterrevolutionaries."[74] In 1954–55 the accelerated effort to socialize China's economy had led to a recrudescence of secret society activity and new measures of repression.[75] The traditional social and spiritual core of the secret societies (their mythology, their network of influence, their style of organization), having survived the demise of their historical and economic functions, was placed at the service of China's antisocialist forces.

The brief historical survey just presented has necessarily been based on materials of very uneven quality. Although certain important questions have been fairly well explored—the activity of secret societies at the time of the great rebellions (1850–70), their participation in the anti-foreign movements of the 1890's (notably the Boxer Rebellion), and to some extent their role in the Revolution of 1911— much remains undone. We have no monographs on particular secret societies studied over time; nothing solid on relations between secret societies and those other heterodox sects the Christian missions; no good provincial monographs, for example on secret society activities in Szechwan or Hunan;[76] and above all only fragmentary information on the functioning of secret societies after 1911. In particular, we know all too little about their relations with the Communist Party and the Kuomintang.

Despite these lacunae, the papers in this volume seem to warrant a number of generalizations. One is that the secret societies throughout modern history have been forces of opposition. Their popular religious beliefs were opposed to the orthodox beliefs, their political efforts directed against a dynasty, their "social banditry" at the expense of the rich, their economic activities carried out in defiance of the state.

Since the studies in this volume tend not to dwell on the secret societies' economic activities as such, it may be helpful to summarize them briefly. Secret societies commonly organized the recruitment of coolies and other manual laborers. They managed a contraband trade in salt and other commodities in competition with the state monopolies, a trade that in some commodities at some times handled as much as half the total volume of exchange. Their piracy and brigandage were profit-making operations, even though part of the booty was commonly distributed to the members. They controlled public markets. They sold their "protection" to travelers, stores, opium dens, and bordellos. They had close relations with pawnshops. In the large, these activities can be seen as exhibiting a tendency toward the primitive accumulation of capital on the part of a class of petty bourgeoisie whose ascension and activity the official system restrained.

According to Feiling Davis, "The history of the secret societies is the history of the formation of the illegal petty bourgeoisie."[77] This statement is largely borne out by Tadao Sakai's study of the Hung Pang in the French edition of this volume. Sakai, who directed Japanese relations with the secret societies in Shanghai during World War II, shows convincingly that many of Shanghai's *lung-t'ou* (dragon heads) had a background in petty commerce. Yet no matter how badly oppressed the secret societies were and how strong their hostility to the established order, they always remained within that order. The *yin* of the underground forces represented by the secret societies opposed the Confucian *yang*, but was at the same time attached to it by bonds of mutual interdependence. In the last analysis, as Wakeman notes in his paper, secret societies were limited to fraternal action within the Confucian world.

Their integration into the old society is apparent, for example, in their local character; in Ella Laffey's words, "They belong to local history." Their emphasis on local ties had several consequences worth noting. One was the tendency toward fratricidal struggles noted by Iliushechkin in the case of the southern societies around 1850. Another was a tendency to be ephemeral, to die out when certain local problems had been solved or become less troublesome and to spring up again when new problems arose. Thus a large number of new secret societies appeared after 1840. The mobility of their organization and of their suborganizations was a consequence of this fragmentation; it was also good protection against the police.

Secret societies also belonged to old China by their ideology. Like peasant movements in other preindustrial societies, they idealized the past, dreaming of the Ming as a bygone golden age just as Russian peasants dreamed of the False Dmitri, Vietnamese peasants of the

fallen Lê dynasty, and Scottish peasants of Bonnie Prince Charlie.
Though the subculture of the secret societies was distinct from the
culture of the ruling classes, it was just as surely founded on tradition. Theirs was Redfield's "little tradition," with its egalitarian
themes and esoteric religious practices, its folklore grown out of the
memory of peasant uprisings of old, its debt to great popular novels
like the *Shui-hu chuan.*

It was a tradition of great age, but by no means closed or rigid.
The study of its internal evolution after the middle of the nineteenth
century, a subject that has only been touched on in this volume,
would no doubt reveal that secret societies had shown themselves
remarkably adept at drawing lessons from the present, the very movement of history, and integrating their experience with their traditional vision of the world. Just as the memory of the Nien has become an integral part of Anhwei peasant folklore down to the present day, so did the natural and political catastrophes of 1920–50 (including the atomic bomb) find their way permanently into the escha-
tology of "archaizing" sects like the Ta-t'ung Hui, the Hsien-t'ien
Ta-tao, and the I-kuan Tao.

The class character of the secret societies is a complex subject. Mrs.
Davis's insistence on their ties with the illegal petty bourgeoisie is
echoed by the perspicacious mandarin who wrote the essay on the
Chin-ch'ien Hui cited earlier: "More and more vagabonds joined up,
but among those who joined were also people who possessed great
fortunes but were at odds with the established powers."[78] As the papers in this volume make clear, however, secret societies found their
greatest support among poor peasants, the urban proto-proletariat,
and rural and urban fringe elements. The close connection between
secret societies and the oppressed is evident in the slogan-refrain
adopted by the Triads in South China around 1840:

> The people up high owe us money.
> The middle class must wake up.
> The people down below, may they come with us.
> That is better than renting an ox to farm bad soil.[79]

The same sense of class is expressed in the songs by which the peasants of Anhwei still perpetuate the memory of the Nien. According
to W. J. F. Jenner, who has studied the popular songs about the
Nien recently collected by the researchers of the Academy of Sciences
in Peking, they show the Nien uprising unambiguously as a war of
the poor against the rich:[80]

> As the moon goes around the sun,
> The poor rebel with the Nien.
> Poor turn to poor, and rich to rich,
> As clearly different as black and white.[81]

> Shining red rises the sun;
> Lao-le is a fine banner-leader.
> The poor men's hearts are happy to see him,
> And the moneybags' bones go soft with terror.[82]

The Nien not only exalted the cause of the poor, but discriminated among different classes of the rich according to their wealth. Jenner justly compares the verse that follows to a passage in Mao Tse-tung's *Report on the Peasant Movement in Hunan*, which describes the richest landlords as fleeing farthest and taking greatest fright at the activities of the peasant associations. In northwest Anhwei, the region of the Nien movement, the big rural landlords fled to the cities while the lesser landlords took refuge in nearby towns:

> Thousand-*ch'ing* bastards flee to Shouchou,
> Hundred-*ch'ing* turtle's eggs stay in Suchou.
> Stinkers with thirty to fifty *ch'ing*
> Hide in the hsien capital and organize militia.
> But the paupers have overrun the whole land;
> As time goes by we'll see that you can do nothing.[83]

The class character of secret societies is thus revealed both inside and outside the "historical bloc" — to apply to China a concept evolved by the Italian thinker A. Gramsci—of imperial China. The societies supported and led the struggles of the poor peasantry, the proto-proletariat (notably transportation workers), and other have-nots against the well-off and their political representatives. But they were also the instrument of economic forces opposed to the state monopolies, of entrepreneurs who sought to break away from the stifling controls placed by the state on economic activity. In this sense China's secret societies embodied the two main lines of class struggle that we find in France in 1789 and most other preindustrial societies: the struggle of the bourgeoisie to free itself of feudal economic restraints, and the struggle of the peasants against their feudal masters. Yet China never had its 1789. And thus we are reminded once again of a fundamental historical problem, the difference between Chinese bureaucratic feudalism and feudalism in the Western sense.

The failure of China's secret societies to bring about a 1789 is not hard to explain: clearly, they were as much havens for alienated or rebellious individuals as instruments of class struggle. Many of their activities were real by any standard; they did in fact strike significant blows at the established order. But as many more were artificial, depending on spiritual mumbo-jumbo, private language, fancy titles, and the like. When they served as the corporate embodiment of individual desires for insurrection or escape, secret societies were capable of extraordinary offensive and defensive efforts. But at the same time they tended to be quickly satisfied with their minor successes; finding in themselves all the answers they sought, they had no ultimate interest in the class struggle as such.

This fundamental duality between the claims of individual rebelliousness and the imperatives of class struggle is in a sense the essence of the secret society. Secret societies had a strong claim to the allegiance of the deprived, but exercised it only sporadically. In a crisis they drew the disaffected like a magnet; but when the crisis was over, for example in the 1870's, they melted away. A leader of the White Lotus Sect made this same point after being captured by imperial forces during the Nien rebellion: "In times of peace, we preach that in reciting the Buddhist sutras and magic formulas, one can become invulnerable to swords and firearms, escape water and fire ... but when there follows a period of chaos and rebellions, we form more ambitious projects."[84]

Because of this discontinuous character, it is hard to distinguish strictly between secret societies proper and more primitive forms of insurrection like banditry and local peasant uprisings. Bandits, vagabonds, discontented peasants—all these forces of opposition were ready to make common cause with secret societies in certain circumstances, only to break away later on. Formations like the Nien, the Hung Hu-tzu, and the Black Flags were at one and the same time secret societies and mass movements.

Capable as secret societies were of mobilizing masses, they were always careful to preserve their own minority organization. One is reminded of the peasant rebels in Mérimée's play *La Jacquerie*. Calling themselves "wolves of the forest," they not only fight the "dogs" (the soldiers of the lord) but on occasion shear the "sheep," docile peasants who refuse to join them and whom they despise.

To what extent were secret societies major instruments, at least in the twentieth century, of the historical evolution of China? Their activities until 1911 were along traditional lines. In 1911 they helped put an end to the dynastic cycle, as the Yellow Turbans had done at the end of the Han, Fang La at the end of the Sung, and the White Lotus rebels at the end of the Yüan. But in 1911 they found themselves in a winning camp directed by a modern political movement foreign to the old China of the secret societies—in the Republican camp, the camp of the T'ung-meng Hui. They helped the Republicans to mobilize the masses, but they remained a "balancing force," at once vigorously opposed to the state and bound to it by many ties and compromises. After 1911 they ceased to serve as a vehicle of political opposition—a function henceforth taken over by modern political parties, labor unions, and peasant associations—and either turned to gangster activities or took refuge in apolitical religious alienation. The change was nowhere instantaneous; and it was generally slower in the countryside, as witness the influence of the Ko-lao Hui among China's poor peasants until around 1940.

What, in the end, is the historical legacy of China's secret societies? For one thing, their traditions of utopian egalitarianism and insurrection have remained popular and prestigious; Mao rendered them implicit homage in his famous letter of 1936 to the Ko-lao Hui. For another, it was the secret societies that for many centuries schooled the Chinese people in the rules and requirements of clandestine political action. Not only were the T'ung-meng Hui and above all the Chung-hua Ko-ming-tang, a revolutionary party headed by Sun Yat-sen in 1914–19, patterned directly on the secret societies, but Marshal Chu Teh in his autobiography equates the cells of the Chinese Communist Party with the lodges of the Ko-lao Hui or the Triads.[85]

Finally, one wonders if it is only by chance that a country in which the Communist Party has so insistently stressed the revolutionary value of protracted armed struggle is also a country in which for many centuries, and down to the present day, political opposition has customarily taken the form of armed revolts led by secret societies and the popular forces that responded to their appeal.

Some Religious Aspects of Secret Societies

GUILLAUME DUNSTHEIMER

Popular character of the religion of the secret societies—
Buddhist and Manichaean elements—The third kalpa*—The*
Eternal Mother—The aspiration to salvation

The groups known in the West as secret societies[1] were classified by
the literati of imperial China as *hsieh-chiao* (perverse, aberrant, or
heterodox sects), *yin-chiao* (depraved sects), *mo-chiao* (demoniac
sects), *fei-chiao* (rebel sects), *yao-chiao* (witchcraft sects), etc.[2] Worth
noting is the fact that each of these Chinese terms contains an allusion to the religious character of the secret societies, a character
discernible in all these groups whether one speaks of the *chiao-men,*
religious sects in the strict sense that propagated a special religious
doctrine, or the *hui-t'ang,* seditious associations or bands in which the
religious elements were restricted to the rites of initiation, to the
sacred area called Mu-yang Ch'eng (City of Willows), to the oaths of
fidelity made by invoking the gods, and to other parareligious acts.

The *hsieh-chiao* were drawn in the main from the popular religions of the enormous mass of the Chinese lower classes. These religions combined the transports of shamanistic ecstasy with elements
drawn from the major religious doctrines and applied the resulting
amalgam, especially in times of political, economic, or social crisis,
to the redress of exploitation by officials or gentry. Such religious
groups were obviously outside the control of the state, given the immense size of the Chinese empire, the difficulty of communications,
and the limited number of agents responsible to the government's
authority.[3] The result was concentrations of forces directed in effect
against the established order. Persecution of the sects by authorities
of the Chinese government derived, consequently, not from religious
intolerance as some have supposed, but from a real fear of subversion
and a concern for preserving the imperial regime intact.[4] This is
also the reason why the documents elaborated by the literati hardly
ever speak of the specifically religious elements of the sects. A work

like the important contemporary study of Huang Yü-pien is an exception.[5] Nevertheless, even in this work, the sixty-eight citations of
heretical texts dating from the late Ming period are presented less
from a desire to furnish an exact idea of the religious doctrines of the
secret societies than from an attempt to refute them by rationalistic
and moralistic reflections and to menace their adherents with the
severe punishments dictated by the laws of the Manchu empire.

The subversive tendencies of the secret societies, whether *chiao-
men* or *hui-t'ang*, were a continual threat to the central authorities.
The societies, especially in troubled times, proposed to establish a
new dynasty that would be more just than the reigning one, or to
re-install, with the support of a corps of honest officials, a dynasty
(Sung or Ming) driven from the throne by foreign forces (Mongol or
Manchu). The theocratic and very ancient idea of the "Mandate of
Heaven" (*t'ien-ming*), a theme fundamental to state Confucianism,
is also found at the core of almost every large-scale peasant uprising
(*ch'i-i*). Whatever importance Buddhist or Taoist ideas may have
had in these peasant uprisings, for the people Heaven was always the
supreme Master of the world. In fighting against the established
order, they always referred to Heaven, which gives and withdraws
the Mandate and which, according to Mencius, speaks through the
people.

The only exception to this rule was the Taiping Rebellion, the
only heretical movement that was strictly anti-Confucian. For the
Taipings, *t'ien-ming* did not signify the "Mandate of Heaven," but
a particular order given by God the Father in a specific case to his
personal representative on earth, Hung Hsiu-ch'üan, divinely or-
dained as "Celestial King" (*t'ien-wang*). The Confucian notion of
t'ien-ming, on the other hand, never implied a commandment by a
god.[6]

In the *chiao-men*, found above all in northern China, we meet Mi-
le-fo (Maitreya, the Buddha of the future).[7] The cult of Maitreya
goes back to the origins of Buddhism in China. His appearance on
earth was expected to restore the *dharma*, the Buddhist law, among
the people. Although since the T'ang period he has been progres-
sively replaced by the general Buddhist devotion to Amitabha,[8]
Maitreya has retained down to our time an important place in the
numerous sects of the White Lotus system. The White Lotus Society
(Pai-lien Chiao) was itself the inheritor of the religion of Maitreya.

Numerous rebellions claimed Maitreya as their inspiration down
to the Yüan period, and even much later.[9] A certain Fu Ta-shih, who

lived in the time of the Emperor Wu Ti of the Liang (502–549), is considered the founder of the Maitreya Society (Mi-le Chiao). He pretended to be the reincarnation of Maitreya but was not active in any of the social disturbances of the time, so far as can be ascertained.[10]

Chi-kung, a Buddhist monk who died at the beginning of the twelfth century and who is the hero of three popular novels[11] and the patriarch of numerous sects, was himself also considered a reincarnation of Maitreya,[12] and as late as 1900 the Boxers circulated messages purporting to be from him. They had allegedly been dictated to a medium during sessions of automatic writing, a phenomenon very commonly found in the lore and practice of secret societies of all periods.[13]

In the course of the rebellions that led to the fall of the Yüan dynasty, Han Shan-t'ung, who belonged to the White Lotus Society and who was declared a direct descendant in the eighth generation of the Sung Emperor Hui-tsung (1101–1125), announced the imminent coming of Maitreya.[14] He was arrested by the authorities in 1351 and executed. Han Lin-erh, his son, was in turn proclaimed emperor and the incarnation of Maitreya.[15]

With the careers of Han Shan-t'ung and his son, a new element seems to have entered the ideology of the Maitreya sect—Manichaean doctrines as propounded by the Mani Sect (Ma-ni Chiao).[16] In the doctrine of Manichaeism, which seems to have been introduced into China in the seventh century A.D., the fundamental phenomena of Darkness and Light lead, in the course of history and in the future of the universe, through three cosmic eras to the final victory of the Light. The doctrine also promises the world that a King of Light (*ming-wang*) will appear.[17] The White Lotus Society itself preached that "when Maitreya descends on earth, the King of Light will be born," a belief that was substantiated by the Sutra of the Birth of the Major and Minor Kings of Light (*Ta-hsiao ming-wang ch'u-shih ching*). By the term King of Light was meant a kind of messiah sent by Maitreya to inaugurate a reign of justice and peace. Han Shan-t'ung and his son were called respectively the Major King of Light (*ta ming-wang*) and the Minor King of Light (*hsiao ming-wang*). And it was under the influence of this complex of ideas of Manichaean origin that Chu Yüan-chang, himself a former member of the White Lotus Society,[18] gave to his dynasty the name of Ming.

The expectation that a holy savior will descend to earth and inaugurate an era of happiness is closely linked to the idea that the duration of the universe is divided into three cosmic eras or *kalpas*. During the first era, that of the Blue Sun (*ch'ing-yang*), Janteng Buddha reigns; during the second era, that of the Red Sun (*hung-yang*), Sakyamuni Buddha reigns; and during the third era, that of the White Sun (*pai-yang*), Maitreya Buddha reigns. The latter epoch is the final one, and the appearance of Maitreya Buddha signals the final salvation, and hence the end, of the universe.

The division of the history of the world into three parts was not new to Buddhist thought. Related concepts had inspired the Sect of the Three Epochs (San-chieh Chiao) founded toward the end of the sixth century, during the Sui dynasty. This sect distinguished the period of the True Law, that of the Counterfeit Law, and that of the Last Law.[19] This division, however, is fundamentally different from the three *kalpas* of the White Lotus Society and affiliated sects, for the final period is not at all a period of millenarian happiness. The Three Moments of Manichaeism consisted of the Former Moment, the Middle Moment, and the Later Moment. In the Former Moment, the earth and the heavens do not yet exist, only the Two Principles, Darkness and Light. In the Middle Moment, Darkness invades the Light, and the Two Principles struggle. This is ended in the Later Moment by the victory of the Light.[20] As in the third *kalpa* of the White Sun, salvation is also achieved here, through the power of Light.[21]

The doctrine of the *kalpas* was given considerable elaboration in the beliefs of the secret societies.[22] The final period of the current *kalpa* and the passage to the following *kalpa* were to be attended by terrible cataclysms wherein humanity suffered endless miseries. Mankind was to be prey to the Three Plagues (*san-hsin*), and the whole earth was to be swallowed up in a cosmic typhoon—a vision of human destiny still entertained by the patriarch of a sect called the Return-to-the-Root Sect (Kuei-ken Men) in Malaysia, who interprets the "cosmic typhoon" as referring to nuclear warfare.[23] To a tormented mankind, the secret societies did, however, hold out one hope—the mercy of Maitreya: true believers alone would escape the apocalypse to enjoy the felicity of the third *kalpa*.

Another strand in the complicated web of secret society religious belief is that of the Eternal Mother (*wu-sheng lao-mu*), a figure given more prominence in some sects than in others. While accounts differ in detail, the most common description of this mysterious deity is of an asexual demiurge who becomes the progenitor of the universe through her offspring Nü Kua and Fu Hsi, the primordial couple.[24]

In some senses complementary to Maitreya in that she occurs at the beginning of the cycle of existence, the Eternal Mother is linked in certain texts to an even more enigmatic divinity, the "Old Buddha of the Celestial Reality of the Unexcellable Who Came Forth from the True Void."[25] After the appearance of the universe, the Old Buddha is believed to have stabilized Heaven and Earth.[26] One might suppose that the Old Buddha and the Eternal Mother were considered on a par, but according to this same work, she is superior to him since she "gave him the order to harvest the fruits of nirvana."[27] The influence of Taoist thinkers can be felt here. In the *Tao-te ching* there appear already the ideas of the maternal and feminine element.[28] These derive from the most ancient traditions of the Chinese people and go back to prehistory.

As embellished by the lore of the secret societies, however, the role of the Eternal Mother is much more than that of the "obscure female" (*hsüan nü*) of Lao Tzu. In its beginning, according to current practitioners, the world was inhabited by men who were indistinguishable from beasts and who did not know how to govern. The Eternal Mother accordingly sent the "Ninety-six Original Sons" (*yüan-tzu*)[29] to establish civilization and to exercise government over mankind. The Ninety-six Original Sons were responsible for such fundamental innovations as architecture, agriculture, writing, music, and rites. A further elaboration on this myth postulates not ninety-six, but 96 times 100,000, or 9,600,000, such "Original Sons."[30] These latter are said to have fallen from grace under the impetus of worldly desires and hence to have lost their primitive divine nature. At this juncture, the Eternal Mother seems to have commanded the great Tao to descend into the world for the purpose of aiding the 9,600,000 to return to their original spiritual paradise (*chia-hsiang*).[31] Into the world were sent a succession of delegates who, though secret incarnations of the great Tao, function as patriarchs of sects and thus prepare the way that leads to the great salvation of humanity.[32] During each of the first two *kalpas*, 200,000 are led to salvation, so that 9,200,000 still remain when the third *kalpa* is announced, which will be governed by Maitreya.[33] Such was the central view of the I-kuan Tao Society. In related traditions, the Original Sons are referred to as "Imperial Embryos" (*huang-t'ai*).[34] The Original Sons are rescued and taken to salvation by a myriad of Boats of the Law to be assembled around the Shadowless Mountain (*wu-ying shan*), that is to say the mountain that exists only in the world of transcendental reality.[35] The Boats of the Law destined to take humanity to the world of salvation are presented in a way that is, as it were, demyth-ologized. They have "neither form nor material appearance" (*wu-hsing wu-hsiang*).[36] They are in fact allegorical figures of acts of merit that open the path of redemption to the faithful, boats of mercy that lead from the sea of sorrows to the world of happiness. For members of the I-kuan Tao Society, these works of merit included the erection of altars, the financing of Society activities, and the printing of tracts, as well as the choice of wise men to lead the group. Filial piety, an exalted virtue for Confucianism, also held an impor-tant place: acts of merit accomplished by descendants were thought to be of definite benefit to the souls of deceased ancestors.[37]

The brief survey set forth above does little more than hint at the complexity of secret society beliefs, a subject that has heretofore been largely neglected. These beliefs reflect both the great imaginative power of the Chinese people and their almost unequaled capacity for synthesis. But we must not become preoccupied ourselves with the discursive content of these beliefs. Whatever that content may be at any given time, they have at all times furnished excellent instruments for interpreting social, economic, and political misery.[38]

Such beliefs have also led to the formation of political factions and, in fact, over the centuries they have effectively stimulated popular revolts against feudal society by offering the discontented masses a moral justification founded on divine will for their discontent. If religion could serve the ruling classes to confirm their privileges, the Chinese secret societies show that religion could also actuate dan-gerous elements in opposition to the established regime. During the period of dynastic rule, the secret societies, while never breaking free from the framework of traditional society, were important ele-ments in the social, political, and economic balance of power. During the last century and until their dissolution twenty years ago, the se-cret societies also occasionally transformed themselves, as did the Box-ers, into movements of national liberation and resistance against im-perialism. But the transformation was never complete; always the secret societies aspired to re-establish a hopelessly outdated state of affairs. For this reason they were finally suppressed.[39]

The Secret Societies of Kwangtung, 1800-1856

FREDERIC WAKEMAN, JR.

Origins of the Triads—"Outer membership" (pirates, criminals, hill bandits) and "inner membership" (dissatisfied peasants and clan members)—The society's loose structure; its social and ideological cohesion—The increase in Triad activities after the First Opium War—Gentry-Triad tension by 1850—The Red Turban uprising in Canton in 1854; its lack of unity and failure

The Triad Society was at first a grouping of marginal and mobile transients, of social "strangers" (*k'o*). As foreign and internal trade soared during the eighteenth century, higher degrees of commerce and urbanization violated the closed political and communal confines of southeastern China. Petty merchants traveled far up the inland river systems. Adventurers roamed the coastal entrepôts. Wherever they went, varying forms of social organization proliferated to receive and protect them: guilds, provincial and district clubs, monopoly hongs. Some of these operated in legal symbiosis with China's official elite. Others did not.

The Fukienese were among the most active in this process of internal migration. Commercially minded, ambitious, even restless, they moved from trading centers like Amoy across mountains and frontiers into neighboring provinces, there to settle and make their way among suspicious and exclusive local residents. One such group, passing over the southern border of Fukien into the prefectures of Hui-chou and Ch'ao-chou, introduced the Triads to Kwangtung.[1]

The "brotherhood" (*ti-hui*) of the Triads was originally engendered of Ming loyalists on the island of Taiwan, and from there had filtered across the Formosan straits to Fukien. Clandestine and closely knit, the secret society offered a perfect form of protection to consignment merchants, smugglers, and petty "strangers" who dared to move into areas like Kwangtung, where native clans and jealous local associations would deny them entrance. Soon—it is impossible to say exactly when—the Triads lost their specific identity as Fukienese, and native Cantonese "strangers" of a slightly different sort began themselves to turn to the brotherhoods for social refuge. The necessity for such protection was obvious: Canton, the greatest port in China, uprooted the peasants of the countryside and drew them to her. By the 1830's some 17,000 workers wove silk there. Another 50,000 manufactured brocades and cottons. Innumerable gangs of coolies collected on street corners, at market places, around the city gates, waiting to unload cargoes, haul goods, construct buildings.[2] Not all joined the secret societies. Some formed local clubs; others, perfectly respectable artisans' associations. But those who followed really marginal professions—those who were neither *nung* (peasant) nor *kung* (artisan)—looked to the Triads. There were three such groups.

First came those who engaged in foreign trade. Obviously, wealthy and respected syndics like the Fu-ch'ao junk merchants or the members of the Cohong had no need for secret societies. But the smaller figures around them—the shroff merchants, compradors, dock hands, and petty shopkeepers—did form illegal brotherhoods, some of which, strongly drawn to the West, even attracted American and Dutch seamen and styled their Chinese leaders "consuls" (*ling-shih*).[3]

The second group, yamen clerks and runners, was often associated with the Triads.[4] Perhaps the clerks, degraded since the Ming period, resented the world of the literati. In any case, they and the yamen police, by profession power-conscious and politicized, were attracted by the Triads' shadow government.

The third type of "stranger," the professional criminal, found the Triads a perfect organizational tool for gambling operations, the control of prostitution, extortion, and even the kidnapping of peasants in the "pig trade" that sent hapless Chinese to California, Latin America, and Southeast Asia.[5] Pirates, at first a distinctly separate nether group, also formed secret societies—especially when they were thrown together with urban gangsters by the illegal opium trade. Eurasians, Chinese junkmen-buccaneers, and compradors distributed the drug by water from "lairs" like Macao and Lintin, and dryland Triads carried it far inland.[6] Confucian moralists of the time were thus partly right when they condemned opium as a pernicious "moral poison." It was indeed responsible for the alarming crescendo of both criminal and secret society activity in Kwangtung after 1820. Not only were river police and yamen clerks corrupted by close contact with the traffickers, but pirate leaders, too, came to control entire stretches of the North and West rivers. Moving far upstream to Kwangsi, they helped spread Triad cells among endemic bands of hill outlaws.[7]

The extent of all this illicit activity suggests a massive criminal conspiracy, coordinated and managed by the secret societies. But there was no *capo mafioso*, no Professor Moriarty, pulling the strings. Although society members had a general term for all Triad chapters—the Hung Men (Hung League; lit., Vast Gate)—there were three separate organizational rubrics: the San-tien Hui (Three Dots Society), the San-ho Hui (Three Harmonies Society; often translated as Triads); and the T'ien-ti Hui (Heaven and Earth Society). These, in turn, were divided into local and fundamentally autocephalous chapters, united by common ritual and a vague sense of brotherhood. Pirate gangs, hill bands, brothel owners, and opium smugglers all retained their separate identities. Therefore, in spite of an exchange of information and favors, the Triads were not a vast overseeing and centralized organization, standing above individual elements and social groupings.

This mixture of unity and independence served the membership well. A Triad member far from home could count on certain small favors and a degree of protection from other members of the Hung Men (who might not even share his dialect) by positioning his teacup or fingering his lapels in certain secretly identifiable ways. But he was not on this account expected to submit to the local lodge's patriarchal discipline. Conversely, no chapter needed to fear the harsh powers or arbitrary interference of a central enforcing agency that might threaten its own autonomy. As Hsiao I-shan has pointed out, this was at once the great strength and the great weakness of the Triads. They were impossible to exterminate because there was no central trunk to be sundered. On the other hand, they found joint action difficult.[8]

Still, there was a potential for joint action if the lodges transcended "peacetime" activities by launching a revolt. At such times small individual bands joined others in ad hoc confederations for the sake of a united assault on local walled cities. The best they could hope for was a day or two of uninterrupted rapine; the worst, being driven back into sparsely settled regions. Such was the pattern in 1801, when a Fukienese named Ch'en Li-nan led his men in an attack on the capital of Hui-chou prefecture. Years of sporadic disorder followed until 1810, when vigorous defense measures taken by the gentry helped restore order.[9] There were isolated resurgences, but not until 1832 did the second great flurry of revolts occur.[10] A Yao tribal revolt along the Hunan border had drawn Kwangtung's provincial garrison away from the Pearl River delta.[11] In their absence, the San-ho Hui rose near Macao in Hsiang-shan hsien (present-day Chung-shan). Farmers were secretly taxed by the society, and entire villages incited to revolt. Once again, the gentry managed to recover their control of the area.[12]

This periodic cycle of revolt and repression seemed to quicken with the Opium War (1839–42). Or perhaps it merely became confused with the general disintegration of Kwangtung province during those years. In fact, it is almost impossible to differentiate the secret societies from other forms of disorder. They were, of course, associated with anti-British militia, which provided them with both a legitimate "cover" and firearms.[13] But did they lead the many mobs that looted Chinese yamens and foreign factories alike throughout the 1840's? Did they, in 1849, play an important role in the anti-foreign agitation of the Canton entry crisis? One simply cannot say. However, there does appear to have been a puzzling change in the nature of the secret society movement itself.

The society's outer "strangers"—pirates along the coast, criminals in the city, endemic hill bandits—continued as before. Then, suddenly, secret societies began to be reported in the wealthy rural districts of Kuang-chou prefecture.[14] This was more than an intensification of Triad activity. It was an extension of the brotherhoods into the densely settled and socially stable villages around Canton itself. Following a blatant secret society feud in Shun-te hsien in 1843, the Triads began to recruit the heretofore unresponsive peasants on a large scale. Several hundred Triads would gather in broad daylight at a crossroads. While guards were posted on all sides, the "Grass Sandal" (ts'ao-hsieh) officer—who acted as paymaster, bagman, and recruiter—would send out runners to round up candidates. Thousands might come, paying three hundred cash apiece for the privilege of joining the brotherhood. Initiations were held in large paper tents on the spot by the "Incense Master" (hsiang-chu), who was selected from among the "White Paper Fans" (pai-chih-shan), literate administrative officers of the chapter. Once initiated, the new member was encouraged with a twenty-cash commission to introduce other recruits.[15]

There was certainly an element of coercion in this form of recruitment. Entire villages sometimes enrolled just to escape the illegal levies of Triad gangs. But self-protection does not explain everything. If the Triads served only the "strangers" described above, what accounts for their success in normally integrated rural areas? What, in other words, was their function in a civil society?

Secret societies among overseas Chinese often acted as mediators between official administrators above and the Chinese community beneath.[16] In China itself, however, it was the gentry, clan elders, and village heads who were ideally supposed to link the hsien capital with the villages around it. As long as these orthodox circuits operated effectively—representing the peasant below to the government above, and vice versa—there was no need for heterodox forms of mediation. But if the circuits were shorted by topography, village nucleation, or the demise of the traditional political system, then secret societies could function in their stead. Such must have been the case during the long civil war that succeeded the fall of the Ch'ing. Aroused peasants turned to the Red Spears (Hung-ch'iang Hui), not to local notables, for protection; and local magistrates could *only* rule through groups like the Elder Brothers Society (Ko-lao Hui). It would follow, then, that during prerevolutionary times, prosperous regions like the Pearl River delta had no need for secret societies in this capacity: the gentry were ostensibly Confucian and the lineage heads sufficiently responsible. Yet Triads did exist in the very villages that these notables nominally controlled.

The most obvious recruits there were the "natural leaders," men whose physical strength or force of personality commanded respect but who lacked the ritual or social status of clan heads or local degree holders.[17] Resenting the stultifying conformity of village life or the dull prospect of peasant toil, such leaders might gather young bachelors or wastrels around them into a gang of "bare sticks." These gangs were wild-spirited but usually quite harmless unless bad times threw them together with actual rebel groups. Then they could tip the local scales toward order or disorder. It was quite clear during the Red Turban revolt (1854–56), for example, that civil order in certain areas depended on the degree of control that "fathers and elders" (*fu-lao*) exercised over their young men. Some local notables literally went from door to door exhorting peasant fathers not to let their sons join the Triads.[18]

Inculcated Confucian values like filial piety did not necessarily make the task any easier. For the major strain in the traditional Chinese family was the relationship between father and son, with the severely imposed discipline of the *yu-nien* age (four to fifteen years old) leading in puberty either to complete submission or to adolescent revolt.[19] The latter phenomenon, a rejection of the father, meant rebelling against many of the norms of village society: respect, obedience, submission to elders. Rejection of the young rebel by the village might then follow, and few could survive that sort of *déracinement* without turning to the secret societies. With its rites of passage, its rebirth into the brotherhood, the Triad Society stood ready to receive the orphan into a group of peers analogous to a kinship group.

Thus the Triads, originally developed for and by society's outsiders, could provide an alternative existence for new types of uprooted individuals, "inner strangers." In the former case, the secret societies were socially dysfunctional. In the latter, they would appear to have been functional equivalents for the communal systems that these young men refused to accept. Nevertheless, informal gangs of the more harmless variety might still have met the needs of the "bare sticks." What precisely drew them to the secret societies?

Secrecy has its own attractions, of course.[20] To that, the Triads added the romance of the *Shui-hu chuan* tradition, with its brotherhoods, its oaths, its league of free and equal men. They were able to evoke much of the glamour of that chivalric past not only by being a brotherhood, but also by becoming associated with Chinese boxing. Every chapter of the Triads had its own "Red Pole" (*hung-kun*) or enforcer, almost always a trained boxer, who led its fighting section. Skill in Chinese boxing proved most useful for warfare, extortion, and self-protection. It also incidentally gave the Triads a certain heroic aura by recalling some of the great popular figures of Chinese history. Yüeh Fei, after all, was said to have been the inventor of South China's most popular boxing style, *hsing-i*.[21]

Of course, boxing was not associated exclusively with the secret societies. Buddhist temples sometimes enrolled young adepts to give demonstrations during popular festivals, and villages even hired perfectly "orthodox" (*cheng*) boxing masters to train their young men in hand-to-hand fighting.[22] The clan elders undoubtedly realized that they were borrowing some of the secret societies' romance in doing this, but their primary motive was much more immediate. A trained body of young kinsmen would stand the clan or village in good stead in the event of boundary wars or blood feuds, which racked Kwangtung during these years.[23] Naturally, such lineage conflicts helped strengthen the elders' mastery over the clan by providing "bare sticks" with an emotional outlet, by increasing their own lineage solidarity, and possibly by acquiring more ritual land for clan use. But at the same time it abetted the very secret societies that lineage leaders and local notables feared. This happened when feuds became so intense that desperate elders decided to push the matter to an awful and bloody conclusion by enlisting the help of the Triads. In the fall of 1853, for example, a clan leader in P'an-yü hsien, twelve miles northeast of Canton, agreed to pay a local secret society chief a reward of four dollars for each enemy head collected.[24] Six months later, another secret society band of 6,000 men near Whampoa stepped between two warring clans and sold its services to the highest bidder. By the time the war was over, a thousand men had been killed.[25]

The martial arts, whether used for "righteous" property wars or for criminal extortion, recalled something else. Yüeh Fei's *hsing-i* boxing had supposedly been invented to fight the Jurced barbarians. This historic resistance to foreign invasion tallied nicely with the Triads' own anti-Manchu slogan, *fan-Ch'ing fu-Ming* ("Overthrow the Ch'ing and restore the Ming"). But Ming restorationism was more than a heroic echo of the past. It gave the Triads political relevance, even providing a form of social respectability that put them a cut above gangsterism. After all, one of the signs of gentry status in Ch'ing China was political activity. Where access to the bureaucratic world was the highest guarantee of local prestige, a pretense of political rebellion made the veriest hooliganism respectable. A peasant boy who audaciously discussed overthrowing the dynasty could thrill at his own grandiloquence.

Thus the raising of a Ming banner provided its own illegitimate "legitimacy." "Local bandits" (*t'u-fei*) would thereupon be regarded as genuine "rebels" (*ni-fei*), a classification that could call down on them a garrison of banner troops and perhaps an Imperial Commissioner or two. Proscribed and hunted, they might even find themselves the object of an all-out suppression campaign. But other societies, attracted by the rebels' political presumptuousness, might swell their ranks and make a large-scale revolt genuinely possible. This, in turn, afforded a promise almost beyond belief. If the political universe stood ready for a change, if the omens were right, the mandate was there for the taking. Peasant boys had become emperors before: why not again?

In its own way, this social myth was as potent as the struggling scholar's examination dream. Instead of inspiring individual cultivation, though, it called for mass action. Moreover, it was implausible when times were good. Bandits could incite disorder, but they could not believe successful rebellion possible unless other large tremors shook the Chinese world order.

Perhaps the Opium War seemed to be such a tremor. In any case, the Triads were inspired in 1844 to enter the hsien capital of Hsiang-shan, demanding money at sword point along the main streets. An indignant magistrate home on mourning leave immediately obtained a warrant from the Governor-General and enrolled the gentry in a mutual defense league that had the right to execute suspects at its own discretion. Defeated, the rebels withdrew.[26] Unfortunately, the provincial authorities, afraid that reports to Peking of such openly rebellious activity would reflect badly on their administration, officially decided to ignore the matter, and banned all references to "secret-society bandits" (hui-fei).* Local magistrates, therefore, could not call for troops from Canton, but had to rely on informal methods of control. Notables or lineage heads were quietly ordered to hand over obstreperous Triad leaders. If they failed to comply, their ancestral tablets were seized and held in the local yamen. But it was difficult for village leaders to challenge the secret societies on their own; the best they could do was to temporize by keeping the brotherhoods quiet, which meant paying their illegal levies. The Triads, in turn, grew bolder. Pawnshops were attacked, and huge meetings were held in all seasons in the White Cloud Mountains (Pai-yüan-shan), just north of Canton. By 1845, Shun-te, Hsiang-shan, Nan-hai, P'an-yü, Tung-kuan, Hsin-hui, and San-shui hsien were all reporting "local bandit" activity.[27]

In 1846 this news reached an alarmed court. On December 17, the Emperor ordered that pao-chia control be enforced throughout the province of Kwangtung: let the registers be brought up to date, each family guarantee the other, and local defense units be organized.[28] Now, with the choice made for them, the local gentry of Kwangtung decided that the time had finally come for a showdown. "Bandits and robbers grew in numbers in every village. . . . The superintending gentry, overseeing each hamlet, raised local militia and cooperated in amassing funds and supplies."[29] This massive effort, barely visible through the official sources, seemed to stay the tide. District by district, the gentry rallied the elders and notables. Village by village, the Triads' activities slowed and finally appeared to subside.[30]

The "outer strangers"—the hill bands, pirates, and gangsters— went back to their old bases. The "inner" Triads, the peasants in

---

* A secret society feud in which at least one hundred were killed was reported by the magistrate of Shun-te hsien (just south of Canton) to the governor. He was advised to keep the matter quiet. However, a censor brought it to the attention of the Emperor, who secretly ordered that an investigation be made. The magistrate thereupon asked the local gentry to sign an affidavit stating that no such feud had occurred. The gentry refused. Finally, a circuit intendant rode out into the district and forced them to sign it. From then until 1853, "bandits" (t'u-fei, tao, or tsei) were mentioned openly, but never "secret societies" (hui or t'ang). See Tseng Wang-yen's memorial cited in note 4.

the delta, simply went underground. "Inner" and "outer" were not permanently separated from each other, since the rich farming counties were not sealed off from the outlying hill districts. Nevertheless, rebellion could be avoided if the political and economic center of the province, Kuang-chou prefecture, remained stable. Around the capital, where *pao-chia* and militia units had been used for so long, it was relatively easy for local officials and gentry to summon resistance to rebels. Therefore, the outer societies would not attack the delta unless they were sure potential allies awaited them. Similarly, peasant Triads within the zone could not hope to challenge the gentry's local hegemony without outside help. It was a standoff until the second great tremor of the nineteenth century shook the South.

The Taiping Rebellion (1850–64) initially blurred deep differences between the rebels and the Cantonese secret societies. The relationship between the unrest of Kwangtung and the explosion in Kwangsi was there for all to see: the pirate migration upriver, economic dislocation when the Canton trade monopoly ended, the growing audacity of the hill bands, the unruly militiamen, Hakka-Punti feuds, even a certain decline in cottage weaving in some of the districts around Canton.[31] Furthermore, the dynasty first believed all rebels to be of the same general sort. Chaos of this magnitude obliterated subtle distinctions in the eyes of the contemporary beholder: why single out one sort of society from another when all seemed to represent an equal threat to public order? In fact, it was not difficult to feel that a universal conspiracy linked the Triad brotherhood with the Society of God Worshippers.* Lo Ta-kang, the Triad leader who began his career on the opium-receiving boats, did figure largely in the rise of the Taiping Heavenly Kingdom.[32] And simultaneous secret society revolts along the coast of China rendered the connection even more plausible.

This confusion of conspiracies and situations did not last long. The Triads soon saw that the rebel emperor, Hung Hsiu-ch'üan, could not tolerate divided loyalties: one was either a true believer or an

---

* This tendency is not confined to the Ch'ing. See Hsieh Hsing-yao, *T'ai-p'ing t'ien-kuo ch'ien-hou Kuang-hsi ti fan-Ch'ing yün-tung* (The anti-Ch'ing movement in Kwangsi before and after the Taiping Rebellion; Peking, 1950). This discussion really lies at the core of another more concretely debatable problem: the identity of Hung Ta-ch'üan. P'eng Tse-i and Hsiao I-shan suggest that the existence of a real Hung Ta-ch'üan confirmed the filiations and links between the Taipings and the Triads. Lo Erh-kang and Jung Meng-yüan, on the other hand, by insisting that the T'ien-te emperor was a fabrication, an apocryphal figure, would deny such links.

infidel. And, as the Taipings bypassed Kwangtung for the North, the dynasty itself realized that southeastern China was but a minor theater of war, that the secret society revolts were merely small whirlpools spinning off the peripheries of the swifter and deeper current. The Cantonese Triads might inspire, but they would never decide, a major rebellion. The crucial battles would always be fought along or above the Yangtze. Imperial claimants had to move to the center of the stage, figuratively and geographically, leaving the minor players of the South to declaim behind them: less grandiose, less important.

In the summer of 1850 the hill bands began to descend.* Fifty thousand Kwangsi Triads poured into Ssu-hui hsien, driving thousands of refugees downriver to Canton. In less than a year, the West River districts had been occupied by another huge force under the infamous Ling Shih-pa. By the spring of 1852, the border city of Wu-chou was under siege by the rebel T'ien Fang. Other Triads closer to the delta were inspired to attack Shao-ch'ing and Tsung-hua, only tens of miles from Canton.[33] To save the city from imminent attack, a thick barrier of garrison troops and hired mercenaries was set up between the delta and the borderland. Hsü Kuang-chin and Yeh Ming-ch'en, successive viceroys of the Liang Kuang (Kwangtung and Kwangsi), personally led armies into the mountains. By August 1852 they had blocked the rebel descent, decisively crushing Ling Shih-pa at Lo-ting.[34]

The government campaign had cost four million taels.[35] These expenses were partly met by the sale of offices, drafts on the provincial treasury, customs revenue, and assessments on the local magistrates. But the borderland had not been totally pacified. Rebellion continued, and soon these sources of revenue were exhausted. The provincial government's only recourse was the delta's wealthy gentry. Some, like the second Kingqua, Liang Lun-shu, tendered the aid willingly.[36] Others were asked in March 1853 to "volunteer" one month's income to the provincial treasury. These extraordinary levies soon became ordinary. Between 1852 and 1855, Shun-te hsien alone was forced to contribute 552,000 taels.[37] Worse yet, a notorious tax scandal rocked the province. In 1850, the Emperor had tried to counter rebellion in the Liang Kuang by first proclaiming a tax moratorium

---

* Along with the topographical distinction between the rich alluvial lands of the "three hsien" nearest Canton (Nan-hai, P'an-yü, and Shun-te) and the rawer and poorer "four hsien" (Hsin-hui, Hsin-ning, K'ai-p'ing, and En-p'ing), there was also a distinction in dialects of Cantonese that probably found expression in differing groupings of Triads.

and then threatening to punish his local officials unless they pacified the region. These commands left the provincial authorities little choice. Pacification demanded revenue, and so, desperately trying to keep the Emperor's remission an official secret, the Provincial Treasurer continued to collect taxes. The gentry were bound to hear of the imperial exemption from friends in Peking. When they did, the hsien of P'an-yü, Nan-hai, Hsin-hui, and especially Tung-kuan were thrown into an uproar. Mobs barricaded magistrates in their yamens. Influential local notables demanded the impeachment of the Provincial Treasurer. Thus, even when the gentry were later mollified by the Governor, they continued to doubt the fiscal probity of the government. What was happening to all the money they had contributed? Why pay taxes at all if those in high places could so meanly defraud them?[38]

Ultimately some of the government's high military costs were passed on to the delta's many tenant farmers, who had endured so much during the prior fifteen years. The insecurity of the Opium War years had been dispelled in 1848, when harvests and prices were better than they had been since 1836; but a surprisingly bad harvest the following year, accompanied by a severe political crisis, had further narrowed their margin of survival. Then, in the summer of 1852, endless monsoon rains had severely flooded several districts. Many died. Others abandoned their villages for refuge in the provincial capital, only to find Canton itself in the throes of a financial crisis caused when the Taiping rebels severed the trade routes north, depressing the city's vital foreign trade.[39] As early as 1849, this economic turbulence had begun to disturb the uneasy peace succeeding the great anti-Triad campaign of 1847. "Strange tales" excited the rural populace. Rumormongers were executed. The Governor-General, seriously concerned, ordered the Salt Commissioner to offer rewards for bandits and to re-enroll militia. Public executions increased. In a single month during the autumn of 1852, some 237 persons were decapitated in Canton, more than for any other such period during the previous twenty years.[40]

By the following spring, Triad activity, hill banditry, and the tax-protest movement had begun to complement each other.[41] In April, anti-official placards first appeared in the streets of Canton. The next month, hill bands cut all communications with the North for ten long days, and there was news of a secret society uprising at Amoy. Bands of armed men openly moved through the countryside. In June, the Triads began extorting taxes from produce farmers only minutes from the capital. Suburban shops were brazenly robbed in the middle of the day. The city gates were strengthened and more militia units formed. The Tartar-General, succumbing to a fit of paranoia, suddenly decided to purge the garrison quarter of all suspicious characters. The civil authorities heard of this plan in time to save the quarter's hapless citizens, but they could not help sharing the old soldier's alarm; something would have to be done. Finally, in November 1853, Yeh Ming-ch'en decided to make an example of Tung-kuan hsien, where tax protestors, secret societies, and warring clans were all flouting official authority. The village elders and clan heads were commanded to turn over local Triads. When this failed, the prefect of Kuang-chou, sent with orders to end the nonsense at all cost, had his troops punish suspect lineages by wiping out entire villages, including women and children. Such indiscriminate ferocity could only benefit the "bare sticks" of the district. On June 17, 1854, one of these—a river smuggler named Ho Lu who had lost his brother in a village massacre near Shih-lung—gathered a motley army of 30,000 vengeance-seekers, Triads, and proscribed peasants and proceeded to seize the hsien capital. Chinese marines retook the city two weeks later, but by then the entire delta was up in arms. The Red Turban revolt had begun.[42]

While the government was still reacting to the Tung-kuan debacle, disaster swiftly followed. On July 4, a force of some 7,000 members of the San-ho Hui astonished the entire province by seizing the great city of Fatshan (Fo-shan), just south of Canton. Their leader, Ch'en K'ai, proclaimed a new era—Ta-ning ("Great Peace")—and the end of the ruling dynasty. Similar rebellions soon broke out north of the capital. By July 20 a great contingent of Triads under Kan Hsien and Li Wen-mao had ringed off three sides of Canton. Within a month the delta was overrun by at least fourteen major bands of rebels.[43]

Under daily attacks from the north and with its delta outposts so suddenly lost, the provincial administration could not but believe that this major rebellion had been organized as a vast conspiracy to arise at a given signal: Ho Lu's assault on Tung-kuan. Some even thought that Ho Liu was an agent sent by the Taipings to form cells (*hung-shun t'ang*) throughout the delta to drape the *hung* ("vast") troops with *hung* ("red") turbans.* Others soon realized, however,

* TKHC, 35: 3b–4a; STHC, 23: 5b (for abbreviations, see notes 5 and 7). This is an enduring myth, difficult to dispel. Chien Yu-wen cites a new (and apparently unpublished) edition of the Hsin-hui hsien gazetteer that distinguishes between

that "each of the bandit [gangs] listened to the wind and responded."[44] "When the Red Turbans rebelled, the local bandits of each
pao one and all acknowledged the greater outlaws as their overlords,
launching surprise attacks on the academies, local schools, and vil-
lage-run militia barracks and public offices, which they seized for
their own lairs."[45]

Bold villagers, usually young men about eighteen years old, hastened to form their own branches of the Triads. These hundreds and
hundreds of smaller chapters then joined the larger confederations
of rebels to attack the cities.[46] Thus the major problem confronting
the rebel chiefs was not the lack of response, but the problem of centralizing their own control over this vast human convulsion. Of
course, there was one great bond between the small-town rowdy and
the professional hill bandit: the prize at stake, the city under attack.
Yet even Kan Hsien's confederation besieging Canton could not remain united for long. As the siege wore on, P'an-yü and Nan-hai hsien
could no longer feed the more than 30,000 rebels encamped there.
When money and food began to run out, individual gang leaders
fell to quarreling among themselves over taxation and looting rights.
By September 5, 1854, the confederation had begun to disintegrate.[47]

Shun-te hsien, farther to the south, saw an even more bitter struggle
between rival leaders. Ta-liang, the capital, was captured on August 5
by a local Triad named Ch'en Chi. After he had held the town for
six months, he received news of a huge "outer" band of Triads moving in from Lung-shan by skiffs and sampans. Its leader, Huang
Fu, had decided to claim his share of the spoils. Unwilling to share
the city with him, Ch'en Chi ignored gentry militia to the north and
east and concentrated on setting up ambuscades and redoubts toward
the west. These preparations frightened off Huang Fu, but they so
weakened Ch'en Chi's other defenses that he lost the city to imperial forces.[48]

Of all the confederations, the San-ho Hui at Fatshan was by far
the most cohesive. Its leader, Ch'en K'ai, fully realized that to retain

---

four major "halls" of Red Turbans in Kwangtung at this time: at Chu-chiang
(near Fatshan), a cell under Ch'en K'ai and Li Wen-mao called the Hung-shun
T'ang; along the East River under Ho Liu, the Hung-i T'ang; along the North
River under Ch'en Chin-kang, the Hung-hsing T'ang; and up the West River, led
by Liang P'ei-yu, the Hung-te T'ang. According to this source, the Taiping rebels
sent Lo Ta-kang to contact Ho Liu while the Small Knife rebels in Shanghai
sent another emissary to enlist the aid of Li Wen-mao and Ch'en K'ai in this
plotted coup. See Chien Yu-wen, *T'ai-p'ing t'ien-kuo ch'üan-shih* (A complete history of the Taiping Heavenly Kingdom; Hong Kong, 1962), 2: 962.

the city he must create a civil network in the surrounding countryside to supplant officials and local notables, as well as organize a
regular but not oppressive system of taxation. Individual rebel patrols
were dispatched to market towns to try to bring local secret societies
under Ch'en's control; or, if such branches did not exist, to use the
"unreliable elements" of the town as their "teeth and claws" in an
attack on yamens, local schools, and other actual and symbolic centers
of resistance. They boldly declared that the gentry and officials had
abnegated their ruling responsibilities and were no longer capable of
protecting the people. Meanwhile, within Fatshan, Ch'en won the
loyalty of the citizenry by making sure that only the wealthiest elements of the city were taxed.

Precisely because he was so reasonable, Ch'en K'ai represented an
enormous danger to the provincial authorities. If he could establish
a viable shadow government at Fatshan, he might come to control the
entire province. And so Canton sent an imperial junk fleet to Fatshan,
which kept the city under continuous bombardment throughout November and December 1854. Simultaneously, Ch'en K'ai found his
carefully woven rural network of political and fiscal control being
challenged by an equally resourceful gentry resistance group operating from a complex of villages around Ta-li. Each side strenuously
fought to restrict the other's control of the countryside; barricades
were flung across major roads, tolls exacted by both sides, passes and
permits required. But on their own ground the rural gentry had the
upper hand. By eventually curtailing much of Ch'en's local tax revenue, the Ta-li resistants forced him to rely almost totally on Fatshan's
resources—just as the costs of his defense of the city were rising
steeply. Sooner or later the rebels would have to risk alienating the
urban populace by upping the tax quotas. The riverine attacks eventually depleted the resources and patience of the city's 20,000 defenders, and in early January 1855 rebel tax collectors began to insist on
heavy contributions from all quarters of the city. When one obdurate
ward went so far as to seize one of Ch'en K'ai's lieutenants and refused to release him until he agreed to lower the quota, the San-ho
Hui retaliated by putting that part of Fatshan to the torch. The fire
raged for over twenty-four hours, and by the time its cinders had
stopped smoking Ch'en K'ai had lost the support of the populace.
On January 18, imperial troops entered the city unopposed. The
rebels, reviled and attacked by the people of Fatshan, had melted
back into the countryside.[49]

Thus each of the rebel movements followed much the same pattern.

The attack on the city brought them together, inviting confederation but not consolidation. Looting, with the single exception of Fatshan, invariably followed. The rebels then might move to a second, more advanced stage: the occupation of the city itself. This could make it possible for a *primus inter pares* like Ch'en Chi to emerge, but that was not always likely. The kind of bravo with sufficient physical magnetism to lead rebels in the first place usually lacked the necessary civil subtlety to realize that order would have to be restored. And even when a leader like Ch'en Chi possessed both traits, his prohibitions against looting were often disobeyed.[50] On the one hand, if he wished to hold his bands together, he dared not enforce his injunctions too severely. On the other hand, there was little hope of attracting gentry support if his men continued to plunder at will. The dilemma was a fatal one for most rebel aspirants, because ultimate success depended upon using one horn to blunt the other: only the coaching and concurrence of the literati could lead to imperial forms of rule, and only such forms would provide enough charisma for the leader to acquire final and unquestioned control over his cohorts. Perhaps this was why men like Chu Yüan-chang, the rebel founder of the Ming dynasty, relied so heavily upon shamans and magicians. Personal magnetism became genuine charisma only when both brutish followers and hesitant literati accepted the same certification: magic omens and prophecies. The antagonistic forces could then be united by shared superstitions, which easily turned into the shared belief that the mandate was truly passing into their hands.

The Red Turbans of Kwangtung never reached this stage. Ming slogans did fill the air, as they tried to summon the past to exorcise the present. "When Hung-wu, the first Emperor of our Ming dynasty, was on the throne, ten thousand countries opened trade, the Superiors and Inferiors harmonized, and there was no war, no conflict with the neighboring countries."[51] But this was designed less to convince opponents of the righteousness of the Red Turbans' cause than to unify the rebel confederation itself. Ming generalissimos and chancellors appeared here and there, trying in vain to secure the obedience of other rebel leaders; but the self-styled "Supreme Commanders" of the glorious Ming were ignored, and the rebellion stumbled along its fragmented and incoherent way.[52] Too much water had passed under the bridge: two centuries of Manchu rule, two decades of conflict with the West. Thus, the dream of recovering the past could unify the brotherhood only on the eve of action. In this sense, the rebels' political opponents—the alien Ch'ing—were no different from the immediate military target, the city.* Both bound men together with hope before the victory was won. But when the walls had fallen and the time for constructive action had arrived, the restorationist fantasy was discarded.

If the restoration of the Ming was an implausible notion to many of the Triads, how much more so to the local gentry! Not, of course, that the conflict was ever reduced to such terms. On the contrary, the Triads represented elements so hostile to the forces of order that the question of gentry support seldom arose. The "clans of the wealthy" were the first to be attacked and to have their leaders seized for ransom. Local notables who dared to shelter magistrates in flight were killed on the spot. A few hardy scholars stayed behind, shutting themselves up heroically in their studios or in the local Confucian temple, but most men of note and influence fled to Canton.[53] Since any form of transportable wealth was in danger of being seized by one Triad band or another, even the well-to-do produce farmers of Canton's suburbs fled behind the city walls. By August 1854 the delta had literally been abandoned to the Red Turbans.[54]

There were but two instances of local degree holders working with the rebels, and these so outraged and horrified other gentry that they quickly got over their initial shock at the sudden violence of the revolt and began to devise ways of recovering their home districts.[55] The government gave them all the encouragement it could, for with a few exceptions those magistrates who had not been killed had been driven out of their yamens and could not rally an effective counterattack. Government arms were supplied to the gentry from arsenals in Canton. Prestigious literati who had taken refuge in Canton tried to contact those few who had remained behind; others returned to their villages bearing official militia warrants.[56] Some of these returnees found resistance groups already operating, especially in areas where clan elders had long been used to leading their lineages in boundary wars. For whereas clans originally abetted disorder, they also represented powerful loyalties, tempered in warfare, that could be used against the secret societies.[57]

Sometimes resistance to the secret societies depended on personal courage, or even sheer happenstance. In one case, the Fatshan rebels

* That anti-Manchu slogans should be sworn to by Triads in Singapore and Hong Kong more than half a century after the demise of the enemy seems to corroborate this. See W. P. Morgan, *Triad Societies in Hong Kong* (Hong Kong, 1960), pp. 201–2, and Maurice Freedman, "Immigrants and Associations: Chinese in Nineteenth-Century Singapore," *Comparative Studies in Society and History*, 3.1 (Oct. 1960): 33.

had sent a patrol out to take over a wealthy marketing town. When they arrived and began executing local worthies in the public square, an elder who had bought himself a *kung-sheng* degree back in 1839 stepped out of the watching crowd and loudly ordered his sons to seize the bandits. When the Triads turned to attack the sons, other kinsmen came to their rescue; soon the entire village was transformed into an angry mob, which finished by drowning the rebel contingent in the river. Thereafter, of course, the village had no choice but to organize militia units to defend itself against rebel reprisals. Eventually, the militia organization spread to become one of the most important in the entire hsien.[58]

Such militia leagues usually centered on the symbols of gentry culture in the countryside: the local academies and schools of the market towns. From there, alliances were forged with clan leaders in outlying towns, after which "unreliable elements" within the perimeters of the league were arrested or killed.[59] As local resistance increased, hundreds of these militia organizations placed themselves between the "inner" Triads at the village level and the huge Red Turban confederations occupying the cities, making it possible for imperial forces to isolate and defeat the larger bands. By December of that year, the tide began turning—decisively so with the recovery of Fatshan in January. Finally, on March 7, 1855, the last great Red Turban force was resoundingly defeated at Whampoa.[60]

The remnants simply pulled out. Ch'en Chi watched gentry militia and imperial troops draw closer to Ta-liang until the day he selected his most reliable adherents, loaded 45,000 piculs of stolen supplies on whatever boats he could find, and slipped into the delta's waterways. Ho Lu, hard-pressed near Tseng-ch'eng, led his men into Kiangsi and Hunan. Li Wen-mao marched upriver to Wu-chou. The hill bands and pirate gangs would continue their ravages away from Kuang-chou prefecture, the former not to be stilled until the Taipings fell at Nanking (1864) and the Ch'ing could look once again to its frontier regions, the latter to face British gunboats from Hong Kong and Shanghai. But the village societies, the tens of thousands who had arisen within the delta, remained behind to survive as best they could.[61]

Some claimed that a million people were killed in the White Terror that followed. No one will ever know. With their well-armed militiamen, their "public offices" to collect likin, their "relief bureaus" to distribute grain to the deserving needy, and even their local courts to try the guilty, the victorious gentry of the Canton region restored their hegemony by exterminating those "unreliable elements" that had come so close to displacing them.[62] In Canton 250 criminals were beheaded every day, and in the rural districts rebel figures were cut down on the spot. Boxes of ears replaced the heads with which military commanders usually certified their kills. Neighbor informed on neighbor, Hakka killed Punti, lineages settled old scores. Winter came and went, and still the massacre went on.

In the late summer of 1856, heavy monsoon rains came once again. The dikes were destroyed, the blood washed away. The Red Turban revolt was over.[63]

While the main acts of the Taiping drama were unfolding in the Yangtze valley, Kwangtung emerged in true perspective. It became, as it had been before the thirteenth century, a kind of frontier region, momentarily expendable while the real struggle for empire took place elsewhere. Half a century later, revolutionaries like Huang Hsing were to learn the same lesson: Canton was peripheral to the centers of power in China. But it was a fertile ground for rebellion, a source of pressure for change. Even the Triads had shown that. Ming restorationism chained them to a traditional past; but their contacts with the treaty-port world associated them with a Sino-barbarian present.

This ambivalence of the Triads corresponded to their diffusion among *both* inner and outer strangers in nineteenth-century China. Other dichotomies, of course, could just as well describe their traditional role in a period of rapid social change: rural-urban, functional-dysfunctional, even native-foreign. Yet they remained fixed in their time. Their native rebelliousness, not the taint of foreignness, condemned them in official eyes. Twentieth-century rebels, ostensibly the Triads' heirs, would find the emphasis reversed. The overseas revolutionary Sun Yat-sen was decried by native allies like Chang T'ai-yen not for his rebelliousness but for his apparent alienation from things truly Chinese. Perhaps that was why Sun picked the secret societies of South China as his historical predecessors: he, too, would use the past to exorcise the present.[64] Thus, his rhetorical victory rites at the Ming tombs in 1912 were more than the payment of a debt that he imagined he owed the Triads. They helped identify him with a long, continuous line of resistance by unimpeachably native Chinese to the Manchus who had usurped *their* China.

Yet Sun's anti-Manchuism was not that of the Red Turbans. Theirs was a dual slogan ("Overthrow the Ch'ing and restore the Ming") designed for a limited end: the preservation of the brotherhood in a Confucian world that they never thought to change. Sun Yat-sen needed only a single goal—overthrow the Ch'ing—and even that was but a means to something larger: the creation of a nation. The line between the revolutionaries of 1911 and the rebels of 1856 had been broken. The Triad uprisings of the mid-nineteenth century were not the first or second failures in a series of ultimately successful revolutionary coups. Rather, they were the last, or next to last, defeats in a much larger series of traditional rebellions. What followed vindicated the past, but did not repeat it.[65]

The Anti-Manchu Propaganda of the Triads, *ca.* 1800-1860

BORIS NOVIKOV

The Heaven and Earth Society as a popular movement—Its influ-
ence—The slogan "Overthrow the Ch'ing, restore the Ming" and its
place in Triad ritual—The theme of struggle against the Ch'ing: its
anti-dynastic and anti-Manchu implications—The theme of the res-
toration of the Ming: its legitimist, nationalist, and utopian aspects

During the first half of the nineteenth century, the social crisis in
feudal Ch'ing China worsened. The fateful consequences of defeat
in the Opium War were still being felt when a secret society called
the Triads awoke to increased activity. The Triads, which included
the T'ien-ti Hui or Heaven and Earth Society, the Hung Men, and
other groups, had been known before only in Chekiang, Fukien, and
Taiwan for their part in the uprisings of Chang I-nien in Chekiang
in 1708 and of Chu I-kuei and Lin Shuang-wen in Taiwan in 1721–23
and 1787–88, respectively. Early in the nineteenth century, however,
the Triads expanded, spreading their influence into new regions
south of the Yangtze River. Armed insurrections led by adherents
of the Triads burst out in various places in the provinces of Kwangtung (1802, 1817, 1832, 1837), Kiangsi (1809, 1814), Kwangsi (1810,
1820–21, 1832), and Hunan (1832), among others.

The insurrections continued, too, in those regions where the Triads
had previously been active: in Taiwan in 1802 and 1832, and in Fukien in 1837. However, by this time, the headquarters of the Triads
had already been transferred to the Kwangtung-Kwangsi area. By
the fourth decade of the nineteenth century, the Triads had apparently become the largest and most influential secret anti-Manchu organization in China.* As emigration increased, new overseas branches

---

* The oldest secret society of China, the White Lotus, and its branches could
be found all over the country during the Ch'ing period, especially north of the
Yangtze River. But after the important uprisings in 1796–1804 and 1813 were defeated, and after these defeats were followed by the cruel repressions of the Ch'ing
feudal authorities, the White Lotus was seriously weakened.

sprang up in many parts of Southeast Asia, including Malaya, Singapore, and the Dutch East Indies, among others.

The activity of the Triads in China accelerated rapidly after the Opium War, as the Ch'ing regime grew steadily weaker and discontent swelled among the people. The armed uprisings of the society became fiercer and more frequent until in the provinces of Kwangtung and Kwangsi, the Triads (and their branches) were in fact after 1842 leading an incessant armed struggle against the local troops of the Ch'ing. These two provinces, and especially Kwangsi, became the principal focus of the insurgents' activities.

Many of the uprisings were launched without sufficient organization, and were more like riots than like battles in a rebellion. Often the insurrectionists indulged in looting and plundering, a tendency encouraged by the great number of social outcasts in their ranks. The localized and isolated character of the uprisings constituted no less serious a weakness. Risings occurred at the same time in the same province, and moreover in neighboring regions, but rarely did their leaders combine forces. This lack of coordination reflected both the tendencies toward particularism and local autonomy so often found in feudal China, and the characteristics of the internal organization of the Triads. The society had no central or unified leadership, and its development consisted of a proliferation of autonomous local branches.

At the same time, just because the armed insurrections led by local groups of the Triads were uncoordinated, one should not assume that there were no links between local chapters. Likewise, just because those chapters had different names, one should not consider them separate organizations. As their own documents show,[1] the branches of the society in various regions of southeastern China saw themselves as part of a single organization, one that was unique in origin, in structure, and in ideological tradition. This view is confirmed by the fact that certain principles were common to all of them; specifically, the principles of anti-Manchu propaganda.

In spite of their great number, the insurrections were in the last analysis merely episodes in the life of the local Triad groups; only rarely did their activities against the Manchu regime take the form of overt armed struggle. Between these brief uprisings there would be much longer periods of secret activity intended to consolidate the strength and influence of the organization. During such periods, which in fact were the ones that determined whether or not the society would survive, anti-Manchu propaganda became one of the most important aspects of its activity. The forms, the media, and the methods of dissemination of this propaganda were largely the same in all the local groups of the society located in Chinese territory.

Propaganda against the Ch'ing rulers found a ready audience among the ignorant and oppressed masses of peasants, the large numbers of poor city dwellers, and the vagabonds without hearth or home. It fell to the society's propagandists to address this audience in an atmosphere of constant terror and persecution by the Ch'ing authorities. These conditions naturally influenced both the form of the propaganda and the way in which it was disseminated. As Sun Yat-sen later put it, "How was the work of the secret society to be organized in such a climate? The only right way to do it was to get across to the masses, by means of the most accessible examples, the idea of a nation. The society's public meetings took the form of theatrical performances, giving the propagandists more opportunities to influence the masses. In their attempt to spread the idea of nationalism* they made use of widespread dissatisfactions and desires for revenge. This was an easy way to arouse the feelings of simple people."[2]

One of the guiding principles of Triad propaganda against the Ch'ing was to put forward everywhere the idea that old Chinese customs were being trampled underfoot. The adherents of the T'ien-ti Hui tried, mainly by personal example, to arouse in their compatriots the spirit of resistance to everything Manchu.

When new brothers enter the society, they have to let their hair down, because our ancestors did not wear pigtails. When the initiates daub their lips with blood and take the oath, they imitate the rites practiced since antiquity by the Han. When the officers of the society perform their official functions and when they visit the local chapters, to set an example they wear old Chinese robes and dress their hair in the old manner. They fashion a doll of tufts of grass or draw a picture to represent the Manchu Emperor. Newcomers to the society have to shoot three arrows into the representation and swear to kill the emperor as a proof that they will never forget the need for vengeance.

Ta-Ch'ing is the name of the Manchu State and has nothing to do with us Chinese. The Ch'ing Emperor is the main enemy, and that is why we do not recognize him as the ruler of our China. That is why when the Hung Men brothers write the character for Ch'ing they drop the element *chu*,

---

* When he talked about the idea of a nation, or nationalism, Sun Yat-sen had in mind throwing off the Manchu domination and restoring the native Han power.

which means "emperor." And not only the emperor, but all the Manchus are our enemies, and we must exterminate them all. That is why the symbol *Man*, which means "Manchu," it written without the *ts'ao*, which means "grass," giving the meaning "the Manchus without heads."[3]

All of the anti-Manchu propaganda of the Triads hinged upon the slogan *fan-Ch'ing fu-Ming* ("Overthrow the Ch'ing and restore the Ming"). As everyone knows, this slogan originated in the first stage of the struggle against the Manchus that was waged under the flag of the last members of the Imperial House of Chu (Ming dynasty). However, the slogan has never been examined in detail by historians. The documents of the T'ien-ti Hui allow us now to evaluate all facets of the meaning of this slogan and of its role in anti-Manchu propaganda.

Fan-Ch'ing fu-Ming runs like a red thread through all the documents of the society that have reached us. It appears in the legend of the origin of the T'ien-ti Hui, on its banners, on the identification cards of the members, on the ritual vessels (for example, on the one that was called the "precious censer"), on the "marvelous peach- and plum-wood sword," on the red cudgel that symbolized the punishment of turncoats, on the magic mirror that "distinguishes the true from the false," on the yellow umbrella that symbolized the imperial power of the Ming dynasty, and on other objects that are reproduced in the publications of original T'ien-ti Hui materials.[4]

But it is in the ritual texts of the society that the slogan and its variations are most often encountered. Most of these texts are rhymed verses, in which the call to overthrow the Ch'ing and restore the Ming serves as an ending or a refrain. For example, during the ceremony of sacrifice to the five legendary founders of the society, the members used to sing the following quatrains:

> *Five men* began fighting against the Ch'ing troops;
> They founded *the invincible Family of the Hung Brothers*;
> After we have taken province, district, and region,
> We shall overthrow the Ch'ing and restore the Ming.

> *The Master orders us to assemble the new members*;
> The steadfast military chiefs will brook no weakness;
> Joyously the troops come to support the Sovereign,
> To overthrow the Ch'ing and restore the Ming.*

* TTH, pp. 10, 32 (see note 1 for abbreviations used in the footnotes). Editor's note: the verses quoted in this chapter from the ritual of the Triads may seem tiresomely repetitive; but "brainwashing" the new members was most likely their purpose. I have quoted them in full and italicized the wording that seems relevant to the points made here and in the following paragraphs.

While burning various kinds of incense, they would recite verses such as this:

> We will give the Manchus no rest:
> In the Hung-hua Pavilion
> We swore in Heaven's name
> To overthrow the Ch'ing and restore the Ming.[5]

A great many such verses contain the so-called "Dialogue with the Vanguard,"* an important part of the initiation ritual for new members and a sort of Triad catechism. Here is one such poem, based on the traditional version of the birth of the organization:

> The sworn brothers find themselves in front of the Hall
>   of Loyalty and Righteousness;†
> Myriads of warriors gather there;
> *In the Temple of Kao-ch'i*[6] *they launched an uprising*
> To overthrow the Ch'ing and restore the great Ming.[7]

The "Song of Mu-yang Ch'eng"‡ that closes the initiation ceremony ends with the same appeal:

> We have newly established the City of Willows
> *And the heroes of Hung are assembled tonight;*
> Swords and spears are piled up high.
> Overturn Ch'ing and, then, restore Ming![8]

The same theme is echoed in the verses that served the T'ien-ti Hui as a kind of watchword.

> The banners hover in the wind
> And under them the glorious heroes gather;
> *Those who call themselves brothers of the Hung family*
> Will overthrow Ch'ing and restore Ming.[9]

Dozens of similar instances could be given, for almost every page of the ritual texts collected by Hsiao I-shan, Lo Erh-kang, and Schlegel contains this appeal to overthrow the Ch'ing and restore the Ming. Thus the original materials of the Triads show convincingly that this was the fundamental purpose of the organization. It was no accident

---

* The Vanguard or Avant-garde (Hsien-feng) was the name of an official post or rank within the T'ien-ti Hui.

† The central part of the building in which the lodge of the T'ien-ti Hui was located was called the Chung-i-t'ang or Hall of Loyalty and Righteousness.

‡ Editor's note: Mu-yang Ch'eng, the conventional name of the society's meeting place, usually rendered "City of Poplars," is translated "City of Willows" by Schlegel. Here and elsewhere, however, in spite of certain obvious difficulties, the wording of Schlegel is usually used verbatim. His *Thian-Ti-Hwui, The Hung League* (Batavia, 1866) is the classic work in the field of these often obscure texts.

that when initiates were asked, at the moment of admission into the society, "Why are you here?" they were required to reply, "To overthrow the Ch'ing and restore the Ming."[10]

As we can see, in its usual form the slogan contained two ideas. The first idea, a negative one, presented the necessity of destroying the Ch'ing dynasty's power; the second, a positive one, was an appeal for the restoration of the Ming. Aside from its purely religious aspects, the necessity for overthrowing the Ch'ing dynasty can be seen to have a triple resonance in the documents of the T'ien-ti Hui. In certain texts describing the traditional origins of the society, it is motivated by a desire for vengeance against the Ch'ing for having treacherously burned the Shao-lin Monastery and all those who lived there.

> For the twenty-eight of the Shao-lin Monastery,
> We will conquer the South and the North,
> We will exterminate the Ch'ing Emperor.
> We hate the unjust Ch'ing ruler
> *For burning the monks, our brothers.*[11]

Such a motivation, based partly on legend and comprehensible only to the initiated, would obviously have a very narrow appeal. It might be useful within the society, but would be nearly useless for bolstering anti-Ch'ing sentiment in the society's external propaganda.

In one series of T'ien-ti Hui documents it is cruelty and injustice toward the people that serve as a basis for the will to overthrow the Ch'ing regime. The Ch'ing rulers are characterized as unjust men, plunderers, man-eating tigers, madmen, etc.[12] Certain poems also reveal this hostility, and develop the motivation further:

> We disperse the soldiers and generals of the Ch'ing dynasty
> *Because the treacherous ministers harm the people.*
> The Hung heroes are going to requite the days of these wrongs;
> They will overthrow the unjust Ch'ing and restore the Ming.[13]

The criticism contained in these lines touched on an important social aspect of the struggle against the Ch'ing, and dimly reflected an anti-feudal trend. However, even taking into account the historical conditions of China in the first half of the nineteenth century, one is bound to conclude that this approach was so vague and so simpleminded that its accusatory resonance and its effectiveness as a basis of the anti-Manchu idea were considerably weakened.

The reason most often advanced in the society's documents for the necessity of overthrowing the Ch'ing was that the regime originated in a nationality different from and foreign to the Han. In many cases this position is briefly expressed, merely by completing or replacing the first part of the usual slogan *fan-Ch'ing fu-Ming* with *mieh-Man* ("Destroy the Manchus"), *ch'ü-Hu* ("Drive out the northern barbarians"), etc.[14]

One series of texts calmly and deliberately sets forth the reasons for opposing the Manchus:

> We have restored the origin, searched the source; and *studied*
>   *the ancient poetry.*
> The Ch'ing people usurped our patrimony.
> We'll now restore the empire, following the instruction of
>   the leader.
> We'll rise by this clear moon and raise the banner of
>   patriotism.[15]

In contrast, some verses devoted to the anti-Manchu theme take on an emotional quality:

> From all directions the troops come to serve under the
>   five generals;*
> The glorious heroes of the universe gather together.
> *Hatred of the Ch'ing dynasty burns them,*
> Assuredly they will turn the bones of the Manchu
>   barbarians to cinders.[16]

Certain documents intended for propaganda outside the society were particularly expressive of this patriotic motive, as witness this Triad recruitment manifesto, found in 1828 in Macao:

> O boundless China, O limitless Heavenly Dynasty,†
> Thousands of possessions sent thee tribute,
> Tens of thousands of ministers came to thy court;
> [Then] the Manchu barbarians seized upon thee—
> Is it really possible to appease the sense of that outrage?
> Join our Hung ranks,
> Let us raise our pikes, rise up,
> And destroy the Ch'ing dynasty.[17]

Analysis of the available documents of the T'ien-ti Hui thus shows convincingly that the anti-Manchu motive formed the main basis of the propaganda directed toward overthrowing the Ch'ing. The anti-Ch'ing orientation of the society signified, at bottom, an anti-Manchu orientation and had, above all, a patriotic content.

Unlike the legendary revenge motive based on the incident at the Shao-lin Monastery, and the diffuse allusions to the injustice of the

---

* These were the so-called Tiger Generals from the legend of the T'ien-ti Hui's origins.

† T'ien-ch'ao ("Heavenly Dynasty"), one of the poetical names of China.

Ch'ing ruler, the anti-Manchu interpretation of *fan Ch'ing fu-Ming* was both convincing and easily comprehensible. A spirited resistance to the Manchu dynasty had resulted from the actual behavior of the regime. As the dynasty continued in power and as its leaders tried in every way they knew to erase from Chinese memory their image as foreign conquerors, this resistance became more significant. It stressed the barbarous, i.e. non-Chinese, origin of the Manchus and the usurpatory character of their rule in China, thus strengthening the native Han opposition to the foreign yoke.

Sun Yat-sen has mentioned the great significance of T'ien-ti Hui propaganda during the period we are considering. Describing the climate that allowed the anti-Manchu movement to develop toward the middle of the Ch'ing reign, he wrote:

As early as the Ch'ien-lung period [1736–95], people were forbidden to use the words *Manchu* and *Han*. Historical works were rewritten, and everything concerning the change of dynasties between Sung and Yüan and Ming and Ch'ing was erased. It was forbidden either to own or to read books containing information about the Manchus or Tartars, and wherever possible such books were not merely forbidden, but destroyed. At the end of this "literary Inquisition," the ideas of Chinese nationalism that had been preserved in literature were completely eliminated. From the middle of the Ch'ing reign onward, the only organization that set forth such ideas was the secret society called the Hung Men.*

The appeal to overthrow the Ch'ing dynasty that echoes throughout the Triad documents could scarcely have failed to arouse a response in the hearts of the Chinese people. In spite of all the Manchu rulers' attempts to win their complete submission, they harbored feelings of hatred toward the Manchus as foreign oppressors, and frequently rose in insurrection against them. Although no concrete data are available about the way peasants received the Triad propaganda, it is reasonable to assume that the society's patriotic anti-

---

* *Sun Chung-shan hsüan-chi* (Selected works of Sun Yat-sen; Peking, 1956), p. 618. The last statement is not historically exact. From the second half of the eighteenth century onward, while the T'ien-ti Hui was active in the southeast, the White Lotus and its branches were very active to the north of the Yangtze; see Hirayama Amane [Shū], *Chung-kuo pi-mi she-hui shih* (History of secret societies in China; Shanghai, 1912), pp. 3–4; E. B. Porchneva, "Narodnoe vosstanie 1796–1803," *Short Reports of the Institute of the Peoples of Asia*, no. 53 (1962), p. 81; Shang Yu, ed., *Ocherki istorii Kitaia* (Sketches of Chinese history; Moscow, 1959), pp. 532–33. However, the T'ien-ti Hui expressed the anti-Manchu idea more clearly and in a way less complicated by the religious considerations that were characteristic of the White Lotus. The southeast, where the T'ien-ti Hui flourished, became the major site of popular movements against the Ch'ing and the cradle of the huge Taiping Rebellion.

Manchu position was one of the most important sources of its popularity among the lower classes of society.

It should be noted, however, that if the people supported anti-
Manchu slogans, it was not only because the Ch'ing regime constituted a foreign yoke, but also because the Manchus, together with
Chinese landlords, behaved like the cruelest feudal exploiters. That
is why the masses of peasants, the poor of the cities, and the ruined
people who made up the rank and file of the society identified with
the struggle against Manchu domination. Thus the above-described
failure of Triad propaganda to appeal more specifically and directly
to the passionately anti-feudal feelings of the people can be seen as
its essential weakness.*

The second part of the slogan *fan-Ch'ing fu-Ming* expressed the
positive idea of restoring the Ming. The available T'ien-ti Hui documents show that this part of the slogan was taken literally, which is
to say that it was taken to refer to restoring the Imperial House of
Chu to the throne. This idea is to be found in the legend concerning
the origin of the society (a scene wherein a descendant of the Ming
emperors appears among the founders of the society and is chosen to
lead them in their attempt to put him back on the throne), in several
verses of the dedication ceremony, and in other texts. Here are some
examples:

> In the West the Merciful One† rejoices extremely—
> Ming rises, Ch'ing disperses,
> And the barbarians are exterminated.
> When we shall have slain and destroyed the Manchus and the
>   Western Tartars,
> *The sons of Hung will restore the old patrimony of Chu.*[18]

> A white and spotless cloud rises
> In sign of a propitious omen.
> The former House of Chu must be restored to the throne.
> Let it be known everywhere that the Sons of Hung will exterminate
>   the Ch'ing dynasty;
> They will cross the Yangtze and *restore the Ming Empire.*[19]

Some of the society's documents contained a broader interpretation
of the slogan, an appeal for the restoration of the native Han power
as opposed to the foreign usurpers, the Manchus:

---

* This failure was most pronounced in the earlier texts of the T'ien-ti Hui.
Later texts, in the second half of the nineteenth century, contain more concrete
anti-feudal statements linked directly to the idea of overthrowing the Ch'ing. See
Hirayama, p. 94.
† The Goddess of Mercy, Kuan-yin.

> Five dragons landed on the earth*
> To accompany the Ming prince;
> In all the universe, the just and charitable
> *Without exception help the Han nation.*[20]

Sometimes the idea is expressed in a concise, slogan-like form. For instance, on a T'ien-ti Hui flag dating from the period of the Taiping Rebellion, now in the Central Revolutionary Museum of the People's Republic of China, appear the words "Mieh-Man hsing-Han," meaning "We shall exterminate the Manchus and restore the Han."[21] The slogan is obviously a paraphrase of *Fan-Ch'ing fu-Ming* with the stress put on the anti-Manchu tendency of the first part and the pro-Han tendency of the second part.

Finally, the society's documents rather often link the restoration of the Ming with the advent of justice, happiness, and good. Different texts express different views of this notion. Some of them explain it in a very narrow sense, as a promise of rewards (titles, offices, etc.) for the faithful supporters of the Ming when its power should be restored. These faithful supporters were of course, in the first place, the members of the society:

> If the sun and the moon appear together, the East will be bright;†
> If millions of warriors rise, they are Hung heroes.
> When we overthrow the Ch'ing and restore the true ruler, Ming,
> *The faithful and the just will become the glorious dignitaries.*[22]

> In the hand we grasp a poniard
> To kill the emperor of Ch'ing and exterminate the Manchus;
> When, some other day, we have assisted our Lord to mount
>   the Imperial Palace,
> The brethren of the Hung family shall get imperial fiefs.[23]

In other documents the period of justice that is expected to follow upon the restoration of the Ming is interpreted in strictly Confucian terms:

---

* The five legendary founders of the society.

† This sentence apparently has an allegorical meaning. The first part of it is often found in Triad texts as a conventional way of referring to the Ming dynasty. The combination of the symbols for the sun and the moon form the character *Ming*. The second part obviously alludes to the "sign" (the red light in the eastern sky) that, according to certain variants of the legend, appeared like a heavenly blessing during the oath-taking ceremony when the T'ien-ti Hui was founded. See, for example, CTSL, ch. 2: 6b. Thus in a global sense the expression could be interpreted to mean "The heavens protect the dynasty of Ming."

The precious nine-storied pagoda stands middlemost;
The founders stand opposite each other [in it] since centuries.
When the Ming dynasty returns, there will be naught but officers
of the Hung Family;
The great dynasty of Ming shall settle the social bonds and virtues.*

A third group of the society's texts links the Ming restoration with a general happiness and with the prosperity of the country:

Let us ride with the single horse and spear to the limit of heaven†
And bear all the dust, to protect our coming lord;
When the true dragon‡ has been created, we'll meet with great
happiness.
Let us assist the lord of Ming to sit on the Golden Terrace.[24]

In the past we shot the Ch'ing soldiers out of cannons,
But no one could ever destroy the Hung heroes.
We remain faithful to the true sovereign, Ming;
We shall exterminate the Ch'ing dynasty,
And *again there will rise a promising dawn.*[25]

The concept of a happy future following the restoration of the Ming is often expressed in the society's documents by the word *t'ai-p'ing,* meaning "great peace" or "great equality," or, as it is usually translated in the Soviet Union, "great prosperity."§

* A model of the nine-storied pagoda usually stood to the left of local T'ien-ti Hui altars; see TTH, p. 17; HMC, p. 121; W. Stanton, "The Triad Society," *The China Review,* 21 (1894–95): 313; J. Ward and W. Stirling, *The Hung Society* (London, 1925), 1: iii, sixth illustration. The quatrain is to be found in CTSL, ch. 4: 11b, 22a, ch. 5: 9a, and in Schlegel, p. 102. The three bonds or relations (often expanded to five) and the five virtues are Confucian. The three bonds (*san-kang*) regulate the relationships between monarch and subject, father and son, husband and wife. The five virtues (*wu-ch'ang*) are the five constant moral virtues or qualities of a gentleman: humanity, justice, endurance, wisdom, and sincerity.

† This expression, based on T'ang legend, has a vivid metaphorical significance: that one who is led by fidelity and love can attain the impossible. See Schlegel, pp. 92, 93, 108.

‡ I.e., the true emperor.

§ *T'ai-p'ing,* a common term in the ideological arsenals of Chinese popular movements, refers to a system of social justice. Dating back to the time of the Eastern Han (A.D. 25–220), it is directly linked to the social utopias of Taoism, in which there would be no rich and no poor, and equality and justice would reign. From these ideas, set forth in a lost religious book attributed to the Taoist preacher Yü Chi, *T'ai-p'ing ch'ing-ling shu,* arose Chiang Chiao's heretical doctrine of the *t'ai-p'ing tao* (way to the great prosperity). This doctrine played a great role in the uprising of the Yellow Turbans at the end of the Han dynasty. See Yang K'uan, "Lun t'ai-p'ing ching," *Hsüeh-shih yüeh-k'an,* no. 9 (1959), pp. 17–26; Yang Yung-kuo et al., *Chien-ming Chung-kuo ssu-hsiang shih* (A brief history of Chinese thought; Peking, 1955), pp. 343–46; Hou Wai-lu, "Social Utopias in Ancient and

Hung rice is the costliest staple, and the City of Willows is full of it.
It feeds the troops of the brothers of the Pavilion of Flowers.
This precious rice must be returned to the authority of the Ming ruler,
And all over the country *a great prosperity* will prevail.*

> From a good tobacco, a white smoke always rises.
> Its white coils remind us of dragons.
> The true dragon is the sovereign of the Ming dynasty;
> Under his power *a great prosperity will reign in the Empire.*[26]

This thing is even (and just) as the stars and constellations are merciful;
Within the City of Willows it weighs clearly;
It adjusts the dynasty of Ch'ing to return to the house of Ming
And the whole country then, surely, will have universal peace.†

From the many examples given above, one can see how varied were the society's interpretations of *fu-Ming.* The expectation of honors and rewards was mixed with the general and patriotic purpose of restoring the native power in the country. Side by side with Confucian dogmas could be found affirmations of a future reign of happiness and justice for all, affirmations that had anti-feudal connotations. All these differing ideals, reflecting the aspirations characteristic of the different social groups represented in the T'ien-ti Hui, depended for their realization on the restoration of the Ming dynasty.

It may be noteworthy that even the positive part of the slogan *fan-Ch'ing fu-Ming* was oriented toward the past. However, such an orientation was not without purpose or precedent. On the contrary, returning to the past to express a challenge to the present was char-

---

Medieval China," *Voprosi filosofi* (Questions of philosophy), no. 9 (1959), pp. 75–86; V. M. Stein, "Iz rannei istorii sotsial'nikh utopii: Daosskaia utopiia v Kitae" (Early history of social utopias: The utopia of Lao-tzu in China), *Vestnik istorii mirovoi kultury* (The herald of world culture), no. 6 (1960), pp. 130–39. In succeeding centuries the idea of the great prosperity continued to be popular among the Chinese masses, and was often used as the symbol of future justice in the struggles against the feudal yoke; see Chung Meng-yüan, *Chung-kuo li-shih chi-nien* (Chronology of the history of China; Peking, 1956), pp. 19, 56, 84, 110, etc.

* "Hung rice" seems to refer to the staples which, during the anti-Ch'ing attacks, the T'ien-ti Hui soldiers seized to feed the followers of the society, the "troops of the brothers of the Pavilion of Flowers." The starving masses that made up the main body of the society regarded this food, rice, as something extremely precious. Schlegel, however, gives another interpretation: he thinks that the term refers to the rice placed on the altar (p. 105).

† Schlegel, p. 44. This quatrain appeared on the scales that were among the appurtenances of the altar, symbolizing the justice that the Ming restoration must bring with it.

acteristic of many popular movements of the proletarian period in various countries. Marx appraised this phenomenon from the view-point of historical materialism:

People make their own history, not arbitrarily or under conditions they themselves have chosen, but under given conditions inherited directly from the past. The traditions of all the dead generations are a heavy burden on the minds of the living. And even when they seem to be engaged in trans-forming themselves and their surroundings into something utterly unprece-dented, it is just in such moments of revolutionary crisis that they will fear-fully evoke the spirits of the past, borrowing their names, their slogans, and their costumes in order to play this unfamiliar scene in history in respect-able disguise and with borrowed language.[27]

Marx's appraisal can be applied to feudal China, where the influence of tradition on the struggling masses was especially strong. The Chi-nese peasants, objectively incapable of expressing their demands on their own behalf without turning to the past, when they rose in re-bellion sometimes made use in their ideological formulas of the tra-ditions of the ruling classes, traditions that were by their very nature foreign to them. Beginning with the insurrections led by Ch'en Sheng and Wu Kuang in the third century B.C., many popular move-ments in China proclaimed the restoration of a former dynasty as a goal of the struggle against the existing regime. This tradition was particularly obvious in the mass uprisings against foreign rulers. Dur-ing the mid-fourteenth-century insurrections led by the White Lotus Society against the Yüan, the society's chief, Han Shan-t'ung, was proclaimed the descendant (eight times removed) of the Sung Em-peror Hui-tsung (1101–25).* The appeal *fu-Ming* stems from such a tradition. Rising against the Manchu power, the Triads declared as their goal the restoration of the former dynasty.

This goal was determined for the Triads by a series of concrete historical circumstances. First, it stemmed naturally from the earlier stage of the anti-Manchu struggle in China that took place under the banner of the last representatives of the Imperial House of Chu. Historically, in other words, *fu-Ming* was directly connected with

---

* See Pi Yüan, *Hsü tzu-chih t'ung-chien* (Peking, 1957), ch. 210: 5719. The pro-Ming position of the T'ien-ti Hui could not have been influenced by the over-throw of the dynasty during the peasant uprisings of 1628–45. First of all, the peasant revolt did not reach the southeastern seacoast of China where later the society sprang up. In those regions, the Ming regime had been overthrown not by the peasants but by the Manchu invaders and their supporters. Thus by the time the T'ien-ti Hui was founded, the struggle had been changed into one against a foreign yoke.

the resistance of the Chinese to the Manchu invaders, and the Heaven and Earth Society appears to have sprung from this source.

Second, the Ming dynasty was the last dynasty before the Manchu conquest. Thus, from the point of view of tradition and legitimacy, which the T'ien-ti Hui used to reinforce their demands, the Ming dynasty was the most suitable on which to pin a movement of opposition to the Manchu regime. Besides this, we must not lose sight of the fact that actual supporters of the Ming helped found the society and influenced its ideology.

Finally, we cannot deny the fact that the Ming dynasty enjoyed a certain popularity in the memory of the Chinese people. The dynasty had come to power when a large popular revolt succeeded in throwing off the Mongol yoke in China, and its founder and first emperor came from the peasant class. Although these facts were far removed from the time of the Triads, although they concerned only the founding of the dynasty and had no connection either with its subsequent history or with its less glorious end, they took on a renewed immediacy when the anti-Manchu struggle began. Thus their effect was to favor the adoption of Ming restorationism as the watchword of the society.

These circumstances served as a kind of historical bridge between the actual Ming dynasty and the idea *fu-Ming* in the T'ien-ti Hui ideology. But the existence of such a bridge explains only the patriotic or anti-Manchu content of the idea. As the society interpreted it, the restoration of the imperial dynasty of the Ming meant not only deliverance from the Manchu yoke, but also the belief that a reign of happiness and justice for all will come afterward. The latter part of this interpretation had nothing in common with the historical reality of the Ming reign. Rather, it clearly reflected the naive monarchistic illusions of the masses—and thus of the T'ien-ti Hui.

The society's documents are thoroughly imbued with this blind confidence in a "good sovereign," as symbolized by the future Ming emperor and as opposed to the present Ch'ing emperor. In verses on the restorationist theme, the proposed Ming ruler is called "the true," "the just," "our own." Sometimes the verses even go so far as to say, "The Ming dynasty is our mother."[28]

It seems remarkable that the society did not bother to substantiate in any way the idea that the restoration of the Ming dynasty would bring great happiness and prosperity. Future happiness and prosperity under Ming authority were presented in the poems and songs of the Triads as something natural and self-evident:

When dawn appears,
The sun naturally rises;
When our sovereign Ming comes,
Again there will be great happiness.[29]

Such an interpretation was founded exclusively on faith, inspired by the natural anti-Manchu hopes of the lower classes, who made up the main body of the society. By virtue of the conditions in China at the time, these hopes were expressed within the framework of the traditional monarchy. According to such an interpretation, the postulated justice and happiness were to be brought about by the same authority whose injustice the lower classes had already experienced.* From the very beginning, this manifest contradiction seriously weakened the idea of restoring the Ming dynasty as a positive program of the anti-Manchu struggle.

In summary, the slogan *fan-Ch'ing fu-Ming* clearly reflected many specific features of the anti-Manchu propaganda which, in the first half of the nineteenth century, was a constant and extremely important part of Triad activity. Among these specific features, one of the most striking may be the dissymmetry between the political elements of the slogan and its socioeconomic elements. The anti-Manchu and pro-Ming political propaganda is extremely vigorous and is expressed very clearly, both in dynastic and in nationalist terms. By contrast, the economic and social ideas, interesting as they may be, appear only fleetingly, with vague criticisms of feudal oppression and sketchy dreams about prosperity to come. The historical consciousness of the masses in the old China was not yet capable of moving from the analysis of political forms to the analysis of fundamental social realities.

* The fact that the pretenders to the imaginary Ming throne that were put forward by the T'ien-ti Hui were actually chosen from among the society's own leaders did not change anything, for they presented themselves to the people as the true descendants of the Imperial House of Chu.

Taiping Relations with Secret Societies and with Other Rebels

C. A. CURWEN

> *The Taipings and the secret societies—Ideological and other influences—Early connections: the Hung Ta-ch'üan contro-versy—The T'ien-ti Hui in Hunan and Kwangtung—The Hsiao-tao Hui of Shanghai—The Taipings and the Nien: subordination, alliance, amalgamation—The Lien-p'eng Tang and the Chin-ch'ien Hui of Chekiang—The new recruits from Hupeh—Conclusion*

Hung Hsiu-ch'üan and Feng Yün-shan, the founders of the Taiping movement, arrived in Kwangsi in 1844, at a time when secret society activity was far more widespread there than in their own province of Kwangtung. In Kuei-p'ing hsien, where they settled for a time, no village was without its secret society, probably affiliated in some way with the San-ho Hui (Triads).[1] During the same year, at Hsin-hsü near Chin-t'ien, where the Taiping rising eventually took place, "ban-dit leaders" assembled several hundred men, and claiming to be mem-bers of a religious association, paraded armed through the streets. In the following year there were risings in T'eng-hsien, and before long, groups of rebels or bandits several thousand strong were active in the province.[2]

This secret society activity was of incalculable benefit to the Pai-shang-ti Hui (Society of God Worshippers), the original Taiping or-ganization. Government officials and forces were far too busy with these extensive and more familiar manifestations of social disorder to give any attention to the apparently innocuous activities of the early Taipings, who were able to organize more or less undisturbed. Official documents do not even mention the God Worshippers until early in 1851, yet within a few months they were recognized as dan-gerous and determined enemies. They were to preoccupy the author-ities for more than a decade and a half. The years between 1847 and 1850, during which God Worshippers' groups were being established in Kwangsi, also marked a peak in Triad activities in Hunan and parts of Kwangtung and the beginning of Triad risings in Kwangsi. The first Pai-shang-ti Hui organization was set up in Tzu-ching-shan in Kuei-p'ing at the height of Lei Tsai-hao's rising, which broke out in Hsin-ning hsien in Hunan, near the border with Kwangsi. A glance at the four supplements to the *Kuang-hsi t'ung-chih chi-yao* (1881) is enough to show the immensity of the social problem in Kwangsi in these years and the extent of secret society and bandit outbreaks.[3]

It would be surprising if the God Worshippers' Society, growing up in this chaotic environment, were not profoundly influenced by the ideology and practices of the secret societies, which had their own long-established traditions and conventions—part of their technique for survival, part of the mystique of brotherhood and secrecy. Traces of these conventions can indeed be found in almost all aspects of Taiping organization and practice. Some examples are striking, implying a fairly direct influence; others are less so, and may mean only that the Taipings absorbed elements of the general tradition of popular revolt. Both the Taipings and the secret societies were imbued with ideas of mutual assistance and brotherhood, sometimes expressed in very similar terms; but these were part of an age-old and indeed universal tradition of social protest that was, in the case of the Taipings, strengthened and given religious authority by ideas borrowed from Christianity. Like the secret societies, the Taipings were influenced by popular novels; but there seems to be little reason to suppose (as V. Y. C. Shih does[4]) that this was the result of direct influence, since novels like *Shui-hu chuan*, *San-kuo yen-i*, and *Feng-shen yen-i* were also part of the Chinese "little tradition" and had long served rebels a sources of inspiration and even as military handbooks.

The Taiping attitude toward women is one area in which the influence of the secret societies was possibly more direct. As another paper in this volume points out, it was not uncommon for men and women to be on more or less equal terms in the secret societies. Thus it is hard to accept the view that the Taiping belief in the equality of the sexes, which as a policy seems so far in advance of the time, was purely the product of imported Christianity.[5] But even here there is no clear evidence that the Taipings were directly influenced by the secret societies; the characteristics of Hakka women themselves, of whom there were many in the early movement, must have played a part in the evolution of Taiping policy.[6]

There is nevertheless abundant evidence of direct influence. Not only was the name of the early Taiping organization—commonly abbreviated as Shang-ti Hui—very similar to that of the T'ien-ti Hui (Heaven and Earth Society), but there were also marked similarities in their initiation ceremonies (although one was polytheistic and the other strictly monotheistic), their predilection for secret code-words—which the Taipings used even in their official publications—their use of riddles, and the style of their proclamations. Like members of the secret societies when they came out in open rebellion against the Manchu dynasty, the Taipings ceased to shave their heads; they too reverted to Ming dress and wore red turbans. The official seals of Hung Hsiu-ch'üan and his son, the "rustic vulgarity" of which was so scorned by contemporary scholar-officials, bear a strong resemblance (as Hsieh Hsing-yao has pointed out) to the passes or belt badges (*yao-p'ing*) given to secret society members. Both contain expressions of superstition or appear to contain riddles. The Taiping seals were carved with Sung-style characters rather than the normal "seal characters," which are more difficult to decipher. (Secret societies sometimes used the two types of script on the same seal.) The Taipings attached great importance to the "royal" seals, making a ceremonial occasion of striking them. Thus it is significant, not that they should have been so different from the imperial seals of tradition, but that they should so closely have resembled those of the secret societies, their debt to whom the Taipings appear to have been anxious to forget. The Taiping "sacred treasury" (*sheng-k'u*) system may well have been influenced by the practice of communal property, at least in food, prevalent among some of the secret societies in Kwangsi before the Taiping rising, and expressed in the appellation *mi-fan-chu* (rice masters) given to their leaders.[7]

These are a few aspects of Taiping ideology and organization that may have been influenced by the secret societies, or by the rebellious tradition common to both.[8] It is when we try to go further, to discover what the actual relations between them were, that we run into difficulty. Aside from the obvious problems connected with studying clandestine organizations, the study of relations between the Taipings and the secret societies is made more difficult by the reticence of the Taipings themselves on the subject. Admission of any debt to the secret societies seems to have been as incompatible with the imperial pretensions of Hung Hsiu-ch'üan as it had been with those of Chu Yüan-chang.

In only one source is there any extensive account of what Hung Hsiu-ch'üan is said to have thought about the secret societies.

Though I [Hung Hsiu-ch'üan] never entered the Triad Society, I have often heard it said that their object is to subvert the Tsing [Ch'ing] and restore the Ming dynasty. Such an expression was very proper in the time of Khang-hi [K'ang-hsi], when this society was at first formed, but now after the lapse of two hundred years, we may still speak of subverting the Tsing, but we cannot properly speak of restoring the Ming. At all events, when our native mountains and rivers are recovered, a new dynasty must be established. How could we at present arouse the energies of men by speaking of restoring the Ming dynasty? There are several evil practices connected with the Triad Society, which I detest; if any new member enter the society, he must worship the devil, and utter thirty-six oaths; a sword is placed upon his neck, and he is forced to contribute money for the use of the society. Their real object has now turned very mean and unworthy. If we preach the true doctrine, and rely upon the powerful help of God, a few of us will equal a multitude of others. I do not even think that Sun-pin, Woo-khi [Wu-Ch'i], Kung-ming [Chu-ko Liang], and others famous in history for their military skill and tactics, are deserving of much estimation, how much less these bands of the Triad Society.[9]

Although it is impossible to be sure whether this was really the opinion of Hung Hsiu-ch'üan, or merely that of his cousin, the ideas expressed do not seem incompatible with what we know of the Taiping leader's character. He objected to the Triads because they wanted to restore the Ming, and because of their polytheism, degeneracy, and ineffectiveness. But it is difficult to believe that in practice the Taiping attitude toward the secret societies and the powerful challenge they posed to the established order in the late 1840's can have been governed entirely by this somewhat lofty disapproval. For instance, the early Taipings did not refuse to have anything to do with individual members of secret societies or even their leaders.

According to investigations carried out in Kwangsi in the 1950's, virtually all Triad members in Kuei-p'ing hsien north of the Hsün River and in the region of Ta-huang-chiang-k'ou and Hsin-hsü had been absorbed into the God Worshippers' Society before the Chin-t'ien rising.[10] But in the period before the Taipings were strong enough to absorb other groups, or could attract secret society leaders by other means, we know nothing about the relationship between them. Not long before the rising, however,

two female rebel chiefs, of great valour, named Kew erh [Ch'iu Erh] and Sze san [Su San-niang], each bringing about 2,000 followers, joined the army of the Godworshippers, and were received on submitting to the authority of Hung and the rules of the congregation. . . . About the same period, eight rebel chiefs belonging to the Triad Society, intimated to Hung siu tshuen

[Hung Hsiu-ch'uan] their wish to join his army with their respective bands. Hung . . . granted their request, but under condition that they would conform to the worship of the true God. The eight chiefs declared themselves willing to do so, and sent their tribute of oxen, pigs, rice, etc. Hung . . . now despatched sixteen of the brethren belonging to the congregation, two to each chief, in order to impart to them and their following some knowledge of the true religion before they had taken the definitive step of joining him. When preparatory instruction had been received, the chiefs dismissed their tutors with a liberal sum of money, as a reward for their trouble, and soon after, they, with all their followers, joined [Hung's army]. Fifteen of the teachers of the laws of the congregation gave the money which they had received into the common treasury; but one of them kept the money for himself without saying a word. . . . As soon as his concealment of the money was proved, Hung . . . and the man's own relatives, who were present in the army, desired to have him punished according to the full vigour of the law, and ordered him to be decapitated as a warning to all. When the chiefs of the Triad Society saw that one of those who had just been despatched as a teacher to them, was now killed for a comparatively small offence, they felt very uncomfortable, and said, "Your laws seem to be rather too strict; we shall perhaps find it difficult to keep them, and upon any small transgression you would perhaps kill us also."

Thereupon [seven chiefs] . . . with their men, departed and afterwards surrendered to the Imperialists, turning their arms against the insurgents. Lo ta kang alone remained with Hung. . . .[11]

The most notable secret society leader to merge his force with the Taipings was Lo Ta-kang. He and his followers were apparently absorbed entirely into the Taiping system, abandoning all Triad organizational forms, banners, and so on and accepting Taiping ideology. Another Taiping leader said to have been a secret society member at one time was Huang Wen-chin, but there is no evidence other than recent oral testimony.[12] As to the connections other Taiping leaders may have had with secret societies in Kwangsi, one can do little more than speculate. As we shall see, there were rumors at the time that Feng Yün-shan and even Hung Hsiu-ch'üan himself were members of the Triad Society. It seems unlikely that Feng, as the real founder of the God Worshippers' Society, would have had no contact at all with secret societies, and their influence on Taiping organizational forms may have come through him, yet there is no more than rumor and unreliable evidence for such a supposition. Yang Hsiu-ch'ing also left a strong mark on the Taiping system, but there is no evidence that he was ever a member of a secret society. On the other hand, in view of what is known of his early career, it would be surprising if he did not have some such connections. Local tradition has it that before joining the God Worshippers he had or-

ganized an armed band to beat up tax collectors; when moving about
the hills at night each man carried four lanterns, in order to give an
impression of great numbers.[13]

The question of the actual relations between the Taipings and the
secret societies, and indeed the whole attitude and policy of the Taipings toward them, is closely tied up with the case of the mysterious
person known as Hung Ta-ch'üan, whose identity has been the subject of controversy for more than a century.[14]

When the Taipings withdrew from Yung-an (Kwangsi) on April
7, 1852, their rear was attacked by Ch'ing troops and a man was captured who was at first mistaken for Yang Hsiu-ch'ing. He was one of
several men wearing chains, in order, it was suspected, to trick the
troops into releasing them by pretending to be prisoners of the Taipings.[15] He was taken to the Imperial Commissioner Sai-shang-ah's
headquarters, where he identified himself as the "T'ien-te Wang
Hung Ta-ch'üan" and "brother of Hung Hsiu-ch'üan."

In a deposition taken down at this time he stated that his name
was not really Hung Ta-ch'üan (he did not reveal his real name),
that he came from Heng-chou in Hunan, and that he was thirty years
of age. He had received an education but had several times failed the
examinations. He had become a monk, and later had made a final,
unsuccessful attempt at the examination. After this, in resentment,
he had started to study military strategy. Several years ago, he stated,
he had been in Kwangtung as an itinerant monk, and had made the
acquaintance of Hung Hsiu-ch'üan and Feng Yün-shan, who had
been traveling between Kwangtung and Kwangsi organizing "vagabonds" into a group which they called the T'ien-ti Hui. Later Hung
Hsiu-ch'üan "invented magical arts and pretended to be able to con-
verse with spirits," and by the time they met again, Hsiu-ch'üan had
changed the name of his organization to Shang-ti Hui.

Hung Ta-ch'üan's account of his position in the Taiping hierarchy
is full of ambiguities. He seemed to imply that he was the equal of
Hung Hsiu-ch'üan—they called each other "brother"—but that
Hsiu-ch'üan "revered him as 'T'ien-te Wang' " and asked his advice
on all military matters. In spite of this he had been discontented; he
had nurtured his own ambitions, but had been prepared to await his
opportunity.

The prisoner was regarded as an important catch, and it was decided to send him to Peking, though in the event he was executed before reaching there. On the way another kind of deposition was writ-

ten, in the form of a memorial from Hung Ta-ch'üan to the Ch'ing Emperor. A third document in the case is the report from the judicial branch of the Grand Council on Hung Ta-ch'üan's evidence, and the discrepancies among the three accounts caused some historians in the past to doubt not merely his veracity and his relationship to the Taiping leaders, but his very existence.[16]

Recent research, however, seems to have solved satisfactorily the question of his real identity. On March 30, 1856, Lo Ping-chang, the Governor of Hunan, reported the capture of two T'ien-ti Hui rebel leaders who had recently led an unsuccessful attack on Kuei-yang. They were Chiao San (or Chiao Yü-ching) and Hsü Yüeh-kuei, a woman. In the evidence they gave after being captured they said that they were the younger brother and the wife respectively of Hung Ta-ch'üan.[17] The historian P'eng Tse-i has found confirmation of their statements in a militia commander's report on the capture of Hsü Yüeh-kuei's sister. This woman, it appeared, had been married to Chiao San, and in her deposition she stated that her sister had been married to his brother Chiao Liang, alias Hung Ta-ch'üan. This in turn was confirmed by investigations connected with her trial, and by other local records.[18]

Hung Ta-ch'üan's real name, then, was Chiao Liang, and he was a member of the T'ien-ti Hui. But what was his position, if any, in the Taiping leadership? What was the significance of his assumption of the title T'ien-te Wang? And what light does the case throw on relations between the Taipings and the Triads?

The most important evidence, apart from his own deposition, that Hung Ta-ch'üan (or Chiao Liang) was a member of the Taiping leadership is found in a memorial dated May 10, 1851, from Chou T'ien-chüeh, Governor of Kwangsi. According to the memorial as cited in one source, the Governor's investigations showed that the leaders of the Taiping rising were Hung Ta-ch'üan and Feng Yün-shan. The Imperial Edict in reply to Chou's memorial repeated this information.[19] The only other evidence is a statement in a book called *Chin-ling ch'un-meng chi-lüeh* by Shen Mou-liang that the Taipings raised a monument in their capital to certain of their leaders, including Hung Ta-ch'üan.[20] It is primarily on the basis of these accounts that the historians Jung Meng-yüan, Jen Yu-wen, and Kuo T'ing-i are prepared to accept Hung Ta-ch'üan's version of his position in the Taiping hierarchy. Lo Erh-kang, however, points out that in other sources containing Chou T'ien-chüeh's memorial the name is given as Hung Hsiu-ch'üan and not Hung Ta-ch'üan.[21] He sug-

gests that the official record was falsified in order to make it agree
with Sai-shang-ah's claim that he had captured an important Taiping
leader. This argument is not entirely convincing, yet there are
grounds for regarding the evidence of Chou's memorial with caution.
There exists in English translation a letter from Chou to a friend,
undated but from internal evidence probably written in the second
half of April 1851, that contains the following passage: "As to these
rebels, they have five great leaders. Hung tseuen is the first, Fung
yun san is the next, Yang sew tsing is the next, Hoo yih seen and
Tsang san sew are the next. Hung tseuen is not a man of the surname
Hung—he is a barbarian of some sort." This last remark seems to
refer to Hung Hsiu-ch'üan, and in quoting the letter Meadows noted
that Hung's Christianity, "and the fact of his having resided some
time with Mr. Roberts, probably gave rise to this belief concerning
him."[22]

The evidence against there having been such a man as Hung Ta-
ch'üan in the top Taiping leadership is mainly negative. Since the
government authorities in Kwangsi had for several years before 1850
been trying to pretend that all was well in the province, and to deny
that anything resembling rebellion existed there, it is not surprising
that they should have been very ignorant about the various subversive groups and their leaders.[23] They were particularly ill-informed,
as already noted, about the early Taipings. Yet the absence of evidence cannot be dismissed. Li Hsiu-ch'eng's deposition, which speaks
at some length of the Taiping leaders, does not mention Hung Ta-
ch'üan's name, nor does any other Taiping document. As far as I
have been able to discover, none of the original documents from the
Liang Kuang Governor-General's archives, which are now in the Public Record Office in London and not really open to the suspicion of
fabrication, makes any reference to Hung Ta-ch'üan before the time
of his capture; nor do any of the depositions of captured rebels that
survive in the same collection.

Apart from documentary evidence, it is necessary to consider
whether, from what we know of the organizations and personalities
involved, the Taiping leadership would have been likely to include
a kind of representative of the Triads, which Hung Ta-ch'üan implied he was. The Triads, as T'ao Ch'eng-chang pointed out, were
made up of individually established groups, without any central
control whatever and often without even any actual connection with
each other, except possibly in time of open rebellion.[24] There could
not therefore have been an overall Triad leader at this time. The

year before the Taiping rising there had been a Triad-led rebellion under Li Yüan-fa in Hsin-ning (Hunan) and this had, it is true, spread into the border regions of Hunan, Kweichow, and Kwangsi. But it had been suppressed six months before the Taiping rising, and there had been no other risings in Hunan until after the Taipings had taken Yung-an (September 1851). Such Triad activity as there was in the Liang Kuang then was sporadic and uncoordinated, and is unlikely to have produced a major leader. If Chiao Liang had been such a leader and had joined the Taipings with his followers, it is possible that he would have been accepted in the same way as Lo Ta-kang was. But had this been the case, we might expect him to have boasted of it, and his existence before he was captured would probably have been better known to the government. It is unlikely, too, that if he had his own followers he would have been vulnerable enough to have been made prisoner by the Taipings at Yung-an. Moreover, there is evidence to suggest that in 1851 and 1852 the Taipings were worried by the apparent willingness of Triad members to enlist in government forces as "braves" (*yung*) and fight against them. Such a situation could hardly have arisen, as Lo Erh-kang has pointed out, if there had been a united Triad organization, and if one of its important leaders had been closely associated with the Taiping command.

To judge from the list of Taiping leaders drawn up by his captors from information given them by Hung Ta-ch'üan, he had a fairly good knowledge of the names, ages, and places of origin of the most important Taiping leaders.[25] This would indicate some kind of association. But it may be that he was merely employed, as a man with some education, as a secretary or drafter of proclamations. This is indeed what an old man of Hsin-ning (Hung Ta-ch'üan's native place) told a Chinese historian in 1951.[26] If his ambitions and his pretension to seniority over Hung Hsiu-ch'üan had become known to the Taipings, this might explain why they put him in chains.

Recent research into early Taiping history has unfortunately done nothing to elucidate the problem of the title "T'ien-te," and there is little one can add to what has already been written on this subject.[27] As Teng Ssu-yü remarked in 1950, there was considerable confusion a century earlier over which rebels were which, not only on the part of the government but even among the rebels themselves. Thus, although the "T'ien-te" title was clearly associated with the Triads, I have seen a Red Turban document stating that it was an "empty title" invented by the "heroes at Nanking" (the Taipings) for organizational reasons.[28] This is another confirmation that secret society members "in scattered areas mistook the victory of others as their own, and responded and made proclamations by using the popular reign title, T'ien-te."[29]

Some of the sources of confusion are not hard to trace: the name of the first-ranking Taiping leader was Hung, his second in command was Yang; Hung was the "sacred" name of the Ming restorationists, after the reign title of the first Ming emperor. The Triads also revered the *hung-yang* (Red Sun), both they and the Taipings wore red turbans, both had an attachment to the term *t'ai-p'ing*, and so on.

It was undoubtedly this confusion that led to the speculation, mainly among foreigners in Canton, Hong Kong, and Shanghai, that the Taiping movement stemmed from the Triad Society.[30] Most of this speculation—which might have produced further information—seems to have been halted by the publication of Theodore Hamberg's book, with its apparently authoritative denial of any such origin. According to Hamberg, the only connection between the two organizations was that the Taipings were prepared to accept recruits from the secret societies, but only on their own strict terms.

As noted above, the Taipings were remarkably reticent about their relations with the secret societies. In the period before they left Kwangsi there is only one mention of the Triads in official Taiping documents. This is in a proclamation circulated before January 1852, appealing to members of the San-ho Hui, by name, not to support the dynasty. Later versions of this proclamation, published after the Taipings had left Yung-an, omitted any direct reference to the Triads.[31] Thereafter in no official Taiping publication now extant can any mention be found either of secret society influence upon the Taipings or of relations between the two groups in any period.

Some historians have argued that before the capture of Yung-an the Taipings were in alliance with the Triads, or even that they were part of the same organization,[32] but that while the Taipings were at Yung-an their policy toward the Triads changed radically to one of hostility and non-cooperation. It is not unlikely that at Yung-an the Taipings gave some thought to the question of their relationship with secret societies and other rebels, since it was during their six-month stay in this town that much of their organizational structure was formalized and many of their policies were worked out. But there is no more evidence of any radical reversal of policy at this time than there is as to the exact nature of their practice and policy beforehand. If Hung Ta-ch'üan was neither the Triad "representative" in the

Taiping command nor the leader of a substantial force of Triad men, it is unlikely that anything in his behavior could have brought about any important change of policy.

Although structural and ideological consolidation at Yung-an may indeed have made the Taipings less disposed to cooperate with organizations holding different religious and political views, practical experience probably had a greater influence on their attitude than anything else. Dogma did not keep the Taipings from cooperating with other rebels in certain circumstances, but the unreliability of the Triads as allies could not be overlooked. A Triad leader and sometime ally named Chang Chia-hsiang threw his lot in with the government and, as Chang Kuo-liang, remained, until his death in battle in 1860, one of the most determined commanders the Taipings had to face. Ta-t'ou Yang (Chang Chao), Ta Li-yü (T'ien Fang), and countless other members and leaders of the Triads also treacherously turned against them.

Yet in spite of such unreliability the Triad Society was still a potential ally. About two months after their withdrawal from Yung-an the Taipings entered Hunan, where thousands of Triad members joined them. Li Hsiu-ch'eng mentioned in his deposition that twenty thousand people joined in Tao-chou, Chiang-hua, and Yung-ming, and twenty or thirty thousand in Ch'en-chou.[33] This figure is probably incomplete, covering only a few places in Hunan; nor are government assessments reliable, since officials were often aware only of those who failed to join up with the Taipings and were captured. Even before entering Hunan, the Taipings must have been well aware of the scope of this potential support—their intelligence system was efficient—and they were not slow to take advantage of the assistance that these allies could give in military operations. There was no question, when military needs pressed, of insisting on adherence to Taiping ideas and discipline before accepting help, and it is clear that secret society groupings sometimes cooperated militarily with the Taipings under their own banners.[34]

Some of the evidence of cooperation between the Taipings and other rebel groups seems very flimsy indeed. One cannot take as evidence of joint action the fact that a secret society rose at a time or place favorable to the Taiping military campaign; nor can one assume that all who used the Taiping name were authorized to do so.[35] On the contrary, those who used the Taiping name without adhering strictly to Taiping protocol were probably unauthorized, even opportunistic, allies. Had the Taipings been in formal alliance with such groups, they would probably have insisted on forms that were in accordance with their own system. As for rebels who had no connection whatsoever with the Taipings, the prestige and appeal of the Taiping name were enough to justify their use of it.

The greatest wave of risings came in the decade after 1854, when hundreds of thousands of rebels, mostly Triads, were active in Kwangtung and Kwangsi. But there is little evidence that the Taipings made any great effort to coordinate this movement or unite with it as a means of depriving the government of the revenue and supplies from the area.

The only definite evidence of contact between the Taipings and the "Red Turban" rebels of Kwangtung is an unpublished letter, apparently from the Taiping commander at Ta-pu-p'ing in Kwangtung to Kan Hsien and Li Wen-mao at Fatshan, which mentions a Taiping gift of gunpowder.[36] There are however certain questions connected with this document that remain to be examined, and it cannot be taken as proof that there was any close connection, certainly not at a high level, between the Taipings and the Red Turbans. Nevertheless there were those who thought at the time that the new rebellion had something to do with the Taipings. Officials in Canton believed that the Taipings had sent men to coordinate the risings.[37] A correspondent signing himself "L. O." wrote to the Hong Kong newspaper *Friend of China* in June 1853, saying that "four head men from the Taeping Wang's army at Nanking" were in Canton "enlisting and training recruits for his service" in preparation for an attack on Canton the following year. He even claimed to have met one of them and seen his credentials, in the form of "an enigmatical name" of Hung Hsiu-ch'üan himself.[38] But this may have been no more than another case in which Triads used the Taiping name for their own purposes.

Ho Lu, who took Tung-kuan, Kwangtung, in June 1854, was said to have been "a follower of Hung Hsiu-ch'üan";[39] but in fact his connection with the Taipings may have been only that he was once a follower of Ta Li-yü (T'ien Fang), who had briefly joined them.[40] New material cited by Jen Yu-wen states that after the Taiping advance on Nanking, Lo Ta-kang sent a man called Cho Chieh-sheng to Kwangtung to make contact with Triad leaders.[41] None of this evidence is very conclusive, however. Unfortunately, for every Taiping publication or document that has survived, thousands of others that might have thrown light on this problem, particularly letters and dispatches, have disappeared.

Jen Yu-wen tends to assume that if secret society rebels showed signs of discipline, or of a relatively constructive policy, they must have come under the influence of the Taipings. He considers, for instance, that the enlightened policy of Huang Ting-feng in Kwangsi in 1857 in forbidding gambling and opium smoking and in insisting on strict discipline and good behavior, together with his economic policy, must have been inspired by the Taiping example, though not necessarily by direct contact.[42] However, among Triad rebels, the quality of a group, the degree of its discipline, and so on depended greatly upon the character of the individual leaders. Some acted in a purely destructive way and behaved like bandits, whereas others tried to win popular support, to "right wrongs," and to establish some sort of effective administration; had they not done so, they would not likely have survived for as long as they did.[43]

If the Taipings did have a policy of absorbing and transforming secret society bands that wanted to join them, Shih Ta-k'ai certainly did not adhere to it while campaigning in Kiangsi in 1855. He enlisted large numbers of Triad members from Kwangtung, many of them disbanded Ch'ao-chou "braves." Numbering, according to some government reports, between twenty and thirty thousand, they constituted an important reinforcement for the Taipings at a critical time. There is strong evidence that they were neither regrouped nor re-educated, but were allowed to retain their own organization, banners, and society names.[44] Official memorials report the appearance of multicolored rebel banners (*hua-ch'i*), in contrast with the Taiping banners, which were yellow. This shows that secret society groups were fighting alongside the Taipings as separate units. A wall painting discovered in Anhwei in 1951 shows such units attacking a town on one side under a banner reading "Yüeh-tung t'ung-i" (United Brotherhood of Kwangtung) while Taiping troops acting as auxiliaries are attacking the town on the other side. The painting was probably done by Triad soldiers under Shih Ta-k'ai's command.[45]

Li Hsiu-ch'eng referred in his deposition to these "Kwangtung soldiers" and the damage they did to the Taiping cause through their lack of discipline.[46] Government officials also noted that the secret society groups were unstable allies, not strictly committed to acting in coordination with the Taipings. Many of them turned coat; but so did many Taiping leaders in the later period, and it is unreasonable to ascribe all the degeneration in the Taiping movement to their influence. Most of the official references to divisive tendencies among the allied rebels refer to the later period, especially after the fall of the Taiping capital, when such demoralization was as common among the Taipings as among their allies.

The rising of the Hsiao-tao Hui (Small Knife Society) in Shanghai in September 1853 gave the Taipings their first real opportunity to show support for another rebel movement. According to a foreign account, when the rising started, its leader Liu Li-ch'uan sent two messengers to the Taipings asking them to dispatch a high official to them.[47] There is some disagreement among historians as to whether the messengers ever arrived, but many believe that help was refused and blame the Taipings for the eventual failure of the Shanghai rising. A. F. Lindley, a friend of the Taipings, stated that the Shanghai rebels wrote "tendering their allegiance to the Tien-wang [Hung Hsiu-ch'üan]. He, however, refused to accept them, despite the enormous advantage he would have derived from the possession of the treaty ports, until such time as they should understand and profess Christianity. . . ."[48] However, when British representatives visited Nanking in June 1853 and presented a number of questions addressed to Yang Hsiu-ch'ing, one of the answers was: "To your enquiry (whether the Canton and Fuhkeen factions in occupation of Shanghai have as yet given their allegiance to us, and whether we will accept their submission) I reply that not only will we permit the factions at Shanghai to yield obedience to our rule, but would wish the myriad nations of the earth to submit to our sway."[49]

Whether or not this was merely a ritual statement, it is clear that the Taipings did not give any assistance to the Hsiao-tao Hui in Shanghai, in spite of an official report that Lo Ta-kang, the ex-Triad Taiping commander, was preparing six hundred small boats to break the blockade and bring aid to Shanghai.[50] There is a fairly convincing argument, however, that they were unable rather than unwilling to do so. The two most distinguished Taiping specialists, Lo Erh-kang and Jen Yu-wen, have pointed out that even before the rising the Shanghai rebels had asked help from Lo Ta-kang, but it had not been given because both the Taiping capital and Lo's own base at Chen-chiang were under enemy attack at the time.[51] At the time of the Shanghai rising the Taipings had three major commitments—their Northern and Western Expeditions, and the defense of their own capital. The Northern Expedition, sent to attack Peking, set out with only 20,000 men, too few for a task of such magnitude. The Western Expedition, launched at about the same time, comprised the main Taiping force, and by the time of the Shanghai rising was already in difficulty and had been forced back to Kiukiang. The only relief available when the Northern Expedition was in danger was the garrison that had been driven out of Lo's base at Chen-chiang. The third major task, which must have taken precedence in the minds of the Taiping leaders, was the protection of their capital, which was threatened by the forces of the Kiangnan Command under Hsiang Jung. In order to send military aid to Shanghai, the Taipings would first have had to fight off the siege of Nanking and destroy the besieging army. This the Taipings were unable to do until 1860, though they drove the enemy as far as Tan-yang in 1856. Leaving aside the question whether they wanted to do so, one must conclude that the Taipings were militarily unable to attack Soochow and Shanghai until after 1860.

Of course it is not impossible that the Taipings, or some of their leaders, were disdainful of the Shanghai rebels, or that they underestimated the importance of being able to control Shanghai; nevertheless the accusation that their attitude was bigoted and uncooperative would seem unproven. Earlier in 1853 there had been a rising in Fukien under Huang Wei. Again, according to Lindley, the Taipings had refused their advances.[52] But a report from Shanghai received in Canton said that the Taipings had sent money and firearms to the rebels in Amoy.[53]

The most fruitful alliance the Taipings had with other rebels was that with the Nien. The existence of groups called *nien-tang* has been traced at least to 1808, though some historians trace their origin back to the period of the White Lotus rebellion.[54] Until 1853, however, their activities seem to have been more or less confined to the traditional occupations of secret societies—banditry of one kind or another, salt smuggling, gambling, rent resistance, attacks on prisons and pawnshops, kidnapping, and so on. This activity greatly increased during the widespread famine in Anhwei in 1851–1852. When the Taipings took An-ch'ing on February 24, 1853, and opened the prisons, it is said, prisoners from north of the Huai River returned home full of praise for their liberators. Shortly afterward, the important Nien leader Chang Lo-hsing came out in open rebellion, and in the months that followed several Nien groups were transformed into armed bands.

In June 1853 the Taipings sent out their Northern Expedition, and this force passed through Meng-ch'eng and Po-chou. This seems to have been the first direct contact between the Taipings and the Nien, and there is no evidence that the Taipings attempted to make an alliance with them at this time. Nevertheless it seems certain that the Northern Expedition was greatly strengthened by the Nien recruits who were absorbed into its ranks. Similar reinforcements strengthened the Taiping relief expedition that set out in February 1854. This force, which at first numbered only 7,500 men, was soon increased, presumably by Nien and other recruits, to a huge army of several tens of thousands. But in this case there is evidence that Nien units fought alongside the Taipings as separate entities. It is possible that this was because the Taiping commanders Huang Sheng-ts'ai and Tseng Li-ch'ang did not have the personality or the authority to insist on their complete incorporation.[55] As far as is known, there was nothing resembling a formal alliance at this time.

A new situation arose after dissension broke out among the Taiping leaders in 1856 and Shih Ta-k'ai defected with thousands of the best troops. In the crisis of leadership and military manpower that resulted, two new commanders, Ch'en Yü-ch'eng and Li Hsiu-ch'eng, came to prominence. Li Hsiu-ch'eng, to judge from his deposition, was certainly less thoroughly committed to Taiping religious dogma than some of his elders; possibly the same was true of Ch'en Yü-ch'eng. So they may have been less inclined to balk at associating themselves with other rebels. On the Nien side, circumstances favored an alliance with the Taipings, in that by this time Chang Lo-hsing had twice been obliged to abandon his base at Chih-ho-chi and move southward. It was at this time (1857) that, using the ex-Nien Li Chao-shou as an intermediary, Li Hsiu-ch'eng persuaded Chang Lo-hsing, "who claimed to have an army of a million," to join him.[56] The two forces met in March, and in spite of a faction among the Nien leaders that opposed the alliance, undertook several joint operations.

The relationship was perhaps more than an alliance, but less than an amalgamation. The Nien leaders were given honorific titles and seals by the Taipings; they also used Taiping flags and let their hair grow. Apart from this, the Nien groups retained their independent command and organization, and the Taipings apparently did not or could not interfere in their internal affairs. Although in his deposition Li Hsiu-ch'eng speaks of Chang Lo-hsing as if he had been a subordinate, he did not address him as such in communications.[57]

Cooperation was limited to military operations between 1856 and 1861, and the Nien kept to the area north of the Yangtze. Sometimes the Taipings acted as auxiliaries for the Nien; sometimes it was the other way round. The Nien had more troops; the Taipings had better troops and better commanders.

The Nien contribution to the Taiping cause, apart from local military support in Anhwei, was to act as a screen protecting the northern frontier of Taiping territory from government operations against it. Taiping aid was of less direct significance to the Nien, who were not really threatened from the south anyway. They were, however, threatened in their home base, and the assistance they gave to the Taipings south of the Huai River meant that they could not adequately protect it. Consequently, much of it was reoccupied by the government during the period of the alliance. This was the main reason for opposition to the alliance among Nien leaders.

This was not the only reason why the alliance ended and Chang Lo-hsing returned to his base late in 1861. He later said that it had happened because of bad relations with the Taipings.[58] For their part, the Taipings were never entirely at ease with their Nien allies. "Although I had enlisted Chang Lo-hsing and his army," wrote Li Hsiu-ch'eng, "[I found that] this type of man accepts honors but not orders." He felt that the Nien allies were greatly responsible for the breakdown of Taiping discipline.[59] This view finds some support in other contemporary sources.[60] Taiping disapproval of the Nien was partly influenced by the unreliable behavior of Li Chao-shou and of the perennial turncoat Miao P'ei-lin, both of whom were thorns in the side of the Taipings—and of the government too—for much of the time.

Relations were not entirely broken off after 1861. When Ch'en Yü-ch'eng was captured in May 1862 (betrayed by Miao P'ei-lin), Chang Lo-hsing attempted to intercept the escort that was taking him to Sheng Pao's headquarters. He failed, and after the death of Ch'en Yü-ch'eng, the Taiping presence in northern Anhwei came to an end. In 1863 Chih-ho-chi was retaken by government forces and Chang Lo-hsing captured and killed.

His nephew and successor, Chang Tsung-yü, together with other Nien leaders, cooperated with the Taiping expedition to the north-west under Ch'en Te-ts'ai and Lai Wen-kuang, and returned with them when they were summoned back to the relief of Nanking. This force, which had been unable to get past government armies in Hupeh, lost heart when the Taiping capital fell, and was defeated in October 1864. After this the key to the survival of both the Taiping and the Nien remnants was to combine their forces. Lai Wen-kuang was put in command of a force in which the Taipings were distinctly in the minority, and a period of amalgamation began.

In this period Taiping procedure was followed in external forms; the leaders were given titles by Lai Wen-kuang in accordance with Taiping protocol. Lai brought to the Nien the military methods and experience of the Taipings, and found new application for Nien guerrilla and cavalry techniques. Li Hung-chang wrote, "The Nien bandits in Meng-ch'eng and Po-chou used to make a living of brigandage and they were mostly stupid and obstinate, lacking any great ambition. . . . Once the Taiping rebel, Lai Wen-kuang, joined them, introducing the military organization and cunning of the Taipings to reorganize the masses, they have been . . . causing us so much trouble as almost to threaten the safety of our capital."[61] The phase of amalgamation continued until the Western Nien were defeated. Lai Wen-kuang surrendered and was executed in January 1868.[62]

We do not know to what extent Taiping cooperation with the Nien was the result of local initiative and to what extent it followed a high-level policy decision. Li Hsiu-ch'eng was certainly instrumental in enlisting Chang Lo-hsing's support, but Chang was officially recognized by Nanking and, it was rumored, had been received in audience by Hung Hsiu-ch'üan and loaded with gifts.

Taiping relations with other rebel movements in the later period seem often to have been of an entirely local nature and dependent on the particular Taiping commander involved. In the winter of 1861 when the Taipings were advancing on Ningpo, a secret society called the Lien-p'eng Tang (Lotus Mat Association) rendered them some assistance.[63] Another secret society, the Chin-ch'ien Hui (Golden Coin Society), rose in August 1861 at P'ing-yang in Chekiang shortly after the Taiping commander Li Shih-hsien occupied Yen-chou. In October the Chin-ch'ien Hui is said to have appealed to the Taipings to attack Wen-chou, only to be told, "You have already stripped the town bare, and now, because you fear the government troops, you ask us for help and want us to take an empty town! If we want to take towns we do not wait for you to ask us. It is disgraceful that you do the looting first and then call on us!"[64]

Another mass enlistment, presumably of secret society members, occurred in 1861: "From Te-an hsien in Kiangsi, and from Sui-chou, I-ning, Wu-ning, Ta-yeh, Hsing-kuo, Ch'i-shui, Ch'i-chou, Wu-chiang, Chiang-hsia, Chin-niu, Pao-an, P'u-ch'i, Chia-yü, T'ung-shan, T'ung-ch'eng, and other places, more than forty leaders of risings sent people with petitions to [Soochow], offering to join us."[65] We do not know how many joined Li Hsiu-ch'eng when he was campaigning in this region in the spring of 1861, but Hu Lin-i, governor of Hupeh, estimated that seventy or eighty thousand had been "pressed" into the Taiping army in I-ning and Wu-ning alone.[66] These recruits seem to have been more or less absorbed into the Taiping ranks, as there is no evidence that they operated thereafter under separate banners. But already there was a certain laxity in the discipline of Li Hsiu-ch'eng's force, now swollen to immense proportions by the addition of a large body of Shih Ta-k'ai's former troops and by Li Hsiu-ch'eng's easy acceptance in the Soochow region of many government soldiers who had been willing to change sides.

According to Li Hsiu-ch'eng, the Taipings had no contact with the Moslem risings in Yunnan, Shensi, and Kansu, but it is not impossible that Ch'en Te-ts'ai had made contact with Moslem rebels in Shensi after his communications with Li Hsiu-ch'eng had been broken. There is no evidence to suggest that the Taipings had any contact with the Miao rebels of Kweichow in the 1850's.

The pattern we see in the development of the Taipings' relations with their most important ally, the Nien, provides a key for a general assessment of their relations with movements of rebellion against the Ch'ing. At times when the Taipings were strong and, above all, full of self-confidence, they seem to have felt no particular need for allies, at least not for the unreliable allies that alone existed, though they were obviously always interested in enlisting recruits. Their attitude toward the secret societies, including the early Nien bands, was probably colored by disdain for those who wanted to restore a dead dynasty instead of founding a new one, for rebels who had neither the Taipings' monotheistic religious beliefs (immensely superior, in their view, to the idolatrous polytheism of the secret societies) nor the strict discipline and exalted bravery that stemmed from this faith. The Taipings scorned the disunity of the secret societies (less marked among the Nien than among the Triads) and their rudimentary organization. The sophisticated administrative machinery and the hierarchy the Taipings themselves had worked out were designed for the realization of far more advanced ideas than the secret societies were capable of.

During the Northern Expedition of 1853, as in the early days in Kwangsi and Hunan, the Taipings had felt strong and confident, able to dictate terms to other rebellious forces that wished to join them. They were able to dominate and rapidly absorb the Nien supporters who flocked to their banners in North China, just as they had done earlier with the thousands of Triad members in Hunan.

By the time that the relief expedition was sent to the north, the situation had already changed appreciably, if the reports about Nien and other rebels operating with the Taipings under their own flags are true. This change may have been partly the result of diminished Taiping prestige, the smallness of the relieving force, and the personality of the commanders. But it may also have been a consequence of a change in the nature of the Nien movement itself. Nien bands were being transformed into units of armed rebellion and were now in a better position to demand a measure of independence as allies.

The Taipings were in difficulties that could no longer be considered temporary, and much of their dynamism and prestige had gone. They were obliged to solicit assistance from the Nien and accept it on terms very different from those they had been able to insist on before. In a situation in which, after the Taiping leadership struggle, there was a marked decline in morale, discipline, power, and central authority, military considerations seem to have taken precedence over matters of principle. There was a tendency for individual Taiping commanders to carve out spheres of influence and act alone. Whether or not they found allies and the kind of agreements they came to depended not only on the nature of local rebellious forces, but also on the character of the Taiping commander in question.

The Taipings have often been blamed for failing to unite effectively with other rebellious movements, but the objective reasons for this failure are often ignored. It is true that they tended to be somewhat "sectarian"; they despised more backward rebels, and not entirely without reason. They often found them very unreliable allies. The Taipings were understandably hesitant about associating with people who might bring their movement into disrepute, for they were anxious to show that they were not just "bandits who harmed the people." By the time they overcame their principled disdain for the secret societies, they had already lost some of the very principles that had made them superior to the others and that offered the only hope of transforming those others into effective allies.

The Making of a Rebel: Liu Yung-fu and the Formation of the Black Flag Army

ELLA S. LAFFEY

The political career of Liu Yung-fu—His impoverished peasant background—First contacts with rebels—Wu Yüan-ch'ing and the Taiping heritage—Rivalry between rebel bands—The rebel campaign of 1866–67 and the formation of the Black Flag Army

One of the aspects of research on secret society activities in modern China that suffers most from the effects of their secrecy and their political failure is that of the individual personalities involved. Although men and not social conditions make revolutions, with few exceptions we know little about how the social conditions of a given time and place affected the lives of individuals so as to make a particular person, at a particular time and place, become a rebel.[1]

Liu Yung-fu was a petty bandit and rebel active in Kwangsi province during the 1860's. Unlike most of his fellows, he survived long enough to become respectable, and he left behind an autobiography that describes both his family background and some of his reasons for becoming a rebel.[2] Although the autobiography glosses over some of the less attractive aspects of his career, it is sufficiently detailed to provide a more intimate perspective than is usually available on the way large numbers of peasants, the most easily oppressed and physically immobile of all social groups, became bandits or rebels.[3]

Born into an extremely poor peasant family in western Kwangtung in 1837, Liu Yung-fu as a young man participated in the banditry and local revolts that occurred in Kwangtung and Kwangsi provinces in the wake of the Taiping Rebellion. Later Liu and his band of followers, like many such groups, were pushed over the Sino-Vietnamese border into northern Tonkin by the Ch'ing armies' mopping-up campaign against Taiping remnants, local bandits, and other disorderly elements in the southernmost provinces of the empire. In the ensuing struggle for survival in the back country of northern Vietnam, Liu's apparently considerable military and administrative talents eventually led to the establishment of a base area along the upper course of the Red River. In the meantime, Liu's Black Flag Army had clashed with Miao tribespeople. When the Vietnamese government attempted to pacify the Miao, Liu and his band fought on the government side, and Liu received official rank and legitimate status for his efforts. From the Vietnamese point of view it was easier, cheaper, and probably more effective to buy Liu's cooperation than to mount a campaign to oust him. During the 1870's and early 1880's the Black Flag Army participated in several campaigns in upper Tonkin, some directed against the ever-present bandits and restless tribespeople and some against attempts by the French to extend their control into northern Vietnam. The last of these campaigns led to Liu's being given Chinese rank and military office and to his repatriation to China. In 1895 Liu Yung-fu and the remnants of the Black Flag Army were stationed on Formosa when the Japanese forces arrived to take over the island as provided by the Treaty of Shimonoseki. There Liu helped organize the military resistance to the Japanese occupation mounted by the short-lived Formosan state. In this, his last great battle, the ex-bandit and former rebel led his forces on behalf of the first republic in the Far East. After returning to the Chinese mainland, Liu spent his remaining years in relative tranquility. He died peacefully in 1916 while dictating his autobiography to his long-time follower, Huang Hai-an.

Although Liu Yung-fu's career spans modern Chinese history from the Taiping Rebellion to the beginnings of republicanism in the Far East, he never achieved the national stature of a Tseng Kuo-fan or Tso Tsung-t'ang. His career never transcended the southernmost provinces, the setting that had made him what he was. Only when the affairs of the South and Southwest moved to prominence in the affairs of the empire as a whole did Liu Yung-fu and the Black Flag Army become part of Imperial history—without losing their essentially regional character. Of course, no clear line can be drawn between local and national history; even if the whole is seen as more than the sum of its parts because it provides the overall structure within which the parts exist, the relationship is still a reciprocal one. The life of a man like Liu Yung-fu can serve as one way of approaching the local setting, and at the same time indicate the concrete effects of the setting on one man's career.

According to his autobiography, Liu Yung-fu[4] was born in 1837 to a poor Hakka family in Hsiao-feng hsiang, a rural area near Ku-sen-tung in Ch'in-chou prefecture,[5] one of the often troubled "four lower prefectures" in the extreme west of Kwangtung province.* Although Liu dutifully acknowledged himself a "Ch'in-chou man," he spent only the first six years of his life there, and he considered his real "native place" Chin-ts'un, a village of Po-pai hsien in Kwangsi province. Chin-ts'un was the birthplace of his father, Liu I-lai, and of his grandfather, Liu Ying-hao,[6] but according to Lo Hsiang-lin, Liu Yung-fu's great-grandfather, Liu Pang-pao, had come to Chin-ts'un as a small boy with his father from Chia-ying-chou in eastern Kwangtung.[7]

The reasons for the Liu family's original move from Chia-ying-chou are unknown. The reasons for their many subsequent moves are plainer and are related to increasing rural poverty in the nineteenth century. By the time Liu Yung-fu's father and his father's younger brother, Liu I-ting, reached manhood in the 1820's, the Liang Kuang were beginning to feel the first pinch of the economic and social decay in the countryside that marked the Ch'ing dynasty's declining years. The long slide down into the conditions that produced the great rebellions of the mid-nineteenth century picked up momentum quickly in Kwangtung and Kwangsi, where ethnic tensions between Hakka and Punti, Han and non-Han tribespeople, increased the friction caused by overpopulation, and where an illegal but lucrative trade in opium stimulated the growth of pirate and bandit groups. The back country of the Liang Kuang, an area generally viewed as insalubrious and uncivilized by outsiders, seems to have been considered a hardship post by Chinese officials, and the quality of local officials may have been somewhat lower there than elsewhere in the empire.

The Lius had been able to make a living in Po-pai as small farmers for three generations. For several years after their parents died, I-lai and I-ting stayed in their birthplace in deepening poverty. They then decided to move to western Kwangtung. Their reasons for selecting this area are not clear, for their existence in Ch'in-chou was even more marginal than it had been in Po-pai. In Po-pai the family had at least been small cultivators, but they never again securely achieved

---

* Laai Yi-faai, "The Part Played by the Pirates of Kwangtung and Kwangsi Provinces in the T'ai-p'ing Insurrection" (Ph.D. diss., Berkeley, Calif., 1950), pp. 130–33, enumerates some of the reasons why this area was particularly disturbed, including its distance from the center of the provincial administration at Canton, its long irregular border with Kwangsi, the existence of river routes of communication into southeastern Kwangsi, and its status as a salt-producing area, which gave rise to bands of salt smugglers. By the 1830's, western Kwangtung already swarmed with an anti-government population.

this status. In Ch'in-chou, I-lai brewed and sold small quantities of liquor, and I-ting worked for a pork butcher. After a decade of scratching out a meager existence, the brothers were able to replace the thatched bamboo shack they had built when they first arrived in Hsiao-feng hsiang with a three-room mud structure. With the achievement of more permanent living quarters I-lai finally married, at the age of forty *sui*. Both the bridegroom's advanced age and the type of bride he procured indicate the poverty of the household: he married a widow surnamed Ch'en from a neighboring village, and when she married Liu I-lai she brought the son of her first marriage with her. When Liu Yung-fu was born in 1837 his father was forty-two *sui*. Shortly thereafter Liu I-ting married.

The death of I-ting's wife initiated a new period of decline in the family's fortunes. I-ting turned to gambling, and his elder brother decided to move his own family elsewhere. They moved first to a nearby village, where I-lai made an unsuccessful attempt at farming. After this unfortunate venture, the family was reduced to going into the hills for mushrooms to dry and sell in the market.

The family moved on again, this time across the border into Shang-ssu chou in Kwangsi province, a move made at the suggestion of a kinsman, who offered Liu I-lai shelter for his family and some of his surplus fields for cultivation.[8] After they had sold all their household possessions to get money for the trip, the Lius heard that their kinsman's son had been imprisoned in Shang-ssu for connections with local bandits. After some hesitation, Liu I-lai decided to move to Kwangsi nonetheless. On their arrival at Pa-chia-ts'un near the New Market of P'ing-fu, they were lodged in the structure that housed their kinsman's oil press, where they remained for several years. The officials at Shang-ssu were "rapacious and corrupt," and the case of the kinsman's son was kept pending until the father sold off his land and possessions to raise the bribe necessary to procure his son's re-lease. This is the first reference in Liu Yung-fu's autobiography to the local officials, the representatives of the Confucian state.[9]

Liu I-lai moved his family again, this time even farther into the back country to the aboriginal area (*t'u-ssu*) of Ch'ien-lung-chou. The family erected a rude shelter of sticks and grass, and Liu Yung-fu's father scratched out a living on the slopes. When Liu Yung-fu was thirteen *sui* he found work on the small boats that plied the rapids of the local rivers, and by the time he was fifteen he was familiar enough with the local hazards to navigation, both human and natural, to serve as a pilot. When Liu Yung-fu was seventeen *sui* both of his parents and his uncle died, and he and Li Pao-ko, his mother's son by her first marriage, could afford to give them only temporary burial. The half-brothers then went to the neighboring village of Kao-feng, where they slept in lean-tos they often had to share with livestock at night, and made a living of sorts by fishing and charcoal-burning during the day.

According to his autobiography, while Liu Yung-fu was at Kao-feng he had a dream, the prophetic nature of which became clear to him only later. While in the hills gathering fuel, he had stopped to rest on a large rock when he saw a very old man. The man asked him, "Why is the Black Tiger General still resting in the mountain groves? Why has he not come out of the hills?" Liu woke with a start and realized the encounter was just a dream. It was only much later that he understood the reference to the "Black Tiger General" as a reference to himself and the color of his army's banners.*

This encounter aside, the years in Kao-feng were bitter ones. Yung-fu was an impoverished young man without parents, wife, children, or fixed abode. There was no permanent place with which he could identify. Even the village he called his "original home" in Po-pai represented a fairly recent migration, and if the Liu family had been able to maintain themselves in Po-pai, they had hardly flourished there; according to the autobiography there was only one heir in each generation until his father's. Even before Liu Yung-fu was born, his father and uncle had had to leave Po-pai, and during his youth the longest time he had spent in one village had been the first six years of his life, spent in the village where he was born. Liu Yung-fu considered himself to be of peasant stock, but by his father's day, and certainly in his own, the family clearly figured among the marginal elements in the Chinese countryside. They possessed few if any attributes of a stable peasant family, save perhaps the ties of kinship, and how fragile a support this could be had been demonstrated in Pa-chia village. Liu I-lai died still trying to make a living from the poor, hilly land in the back country along the Kwangtung-Kwangsi border. Liu Yung-fu himself evidently did not even try to make his living as a farmer. Instead, he found odd jobs along the rivers as a boatman or fisherman and in the hills as a fuel-gatherer and charcoal-

* LST, p. 29; *Chuan*, pp. 8, 9. (See note 2 for these abbreviations.) Whether or not Liu Yung-fu actually had such a dream is irrelevant. What is significant is that he saw fit in 1915 to say that he had and to note its significance with respect to the color of his banners. Such portents and omens did, of course, play a role in Chinese folk traditions and in the beliefs and mythology of the secret societies.

burner. These latter occupations were known for being riddled with brotherhoods and secret societies. Liu's autobiography does not mention any contacts with such groups during his early days, but as a vigorous young man without any real roots in the traditional, more stable rural order, he was ideal material for recruitment into the ranks of an illegal group.

Liu Yung-fu's first recorded contact with the bandits and rebels operating in the Liang Kuang in the wake of the Taiping Rebellion came in 1857, when he was twenty-one *sui*. In that year, "The long-haired ones were everywhere, calling for the destruction of the Ch'ing and the restoration of the Han; there was no place that did not have them."[10] As a modern historian has observed, it is difficult not to sympathize with the reasons Liu put forward in his autobiography for joining the rebellion: "It would have been shameful if I did nothing to benefit the people; besides, I could not continue night and day eating thin rice gruel to soothe my hunger."[11] If Liu's motives for joining the rebels were grounded in both idealism and self-interest, the way the initial contact was made seems almost appallingly casual. Liu Yung-fu, his half-brother, and four fellow villagers simply went in a body from their village to the town of Ch'ien-lung-chou itself to explore the possibility of joining the rebel army there. After several days in Ch'ien-lung-chou, three of the six young men decided to return home, but Liu Yung-fu, his half-brother, and one other man decided to join the rebels. Apparently Liu and the others initially went to Ch'ien-lung-chou because it was the closest rebel-held town, one that had been taken fairly recently. After deciding to join the rebels, the three young men left Ch'ien-lung-chou for the village of Fu-lu, a rebel stronghold that had been occupied for several years by a band of slightly over one hundred men, led by four brothers surnamed Cheng. The brothers' original home was Na-liang in Ch'in-chou prefecture, the area in western Kwangtung where Liu Yung-fu had been born. Whether the ready acceptance of Liu Yung-fu and his two companions came as a result of prior acquaintance or home-area ties, or simply because of the new recruits' keenness, it is now hard to tell, but in a very brief period the three young men seem to have been accepted into the vanguard (*hsien-feng*) alongside the Cheng brothers.[12]

The whole affair seems strikingly low-key. There are no blood oaths, no awesome initiation rites,[13] just six disaffected young men walking to the nearest rebel-held point to look over the situation and see whether they cared to join the dissidents. Three of them decided against it and went back home. The remaining three also walked away from Ch'ien-lung-chou, but it was to join another rebel band elsewhere. At the very least, the entire episode indicates conditions of widespread and profound social anarchy; under anything approaching settled social conditions, men do not in effect go window-shopping for a congenial band of rebels to join.

The following year, 1858, Li Pao-ko fell ill and died, leaving Liu Yung-fu alone in the world. In this same year, when he was twenty-two *sui*, Liu had his first recorded contact with rebels who had stretched a tip of the Taiping mantle over their activities.[14] Wu Yüan-ch'ing, also known as Wu Ssu and as Wu Ling-yün, was a major figure among the bands of rebels and bandits that boiled up in Kwangsi in the 1850's.[15] Wu Yüan-ch'ing's once wealthy family had been ruined by avaricious officials, and he became a rebel in the summer of 1852. For about five years thereafter he operated from a base in Lung-lo, a market town in his native hsien of Hsin-ning.[16] In 1857 he joined forces with other rebel groups to attack the Hsin-ning hsien capital.[17] Wu Yüan-ch'ing's ambitions clearly went beyond simple banditry. While still at his original base in Lung-lo, he set up his own administration and gave official ranks to his subordinates and allies.[18] From 1857 on, Wu Yüan-ch'ing's theater of operations seems to have grown rapidly, and his claims to legitimate status along with it. It is not clear whether he began using the title *wang* (prince) in 1858 when he occupied Lien-lo, or in 1860, when the combined rebel forces attacked the city of Yang-li-chou in T'ai-p'ing prefecture and threatened the prefectural seat, T'ai-p'ing, itself.[19]

Whatever Wu Yüan-ch'ing's actual connection with the Taiping Rebellion, in 1858 the band led by the Cheng brothers and Liu Yung-fu learned of Wu's victories in Hsüan-hua. They went to Wu's camp and offered their support and then returned to Ch'ien-lung-chou. Not long thereafter, some of Wu's military chiefs began operations near the New Market of P'ing-fu. One of them, Wu Erh, from Ling-shan hsien in Kwangtung province, had connections with the Chengs, and the Cheng band joined what became a combined force of about three thousand men for several months of campaigning in the P'ing-fu area.[20] The bands roamed almost at will: "At that time, the officials in the districts of Shang-ssu, Hsia-ssu, Ning-ming, and Ssu-ming had all run away."[21]

There was little more order and cohesion among the rebels than among their enemies. Within the larger drama of revolt and rebellion, the smaller fry in the border areas engaged in confused, bloody strug-

gles among themselves that were more like gangland warfare than concerted efforts against the comon enemy. Local bands staked out terri-
tories in the vacuum left by the virtual disappearance of the regular
authorities; they moved in with a few thousand men, holding on as
long as possible and expanding when they could. The leader of one
such band, Wu Pi-ling, moved into Shang-ssu with a force of several
thousand men and then marched on Ch'ien-lung-chou. This brought
him into conflict with the other large bandit force in the area, the
combined bands of Wu Erh and Ling Kuo-chin. After participating
in some of the initial clashes between the rival forces, Cheng San, Liu
Yung-fu's chief, returned to his own encampment at Fu-lu, and Liu
and "several tens" of his men accompanied him. Back in Fu-lu, Cheng
met another Ch'in-chou man, one Hsü Wu, who had spent a good deal
of time in Kwangsi and had camped with several hundred men in a
temple enclosure near Fu-lu. The two leaders decided to establish a
joint camp.

The times were beginning to change, however; men who had let
their hair grow long in rebellion began "to shave the hair," i.e., cast
their lot with the Ch'ing dynasty. Cheng San may have been a far-
sighted man. He withdrew and left only part of his force, led by his
two brothers and Liu Yung-fu, in the fortified village at Fu-lu. According to Liu Yung-fu, the Chengs were betrayed by men inside the
village. When Wu Pi-ling attacked at night, the Cheng brothers were
killed and Liu Yung-fu was badly wounded.[22]

For several months Liu Yung-fu convalesced; he had only a few
companions, men who like himself had survived the debacle at Fu-lu.
Meantime, the turning of the tide in the dynasty's favor was becoming
clearer, even in the southern hinterland. While petty squabbles over
territory preoccupied the bandits and rebels, loyalist forces gathered
to break the power of the major rebel leader, Wu Yüan-ch'ing. Early
in 1862 one of Wu Yüan-ch'ing's most important generals was killed
in battle, and the Imperial forces moved to invest T'ai-p'ing. In
March 1862 T'ai-p'ing was recaptured by the Imperial forces and Wu
Yüan-ch'ing was forced to flee to his old base at Lung-lo.[23] While
other rebels were being routed elsewhere in Kwangsi, the Imperial
forces surrounded Lung-lo. In February 1863 they captured Lung-lo,
slaughtering those who attempted to flee and putting the town to the
torch. Wu Yüan-ch'ing's son Ya-chung was one of those who escaped
the general destruction.[24]

In the meantime, Liu Yung-fu had rejoined Wu Erh's forces in time
to be caught in the general reversal of fortunes suffered by the adher-

ents of the ephemeral Yen-ling kingdom. With the resurgence of the dynasty, the various rebel and bandit groups were caught in a pattern of ever-shifting alliances within an increasingly circumscribed area. Wu Erh had joined forces with one Wang Shih-lin and his band, and at one point the joint band even became involved in a Hakka-Punti feud similar to those of pre-Taiping days.[25] As former friends and rivals were picked off one by one by the official forces, the existence of the remaining outlaws became increasingly miserable. For these years, Liu Yung-fu's account lays as much stress on the problems of supply and sustenance as it does on actual fighting.

Hunted and harassed, Wu Ya-chung managed to keep his own force in being in the back country of Kwangsi, perhaps because he was more gifted at warfare than his father, perhaps because the obscurity of an uprooted guerrilla band proved a blessing in disguise. Although Wu's band was steadily pushed ahead of the advancing Imperial armies, it continued to exist and was one of the major remaining rebel groups in 1867, when it was attacked in the vicinity of Chen-an Pass between China and northern Vietnam.[26] Under the direction of Feng Tzu-ts'ai, an old "disorderly element" who had led bandits in Po-pai himself before going over to the dynasty during the Taiping Rebellion,[27] Wu Ya-chung and others like him were pushed across the frontier into Vietnam. In October 1869 Feng marched into Vietnam and met Wu's forces in a final battle in the Vietnamese province of Lang-son (Ch. Liang-shan). Wu died on the battlefield, and the remnants of his band scattered all along the Sino-Vietnamese border.[28]

During 1864 and 1865 Liu Yung-fu was conducting his own search for relative security within the general melee of competing bandit groups. As the larger bands broke up, Liu Yung-fu found himself and his few hundred followers entirely out of money and rations. His autobiography strongly implies he was so desperate that he had no recourse at this point but to rejoin Wu Ya-chung. This may be a later rationalization of his renewed association with a major rebel figure, but it also reflects Liu's aversion to close association with any-one strong enough to restrict his freedom of action. His reluctance may also have stemmed from the recognition that Wu was too promi-nent a figure, one that the Ch'ing forces might be inclined to pursue to the end. In an effort to fathom what looked like an increasingly dark future, Liu consulted oracles. The absolute exhaustion of his own resources brought him back to Wu Ya-chung's camp, where he was given money and supplies.[29] Liu Yung-fu soon left Wu's encamp-ment, however, and underlined his implicit claim to equal rather than subordinate status by setting up his own banner. In memory of his dream, it was black, with seven white stars. Appropriate omens accompanied the dedication of the standard—an apocalyptic darkening of earth and sky, rolls of thunder, and a pouring rain. The Black Flag Army had been founded.[30]

Whatever the long-term portents, the signs for the immediate future were not auspicious. In 1865 Liu Yung-fu led about two hundred followers across the border into Vietnam. He was thirty *sui*, and he had been raised in an exceptionally hard school for survival. As his later career was to indicate, he had learned his lessons well.

The outlines of Liu Yung-fu's subsequent career have been sketched in above, and will not be repeated here. His considerable military talents and keen eye for his own advantage in the struggle for existence among bandit groups in the northern Vietnamese hinterland eventually put him in a position where his allegiance was worth accepting, first by the Vietnamese and later by the Chinese themselves. There is little indication on Liu's part of any overriding political or ideological principles that precluded his offering it. It was in fact his willingness to cooperate with the Vietnamese and Chinese authorities in the suppression of former rebels like himself, some of whom had been his comrades-in-arms back in China, that paved the way for his rehabilitation. The details of his career in Vietnam need no further enlargement here; they are not central to the picture of Liu Yung-fu as a rebel in the making.

The making of a rebel in nineteenth-century China was not necessarily a colorful process; despite the drums, bells, and banners, a large portion of Liu Yung-fu's own account is taken up with the dreary mechanics of the struggle for existence in a declining age—first of his family and then of the outlaws he joined as a young man. He remains, of course, an individual and not a Chinese rebel version of Everyman, but the forces that produced him also molded the lives of many other Chinese of his time, and even a truncated description of the process by which he became an outlaw may raise more general questions bearing on an assessment of the role of secret societies in modern Chinese history.

First, an examination of Liu Yung-fu's background and early career suggests that the Kwangtung-Kwangsi border area was a coherent unit unto itself, and that in many ways it was the border area that was the real functional unit rather than its component provinces. There was a remarkable continuity of personnel from one crisis to another in the southwest, on both the rebel and loyalist sides. Liu Yung-fu participated in the rebellions of the 1850's and 1860's; in the 1870's he participated as a Vietnamese official in bandit-suppression campaigns mounted jointly by the Vietnamese and Chinese against men like himself, and in the 1880's his forces fought the French. Similarly on the official side, one low-ranking man, Chao Wo, who helped sweep the rebels out of Kwangsi, reappears leading Kwangsi troops in Chinese bandit-suppression expeditions in Vietnam in the 1870's and again in the 1880's. One consequence of this continuity of personnel in the southwest complicated the Chinese operations of the 1880's: evidently Feng Tzu-ts'ai never overcame the low opinion he formed of Chao in the 1870's, and it affected relations between the two men in the 1880's, when both were commanding troops for the Chinese. Feng Tzu-ts'ai himself, who was from Ch'in-chou and who began his career as a bandit leader, likewise reappears more than once in the history of his native region.

Among the rebels, it is striking how many men from western Kwangtung were active over a fairly long period in southeastern Kwangsi. The picture is doubtless colored by the fact that much of the information on the subject comes from the account of Liu Yung-fu, who considered himself a Kwangtung man. Still, the large number of rebels he identifies as Ch'in-chou men suggests that the rebel fish found the same water on both sides of the provincial boundary. A cross-checking of bandit groups' native villages, where known, against local gazetteers and maps might indicate the relevance of even smaller units—for example, the primary marketing area—as basic building blocks of large-scale rebellion.[31] In any case once rebellion became widespread, alliances transcending local loyalties had to be formed if the rebellion was to grow, but again a study of Liu Yung-fu's activities suggests that much of the rebel infrastructure retained its local nature. This, in turn, may help account for the rapidity with which secret society rebellions dissolved into fratricidal factions in the face of their acknowledged common enemy, the dynasty, as well as the general absence of any unifying ideology among such groups. The acceptance of similar beliefs and superstitions and traditional standards of legitimacy, together with the usual evocation of avaricious officialdom, does not add up to a coherent and compelling ideology that can bind men together in a common cause. Even when the original motives for revolt were the traditional righteous ones, the lack of a unifying ideology hastened the process of demoralization in adversity. It is all too evident that in the deteriorating conditions of the

1860's in the Liang Kuang, rebels survived by preying on one another and on the surrounding population, and ultimately degenerated, no matter what their origins and pretensions, into essentially predatory forces.

Liu Yung-fu's account of his rebel years cannot answer all the questions posed above; it can only suggest the level on which some of the answers might fruitfully be sought.

Some Notes on the Ko-lao Hui in Late Ch'ing China

CHARLTON M. LEWIS

Origins of the Ko-lao Hui: possible relationship to the Taiping Rebellion—Organization: lodges, hierarchy, ceremonies, initiation practices, and prohibitions—Activities: quest for wealth and power, pillage, and popular justice—Political significance: roles in the Yangtze valley riots, the Mason case, and the Revolution of 1911

During the last fifty years of the Ch'ing dynasty the Ko-lao Hui (Elder Brothers Society) became the predominant secret society in central China. It flourished first within the ranks of Tseng Kuo-fan's Hunan Army. Later it spread down the Yangtze valley into other sectors of the Chinese population. By the end of the Ch'ing dynasty in 1912, its network stretched from the province of Szechwan in the west to Kiangsu and Chekiang in the east, with offshoots in the north that included Kansu, Shansi, and even Shan-hai-kuan, on the border of Manchuria.

Scattered sources provide a fragmentary portrait of a loosely knit association diffused through the towns and villages of the countryside, an integral part of Chinese rural life. Locally, the Ko-lao Hui controlled a number of legitimate and illegitimate economic activities, notably gambling and salt smuggling. Its members sometimes became outlaws and bandits, extorting protection fees from merchants and travelers. It thrived within the provincial garrisons of Hunanese troops stationed along the Yangtze River, and it shared in the perquisites of Hunan's regional power in central China. It collaborated with Hunanese officials and military leaders in the lower Yangtze, and shared the anti-foreign attitudes of the Hunanese literati. For most of the nineteenth century it remained a politically moderate organization.

During the historical transition from Confucian orthodoxy to nationalist revolution that preceded the demise of the Ch'ing state, the Ko-lao Hui played an ambiguous role that is as yet little understood.

Relations between the scholar-elite and the society took new forms as literati nationalists courted Ko-lao Hui support for insurrections against the government. The Ko-lao Hui shared the rising anti-Man-chu feeling of these literati activists, but its ignorant and isolated rural membership was not easily indoctrinated with the ideology of revolution. The society was too dispersed, too loosely organized, and too closely bound to traditional institutions. Its political objectives were vague and its political role circumscribed by the conditions of its existence. In 1911 it played only a minor part in the revolution that destroyed the dynasty.

Origins and Development

Evidence is growing to refute the traditional view of T'ao Ch'eng-chang and others that the Ko-lao Hui originated as a branch of the Hung Men (Hung League, lit. "Vast Gate").[1] Tadao Sakai states that there is a clear distinction between the various branches of the Hung Men, well-known in southern and eastern China since the seventeenth century, and the Ko-lao Hui, which flourished in Hunan, Hupeh, Szechwan, and Kweichow during the late Ch'ing. He believes that the Ko-lao Hui originated in a coalescence of White Lotus remnants, which during the 1860's mingled with branches of the Hung Men and assumed some of their characteristics.[2] Jerome Ch'en in a recent study notes that the Ko-lao Hui replaced the T'ien-ti Hui (Heaven and Earth Society, a branch of the Hung Men) in Hunan during the 1850's, and that the former borrowed organizational and nomencla-tural features from the latter. He also points out that they worshiped separate sets of deceased masters (tsu) "in a way contradictory to the theory that these two societies were one."[3]

To these findings may be added some contemporary materials from Hunan which suggest that the Ko-lao Hui originated in western China—Szechwan and Kweichow—remote from the traditional cen-ters of the Hung Men in the south and east. For example, an appen-dix on the Ko-lao Hui in the Pi-hsieh chi-shih (A record of facts to ward off heterodoxy), first published in 1861, states that the society was most extensive in Szechwan, followed by Kweichow, Yunnan, and Kwangsi. It blames Ko-lao Hui infiltration of the Hunan Army on soldiers recruited from Szechwan and Kweichow.[4] Similar informa-tion is contained in an 1867 memorial from Liu K'un, the governor of Hunan. Liu states that the expansion of the Ko-lao Hui began in Szechwan and then spread to Kweichow. He believes that the society then infiltrated Hunan and spread to the provinces of the southeast.[5] A third source, the gazetteer of Liu-yang hsien (Hunan) compiled in 1873, also designates Szechwan and Kweichow as the main origin of the Ko-lao Hui's expansion into Hunan.[6]

It appears, then, that the Ko-lao Hui took its rise in western China, far from the Hung Men's center of power in the south and east, and that its main flow of expansion was eastward from Szechwan. It remains to be seen whether mid-nineteenth-century documents from southwestern China will confirm the Ko-lao Hui's origins in that region, and to what extent the Ko-lao Hui's organization and ideology are comparable to those of the White Lotus sect. In the meantime, the Ko-lao Hui must be carefully distinguished from other "branches" of the Hung Men and subjected to separate study.

All sources agree that Tseng Kuo-fan's Hunan Army was the main vehicle for the Ko-lao Hui's expansion. In the early 1850's, Tseng may even have encouraged Ko-lao Hui infiltration to offset the influence of the T'ien-ti Hui.[7] By 1861, however, the *Pi-hsieh chi-shih*, which was probably printed by Tseng or other high officers of the Hunan Army,[8] was bitterly condemning the Ko-lao Hui as an obstruction to the campaign against the Taipings. It reported that 30 or 40 percent of new recruits to the army were being lured into the society. Ko-lao Hui members within the army were leading a double life: government soldiers when in camp, robbers and thieves when off duty. Wearing their military uniforms to allay the suspicions of their victims, they robbed large numbers of travelers in the countryside. The Ko-lao Hui had by now absorbed elements of the T'ien-ti Hui and other societies in Hunan.[9] As it spread with the Hunan Army down the Yangtze valley, it encountered and to some extent became identified with the Ch'ing Pang and the Hung Pang (Green and Red Gangs), branches of the Ch'ing Men (Ch'ing League, lit. "Pure Family") that were engaged in transport and smuggling.[10] All these activities threatened government control, and they probably constituted a major reason why Tseng Kuo-fan felt it necessary to disband the Hunan Army immediately after the end of the Taiping Rebellion in 1864.[11]

The breakup of the Hunan Army brought new opportunities for Ko-lao Hui expansion. Restless after the travel and excitement of military service, disbanded soldiers were soon dissatisfied with the quiet life on Hunanese farms, and many sought more interesting occupations in the cities along the rivers.[12] Those who were already Ko-lao Hui members quickly recruited others, among them artisans, merchants, and peasants.[13] In 1867 Governor Liu K'un reported that in Hunan the members of the society were "uncountable" and that they were "tempered by battle." Some of them, because of military valor, had been promoted to the rank of fourth, third, or even second officer. Others, well-to-do persons with commercial interests along the provincial waterways, joined the Ko-lao Hui to protect their wealth. Liu's memorial thus indicates that numerous persons of elite status who were by no means inclined to social disorder had become members of the Ko-lao Hui.[14]

During the next quarter century the society continued to thrive in central China, though its existence entered the historical record mainly when its activities spilled over into violence. In 1870, three years after Liu K'un's memorial, the Ko-lao Hui was blamed for uprisings in seven districts of Hunan,[15] and in 1871 there was an additional disturbance near I-yang.[16] In 1875 Tso Tsung-t'ang led an army out to Lanchow in Kansu on his way to pacify rebellion farther west, which probably accounts for the spread of the society to the Kansu region. One popular story even declares that Tso's army was made up entirely of Ko-lao Hui members.[17] In 1876 the *Peking Gazette* contained a report from the governor of Kweichow that the Ko-lao Hui was active throughout Hunan, Hupeh, Fukien, Yunnan, Kweichow, Szechwan, Shensi, Anhwei, and Kiangsi.[18]

In 1891 the Ko-lao Hui gained double notoriety, first for its alleged fomentation of the Yangtze valley riots in the spring and summer, and then for a conspiracy involving C. W. Mason, a British customs employee who was arrested in September for smuggling arms to members of the society along the Yangtze River.[19] By 1900 dissident literati had begun to encourage anti-Manchu sentiment in the Ko-lao Hui. In the summer of that year T'ang Ts'ai-ch'ang and other veterans of the Hunan reform movement recruited a large Ko-lao Hui army in Hunan and Hupeh for an attempted revolt against the Ch'ing Court. In 1904 Huang Hsing and other revolutionaries used similar techniques in the same area to mobilize a Ko-lao Hui force. Their attempted insurrection, with its center at Changsha, was detected and suppressed, but it engendered anti-Ch'ing sentiment within the society that carried over to the P'ing-Liu-Li uprising of December 1906. This massive outbreak on the Hunan-Kiangsi border was by far the most significant political action of the Ko-lao Hui during the Ch'ing period.

Organization and Activities

The role of the Ko-lao Hui during the late Ch'ing can be understood only in terms of its organization and functions. The brief glimpses we have of the society suggest a loose network with no single head-quarters or leadership. Individual lodges, located all over central China, wove themselves into the fabric of rural life and solicited mem-bers as widely as they could. They shared a quasi-religious heritage drawn from Chinese folklore, rich in moral and ethical idealism and in clandestine ritual. Individual chieftains gained power by personal charisma and by their ability to fulfill the economic and social needs of their immediate followers.

One source on Ko-lao Hui organization dominates all others: the article by Hirayama Shū (Amane)[20] entitled "Shina kakumeitō oyobi himitsu kessha" (The Chinese revolutionary party and the secret so-cieties). Published in Tokyo in 1911, just as the revolution was burst-ing across central China,[21] Hirayama's article was quickly translated into Chinese under the title *Chung-kuo pi-mi she-hui shih* (A history of Chinese secret societies; Shanghai, 1912). Later it became the main source for other treatments of the Ko-lao Hui, in which it is some-times quoted at length without citation.[22] Hirayama's reliability has been praised by as eminent an historian as Lo Erh-kang,[23] but his treatment of Ko-lao Hui history must be used with discrimination.[24] I have drawn from his article here, and from another important source, Matsuzaki Tsuruo's *Jiufu zuihitsu* (Essays of the tender father; Tokyo, 1943).[25]

The basic organizational unit of the Ko-lao Hui was the lodge (*t'ang*), a term traditionally used for a Buddhist temple or monastery and also hallowed in popular thought by the fictional Liang-shan and Chung-i lodges, headquarters of heroic bands in the novel *Shui-hu chuan* (Water margin). Each Ko-lao Hui lodge was designated by four different names: a "mountain name" (*shan-ming*), patterned after the practice of Buddhist monasteries; a "lodge" name (*t'ang-ming*), in the style of the *Shui-hu chuan* heroes; and a so-called "water name" (*shui-ming*) and "incense name" (*hsiang-ming*), which were drawn from Buddhist or Taoist practices or otherwise related to the ceremonies of the particular lodge. There were also "inner" and "outer" code terms (*k'ou-hao*) that served as passwords, and certain metrical verses peculiar to the lodge or expressive of its ideals. An example of lodge nomenclature follows:

A Hunan Ko-lao Hui Lodge[26]

MOUNTAIN NAME: Chin-hua Shan (Embroidered flower mountain)
LODGE NAME: Jen-i T'ang (Benevolent and righteous lodge)
WATER NAME: Ssu-hai Shui (Water of the four seas)
INCENSE NAME: Wan-fu Hsiang (Incense of myriad fortune)
INNER CODES: I-chung (Righteousness and respect)
                  T'ao-yüan (Peach garden)
OUTER CODES: Ying-hsiung (Heroes)
                  K'o-li (Able to stand)

VERSES:

> Chin-hua Shan shang i-pa hsiang
> Wu-tsu ming-erh tao-ch'u yang
>
> (When incense burns on Chin-hua Shan
> The names of the Five Patriarchs are everywhere raised)
>
> T'ien-hsia ying-hsiung ch'i-chieh i
> San-shan Wu-yüeh ting chia pang
>
> (When the heroes of the empire unite their righteousness
> The Three Peaks and Five Sacred Mountains assure stability in
>   home and country)

Lodge members were bound in fraternal association with a complex hierarchy.[27] The highest office was that of the *cheng lung-t'ou* (chief dragon head), under whom was a *fu lung-t'ou* (deputy dragon head).[28] Next came five *t'ang* (lodge) offices: the *tso-t'ang* (seating-the-hall), *p'ei-t'ang* (deputy seating-the-hall), *hsing-t'ang* (supervisor of punishments), *li-t'ang* (manager), and *chih-t'ang* (registrar). Separate but apparently equal were two officers charged with ceremonies, the *meng-cheng* (oath taker) and the *hsiang-chang* (incense master). The five *t'ang* officers also conducted ceremonies when occasion demanded. In addition, there was a subordinate group of five officers that served in military capacities. These were the *hsin-fu* (adviser, lit. "mind and belly"), *sheng-hsien* (sage and worthy), *t'ang-chia* (the *t'ang* household), *hung-ch'i* (red banner), and *hsün-feng* (lookout, lit. "patroller of the wind"). Sometimes these officers were grouped under the heading of *hsiang-chang* (incense masters).

All officers listed so far were considered leaders (*t'ou-mu*). Sometimes the two *lung-t'ou*, the five *t'ang*, and the *meng-cheng* were grouped separately as a controlling body, and were known as the *nei-ko ta-ch'en* (high officers of the inner council) or as the *nei-pa t'ang* (lodge of the inner eight). Below these officers were many additional ratings, with titles such as *ta-chiu* (great nine), *hsiao-chiu* (small nine), *ta-yao* (greater youngest), *hsiao-yao* (lesser youngest), *ta-man* (greater sufficiency), and *hsiao-man* (lesser sufficiency). Sometimes eight of these were distinguished as a separate body and called the *wai-pa t'ang* (lodge of the outer eight). Promotions were granted according to achievement. Outside the regular membership there was an outcaste group, likened by Hirayama to the Eta in Japan. This was called the *pa-p'ai* (eight placards) and comprised members from so-called unclean trades such as cobblers, leather workers, clothiers, and armorers. Such persons were not eligible for promotion. It should be emphasized that the above-mentioned hierarchies were subject to many variations and alternative usages.

Ko-lao Hui ritual is said by Matsuzaki to derive in about equal parts from Buddhist and Taoist practice.[29] The following examples illustrate the heady mystique and quasi-sacred character of the organization.

Opening a New Lodge. An auspicious day was selected and the ceremony conducted in a deserted area, ideally at an old temple deep in the mountains. An altar was erected and various deities enshrined, sometimes including Yüeh Fei, the Southern Sung general who became a martyr to resistance against foreign domination. Pledges to the gods, written in ritual form on specially designated slips of red paper, were placed on the altar; and when all the members were assembled, the *cheng lung-t'ou* faced the altar and chanted the pledges aloud. There followed a form of the ceremony called *tou-hai* (shaking the seas), probably including a blood oath, in which members pledged their common purpose.[30]

Initiation. This ceremony was best conducted in an environment similar to that for opening a lodge. Each initiate was introduced by an old member called a *pao-chü* (sponsor)—sometimes called a *ch'eng-hsiung* (mature brother)—who was responsible for the initiate's character. When lodge members were assembled, the sponsor introduced the initiate to the *kuan-shih-che* (presiding officer), who was one of the lodge leaders. The *tou-hai* oath of common purpose was then administered with the aid of another member called the *pang-hsiung* (state brother). The initiate then knelt before the altar and the presiding officer formally interrogated him:

P. Why have you come?
I. In order to enter your esteemed Society.
P. By whose instructions do you come?
I. By those of Mr. So-and-so.

The presiding officer then turned to the sponsor and asked for confirmation, after which he again questioned the initiate.

P. Do you know the ritual of this Society?
I. I shall follow as taught by the mature brother and the state brother.
P. Why are you entering the Society?
I. For loyalty and righteousness.[31]
P. If the officials know that you have entered the Society, you will be killed. Or if you violate rules of the Society, you will be killed.
I. When it is known that I have let out a secret, I shall assume all the blame myself and never implicate the brothers. Moreover, if I should violate the Society's rules or have collusion with officials, turning my back on Society ritual, I shall receive the punishment of the three swords and the five axes.

To climax the ceremony, the presiding officer, standing to the left of the altar, decapitated a white cock with his sword, shouting, "You will become like this cock!" He then offered it as a sacrifice, lighting candles and burning incense. Next he bound a stick of incense in a piece of colored silk and cut it in two, shouting, "You will become like this incense stick!" When this ritual was completed, the brothers joined in ceremonially shaking hands with the new member.

At the end of the ceremony, the presiding officer inserted the new member's name on an identification ticket called a *pao* (treasure). The ticket was handed to a subordinate, who received it respectfully in both hands while he called in a loud voice, "The Great Brother orders me to hand over this treasure." He then bestowed it upon the new member, who also received it in both hands replying, "Thank you, Brother So-and-so, for this treasure." The new member then paid an initiation fee of 108 cash.[32] All the members then offered congratulations. Matsuzaki states that the Ko-lao Hui initiation ceremony was strict, serious, and impressive, and that no equivalent could be found among other societies.[33]

Once initiated, the new member shared a fraternal relationship with his comrades. In theory, at least, he was bound to a high standard of behavior by a set of ethical precepts called the *shih-chieh* (ten prohibitions). The prohibited offenses were *wu-ni* (disobedience), *ch'iang-chien* (rape), *tao* (robbery for private gain), *tsei* (thievery), *p'a-hui* (incest with a daughter-in-law), *ch'ih-shui fang-shui* (self-seeking, lit. "to drink and throw out water"), *hsü-chiu tzu-shih* (being drunk and disorderly), *sha-jen fang-huo* (murder and arson), *ma t'ien-ti* (cursing), and *hsiung-ti pu-ho* (disharmony with the brothers). In Hunan violators were subject to execution or other severe punishment.[34] In return for his obligations to the society, the member enjoyed the protection of his brothers against outsiders and assistance from Ko-lao Hui lodges wherever he traveled. This assistance could be in the form of lodging, money, or an introduction for employment.

Business. Elaborate ritual often accompanied business relations within the society. A favorite device for recognizing members and exchanging information was a tea-drinking ceremony in which messages were conveyed by the way teacups were offered and received.[35] There was also an elaborate language of hand and body movements used to greet and communicate with comrades of various ranks. Code terms, subject to infinite variation, were also used to exchange information. Some examples follow:[36]

Term	*Meaning*
ch'üan-tzu (ring)	affairs of members
hsin tsai hsüan (new in the occult)	a new member
k'ai shan (open a mountain)	gather for a meeting
chin pu huan (gold not exchanged)	secret documents
ma-tzu (colt)	an outsider
hsün lao (age from smoke)	opium
hsien (thread)	a road
ch'uai hsien (walk or trample on thread)	follow a road
k'ao hsün (rely on smoke)	an opium smoker
hung hua (red flowers)	liquor
ping-tzu (cakes)	silver money
pei (passive of "to be")	be captured (pei-pu)
shu (book)	prison
wei-wu yao-tzu (war-threatening brothel)	a yamen

A common way of extending the influence of a lodge was by running a gambling house, which provided both revenue and new recruits.[37] During the last decade of the Ch'ing, for example, the Ko-lao Hui controlled many gambling houses along the Hunan-Kiangsi border. Every morning the houses sent out men to collect bets from peasants in surrounding villages; in the afternoon a drawing was held and the house paid five-sixths of the total stake to the winner. A flourishing gambling enterprise could bring commercial prosperity to a large area. In the late Ch'ing period, the trading town of Lu-k'ou on the Hsiang River in Hunan contained dozens of gambling houses. During the great festivals in the first, fifth, and eighth lunar months, wealthy merchants came from far away and won or lost enormous sums. In the 1890's Ma Fu-i, the preeminent Ko-lao Hui leader in Hunan, built this area into a major power base for the society. Many new recruits joined, and Ma Fu-i's fame spread widely through the province.[38]

By such methods, the Ko-lao Hui gained wealth and power. Once established, a network of lodges could dominate all levels of rural society. In Szechwan during the Republican period, for example, the society controlled the markets in many communities. According to Skinner, the positions of grain measurers, pig weighers, livestock middlemen, and other commission agents were reserved for Ko-lao Hui members, and a portion of each agent's fees went to the lodge treasury.[39] A similar example comes from the town of P'u-chi in Liu-yang hsien (Hunan), where a six-day livestock fair held every September attracted tens of thousands of farmers from all over the province. During the late Ch'ing, the Ko-lao Hui dominated the fair, and in 1904 used it as an organizational headquarters for an uprising in cooperation with the Hunanese revolutionary Huang Hsing.[40]

As a Ko-lao Hui network became stronger, the pattern of aggrandizement described above could be supplemented by armed robbery or other kinds of organized violence. According to Matsuzaki, tactical preparations were divided into two categories. The first, relating to the assault force itself, was supervised by a *nei kuan-shih* (internal affairs director) and was concerned with discipline. The second was under a *wai kuan-shih* (external affairs director) and was concerned with reconnaissance. This latter function was greatly emphasized. In planning a highway robbery, for example, exact information was obtained on who the traveler was, where he was stopping, and the weight and contents of his baggage. In areas where the Ko-lao Hui was strong, its members invariably included the servants of the wealthy scholar-elite and high officials, and the houseboys of foreigners.[41]

Oaths of brotherhood, which underlay all Ko-lao Hui activity, were reaffirmed in preparation for armed violence. Members symbolically declared their unity of purpose by sacrificing a cock and drinking from its blood. Sometimes a feast was held before the men departed on their assignments. Tactics included such guerrilla techniques as carrying minimum equipment to ensure high mobility, stationing crack marksmen as a rear guard during retreat, and sending messages by placing twigs on the trail in different ways.[42] Sometimes armed robbery was undertaken on a grand scale. According to Hirayama, the high official Li Hung-tsao (possibly a mistake for Li

Han-chang) was once returning from Kwangtung to Peking along the Hsiang River in Hunan when the Ko-lao Hui plundered eighty of the hundred-odd ships in his retinue.[43] Such forays against government officials raise questions about the political ideals of the Ko-lao Hui and its influence on anti-dynastic activity during the late Ch'ing period, to which questions we turn next.

The Yangtze Valley Riots and the Mason Conspiracy

During the nineteenth century, the ideals of the Ko-lao Hui were roughly consistent with the conceptions of social justice and resistance to foreign encroachment contained in the *Shui-hu chuan*, the novel whose influence is so apparent in Ko-lao Hui ritual and nomenclature. The model of political action established in the *Shui-hu chuan* stresses social solidarity, not class struggle. Members of the elite who practice *noblesse oblige* are as welcome in the fictional brotherhood as are peasants, fishermen, butchers, and other commoners. The emphasis on comradeship and fraternity that pervades the novel is not incompatible with the hierarchical distinctions of a Confucian world. Men have different stations, but they share universal attributes as human beings.[44] The heroes of this novel, C. T. Hsia has observed, strive to honor their family name and achieve fame in the service of the state. They hate bad officials and unjust men, but "they are incapable of the kind of abstract hatred that motivates revolution."[45]

The Yangtze valley riots and the Mason conspiracy of 1891 demonstrate that the Ko-lao Hui was too decentralized and too enmeshed in the existing political system to mount a unified movement against the dynasty. Both these affairs, as Guy Puyraimond points out, reflected the "social and economic malaise" that gripped central China at this time.[46] Restlessness was widespread, ranging from Shanghai to Szechwan, and capable leaders could exploit it for particular purposes. But the anti-Manchu sentiment that was to engender unity against the government a decade later was largely absent in 1891.

The Yangtze riots of 1891 were part of a deliberately organized anti-foreign campaign, inspired by Hunanese literati and carried out, at least in part, by members of the Ko-lao Hui. The interpretation of these outbreaks is complicated by the fact that a new Liang Kiang governor-general, Liu K'un-i, had just taken office, with orders to reduce the swollen government garrison at Nanking.[47] Ko-lao Hui members within the garrison participated in the riots in part to embarrass Liu and to prevent his implementing this government policy.[48] Taken as a whole, however, the riots were anti-foreign, not anti-official. This was dramatically true in the Wu-hsüeh riot of June 5, where two foreigners were killed by an angry mob,[49] and the I-ch'ang riot of September 2, where responsible officials failed to take action and the collusion of important persons was widely suspected.[50] Both of these outbreaks, significantly, occurred in the province of Hupeh, outside the jurisdiction of Liu K'un-i.

The limited nature of the protest against Liu K'un-i, and the anti-foreign emphasis of the riots, cast doubt on sources from a later period that try to read back into these events a Ko-lao Hui plot to overthrow the Ch'ing dynasty.[51] A more probable interpretation is that elements of the Hunanese provincial elite acted in concert with military units dominated by the Ko-lao Hui in order to preserve regional interests that the two groups shared in the Yangtze valley. These interests, which dated from the period of the Taiping Rebellion, were in no way incompatible with loyalty to the Ch'ing dynasty.

The Hunanese generally had more to fear from encroaching foreign interests in central China than from the threats of a governor-general, himself a Hunanese, to reduce the Nanking garrison. Since 1860 foreigners had enjoyed privileged status in four inland Yangtze treaty ports, and since 1876 they had traded at six additional ports of call. Foreign shipping had disrupted junk commerce, throwing thousands of boatmen out of work.[52] Catholic and Protestant missionaries from several foreign countries had established churches, orphanages, and schools in many parts of rural central China. During the 1880's huge quantities of Christian tracts, pamphlets, and books had been distributed in the region.[53] In 1890 Chungking had been opened as a treaty port, drawing the vast interior province of Szechwan into the growing treaty system.[54] Missionary pressure to open Hunan itself was increasing.

A series of vituperative anti-foreign pamphlets, published by an expectant taotai named Chou Han and a coterie of literati supporters at Changsha, provided the primary inspiration for the riots of 1891. Similar in style and content to material that Hunanese had been circulating through the empire since the *Pi-hsieh chi-shih* was first published in 1861, these pamphlets used large woodblock cartoons to attract the illiterate and pandered to popular superstition in order to arouse fear against missionary practices. They constantly urged loyalty to Confucian moral values and to the Ch'ing government. Their authors expressed a firm literati faith that an aroused populace would vent its wrath on foreigners, not on the dynasty.[55]

The near simultaneity of the riots suggests literati leadership. Griffith John, the British missionary at Hankow, argued at the time that agitators acting on orders from members of the Hunan provincial elite were responsible.[56] In the Peking protocol of September 9, 1891, nine foreign nations blamed "anti-foreign and anti-Christian members of the literati class, whose head-quarters and centre must be considered to be the province of Hunan, but whose acolytes are distributed over the whole Empire, and are represented even among the highest officials of the realm."[57] The participation of Hunanese ran as a single theme through the entire riot sequence. Propaganda distributed at the riot scenes seems to have come exclusively from Hunan, and testimony from up and down the Yangtze laid the blame on Hunanese instigators.[58] The Ko-lao Hui, by joining in this movement, acted in support of the long-standing Hunanese military presence in the Yangtze region, and in accord with *Shui-hu chuan* ideals of social solidarity.

The conspiracy involving C. W. Mason was very different, as a closer examination suggests. After Mason was seized at Chen-chiang on September 13, government officials initiated a widespread search for his Chinese accomplices. Arrests were made from Hunan to Fukien, but leadership in the plot was finally attributed to two men. One of these was an expectant prefect named Li Hung (Li Hsien-mo), known as the Grand Marshal (*ta yüan-shuai*), who was said to control an alliance of Ko-lao Hui leaders along the Yangtze.[59] The other was K'uang Shih-ming, who admitted to Ko-lao Hui associations in Kiangsu and Fukien. Li Hung allegedly provided money for the arms, 60,000 taels of silver, and K'uang Shih-ming, through various intermediaries, acted as a liaison between Li and Mason. An uprising was scheduled for November 16 at Sha-shih (Hupeh) to revenge the death of Li Hung's father, Li Shih-chung, who after defecting from the Taiping army to become a general in the government forces had fallen under suspicion and been executed.[60] The conspiracy dated from at least 1889, when Mason had agreed to supply weapons to the leaders, but it was not until 1891 that the weapons were shipped and the plot discovered. Li Hung and K'uang Shih-ming were finally apprehended. Li poisoned himself in prison and K'uang was executed.[61]

The Mason conspiracy, like the anti-foreign riots, reflected endemic discontent in the Yangtze valley. Its leaders included at least one member of the scholar-elite. But there is little evidence to suggest that the two affairs were linked in any way or shared a common objective. Li Hung, who was from Honan, seems to have had no connection with the largely Hunanese network that controlled the riots. Motivated by a personal grudge, he financed the plot with his own funds. Others were ready to join him in his proposed insurrection, but they do not seem to have been part of the anti-foreign movement.

The Ko-lao Hui and the Revolutionary Movement

After 1895 the political role of the Ko-lao Hui became increasingly anti-Manchu. China's defeat by Japan, the concessions scramble, the collapse of the imperial reform movement, and the Boxer disaster all brought the Ch'ing dynasty into increasing disrepute. Anti-dynastic sentiment nurtured within the literati class filtered into the ranks of the Ko-lao Hui, and reformers and revolutionaries in search of popular support began to cultivate acquaintance with Ko-lao Hui chiefs. In 1899 the Hunanese revolutionary Pi Yung-nien escorted a group of them to Hong Kong to meet with other revolutionaries and with members of the Triad Society. The resulting organization, the Hsing-Han Hui (Society for the Restoration of the Han),[62] proved ephemeral, but it initiated a collaboration between anti-dynastic literati and the Ko-lao Hui that continued until the end of the dynasty.

This collaboration was limited by Ko-lao Hui decentralization and parochialism. Local chiefs were more easily mobilized by hard silver than by ideological abstractions, and literati activists were never able to control them adequately. In 1900 several of the chiefs who had followed Pi Yung-nien to Hong Kong deserted the revolutionaries to join the reformist Tzu-li Hui (Independence Society), led by T'ang Ts'ai-ch'ang, which was planning an insurrection against the Ch'ing Court with the object of establishing an independent state in South China under the Kuang-hsü Emperor. The Ko-lao Hui chiefs believed that T'ang was lavishly financed from abroad by K'ang Yu-wei's Pao-huang Hui (Society to Protect the Emperor).[63] In August, when the anticipated funds failed to arrive, some of the chiefs deserted T'ang, thereby contributing to the failure of his movement.[64]

Collaboration between literati and the Ko-lao Hui was mainly conducted on the secret society's terms. In part this was because the young reformers and revolutionaries relished the romantic role of popular hero (chieh) and failed to stress political organization.[65] It was also because familiar recruiting techniques appealed readily to the unsophisticated society membership. T'ang Ts'ai-ch'ang, for example, recruited Ko-lao Hui members with tickets printed in secret society style. These were issued from a "lodge" in Shanghai (the Fu-yu Shan or "enrichment lodge"). K'ang Yu-wei, Liang Ch'i-ch'ao, and other literati associated with the insurrection were referred to as "dragon heads" or by other Ko-lao Hui code words.[66]

In 1904, when Huang Hsing was preparing his Hua-hsing Hui (Society for China's Revival) revolt at Changsha, he too solicited the Ko-lao Hui's support on its own terms. Huang and his lieutenant, Liu K'uei-i, made long trips into the countryside to arrange an alliance with the Ko-lao Hui chief Ma Fu-i. A special organization, the T'ung-ch'ou Hui (Society Against the Common Enemy), was created for liaison with Ko-lao Hui personnel.[67] Ko-lao Hui forces were organized separately from the literati leadership to foment sympathetic uprisings in five districts of Hunan. The plot was discovered before it could be carried out, in part because some of Ma Fu-i's subordinates were captured and revealed the plans.

During the two years after the Hua-hsing Hui's failure, anti-Manchu sentiment spread through central China. In April 1905 the Manchu governor of Hunan, Tuan-fang, brutally tortured and executed Ma Fu-i, leaving Ma's Ko-lao Hui lieutenants bent on revenge.[68] Later in the year revolutionaries in Tokyo organized the T'ung-meng Hui (Revolutionary Alliance) and distributed the anti-Manchu *Min-pao* (People's report) on the mainland. Yet the P'ing-Liu-Li uprising that broke out on the Hunan-Kiangsi border in December 1906 again demonstrated the relative inability of anti-dynastic literati to control Ko-lao Hui ideology or organization.

The uprising was born of flood and famine, of Ko-lao Hui anger at the execution of Ma Fu-i, and of oppressive conditions at the An-yüan collieries in P'ing-hsiang (Kiangsi). It was precipitated by a handful of young student revolutionaries, newly returned from Japan, who preached the sins of the Manchus in the border districts of P'ing-hsiang, Liu-yang, and Li-ling; but once the insurrection began, the literati instigators lost control. Leadership of the rebels fell to two Ko-lao Hui chiefs, former subordinates of Ma Fu-i, who published separate manifestos, both bitterly anti-Manchu but contradictory in their ultimate aims. One, following pronouncements of the T'ung-meng Hui, called for a people's republic that would provide equal benefits for all. The other called for a "New Chinese Empire" and the restoration of a Chinese imperial line.[69] The lack of organization that gave rise to this confusion doubtless contributed to the rebel defeat.

The P'ing-Liu-Li uprising was the largest of the decade and required the armies of four provinces to suppress. When it was over, the Ko-lao Hui had lost much of its political vitality in central China.

Abandoning the attempt to combine student idealism with secret society discontent, revolutionaries turned their efforts to the conversion of rank-and-file members of the new government army. As a result, the revolution that broke out in Wuchang on October 10, 1911, was very different from the earlier uprisings based on alliances between literati and secret societies. In the final showdown the Ko-lao Hui, except for members of the army, played an insignificant role.[70]

The Ko-lao Hui and the
Anti-Foreign Incidents of 1891

GUY PUYRAIMOND

*The riots of May–July, 1891—The question of the responsibility
of the Ko-lao Hui—The moving force behind the popular anti-
foreign agitation—Economic and social malaise in the Yangtze
basin—Hypothesis of a deliberate overall design—Hostility of
the literati toward both Christianity and the Ko-lao Hui*

When the Yangtze valley was opened by treaty to Western commerce
and residence, the missionaries became indirect beneficiaries. With
the Peking Convention of 1860 and, more important, the Berthemy
Convention of 1865, their position in the area was rapidly transformed. Catholic missionaries became authorized to buy land on
Chinese territory and to construct buildings there. In accordance
with the "most-favored-nation" principle, this privilege was extended
to the Protestant churches as well, particularly those of British certification.

From this time onward, the security of foreign lives and possessions
was linked, inversely, to the extent of foreign penetration into the
interior of China. The advance of missionary activity unwittingly
fanned into flame a Chinese anti-Christian tradition that had smol-
dered since the seventeenth century. The deeper the Western penetration went, the more the foreign communities in the hinterland were
threatened. A series of anti-foreign uprisings was precipitated that
created diverse and often unrelated lines of force within Chinese
society.

One of these lines of force can be seen in the series of incidents
that swept through the lower and middle Yangtze regions between
May 2 and September 2, 1891. Although they lasted only a few
months, they extended from Wu-hsi on the Grand Canal to I-ch'ang
in central Hupeh, and involved the provinces of Kiangsu, Anhwei,
Kiangsi, and Hupeh. Moreover, incidents appeared to contemporary
observers to be very well organized. The subversive propaganda of

the literati, strongly attached to the traditional socioeconomic order, was not in itself sufficient despite its incontestable influence to account for the rational progression of these uprisings. Even contemporaries searching for a common denominator underlying the various incidents were disinclined to dwell very long on the possibility that these armed popular revolts were inspired principally by ultra-Confucian pamphlets.[1] It was rather the Ko-lao Hui (Elder Brothers Society) that became the primary object of their suspicions.

The secret society known as the Ko-lao Hui, which counted among its membership a considerable number of soldiers, boatmen, peddlers, and the like, was the most powerful of the secret societies of the Yangtze basin.[2] The central government had taken coercive measures against it, as it had against other secret societies hostile to its rule, but without tangible result. The anti-Christian, anti-Western literature mentioned above, flowing into the region of the Ko-lao Hui's influence,[3] no doubt helped set the stage psychologically for violence on the part of the local populace, but it was the presence of the Ko-lao Hui that was to prove decisive.

It was at this critical moment of heightened anti-Western agitation that Liu K'un-i took up his responsibilities as the new governor-general of the Liang Kiang (lower Yangtze). He replaced Tseng Kuo-ch'üan, the brother of Tseng Kuo-fan, whose army had vanquished the Taipings. Tseng Kuo-ch'üan, wanting to retain the loyalties of his former troops, now discharged, had granted them half-pay pensions that had been paid more or less regularly as long as he was in office. The majority of these ex-soldiers, for the most part Hunanese like their commander, were affiliated with the Ko-lao Hui, one of whose primary goals, it seems, was to obtain the regular payment of their pensions. Liu K'un-i, no doubt thinking the expense too great,[4] soon put an end to the pensions, and set out to abolish the Ko-lao Hui as well. In the meantime, on May 2, 1891, the Catholic orphanage at Yangchow was attacked by rioters, an event that sparked a series of anti-foreign outrages. Having begun in the lower Yangtze basin, these riots were to be directed back toward the middle region of the river, finishing finally at I-ch'ang.

At Wu-hu, where the headquarters of the Jesuit mission for Anhwei was located, the revolt lasted for two days, May 12–13. The people moved against the church, the English consulate, and the customs house. Only the church was destroyed, and, although there were some six thousand participants in the riot,[5] no loss of human life is known. A proclamation signed by "The Community of Wu-

hu" called for another uprising on May 20. It recommended that
the inhabitants "destroy the Catholic and Protestant churches and
the property of the missions," but it urged no taking of foreign
lives.[6] It is clear, however, that the objectives envisioned were not
limited to an attack merely upon the missions, but included the
property of the entire Western community—except for the customs
house. Wagner, the consul general of France in Shanghai, who followed the incident with close attention, maintained that the anti-
Christian propaganda by itself could not have sufficed to account for
the scope and organization of the attacks. Moreover, he wrote, "it
has been verified that the rioters obey a discipline and proceed according to a definite method."[7] Further on, his account implicated
the Ko-lao Hui, even insinuating that this society in acting as it did
had been pursuing a plot against the Manchus. Yazawa Toshihiko
has emphasized, "If there had been no method behind the execution
of the revolt, it would without doubt have been impossible to contain the crowd and to prevent it from killing anyone."[8] The Reverend John Walley of the Methodist Episcopal Mission thought in
fact that the proclamation signed "The Community of Wu-hu" had
been the work of the Ko-lao Hui.[9] Father H. Havret, also implicating
the Ko-lao Hui, noted a connection between the riot at Wu-hu and
the attempt of May 2 against the orphanage of Yangchow.[10]

Other less serious riots followed. In his dispatch dated May 24,
Wagner reported that the orphanage at Ho-chou to the north of
Wu-hu had been pillaged on May 16. Notices dated May 14 at Ning-
kuo-fu reported that this populous town situated to the south of
Wu-hu had been filled with unauthorized people and with members
of the Ko-lao Hui. The mission at Ning-kuo-fu was actually attacked
on the following day, May 15, but the authorities were able to maintain order. Although the attack was a failure, participation by members of the Ko-lao Hui was considered worthy of special notice.[11]

When strong security measures were taken, whether by the representatives of foreign powers or by local authorities, the riots failed.
This was the case at An-ch'ing, the capital of Anhwei, but it was not
to be the same everywhere, as Wagner reported on June 4. At Kuang-
te, buildings were damaged on May 23. The same day, the church
at Pi-chia-ch'iao was invaded, while at Chih-chieh-tu some soldiers
returning to Wu-hu joined the populace in destroying the church.

The rioters were never content to limit their attacks to Catholic
establishments, except of course where they alone represented Western power. That all foreign possessions were considered fair game

was confirmed by the events of May 25 at Nanking. Wagner notes that in this city "starting on the evening of May 24, American missionaries were informed that they would be attacked in earnest and that the viceroy was in no position to protect them. They were urged to provide for the safety of their pupils and orphans, etc."[12] The next day, May 25, fires and pillage broke out within the Protestant community as well as the Catholic. Both attacks were ordered, according to Wagner's information, by the Ko-lao Hui.[13] It is worthy of notice that the Ko-lao Hui, the apparent instigator of the riot, took measures to forewarn the missionaries, permitting them to escape and thus to avoid serious injury.

An abortive uprising at Chen-chiang on May 31 was followed by another, this one successful, at Tan-yang on June 2. In this town, the same procedure was followed: fires were lit but no killing took place. The demonstrations at Wu-hsüeh, however, were not bloodless. There, the rapid and violent sequence of events supports the assumption that an explosion of genuine popular indignation had occurred, arising as much from the news coming from Wu-hu and elsewhere as from anti-foreign propaganda itself.[14] Women and children were molested; a Wesleyan preacher, Argent, and a customs agent, Green, were killed. Nor were Westerners the only targets. The Chinese police, obviously surprised and overwhelmed, also suffered. But this case was exceptional. Everywhere else, the same pattern was followed, with the attack limited to destruction of property alone.

Wu-hsi, on June 8, was the fourth town on the Grand Canal to be affected by the riots, after Yangchow, Chen-chiang, and Tan-yang. On June 13 it was Wu-chen near Lake Taihu; on June 29, it was Ju-kao in Kiangsu; the first week of July, it was Fu-chou and then Nan-ch'ang; on July 22, it was Feng-li near Ju-kao. The last and most important riot in this series took place in the middle Yangtze region at I-ch'ang in Hupeh. The American and Catholic churches were burned, as were the building housing the Scottish mission, the new English consulate then under construction, and the homes of the English customs officials. But here, too, there were no murders.

If one observes the course of these events closely, one cannot but recognize in them a certain unity both of conception and of execution. Witnesses like Consul Wagner held the Ko-lao Hui responsible, and in fact the strength of the Society in the region at that time lends credence to this assumption.

Contemporary witnesses, both Chinese and Western, were divided into two groups on the question of the causes of the riots. One, represented principally by the Rev. Griffith John, believed that the riots were inspired by the traditionalist gentry of Changsha, who remained faithful to the Ch'ing. Without denying the importance of the Ko-lao Hui in the Yangtze basin, Griffith John was firmly convinced that the source of all the trouble was the Hunanese literati and their "poisonous literature." In addition, he was persuaded that the higher Chinese authorities, composed also of literati, had done practically nothing to put an end to the spread of the movement.[15]

In contrast to John, a good part of the European community agreed with the official Chinese explanation, which placed the blame on roving bands and brigand societies, specifically the Ko-lao Hui. The French diplomats, Wagner in Shanghai and Ristelhueber, the chargé d'affaires in Peking, shared this opinion.[16]

In the same regions that had twenty years before been the theater of Taiping battles, the Ko-lao Hui, gathering together discharged soldiers now deprived of their pensions, boatmen on Chinese junks unhappy about totally new competition from steam navigation, petty merchants, and peddlers, as well as a large number of social outcasts, no doubt constituted a grave threat to public order.[17] In a report to the throne concerning the riots, Liu K'un-i wrote: "Groups of rebels are plotting together and fomenting trouble. After I assumed the responsibilities of my post, all the local officials to the north as well as to the south of the Yangtze called to my attention in their reports cases of pillage, the frequency of which is growing day by day."[18] The ministers of the Tsungli Yamen were aware of the situation as well. In a memorial to the emperor, they stated: "Secret society bandits are spread throughout each province along the Yangtze. . . . They take advantage of opportunities to cause disorder. Their conduct is exactly contrary to that of loyal subjects."[19]

Hsüeh Fu-ch'eng, the Chinese minister in London and Paris, stated to the Marquess of Salisbury that the Ko-lao Hui was the instigator of these revolts and that it was composed of the discharged soldiers of disbanded armies, originally from Hunan.[20] Chang Chih-tung, governor-general of the Liang Hu (Hunan and Hupeh), stated: "This year, in the fourth and fifth months, secret society bandits caused disorders among the churches all along the Yangtze."[21]

At a conference in 1891 before the Geographical Society of Manchester, F. H. Balfour expressed the opinion that the Ko-lao Hui was in battle against all foreigners, "including the reigning dynasty." As Balfour put it, "the bulk of the confederacy consists of soldiers, disbanded braves, etc. The agents of the Society generally travel as itinerant doctors professing to sell nostrums, really engaged in conveying news from chief to chief and keeping up the fire which without fermentation would, I fancy, be very likely to die out."[22]

At Wu-hu, Tournade, Havret, the head of the Catholic mission,[23] and Walley, of the local Methodist Episcopal mission, all held the Ko-lao Hui responsible. The Jesuit Colombel had recognized some Hunanese among the leaders of the incidents at Tan-yang on June 1 and at Wu-hsi on June 8.[24] Were these men representatives of the traditionalist literati or of the Ko-lao Hui, which was very strong in Hunan? Yazawa inclines toward the latter possibility,[25] but his conclusion, made by analogy only, is without definitive proof. At I-ch'ang on August 23, three Chinese had broken into the Scottish mission.[26] This was an indication that the revolt was already germinating, that discreet preparations were already under way. Who was making these preparations? According to the English consul Everard, it was strangers to the region—natives of Szechwan, Kweichow, Hunan, Hankow, and the nearby island of Hsi-pa.[27] There were, in addition, a large number of Hunanese soldiers under the magistrate of I-ch'ang, a Hunanese named Lo Chin-shen, who himself went over to the insurgents. When one considers that the majority of these elements were probably affiliated with the Ko-lao Hui, the assertion that those who prepared and participated in the revolt were very closely connected with the Society can hardly be said to be without foundation.

The final piece of evidence—and not the least important—connecting the Ko-lao Hui with the riots of 1891 is furnished by the arrest, on September 14, of a British employee of the customs office of Chen-chiang, one C. W. Mason. He was caught red-handed trafficking in illegal arms. The customs office seized some thirty-five cases of various munitions imported from Hong Kong and destined for the Ko-lao Hui.[28] Mason was sentenced to a mere nine months in prison, but the incident permitted the Ch'ing government to maintain a closer watch on the Ko-lao Hui.

The testimony presented above does not, of course, pretend to be an exhaustive survey of all the evidence available. Nonetheless, at this point it seems not unjustified to believe that the Ko-lao Hui, as numerous contemporaries affirmed, were the "common denominator" of these various uprisings.

A number of separate causes underlay the riots and attacks on Western property. The most conspicuous of all was certainly the mass of libelous anti-foreign literature that abounded in the Yangtze basin. These pamphlets were composed by members of the literati, the best known being Chou Han, a native of Hunan and an expectant official.[29] The contents of these tracts were well calculated to arouse the xenophobic emotions of their readers, but other motivating factors, less conspicuous, are to be found in the secret societies and the Ko-lao Hui. That is to say, both the anti-Manchu secret societies and the traditionalist anti-Christian literati were capable of conceiving a program of action and carrying it out through physical assault and the destruction of property.

When one examines the attitude of the rioters wherever these incidents took place, certain constant features appear. First of all, it was the orphanages directed by the missionaries—and specifically the fact that these orphanages tended to deal with all aspects of the child's life—that most aroused the anger and mistrust of the local populace.[30] Another constant was the belief that the foreigners, and particularly the priests, tore out the eyes and entrails of Chinese children and of the dying.[31] These common features were not exclusive to the events of 1891; propagated through the works of the isolationist literati, they had figured in almost every anti-foreign outburst in China since 1840. Historically, moreover, these curious rumors do not date only from the new wave of proselytism that swept China beginning around 1860. They had been spread by various works of literature since the first attempts to implant Christianity in China.[32] In addition, the fact that alchemy had been honored in China since ancient times[33] allowed rumors to be spread that a new, demonic form of this science was being practiced by Occidental masters, now ranged on an equal footing beside the *tao-shih* of popular Taoism. There is little likelihood that the literati believed the legends they helped to propagate, but the stories were useful in alienating the people from the Europeans.[34] In the words of a contemporary Chinese official, "This gossip made of the crowd a flammable mass ready to burst into flames at a single spark. Should the occasion arise, all the accumulated hostility would surge to the surface."[35] It was to the exploitation of this situation that the Ko-lao Hui devoted itself in 1891. It remains to determine what could have incited this society to act as it did and what might have been its goals.

The region in which the disorders developed was at the time in the throes of a continuing moral and economic crisis. It had just begun to recover slowly from the conflict and devastation it had suffered during the Taiping insurrection twenty years before.[36] Soochow had, for example, been sacked by the Taipings in 1860. Chen-chiang and Chin-chiang had been equally affected. All of this resulted in a serious impoverishment of agriculture. And to the terrible state of agriculture was added the decline of a vital commercial activity. The export of tea, which had provided a livelihood for more than a hundred million people, was steadily shrinking in the face of competition from the much cheaper Indian and Senegalese teas.[37] It was easy for the Ko-lao Hui to place the blame for this situation on the Manchu dynasty, and it was equally easy to recruit strong contingents of determined partisans among the discontented. Recruitment was also widespread among the considerable unsettled riverine population of the Yangtze. An atmosphere of malaise had developed among the boatmen, who by then were already suffering from the introduction of steam navigation.

Among the immediate motives that impelled the Ko-lao Hui to act was Liu K'un-i's cutting off the pensions to Tseng Kuo-fan's former soldiers, mentioned above. This almost certainly prompted the Ko-lao Hui to take countermeasures, especially as the membership of the Society was recruited so widely among the ranks of soldiers and ex-soldiers. In his dispatch of June 19, 1891, Wagner writes: "[The Society would like] to force Liu K'un-i to continue the payment of the pensions given to the old troops of Tseng Kuo-fan, which he had eliminated immediately upon taking up his duties as governor-general of Liang Kiang. . . . This may be only a means of making the Viceroy pay amounts far greater than those he wanted to save."

Social and economic malaise thus touched all the various groups that ordinarily made up the clientele of the Ko-lao Hui, and responsibility for it could easily be imputed to a foreign dynasty accused of abdicating without a struggle before those other foreigners, the Westerners. It does not seem, however, that the action undertaken by the Ko-lao Hui in 1891 was catalyzed only by the appearance of an opportune moment or by the hope of realizing economic objectives. Rather, it seems likely that the disturbances of 1891 were the continuation of the riots of 1890 led in Szechwan by Yü Man-tzu,[38] the leader of the local secret society. These riots had succeeded in throwing the Szechwanese branch of the Société des Missions Etrangères of Paris into such disorder that several Christians had had to seek refuge at Chungking. The Father Superior of the Apostolic Vicarate of Eastern Szechwan, Father Blettery, in making a connection between the riots of Chiang-nan and those of Szechwan, regarded the

latter as forewarnings. Father Palissier, assigned to Kweichow, noticed that "the local secret society called the Ko-ti [another name for
the Ko-lao Hui] reacted in response to the secret societies in Szechwan
and in the neighbouring provinces. Ever since the disorders in the
neighbouring areas broke out, the reaction has made itself felt in
Kweichow." Lastly, Msgr. Chausse, in Kwangtung, warned his col-
leagues of the fact that "noises from the North" were arriving in
Canton and that the population thought the hour had come to begin
anew the incidents of 1884—this in a message dated July 12, 1891.
As far away as Fukien and Kiangsi, Father Rey had also had a moment of worry, in the form of some posters inviting the populace to
destroy the Catholic chapel and the Protestant church, but the local
magistrate prevented this from taking place.[39] In each of these cases,
we find ourselves in the presence of activities identical to those that
the Ko-lao Hui had apparently carried out in the Yangtze basin. The
procedure was the same: placards or proclamations calling on the
people to rise up; then, insofar as the local officials did not pose any
opposition, the destruction of foreign establishments.

It seems quite plausible, then, that a large-scale movement had
been envisaged by the secret societies and that it had begun with the
uprisings of Yü Man-tzu in Szechwan. Szechwan was at the time the
great center for the manufacture of drugs and medicines for China,[40]
and one of the "professions" commonly practiced by the agents of
the Ko-lao Hui was that of drug peddler.[41] Moreover, the Yangtze
provided an ideal means of communication.

In light of the foregoing, it would not appear unreasonable to
speak of a general plan, coordinated by the secret societies, in which
the Ko-lao Hui and its activities played a major role, designed to put
the Manchu government in a difficult position by dragging it toward
serious differences with the Western powers. The historian Liu Lien-
k'o sees it this way, at least concerning the Ko-lao Hui. He writes:
"[The Ko-lao Hui] wanted to weaken the Ch'ing still more by creating disorder in the dynasty's relations with the foreigners. It is for
that reason that at that time [1891] along the Yangtze valley incidents
directed against churches, consulates, customs offices, etc., broke out.
All were instigated by the Ko-lao Hui with the goal of overthrowing
the Ch'ing."[42]

The interlude provided by the Sino-Japanese War did not bring
about an end to the activities of the secret societies. In 1898 a new
wave of popular anti-foreign agitation swept through China from
Kwangtung to Kiangsu, finally reaching Szechwan, where Yü Man-

tzu re-enters the scene. Father Flachère, the biographer of Msgr. de Guebriant, who was stationed for many years in Szechwan, stated in 1898 that "the secret societies, whose adherents are rapidly multiplying, do not want to cease their intrigues against the present foreign dynasty. . . . They play their cards well in accusing it of causing all the present ills of China and the humiliating position that China is in with regard to Europe. Thus, to harass both the Europeans and the Christians, and thereby to place the ruling dynasty in a difficult position, to profit from disorder by fomenting civil war, and to transfer power to an emperor of the Chinese race very clearly appear to be the components of their program."[43]

The attitude of the literati was simply anti-foreign; in all other respects, they remained completely loyal to the dynasty. By contrast, the Ko-lao Hui of the Yangtze region and elsewhere, together with the other secret societies to which it was allied, in exploiting a situation favorable to anti-foreign agitation sought a weapon for the overthrow of the Manchus.[44] This was the fundamental difference. Like the Triads, the Ko-lao Hui was one of the offshoots of the Hung Men. Liu Lien-k'o states: "Although comprising two different denominations, the Triads and the Ko-lao Hui had identical aims."[45] The aims of the Triads were very well known: "Overthrow the Ch'ing, restore the Ming." This was not at all true for the literati, who, whether pure traditionalists or advocates of a kind of *yang-wu yün-tung* westernization, were all dynastic loyalists to one degree or another. Their lot during this troubled period became more and more wedded to that of the foreign dynasty. The literati's attitude toward the Ko-lao Hui strongly resembled that of the *Ta-Ch'ing lü-li* (Code of the Ch'ing dynasty). In defining the secret societies as heterodox, the Code rejected them entirely and decreed very severe penalties against their members.[46]

In this regard we may also take note of the opinion of the author of the *Pi-hsieh chi-shih* (A record of facts to ward off heterodoxy) with respect to the Ko-lao Hui.[47] These "facts" are developed in an appendix entitled "Ko-lao Hui shuo" (On the Ko-lao Hui). The hostility of the author, a spokesman for the literati class, is stated in a most unequivocal and striking fashion.

Such hostility was of course only normal. The Confucian authorities had always considered heterodox sects as threats against the established social order.[48] This had been the case with Buddhism and Taoism before they became recognized as a part of the orthodoxy. Living an existence perpetually threatened, the various sects found safety only at night and only by remaining secret. Always exposed to persecution, they frequently tried to protect themselves by launching attacks. Beginning with the uprising of the Pa-kua Chiao (Eight Trigrams Sect) in 1813, the nineteenth century was filled with such uprisings, either successful or abortive, among which one can place that of the Ko-lao Hui in 1891. In their desperate attempts to repel heterodoxy and to re-establish state control over religion, the literati in their diatribes encompassed both the Ko-lao Hui and Christianity in a single condemnation, thus placing them on a more or less equal footing. From the perspective of Confucianism this classification was normal. Without any real awareness of the confusion they were causing, the missionaries had cast their churches in the same mold, in effect, as the Chinese heterodox sects, and, like the latter, became a threat to orthodox authority. "The Christians in China," said Pierre Maybon, "adopt without difficulty the status of numerous Chinese societies. . . ."[49] But what rendered this new "society" considerably more threatening than the others was the active support it received from the Western powers.

There was also a similarity between the social composition of a secret society like the Ko-lao Hui and that of the Christian churches. In both cases, the lowest strata of the population were involved;[50] hence the astonishment shown by certain missionaries when they perceived that the part of the population that seemed most ready to embrace the Christian faith belonged already to a secret society. In fact, in the China of the late nineteenth century,[51] the presence of the Western churches, at once subversive and incongruous, revealed itself as useful to the Ko-lao Hui in realizing the anti-dynastic intentions of the Hung Men in the Yangtze valley. Thus the Ko-lao Hui set in motion the series of uprisings that we have just described.

The movement had a double intent: it was at once a movement of protest against the unpopular measures of Liu K'un-i and, beyond that, a movement of protest against the foreign Ch'ing dynasty. The acts of violence began shortly after Liu took power and were at first limited to the provinces directly under his jurisdiction. Beginning with July 1891, however, the disturbances swept in sequence up the Yangtze, to terminate at the port of I-ch'ang in Hupeh. Finally, as noted above, on September 14, C. W. Mason, a customs employee, was arrested for dealing in arms destined for the Ko-lao Hui.

The Ko-lao Hui disturbances of May–September 1891 were one of a long series of popular outbursts prompted by the economic, social, and political ills endemic to a dynasty on its last legs. But that was not all. The Ko-lao Hui, through its acts and by its very organization, was also making one of the earliest attempts to strike a new equilibrium in a Chinese society trapped in a rigid socioeconomic order and faltering before the incursions of rapacious Western powers. The Ko-lao Hui uprisings were one attempt to bring a measure of certainty to what must have seemed a most uncertain future. Their failure both demonstrated the bankruptcy of the traditional secret society in dealing with essentially unprecedented problems and helped initiate the subsequent era of bourgeois revolution.

The Hung Hu-tzu of Northeast China

MARK MANCALL AND GEORGES JIDKOFF

Origins of the Hung Hu-tzu—"Pai-ma" Chang's thirteen regulations—The political structure and economy of the Zheltuga Republic—European views of the Republic— Characteristics of the Hung Hu-tzu

From the earliest days of outside exploration and settlement of the Amur River system, which by the middle of the nineteenth century had become the frontier area between Russia's Siberia and the Northeastern Region of the Chinese Empire, the population of northern Manchuria had been made up of a mixture of groups. Some had settled as colonists in the area with official aid or sanction; others were illegally engaged in the exploitation of northern Manchuria's natural resources or in banditry. At first, both the officially sanctioned and the unsanctioned groups were composed primarily of Russians. After the middle of the nineteenth century, however, and particularly after Manchuria (hitherto closed to Han Chinese) was officially opened to Chinese settlement by the Manchus for purposes of economic exploitation and defense against increasing Russian encroachment, the Chinese population of northern Manchuria increased rapidly in both categories. The appellation Hung Hu-tzu ("Red Beards"), though used elsewhere in China strictly to mean "bandits," came to be applied generically to all Chinese who lived and worked in northern Manchuria without the official sanction of the Chinese state. Although some Russians, Mongols, and Manchus were occasionally found in Hung Hu-tzu groups, they were composed primarily of immigrants into Manchuria from the provinces of Shantung and Chihli.[1]

Geographically, the Hung Hu-tzu ranged throughout most of Manchuria, across an area almost twice the size of France. In the east they were known in the mountains and the river system of the Ussuri region;[2] in the northwest they were active as far as the Argun River and the upper reaches of the Amur; in the north they centered

around the Zheltuga, a tributary of the Amur, and in the region of
the Amur town of Mo-ho; in central Manchuria they were well
known in the region of the Chinese Eastern Railway. Nor did they
restrict their activities to the highways, the forests, and the countryside: such major population centers as Mukden, Kirin, Dairen, and
Port Arthur came under attack by the Hung Hu-tzu or were centers
of their activities at one time or another. We cannot date their emergence with any degree of precision, but groups known as Hung Hu-
tzu raided towns as early as 1866, and Hung Hu-tzu groups encouraged anti-Japanese guerrilla activities in the 1930's.[3]

The best-known groups of Hung Hu-tzu were active in the gold-
mining areas of northern Manchuria beginning in the 1860's. By
Ch'ing law, the subsoil and its contents were the property of the
emperor; consequently, northern Manchuria's gold-mining industry
was initiated and directed by the state. Working conditions in the
mines were primitive and were kept that way by bureaucratic ineffi-
ciency and corruption, with the result that many of the laborers recruited from the peasantry of North China deserted. Finding it difficult to replace them with further peasant volunteers, the state turned
to deported criminals and "antisocial" elements as a source of labor;
but these too were quick to desert the mines. Some deserters took to
mining gold on their own, thus placing themselves doubly outside
the law, for desertion and for poaching. Others became bandits. Most
Hung Hu-tzu were of these two types. Another group, particularly
prominent in leadership positions, was composed of Ch'ing bureaucrats who had been exiled to work in northern Manchuria for various
reasons or who had fled to the region to escape prosecution in China
proper. Finally, there were some Siberians, Mongols, and Koreans,
though they were never numerous.[4]

The general term "bandits," used most often in the historical and
journalistic literature to describe the Hung Hu-tzu, tends to mask the
wide variety of their social origins. One group of Hung Hu-tzu, for
instance, included the following members: a ruined merchant, who
had been arrested for his debts by the Chinese police but escaped by
bribing a guard; the son of a Chinese whose relations with the Hung
Hu-tzu had led to his violent persecution by the Chinese authorities;
a peasant who had been ruined by a swindler; a man who had killed
another in a robbery; a carpenter who had fled from local oppression; a Chinese Eastern Railway worker who sought more personal
independence than the railroad's management permitted; and a Chinese patriot-populist from South China who had fled, with a reward

of 5,000 ounces of silver on his head, because of his opposition to the Manchus.[5] One is reminded of the cast of characters in the famous Chinese "bandit" novel *Shui-hu chuan.* As might be imagined, this and similar groups were engaged in more than simple banditry. The very fact that Japanese and Russian as well as Chinese enterprises, authorities, and subjects were objects of the Hung Hu-tzu's attention inevitably gave their activities a political character.[6]

This political character is plainly apparent in the thirteen rules established for the conduct of one Hung Hu-tzu band by its leader, known as "Pai-ma" Chang ("White Horse Chang").[7] To join the group, a new member had to be presented by at least twenty other members. To gain full membership, he had to declare his willingness to accept the leadership of the head of the band, to pass through an initiation ceremony conducted by the leader, and to prove himself by participating in an expedition.

Members were enjoined to help their comrades whenever necessary, to maintain the band's secrets, to undertake any duties assigned them, and to behave justly. Any member who engaged in antisocial action (as defined by the band) was to be severely punished. Clearly, the members of "Pai-ma" Chang's band did not consider themselves bandits.

The band's rules further distinguished between practitioners of what it considered socially acceptable and socially unacceptable professions. The former were permitted to continue to practice their profession after joining the band; the latter, notably fortune-tellers and astrologers, were not. Furthermore, members who were too strongly attracted by these "parasitical professions" were forbidden to hold leadership positions. That this was a serious matter is clear from the rule that failure to exercise leadership when assigned by the group was punishable by death.

Other regulations distinguished between those whom the band considered legitimate enemies and subjects for plunder, and those whom it regarded as meriting protection. Women, children, old people, and isolated individual travelers were excluded from attack. Bureaucrats and other official personages, whether good or corrupt, were legitimate objects for attack when they passed through the territory under the band's jurisdiction. A corrupt official, however, was to lose all his possessions, whereas an official of good reputation was to have only half his goods confiscated. Another group officially excluded from attack were foreigners; they were even to be protected "discreetly" so as to avoid complications with the Treaty Powers, though this provision appears to have been honored rarely if at all.[8] During expeditions, the violation of women was punishable by death, as was plunder for individual gain as opposed to the gain of the group as a whole.

"Pai-ma" Chang's rules established two mechanisms for the promotion of group cohesion and solidarity. One was a recognition ritual: a particular way of smoking cigarettes that allowed Hung Hu-tzu members to recognize each other. Once his identity was established, any Hung Hu-tzu traveling outside the band was expected to extend to a fellow member whatever aid the latter required. The other was a resolute insistence on the primacy of group loyalties over personal ties. Executions of members for infraction of the regulations were to be carried out by the band's members, chosen by lot. Anyone who defaulted in this assignment, even if he were required to execute a close relative, was himself punishable by death.

The income received by the band from any particular expedition was to be divided into nine equal parts: two parts for the satisfaction of the band's needs as a group, one part to whoever had furnished the information leading to the expedition, four parts for distribution among all the members of the band, one part for distribution among those who had taken part in the expedition itself, and one part for distribution to the families of band members who had been killed or wounded in the service of the band—a kind of rudimentary social security system.

It is clear from these thirteen regulations that the Hung Hu-tzu, or at least one group of them, not only made decisive distinctions between themselves and outsiders but enforced certain social and moral values as norms of behavior within the group. Moreover, they were conscious of themselves as a group *in time*, as is clear from their procedures for replenishing and increasing membership and for contributing to the care of families of members who had fallen in the group's service. As rudimentary as these characteristics may appear to be, they suggest a sort of "Hung Hu-tzu consciousness" that went beyond that of the average Chinese bandit.[9]

This Hung Hu-tzu consciousness—this sense of being something other than outlaws from Chinese society—found its clearest expression in the history of the so-called Zheltuga Republic, a highly self-conscious and rudimentarily communistic society that developed in the gold fields along the Zheltuga River in northern Manchuria in the latter part of the nineteenth century. European travelers in Manchuria around the turn of the century, especially those with utopian socialist or anarchist leanings, saw the Republic as a vindication of their belief in the naturalness of a socialist or anarchist society, the more so since it had seemingly developed without political or ideological influences from the West. As Alexandre Ular remarked:

The work and life-style of these men, who could be described as antisocial and resembling the cannibals of Fiji, recalls the system dear to Jean-Jacques [Rousseau]. . . . To be sure, it is strictly fear on the one hand and economic conditions on the other that produced the republic. But it must be remarked that one does not find there the "unhappy individual" described by European socialists, who claims to be leaving one social order for another that he deems better. Rather, the citizen of the republic is a vigorous individual who stands up courageously against society and liberates himself from it, in the various senses of the word *liberate*, and then deliberately becomes a cog in a machine that runs by itself.[10]

Although we do not know exactly when the Zheltuga Republic was founded,[11] it clearly developed at about the same time as the more nomadic Hung Hu-tzu bands, and in response to the same conditions. Deserting miners were constrained by two conditions to organize themselves contractually into proto-cooperative communities: the need to survive in a region highly inhospitable to individual survival, and the need for mutual defense both against the authorities of the Chinese state and against the pressure for admission of newly arrived miners, who would have taxed the group's resources beyond its ability to survive.

With a population of perhaps 25,000[12]—preponderantly male—the Republic had to develop a social structure that could provide the services of the state from which its citizens, as outlaws, were excluded, while at the same time reaching a modus vivendi with the surrounding population. Although more numerous and better armed than the Hung Hu-tzu bands outside the Republic, the Zheltuga Hung Hu-tzu were eager to avoid a battle that inevitably would attract the attention of the Chinese and Russian authorities. Consequently, the Republic's leaders began negotiations with the surrounding Hung Hu-tzu for the founding of a settlement near the source of the Sungari River, far to the east of the Zheltuga.

Lack of food supplies, an unfavorable climate, and the presence of man-eating beasts had kept the gold fields of the Sungari region from being exploited, but it seemed clear that a group suitably supplied with arms and provisions could develop an agricultural and commercial organization capable of providing the necessities of life. Accordingly, the Republic, in exchange for an undertaking by the surrounding Hung Hu-tzu bands not to engage in aggressive actions against it, agreed to provide guides to the Sungari gold fields and six months' provisions to enable these bands to establish a settlement there. In due course a second miners' republic, on the model of the first but with a much smaller population, was established on the upper Sungari, where it evidently flourished.[13] As Alexandre Ular remarked:

What is really extraordinary is that the fatal antagonism between the two groups never led to open warfare, even at the beginning. Nothing is more sound or more admirable than the vigorous logic of these criminals—these degenerates, as the simplistic would call them—who, in this era of rigid alternatives, *reflected*.[14]

The institutions of the Zheltuga Republic were based largely on two principles, universal suffrage and a kind of absolute communism. Its legislative functions were performed by a council of thirty elected members, whose function it was to define the republic's general policies.[15] The council in turn named an executive committee that consisted of two presidents, two judges, a supply officer, a production officer, and a trade officer.

The two judges were responsible for the administration of a severe legal code, but their actions were taken in consultation with district committees, similar to the French *conseils de prud'hommes*. Murder was punishable by death, assault by corporal punishment, and many other crimes by exclusion from the Republic, which, in the difficult conditions of northern Manchuria, was tantamount to a death sentence. It is interesting to note that theft was also punishable by death; according to Ular, this was because it implied the negation of the fundamental characteristics of the Republic itself.

The supply officer was a kind of minister of economics. He was responsible for agriculture, fishing, and transportation as well as for the storage and distribution of food supplies, which were kept in official entrepôts. The production officer oversaw the Republic's gold-mining industry, its basic industry and the major source of its income; he paid particular attention to its technical development. The trade officer was responsible for the Republic's foreign trade, that is to say, for the sale of its gold production in China and Siberia. He was a figure of some importance, capable of exercising influence over local Siberian and Chinese authorities owing to their own, often private, interest in the Republic's traffic in gold.[16] The Republic's governmental apparatus was completed by an armed police force of approximately two hundred men under the direction of the production officer.[17]

The principle of communism operated chiefly in matters of distribution. The masses were employed in gold mining, agriculture, transportation, and other pursuits. Those who were engaged in administrative work were chosen by the district committees. But all the Republic's citizens, from the gold miners up to the two presidents, who were charged with overall administration, received the same income. Moreover, as a further step to prevent people from accumulating wealth by savings, all payments were made in bills of credit that expired at the end of one year. Thus, whereas each individual was free to use his bills of credit as he saw fit, no one could achieve a superior socioeconomic position.

Used merchandise could apparently be exchanged on the open market, but new merchandise, whether produced within the Republic or purchased elsewhere with the proceeds from the sale of gold, could be sold only at community-owned stores. Any income that resulted from a favorable balance of trade remained in the state treasury for periodic distribution to the population in the form of the Republic's annual bills of credit. These bills of credit were not redeemable either in gold or in any foreign currency, thus making it impossible for anyone to take money out of the community. Ular reports that the violent repression of the Republic by the Manchu authorities prevented any final distribution of profits to the populace; presumably these profits fell into the hands of Manchu officials.[18]

The Republic's strict economic communism extended to its social life as well. Its relatively few women, who were mostly engaged in agriculture and fishing, were completely equal with men in community membership and activities. According to Francis Mury, some of the women had joined the republic voluntarily and others had been abducted from their native villages by the Hung Hu-tzu. Those abducted, while free and equal members of the Republic, did not have the right of departure. Free love was customary, and neither family nor marriage law existed. Marriages, such as they were, were consummated without formality or intervention by the Republic's authorities. For reasons that are not altogether clear, children were few. Evidently, all-male households existed; Ular remarks, "Since homosexual relations are considered merely an addition to normal sexual relations by the average Chinese, he is capable of living almost equally well with or without women."[19]

Mury claimed that the Republic's communism was inhumanly strict:

Among these outlaws, who live outside of humanity and who are faced by incessant difficulties and dangers, no one could escape the law of work and

survive. Pity and compassion were unknown sentiments. A person incapaci-
tated by sickness or accident could expect no assistance. He could perhaps
convalesce for several months if he had had the foresight to put aside a certain number of those bills of credit that constituted wages in this federation
where gold was an instrument of exchange only with the outside world. But
even then he could not prolong his inactivity beyond certain limits. The
bills of credit expired one year from the date of issue. If they were not
cashed by that time, their value reverted to the federation's treasury. . . . The
ill who had saved no wages or whose bills of credit were used up knew that
no one would come to their aid and could only await death in their huts.
The fear of a similar fate prevented their fellow workers from assisting
them.[20]

Nevertheless, although Mury obviously deplored this harsh aspect of
life in the Republic, he could not help feeling a grudging admiration
for it. He wrote in 1912:

This federation was the most curious experiment in communism that has
ever been tried. Thanks to the perfection and, at the same time, the simplicity of its organization, it attained an extraordinary prosperity, despite
or perhaps because of its inflexible severity toward individuals. Our European collectivists would certainly have learned a lot from a sojourn in this
small republic. They would have noted that each of its citizens owed the
federation his maximum effort, and that in this environment where all property was held in common, communism in no way favored the sloth of individuals at the expense of society.[21]

Writing some eleven years earlier, in 1901, Ular had been even
more enthusiastic and sympathetic:

This republic, built from scratch, launched an experiment in collectivism
far broader than Europe's socialists—even those who emigrated or held more
or less scientific theories—have ever been able to carry out. Its relative prosperity and astonishing economic development, achieved without outside aid,
in a sterile land, and in a climate said to be deadly, attest at the outset to
the marvelous genius, still unknown among Europeans, that even the least
cultivated Chinese have for organizing themselves and serving an organization to which they freely acknowledge allegiance. Indeed, the simplicity of
the Republic's legislation, the efficiency of its administrative services, and,
most interesting of all, the administration of common property seem to prove
that given a sufficiently limited population and the necessary minimum of
laws and institutions, communism can achieve both maximum production
and maximum security for the private citizen. . . .
Because of the primitive living conditions of the outlaws of the Feltuga
[sic], their experience bears little relation to the socialist theories of Europe.
Yet at the very least it is heartening to observe a group of humanity's most
wretched specimens creating a functioning society out of nothing. From the
scientific point of view, the destruction of this center of spontaneous socialist
experimentation is most regrettable.[22]

Founded in the 1860's and flourishing by 1883,[23] the Zheltuga Republic lasted until shortly after the turn of the century, when its territory became important to the Russians constructing the Chinese Eastern Railway and the spread of its influence came at last to annoy the Ch'ing bureaucracy. On learning that many Ch'ing officials in the area traveled and exercised their functions only at the will of the Hung Hu-tzu, the Peking government finally decided to take decisive action. With the cooperation of the Russian authorities, who sealed off Siberia as a possible refuge for the Hung Hu-tzu, Manchu forces quickly scattered the Republic's defenders. Many Hung Hu-tzu were massacred. Others (perhaps as many as half of them) escaped to the Sungari Republic. Still others joined existing bandit forces or formed their own.[24]

"Pai-ma" Chang's thirteen rules and the rudimentary structure of the state that developed along the Zheltuga River shared two common denominators. First, both were marginal to Ch'ing society. The Zheltuga Republic and its sister republic on the Sungari were literally beyond the reach of Ch'ing military and bureaucratic power and Ch'ing law. "Pai-ma" Chang's group and groups like his, though operating within the political limits of Ch'ing power, were outside the formal legal and social structure of Chinese society. The roving Hung Hu-tzu bands are roughly analogous to secret societies inside China itself, with their regulations for membership, their conduct of operations, and their maintenance of group loyalty. The Zheltuga Republic, on the other hand, is analogous to groups that establish permanent societies in geographically marginal areas, areas where the physical and social environments are hostile.

The second common denominator shared by both Hung Hu-tzu groups was their remarkable social consciousness. In the absence of traditional social forms, both developed membership rules, systems for acquiring and distributing wealth, and ways of maintaining the community through time. Conceivably "Pai-ma" Chang may have been influenced by Hung Hu-tzu who fled the Zheltuga Republic after its destruction. But neither group appears to have been influenced by European utopian socialism, and neither seems to have developed the politico-religious symbolism characteristic of Chinese secret societies and popular movements like the Taiping. Seemingly the Hung Hu-tzu's primitive egalitarianism was a response to the specific conditions of northern Manchuria in their time, notably to the legal and geographic isolation of heterogeneous populations in an economically marginal region. Neither the Zheltuga Republic nor "Pai-ma" Chang's band was by any normal definition a bandit group in opposition to Chinese society. In a rudimentary fashion, both developed rules and institutions parallel to those of the society from which their members had withdrawn or been excluded; their lives related economically to Ch'ing society but were socially and politically independent of it. The Hung Hu-tzu were born out of protest against the injustices and inefficiencies of the late Ch'ing, but they grew into something more.

Notes on the Early Role of Secret Societies in Sun Yat-sen's Republican Movement

LILIA BOROKH

Sources for studying the relationship between the Hsing-Chung Hui and secret societies—The personal ties of some founders of the Hsing-Chung Hui, in particular Cheng Shih-liang, with secret societies—The influence of secret societies on the political program of the Hsing-Chung Hui—The participation of the hui-t'ang in the insurrections of 1895 and 1900

The influence of traditional secret organizations (*hui-t'ang*) on the early stages of the bourgeois revolutionary movement can be studied in the history of the Hsing-Chung Hui (Restore China Society), the first political association of Chinese revolutionaries.[1] It is possible to get some idea of the nature of the ties between the Hsing-Chung Hui (hereafter HCH) and secret societies from the official oath and from membership lists of the association, from Ch'ing edicts promulgated in response to uprisings led by the HCH,[2] and from the writings of Sun Yat-sen. Sun's opinion of the secret anti-Manchu movement was expressed in his first works, which were published in London and had a large European audience. In the article "China's Present and Future," Sun speaks of "hidden forces at work in China" (literally, hidden forces that roam about in China). In the pamphlet *Kidnapped in London* he not only mentions the existence of a "strong underground current of popular discontent," but also gives his first published description of the Canton uprising of 1895, in which members of secret societies took part. In his conversation with the Russian translator of this pamphlet Sun spoke more clearly of the nature of these "hidden forces." On the subject of the possibility of a popular progressive movement, he noted the widespread system of secret societies and their mass character, and sketched the areas in which they were active.[3]

More detailed information on the ties between the HCH and secret societies can be found in Sun Yat-sen's works *Plan for Establishing* *the State* and *History of the Revolution* (1923)[4] as well as in the official Kuomintang editions of the history of the party.[5] Certain episodes of cooperation between the HCH and secret societies are also described in the memoirs of Ch'en Shao-pai, Ch'en Ch'un-sheng, and Miyazaki Torazō.[6] In their time these men either personally planned uprisings with the participation of secret societies or took part in negotiations with the societies on behalf of their organization.*

Almost all those who formed the core of the HCH were natives of the southeast provinces, where secret societies were very widespread.[7] Yu Lieh, who before enrolling in the cartography school at Hong Kong had visited Korea and Japan and had lived in Peking and Shanghai, had belonged to a local secret society in Shanghai.[8] Since his childhood, Hsieh Tsuan-t'ai had been initiated into the secret of the anti-Manchu societies, for his father was the head of a section of the Triads among Chinese émigrés in Australia.[9] The most numerous documents on ties between leaders of the HCH and secret societies, however, concern Cheng Shih-liang. Son of a rich Shanghai merchant, Cheng not only belonged to a society, but was a powerful figure in the Triads in his native area (Kuei-shan hsien, Kwangtung province). He was in touch with leaders of the *hui-t'ang* in Kwangtung, Kwangsi, and even Southeast Asia. At the Canton Medical School, Cheng Shih-liang was known as a man who "had lots of contact with people who had been around."[10]

Only indirect indications remain of the secret-society ties of the group of young men who later entered the HCH: some took the life-and-death oath together; others called each other half-brother.[11] As a child, Sun Yat-sen already knew of the existence of anti-Manchu secret societies, but during the course of his studies at Po-chi, with the aid of Cheng Shih-liang and Yu Lieh,† he significantly developed his knowledge of the societies' activities.[12] Later, he attributed great importance to his relations with Cheng Shih-liang. In identifying the principal landmarks of the revolution—very seldom documented— Sun stressed this friendship, recalling it in all its details. "None of

---

* Ch'en Shao-pai was an HCH leader who took part in the 1895 action. He represented HCH in the negotiations with San-ho Hui and Ko-lao Hui leaders in Hong Kong in 1899, and directed *Chung-kuo jih-pao*, the HCH organ that was central to preparations for the second uprising. Ch'en Ch'un-sheng was on the paper's editorial board. Miyazaki was a Japanese politician who joined the HCH in 1896 and took part in the *hui-t'ang* negotiations in 1899.

† Yu Lieh met Sun Yat-sen through one of Sun's relatives, a graduate of Po-chi Medical Institute. Sun Yat-sen, *Kuo-fu Sun Chung-shan hsien-sheng nien-p'u ch'u-kao* (A preliminary draft of a chronological biography of Sun Yat-sen, the founding father; Taipei, 1958), 1: 35.

my schoolmates was like him. He impressed me from the first meeting," he wrote, recalling the impression Cheng had made on him.
Shortly after they met, Cheng told Sun that he belonged to a secret
society and if necessary could find useful people there.[13] Ch'en Shao-
pai also recognized the importance of this friendship. In his recollections of the history of the HCH, the chapter on the formation of
revolutionary ideas begins with an account of the meeting.[14]

In 1887 the future organizers of the HCH met with an 80-year-old
hermit named Cheng An, a former adviser of Lin Tse-hsü. He apparently explained the organization and aims of the *hui-t'ang* to the
young men and persuaded them that it would be necessary to unite
with the *hui-t'ang*.[15]

It is difficult to assess the effect of contacts with members of secret
societies on the future leaders of the HCH. The noble sentiments
and boldness of the *hui-t'ang* leaders certainly impressed the young
men, as did the chivalrous spirit and the calls for mutual aid, devotion, and abnegation to be found in the societies' statutes. The political convictions of the societies, too, seem to have had their effect.
After China was defeated by France (1884–85), the climate of opinion
among the youth was in any case opposed to the reigning dynasty.
Inspired by the proposals of Wang T'ao, Cheng Kuan-ying, and Ho
Ch'i for the peaceful "Europeanization" of China, by the events of
the Taiping uprising, and by the revolutionary experience of Europe
and America, the future organizers of the HCH asked themselves
which road to take to save the country: reform or revolution? In this
period of search and hesitation, the group found that the members
of secret organizations were responsive to and shared their anti-
Ch'ing bent. Later Sun Yat-sen admitted that "only secret society
members were not confused by conversations on the revolution and
the overthrow of the Manchus."[16] In the widespread network of
secret organizations in China, the youth of that day saw real forces
rising in opposition to the dynasty. Cheng Shih-liang's offer to "find
useful people" and old Cheng An's advice to unite with the *hui-t'ang*
opened the way to relations with anti-Ch'ing forces.

Cheng was given the task of recruiting *hui-t'ang* members in
Kwangtung for the future revolutionary organization.[17] In his *History of the Revolution* Sun Yat-sen writes that on the eve of the
foundation of the party, improving contacts with the San-ho Hui
seemed to him the most important task.[18] The Ts'an-chün Hui (Society of Splendid Equality) participated directly in the founding of
the HCH in Honolulu (1895). The head of the local section of the

society, Teng Yin-nan, using his influence in the Chinese community, helped Sun establish ties with Chinese émigrés and draw them into the revolutionary organization.[19]

Many of those who joined the HCH in Hong Kong and Canton in 1895 also belonged to secret societies. Cheng Shih-liang, Yu Lieh, and Hsieh Tsuan-t'ai were Triads, for example. However, the official membership lists for 1895 show only thirteen members specifically categorized as secret society members. For these thirteen, their secret society activities were apparently their major or even their only occupation: the notation of their *hui-t'ang* membership appeared in the documents in the space where social position would normally have been indicated. Nine of these thirteen men were already connected with Sun Yat-sen in 1892: they had worked at various times in his pharmacy in Ao-ming. As for the others, they had a certain amount of influence in their local *hui-t'ang* as well as occupying a leadership position in the HCH. Liang Ta-p'ao was one of them, a leader in Pei-chiang hsien.[20] In 1895, on the orders of HCH headquarters, he directed preparations for the uprising in this region. Sun spoke of two other such men, Chu Kuei-ch'üan and Ch'iu Ssu, in his recollections of the revolution.[21] During the uprising of 1895 they headed a detachment of 3,000 men who tried to take Canton. When the attempt failed, the two leaders were arrested and subsequently executed.

According to the HCH membership lists for 1900, there were 23 *hui-t'ang* members in the association at the time of the second major uprising, at Waichow. They were leaders of local sections of secret societies active in the coastal districts of Kwangtung, and in the HCH documents are referred to as marshals and generals. A number of them died in skirmishes with Ch'ing troops. The most important figure in this group was Huang Fu, the most competent Triad leader in the region.[22] Huang Fu was in Borneo when preparations for the uprising began. Cheng Shih-liang sent one of his men to get him.[23] The leader of the San-tien Hui of Kuei-shan belonged to the HCH; his grandson, who also held an influential post in the San-ho Hui, joined the HCH as well. On the eve of the second uprising the grandson recruited members in the region of P'ing-hai.[24] *Hui-t'ang* leaders of Ssu-nan hsien who had been brought into the HCH are known to have commanded groups of *lü-lin* (forest bandits).[25]

The *hui-t'ang* members who took an active part in the uprisings led by the HCH in 1895 and 1900 were obviously not ordinary members of secret fraternities. Only leaders of local secret societies actually entered the organization; that is to say, those who were educated and rather well off.* Examples include Cheng Shih-liang, son of a merchant as already noted; Huang Yao-t'ing, owner of an inn in Singapore; a pharmacist from Po-lo hsien; and a student from Tientsin.[26] Relying on such leaders, the revolutionaries took great advantage of *hui-t'ang* detachments to achieve their own ends during the uprisings.

The quest for contacts with Kwangtung secret societies and the entry of *hui-t'ang* leaders into the HCH were not chance events. The HCH program contained ideas that were widespread among members of the secret anti-Manchu movement, and calculated to be attractive to them. Members of secret societies took an oath to devote themselves "to the restoration of the Ming dynasty, which originates in Heaven and Earth and all that exists; to the extermination of the barbarian bandits; and to waiting for the real mandate of heaven." In their statutes, they spoke of their resolution to overthrow the Manchu regime.[27] In their ritual dialogue, Triad initiates repeated that they, like the members of the fraternity they were joining, wanted to "overthrow the Ch'ing and restore the Ming." The HCH admission ceremony also included the rite of the oath. Those who entered the organization promised to struggle to "chase out the Tartar slaves [the Manchus], reestablish China, and found a democratic government."[28]

This first requirement of the revolutionaries repeated the most popular slogan put forward by the spontaneous anti-Manchu movement; nor was the HCH interpretation of the slogan original. It preserved traditional notions about foreign domination and the imminent punishment of the Manchus for their "villainous deeds."[29] Unlike other documents of the organization, the HCH oath—which might not have existed at all but for the strong secret society precedent—is couched in a form similar to that seen in Triad documents. The very words of its anti-Manchu slogan ("chase out the barbarian

---

* The HCH welcomed secret society leaders into its ranks, but adopted a different position toward the mass base of the anti-Manchu organizations. Nevertheless, among the *hui-t'ang* leaders close to the HCH there were, to cite Miyazaki Torazō, people who were not literati at all. Describing the Ko-lao Hui leaders who came to the negotiations in Hong Kong in 1899, Miyazaki observed that they differed markedly from intellectuals in their bearing and in their speech (HHKM, 1: 110). (See note 2 for HHKM.) Apparently, *hui-t'ang* leaders who rallied to the organization came from extremely varied social positions, so that it is impossible to make an overall statement about the social composition of the group.

slaves") are found in *hui-t'ang* proclamations and in Taiping documents, which disdainfully call the Ch'ing "Tartars."[30]

The anti-Manchu slogan was the ideological basis for the affinity between the HCH and the secret societies, even though as the HCH used it, it was combined with ideas of "the restoration of China" (*hui-fu Chung-kuo*) and "the establishment of a democratic regime," and thus substantially transformed.

The HCH intended to take power in 1895 with the help of mercenary detachments recruited among the *hui-t'ang* of Kwangtung.[31] On the day of attack, these detachments, which totaled 3,000 men, were to enter Canton from various directions. According to Sun Yat-sen, they were assigned the role of shock forces.[32] The HCH obtained arms for the societies to distribute to their members, and paid each participant in the operation. When the news of failure reached headquarters on the day of the attack, Sun and Ch'en Shao-pai distributed money to the leaders of the detachments and dismissed them. On the exact terms of the financial arrangement, the decree made public by the local administration in Kwangtung at the time of the uprising stated: "His [Sun Yat-sen's] followers went everywhere to recruit people. They recruited fighters in his name, promising the imbeciles they would pay each one ten pieces of foreign coin. And the people rushed to hire themselves out."[33]

In Sun's account of this first insurrection there is an interesting detail that reveals a great deal about the nature of the relationship between the HCH and the secret societies. Members of the revolutionary organization were sent to negotiate with *hui-t'ang* in districts that differed linguistically from Canton. Sun explains that "it made sense to bring people from another area in to fight, since, unable to speak with the people of Canton, they could not fall under any other influence, and therefore could be expected to be more dependable." They could "neither desert nor totally abandon the fight, for it would be easy to recognize them, and those who remained in Canton after the event would inevitably be under suspicion."[34]

In making their plans for the insurrection, the HCH leaders did not omit the habitual accessories to such actions for secret society members. They chose a color venerated by the societies—a red turban was to be the mark of the uprising's fighters—and they instituted a system of passwords.[35] Likewise, they chose a slogan in accord with the spirit of the societies: "Chase out the tyrants; assure peace to good men" (*ch'u-pao an-liang*). In so doing the revolutionaries might seem to be very cleverly taking advantage of past experience in uprisings against the Ch'ing. In fact, however, they had very little choice but to adopt the forms most familiar to the mass of their fighters.

The organization was paralyzed for a time by the first defeat. Not until four years later did the HCH try to build up the base for a new insurrection in China. At this stage in their history, the revolutionaries turned again to the secret societies. They sent Ch'en Shao-pai to Hong Kong in 1899 to arrange for the publication of a journal, *Chung-kuo jih-pao*. Trying to establish himself in China, Ch'en Shao-pai decided to join the San-ho Hui. He explained later in his memoirs that this was the only way open to him for establishing solid ties with the *hui-t'ang*.[36] Through the intermediary of another HCH member, Ch'en Shao-pai invited the oldest Triad leader from Hop'ing hsien to Hong Kong to preside over his initiation ceremony. After the ceremony, Ch'en was raised to the rank of *pai-shan* (white fan), an honorific title (the equivalent of "military counselor") normally given only in recognition of great merit to the oldest members of the San-ho Hui.[37] Ch'en Shao-pai was very conscious of the importance of this event. He believed that his joining the San-ho Hui opened great possibilities for the development of activities in Kwangtung.[38]

At the same time, the HCH succeeded in attracting the *hui-t'ang* of the Yangtze basin. Pi Yung-nien, a member of the HCH since 1898 who had previously participated in the reform movement, helped cement relations with them. A group of Ko-lao Hui leaders came to Hong Kong with a letter of recommendation from him. These men were the most powerful leaders of the sections of this society in the Hunan-Hupeh region.[39] They expressed an extraordinary interest in joint action with the HCH. During the meeting they explained this interest, and why they had come, as follows: "Not to know what is going on right now, but just to throw ourselves precipitously into fights—isn't that just prolonging for another hundred years our present unlimited woes?"[40] Ch'en Shao-pai, who as HCH representative was conducting the negotiations, was probably able to speak the same language as this group of *hui-t'ang* leaders. He was accepted into the ranks of the Ko-lao Hui and proclaimed "dragon head among dragon heads" (*lung-t'ou chi lung-t'ou*).[41]

The Ko-lao Hui leaders stayed in Hong Kong more than two months. The result of these long negotiations was a conference in

October 1899 at which the three representatives of the HCH, the two representatives of the San-ho Hui, and the seven representatives of the Ko-lao Hui decided to found an association, the Hsing-Han Hui, with Sun Yat-sen at its head.[42] The conference participants set out the zones of future uprisings (Kwangtung-Kwangsi, Fukien-Chekiang, Shanghai). They decided to inform local *hui-t'ang* of the results of the negotiations. The conference participants consolidated their unity with an oath according to Ko-lao Hui custom, drinking wine mixed with the blood of a rooster.[43]

Thanks to this agreement of 1899, the revolutionaries had closer and more extensive ties with the secret societies on the eve of the Waichow uprising in 1900 than they had had in 1895.* This time, the focus of the uprising was shifted from Canton to the maritime regions of Kwangtung. This mountainous, forest-covered terrain, long known as a bandit hideout, as the "nest" of the San-ho Hui and the "refuge of members of revolutionary organizations," was deliberately chosen: the HCH leaders counted on a massive intervention by the secret societies. San-ho Hui members in the districts of Hsin-an, Waichow, and Kuei-shan were given the role of "main force," in the words of Ch'en Shao-pai. That the *hui-t'ang* did indeed participate in the uprising is indicated in several reports by the authorities. In answer to the Emperor's inquiry about the revolt, Governor Te-shou of Kwangtung described the Waichow events as "an agreement between Sun Wen and local bandits." Reports from individual districts repeat again and again that "the rebel army is entirely made up of secret society members," and that *hui-t'ang* forces were growing continually. During the uprising the insurgents themselves openly declared that they belonged to secret societies. Their declaration was published in a Hong Kong newspaper: "We are not Boxers, we are great *hui-t'ang* politicians, members of the I-hsing Hui, the T'ien-ti Hui, and the San-ho Hui."[44]

HCH leaders worked out a general plan for revolt. They obtained the support of Japan and negotiated with the British on the subject of the independence of Kwangtung and Kwangsi. They provided the *hui-t'ang* with arms and sent a small group of military instructors to their detachments.[45] HCH members also prepared propaganda materials for the insurgents. Sun Yat-sen wrote a poem on the eve of the Waichow uprising:

* This new HCH action occurred at the same time as that of the "Independence Army," which was composed of reformists supported by the secret societies of the Yangtze valley.

> In endless whirlpools of darkness there is no ray of light,
> Years of woe roll by, one after the other.
> But the glorious heroes have now achieved manhood,
> Ready to carry out the revolution of Heaven and Earth.[46]

The poem was made into a song and was distributed to the *hui-t'ang* as a call to action.

The declaration of the insurgents of Kuei-shan hsien, which was made public in Hong Kong, was doubtless written with the help of HCH members. In this document, traditional ideas on the will of Heaven are interspersed with the demands of the revolutionary program for a democratic government: "We, Chinese living in China and abroad, swear to chase out the Manchu government and establish a government of popular sovereignty."[47] The slogan calling for restoration of Chinese power ("the realization of unfulfilled hopes three hundred years old") was combined with propositions for the development of Chinese international commerce. The traditional *hui-t'ang* slogan of self-sacrifice, "Don't spare blood in the name of the great work," is followed by an appeal to the great powers for neutrality, in the spirit of the HCH program.[48]

Although they contributed actively to the preparations for the uprising of 1900, the heads of the HCH played almost no direct role in the action. In the initial plan, they projected a much more salient role for the secret societies of Kwangtung than they had played in 1894. The detachment under Cheng Shih-liang, who had led the Waichow uprising, was the insurgents' *avant garde*. Likewise, local *hui-t'ang* detachments under their own leaders carried out military operations. Sometimes they hid in the most inaccessible regions; sometimes they attacked the hsien capital. The fighters in the uprising, following secret society tradition, wore red turbans or dressed in white outfits with a red border. *Hui-t'ang* members did not go into action under the HCH flag ("white sun in a blue sky"), but under flags bearing the names of leaders such as Sun and Cheng, and the slogans "Protect the foreigners, annihilate the Manchus" (*pao-yang mieh-Man*) and "For Great China."[49]

The historian Lo Hsiang-lin, author of many works on Sun Yat-sen, has declared that "if there had been no Hung Men, there would have been no Hsing-Chung Hui."[50] It is impossible not to share this opinion. The anti-Manchu ideas in the organization's program are proof of the influence of the secret movement on the political convictions of HCH members, and the first practical actions taken by the revolutionaries were linked to *hui-t'ang* support.

Nevertheless, the role of the *hui-t'ang* in the revolution should not be overestimated, as Sun Yat-sen himself warned: "Even though nationalism is greatly expanding in the secret societies, they are very despotic, with sharp hierarchical differences; there is no trace among them of the republican principle or the idea of popular sovereignty."[51] He stressed that the *hui-t'ang* had little ideological influence on the new leadership, and insisted that the limits of this influence should be precisely noted.[52]

More precision is also necessary on the subject of the nature of the secret societies' influence on HCH tactics. The revolutionaries saw the *hui-t'ang* as a ready-made instrument for revolution. They were able to hire armed detachments from the *hui-t'ang* for predetermined amounts of money (1895) or enter into agreements with their leaders in preparation for the insurrection (1900). These possibilities influenced HCH actions during the uprisings to a considerable extent. Thanks to the easy availability of aid from the *hui-t'ang*, for example, the organization was not moved to look further for support and thus limited its base.

The history of the Hsing-Chung Hui does not enable us to make a definitive evaluation of the influence of secret societies on the bourgeois revolutionary movement. The relations between the two groups are complex, as is evident from the HCH program itself and from the tactics chosen by the organization's leaders.

Triads, Salt Smugglers, and Local Uprisings: Observations on the Social and Economic Background of the Waichow Revolution of 1911

WINSTON HSIEH

Précis of the findings—Triad forces in the Waichow Revolution—The tradition of secret-society-sponsored uprisings in Waichow—The Triad network and the urban hierarchy—Salt monopoly and salt smuggling in Waichow—The tightening up of salt administration on the eve of the Revolution

The most significant aspect of the Chinese secret societies appears to have been their capacity to organize, to support, and on occasions of violent collective action to mobilize the scattered fragments of power that existed outside the realm of formal governmental administration. Their capacity to fulfill such political functions seems to have derived mainly from their key role in satisfying the social and economic needs of various groups at the local and regional levels, needs that were not adequately satisfied by legitimate organizations.

These observations are based on my study of secret-society-sponsored uprisings in general and the Waichow Revolution of 1911 in particular.* The activities of the Triads formed perhaps the most obscure thread in the tapestry of the social and economic life of the Waichow region, a thread that caught the eye only occasionally, with the outbreak of local uprisings and rebellions. Even for such occasions, the reliable information on the Triads is always spotty. In order to piece together the various bits of information on the Triad involvement in the Waichow uprisings, I shall attempt to link these uprisings to local conditions and, in particular, to study them in the context of

* This paper has been condensed from a much longer study, each of its five sections containing the substance of a separate chapter or an independent article. Special thanks go to Messrs. John K. Fairbank, Thomas A. Metzger, G. William Skinner, Charles Tilly, Frederic Wakeman, Jr., and Wang Yeh-chien for their comments on earlier versions of the study, and to editors J. G. Bell and Autumn Stanley for their admirable efforts and skill in trimming the work to a size publishable as a single chapter in this volume without sacrificing any of the essential points.

the interpenetration, or articulation, of two systems of hierarchies, that of formal administrative centers and that of marketing centers.[1] Against this defined and structured background, the actions of various Triad forces no longer appear random but seem to have a sense of purpose and of organization. The picture is necessarily an incomplete one, with large areas still left blank, but the otherwise isolated and meaningless data are now part of a fascinating drama, appealing to the historical imagination.

Specific findings will be presented in the following sections, but I should like to summarize in these introductory paragraphs the major themes suggested by the findings. First, the Triad uprisings were found to occur only at certain types of places, namely, towns and markets. In other words, the revolutionary potential seems to be selective rather than permeating the countryside or the peasantry as a whole. Second, when one's attention is focused on those localities that served as the central stage of the uprisings, an interesting pattern of revolutionary mobilization begins to emerge. This pattern may be viewed as (a) a series of centripetal movements of the insurrectionary forces— gathering first at the smaller towns on the outer ring of a central market town, e.g. Tan-shui, then congregating at this town, which in turn is located on the outer ring of a larger urban center, e.g. the city of Waichow, and finally joining forces with bands from other large towns to conquer the city—that can also be seen as (b) an ascending movement (or a descending movement in the moment of defeat) along the hierarchy of economic centers from market towns to local cities and finally to the metropolis serving as the capital of the regional economy.

The discovery of such a pattern is significant for a number of reasons. In the first place, it provides some basis for distinguishing secret-society-sponsored forces from some other types of revolutionary forces. Thus whereas the Triads appear to have been most active in the middle-level centers (market towns and local cities) of the hierarchy, village- and lineage-sponsored forces ordinarily operated only in the bottom-level markets and villages, and coups d'etat led by regular troops commonly occurred at the great administrative capitals, which usually occupied a high position in the economic hierarchy. This possibility of delineation, in turn, helps to provide a focus for studying the social and economic basis of the Triad forces. In particular, since the channels of trade and commerce that connected the various levels of economic centers were crucial in bringing the Triad forces to the central stage of the drama, an investigation into the region's economic and social conditions seemed to be called for, in order to understand the rampant activities of the Triads in Waichow.

The results of that investigation point overwhelmingly to an association between the Triad organization and the salt-smuggling network in the region. The last part of this paper contains a brief survey of the salt monopoly in Waichow—a subject of interest in its own right because it has received far less attention than the salt monopoly in Liang-huai and many other places. My investigation indicates that administrative efforts to tighten control over the salt trade and to exact ever more revenue from it provided the immediate cause of the popular uprisings in Waichow.

In the transformation of resentment against the tax squeeze into violent collective action, the Triad network played an important role. This point should be stressed, especially since the theory that the stimulus to revolution comes largely from men's anxieties and resentments has been called into question by the recent works of Charles Tilly, who has pointed out that violent protests seem to grow most directly from the struggle for an established place in the structure of power.[2] In Waichow, it was the existing Triad operation that gave merchant leaders and T'ung-meng Hui agitators an instant insurrectionary army.

The Triad Forces in the Waichow Revolution

In speaking of the Waichow Revolution, a natural association that comes to mind is the Waichow Uprising of 1900, when Triad leaders loyal to Sun Yat-sen succeeded in organizing a rebellion that swept over the East River region and onward to coastal Fukien in two weeks.[3] Although the uprising was soon suppressed, the Triad network apparently survived, because a number of uprisings subsequently occurred in the East River region. In June 1907, for instance, another Triad rebellion erupted at Ch'i-nü-hu, near Waichow.[4] According to the available records, the Triad forces were no match for the disciplined regular troops, but they demonstrated a fierce fighting capacity, at least at the initial stage, and they enjoyed popular support in the local communities. From such uprisings the revolutionary activists around Sun Yat-sen learned lessons. And afterwards many T'ung-meng Hui members began to devote much of their attention to cultivating relationships with the Triad leaders in this region.

In the years immediately preceding 1911, Ch'en Chiung-ming and several of his comrades in the T'ung-meng Hui worked hard to contact Triad forces in Kwangtung.[5] Apparently they succeeded, because they brought men to Canton from the East River region to participate in the March 29th Uprising* in 1911. One of the "seventy-two martyrs" of this uprising was eventually identified as a peasant from Hai-feng who had belonged to the Waichow band under Ch'en's command.[6] Simultaneous uprisings were also attempted in Waichow.[7] In many respects, this abortive spring uprising paved the way for the Revolution that followed in the autumn. The Triad fighters who had been driven back to their home towns were now more than ever prepared to take up arms again. The "pacification" campaign by government troops in the wake of the uprising spread more seeds of resentment and revolt. The ringleaders who escaped to Hong Kong, Macao, or the Chinatowns of Southeast Asian cities were to come back to stage uprisings again after Wuchang rose. Also, the T'ung-meng Hui intellectuals had learned how to arouse local forces, and a common hatred now bound them closely to many of the Triad leaders.

Although Ch'en Chiung-ming commanded the insurrectionary forces in the whole Waichow region during the Revolution, the initial uprising at the great town of Tan-shui was masterminded by Teng K'eng, a young revolutionary whose wealthy Hakka family was associated with the salt business. Relying upon secret society ties among the Hakka, Teng not only succeeded in taking over the town of Tan-shui, but also assisted Ch'en in organizing a huge revolutionary army to march on Canton following the conquest of Waichow.[8]

Recently unearthed sources tell of another revolutionary force, commanded by the Triad leader Liang Chiu-hsi, that established itself near the town of Shih-lung, at the junction point of the East River and the Canton-Kowloon Railroad. This force was recorded as having intercepted a junk fleet carrying some three thousand packages of rice to the government troops in Waichow. Liang's men kept most of the rice, but they did give 50 packages to the revolutionary troops arriving from Hsin-an.[9] No sooner had the Ch'ing forces retreated from Shih-lung than a band of a hundred T'ung-meng Hui revolutionaries arrived from Hong Kong, including more than thirty waiters and porters presumably recruited through Triad channels from the big hotels in Hong Kong.[10]

More details are found about one particular group of Triad bands that was quite active along the lower East River valley, particularly

* The March 29th Uprising was actually staged on April 27, 1911, the twenty-ninth day of the third month of the Chinese lunar calendar. Officially the lunar calendar was abolished right after the Revolution of 1911, but the event is nonetheless traditionally called the March 29th Uprising.

in the hsien of Tzu-chin and Kuei-shan, before 1911. The original
organizer of these bands was Ch'en Ya-hsiang, a Triad leader from
Tzu-chin who had participated in the 1900 uprising, taken refuge in
Hong Kong after the defeat, and later joined the T'ung-meng Hui.
By late 1907, subsidies from the T'ung-meng Hui had enabled him
to sneak back to Tzu-chin to organize more uprisings. This time he
tried to reinforce the secret society ties by the superstitious teachings
of a White Fan Sect, or Pai-shan Chiao, which he created after the
Boxer model. By waving a white paper fan and reciting certain incantations, his followers were supposed to be possessed of a magic spirit
and to become impervious to knives and bullets. But this was the
post-1900 era, and the anti-missionary, anti-foreign cries of the Boxers
were dropped. Ch'en's two rallying slogans were "Plunder the rich
and aid the poor" (*chieh-fu chi-p'in*) and "Overthrow the Ch'ing and
restore the Ming" (*fan-Ch'ing fu-Ming*).

The movement was so popular that within a few months Ch'en had
a band of over three hundred fighters stationed in the mountainous
area of T'ang-k'ang-shan (in Tzu-chin) and huge masses of followers
in the surrounding villages of Hao-i, Lan-t'ang, Ku-chu, I-jung, and
Feng-an. One government troop commander, returned from a campaign to suppress the movement, testified, "In these villages you can
just reach out your arms and anybody you touch will be a secret society member."

Attacking rich landlords provided both a popular rallying point
and a convenient way to obtain supplies for this ever-growing band,
now too large to be supported by neighboring villages. In the winter
of 1908, for instance, a mob of over a thousand men joined Ch'en's
band in laying siege to a rich landlord's heavily guarded mansion.
After "three days and three nights," they broke in, occupied the building, and opened up the rice depot as well as the treasury. Everyone
who had taken part in the siege and who could identify himself as a
member of Ch'en's society received a hatful of silver from the treasury.

To obtain arms and munitions, Ch'en's band occasionally attacked
local militia forces. In early 1909, for instance, a mob of 700 men accompanied by Ch'en's striking force routed a contingent of militia
from Ku-chu hsiang and seized twenty Mauser rifles along with other
spoils.

Before Ch'en's band grew to uncontrollable size, however, the government forces began to move in. Guided by an informant from
among his followers, they soon searched out his headquarters in

T'ang-k'ang-shan. One spring morning Ch'en rose to find his headquarters encircled by a government force of over three thousand men.
Outnumbered and outmaneuvered, Ch'en's band found that the
"white fan" magic was no protection against modern bullets. But
the ruthless conduct of the government forces served to unify the men
under Ch'en's command, who retreated as a unit to Kuei-shan hsien,
where they were welcomed by the Triad forces under the command
of Chung Tzu-t'ing and his brothers. The following summer, they
marched back to Tzu-chin and destroyed the militia bureau of Lan-
t'ang hsiang as a public gesture of revenge for their beheaded sworn
brethren.

Although Ch'en himself was caught by government troops at Tan-
shui and executed in the fall of 1909, the Triad forces survived. They
were commanded by the Chung brothers in Kuei-shan and by others
in Tzu-chin. It was thus natural for the T'ung-meng Hui agitators
to contact these forces for the 1911 uprisings. The bands led by the
Chung brothers participated in the Waichow Revolution, and the
Triad forces remaining in Tzu-chin took an active part in the conquest of their hsien capital.[11]

Two other major revolutionary troops from the Waichow area that
were known for their Triad connections were the forces led by Wang
Ho-shun and by Kuan Jen-fu. Wang Ho-shun was among the most
colorful of the "people's army" (min chün) commanders.[12] Born into
a poor family in Kwangsi, Wang was illiterate. In his youth he had
served in Liu Yung-fu's Black Flag Army, which was active in the
border area encompassing southern Kwangsi and southwestern
Kwangtung on the Chinese side and northern Tonkin on the Annamese side (see Laffey's paper in this volume, pp. 85–96). It is uncertain whether Wang actually participated in any of the battles—
much eulogized by Chinese historians—against the French forces in
the 1880's. According to Feng Tzu-yu, Wang had become so much involved in Triad activities and so deeply concerned about the suffering of the people that he left the army and devoted himself to secret
society organization work.[13] However, since the Black Flags were
themselves irregular forces with secret society ties and since they had
quit the Kwangsi-Kwangtung-Tonkin border area as early as 1885,
when Wang was no more than sixteen, it is likely that Wang was
among the soldiers Liu Yung-fu left behind in this area when he was
pressed by the Ch'ing authorities to cut his irregular forces from several thousand men to one thousand, and to move them from the
Annamese border to Canton.[14]

In any event, Wang turned out to be a daring and able commander of Triad forces in the border area, stirring up or taking part in many uprisings there between 1902 and 1911. Following one such uprising in 1905, Wang took refuge in Saigon, where he met Sun Yat-sen in 1906. Having a common interest in secret society activities, the two liked each other immediately. Wang joined the T'ung-meng Hui. Although he got along poorly with many of the intellectuals of the group, he was among Sun's entourage when they moved to Hanoi, stayed in Sun's household for several months, and from then on participated in every uprising in the border area of Kwangtung, Kwangsi, and Yunnan in which Sun claimed some leadership.

Kuan Jen-fu was another senior Triad leader.[15] He had a background similar to Wang's and participated in many of the uprisings that Wang commanded in the border area in 1907–8—notably the 1907 uprising at Chen-nan-kuan, near the Kwangsi border, in which Sun Yat-sen and many T'ung-meng Hui leaders participated as well.

When the Wuchang uprising broke out in October 1911, both Wang and Kuan were hiding in Southeast Asia. They hurried to Hong Kong and actively supported the T'ung-meng Hui's effort to raise "people's armies." Moreover, through their Triad connections, Wang and Kuan independently raised funds and each recruited a sizable "people's army" in the East River area. There is evidence that Wang's troops participated in the Tan-shui uprising. After the conquest of Waichow, the forces under the command of Wang and Kuan absorbed a still larger number of secret society members, smugglers, vagabonds, and *yu-min* (idle wanderers) along the way toward Canton. Wang's public proclamation in his capacity as "Commander of the People's Corps from Waichow," which is preserved in the Kuomintang archives, suggests a mixture of the Triads' anti-Manchu and anti-administration tradition with the slogans borrowed from the French revolutionary cry of *Liberté! Egalité! Fraternité!*[16]

Ch'en Chiung-ming, the top commander of the revolutionary forces at Waichow, apparently also had established solid ties with the Triads in the Waichow region. The huge sums of money Ch'en brought to Canton after the victory at Waichow[17] were probably borrowed from the salt merchants through Triad connections. When Ch'en and other revolutionaries took refuge in Southeast Asia[18] after the "second revolution" of 1913, they were probably supported by overseas Triads.*

* Such possibilities, raised mainly in personal interviews, do shed light on Ch'en's intimate relationship with the Triads after 1911. For instance, Ch'en and **Huang San-te**, the top Triad leader in America, made a joint statement in 1915

While the battles over Waichow dragged on, a number of neighboring towns and cities were taken by the Triad forces. The hsien capital of Po-lo, for instance, was conquered by the forces commanded by Lin Chi-cheng, Ch'iu Yao-hsi, and other revolutionaries, many of whom were Triad leaders. From Po-lo, they recruited more volunteers to reinforce the troops attacking Waichow.[19] In Mei hsien the main revolutionary troop, which helped in the takeover of the hsien capital and stabilized the conditions there in the post-revolutionary period, was a Triad band from the market town of Sung-k'ou.[20]

From these various bits of information there emerges a picture, incomplete as it is, of a "confederation" of secret society bands, essentially independent of each other but sharing common traditions, beliefs, and codes of behavior, now united in the struggle against the Ch'ing authority. Ch'en Chiung-ming, Wang Ho-shun, and other commanders of these large troops of several thousand men were actually serving as the heads of a congregation of smaller fighting bands, separately commanded by their own leaders. The Triad preeminence here will seem less surprising after a brief look at the history of the Triads in the Waichow region.

A Tradition of Secret Society Rebellion in Waichow

Local gazetteers reveal that the Triad network had probably existed in this region for at least a century. Even if the uprisings during the beginning phase of the Ch'ing dynasty—those of 1651 and 1674, both involving some secret society or secret religious sect—are not counted, the disturbances specifically attributed to the Triads under such names as T'ien-ti Hui, San-tien Hui, and San-ho Hui may be traced back as far as the first years of the nineteenth century.[21]

In 1801 the Tung-kuan authorities suppressed a T'ien-ti Hui organization, and allegedly had the leaders executed and all the followers exiled to distant frontier provinces.[22] In spite of such rigorous

---

denouncing Sun Yat-sen's unscrupulous way of securing Japanese support for his struggle against Yüan Shih-k'ai. Ch'en, Huang Hsing, and many other leaders among the revolutionary refugees had urged that all campaigns against Yüan should be stopped as long as he was facing the crisis of Japan's Twenty-one Demands. After Yüan's downfall, Ch'en Chiung-ming was recommended to Peking by the Chih-kung T'ang (Triad lodges in America) as an overseas Chinese candidate for Parliament. In his later challenges to Sun Yat-sen's power in Canton in the 1920's, one of the major sources of Ch'en's financial support was contributions from overseas Chinese communities through Triad channels. In 1926, he formally reorganized the overseas Chih-kung T'ang networks into a Chih-kung party, or Chih-kung *tang*, and served as its director.

suppression, however, a large-scale Triad rebellion broke out the following year. Its leader, popularly known as Ch'en Lan-ssu-chi (Ch'en the Fourth [who wears] Rotten Pattens), was from a wealthy and rapidly rising Ch'en family in Po-lo. Although probably none of his family had acquired a regular degree, his father had purchased a high official title, that of judicial commissioner at the provincial level. Already deeply involved in Triad activities, Ch'en was drawn into organizing a revolt when a Triad band in neighboring Kuei-shan hsien was ruthlessly suppressed and its leader took refuge in his household. Several thousand men were gathered at a hilly place near the Kuei-shan hsien border. They first struck westward at the capital of Tung-kuan hsien, but were defeated. They then moved toward the Lo-fu Mountains in Po-lo hsien, and finally entered a fourth hsien, Tseng-ch'eng, where they were routed.[23]

In the meantime a number of other Triad disturbances were reported to Peking by Governor-General Chi-ch'ing in Canton, with the alarming news that a still larger troop of Triads had risen up in response to the invasion of the East River basin by several thousand Red Turbans from southwestern Fukien. Suspicious, the Court dispatched a special envoy to investigate, stripping Chi-ch'ing meanwhile of all titles and ranks of honor. Upon arriving at Canton, the envoy, Na-yen-ch'eng, found not only that Chi-ch'ing had committed suicide in protest and that all the reports had been true, but also that a still larger rebellion was waiting for him. The Red Turbans from Fukien were now reinforced by followers of the White Lotus Society wearing white turbans and by native Triad bands in Kwangtung. The rebellion was not suppressed until after Na-yen-ch'eng mobilized all the government troops in Kwangtung in 1804.[24]

Although the major Triad bands were suppressed at this time, the Triad network of the region apparently survived, because less than two months later we find the troops under the provincial commander-in-chief chasing some Triad forces from Waichow to the east side of the Canton delta.[25] In 1805, several thousand men were organized by Triad leaders in Hai-feng and Lu-feng.

Although the gazetteers of the Waichow region record few disturbances in the decades following 1810, the archival materials of the central government suggest that the Triads in South China were still a headache to the authorities in the 1830's and 1840's.[26] Then, in mid-century, there occurred the great Red Turban revolt that laid siege to Canton.

There is no need to go into detail about the Red Turbans in the

Canton delta, whose activities are described in Frederic Wakeman's essay in this volume (pp. 29–47), but it is worth observing that the revolt started in the Waichow region in June 1854.[27] The Turbans' first move was to occupy Shih-lung, the town downstream from Wai-chow on the East River. Their most famous leader, Ho Lu, was a salt smuggler and a Triad leader of Tung-kuan whose brother and rela-tives had been killed by government troops. In revenge, Ho Lu's forces not only occupied the market town of Shih-lung, but also conquered the Tung-kuan hsien capital. A huge mob burned down the yamen, opened the jail to release all the prisoners, and searched out the hsien magistrate and the battalion commander of the govern-ment troops stationed there. The Triads only teased the magistrate and set him free, but they killed the battalion commander and dis-membered him. More essential to the growth of the Triad forces, the crews of the whole fleet of patrol boats that had been stationed at Tung-kuan to suppress smugglers now joined forces with Ho Lu.

In the meantime, other Triad bands nominally affiliated with Ho Lu's central forces occupied Tseng-ch'eng, Po-lo, and other neighbor-ing hsien. The only resistance in this area came from isolated villages under the control of clan-based and gentry-commanded militia forces, and from a larger fleet of patrol boats based at Canton, which had been in bitter rivalry with the Tung-kuan fleet in its dual role of sup-pressing and patronizing the lucrative salt-smuggling business.

Before the federation of Triad forces under Ho Lu was wiped out, another Triad army rose under the command of a savage female smug-gler-gambler, Chai Ho-ku (Chai [the Lady of] Burning Temper). Im-prisoned for gambling, Chai broke out of jail and joined Ho Liu's troops for a while. Then she became the leader of several independent Triad bands in Kuei-shan hsien. In the half-year following August 11, 1854, when her forces first took over the market town of San-tung in Kuei-shan, her troops and their affiliated bands were a powerful threat to the government forces in this region, attacking the Kuei-shan hsien capital twice, besieging the prefectural capital for more than twelve days, occupying the hsien capitals of Po-lo, Tseng-ch'eng, Ho-yüan, Ho-p'ing, and Hai-feng for various periods, and dominating Tan-shui, Ma-an, Pai-mang-hua, Heng-li, and a number of other market towns. It took two years for government troops to subdue the rebellions in this region.

In general, my impression of such activities at the local level is not quite the same as the one that the official gazetteer compilers tried to give their readers. Instead of premeditated and well-coordinated revolts, the Triad uprisings were mostly spontaneous and sporadic. Uprising sparked uprising, and the more signs of weakness and uncertainty the government authorities showed, the more volunteers joined the rebellion.

As one might infer from the spontaneous, autonomous, and occasionally conflicting movements of the Triads, a widespread network of loosely connected secret societies existed in this region before the outbreak of open rebellion. The government forces could suppress the rebellion of the moment but never succeeded in wiping out the organization itself, interwoven as it was with the social, economic, and political life of the people at the sub-hsien, or sub-administrative, level. Every few years or every few decades, whenever conditions favored open rebellion, the Triads would rise again.

Secret Societies and the Urban Hierarchy

By piecing together the various bits of reliable information on the movement of secret society forces and by plotting this information on local maps, it is possible to show a fascinating pattern in the development of revolutionary insurrections.

The Waichow Revolution, for example, began at the central market town of Tan-shui. In the first two days following the takeover of the police station by Teng K'eng's Triad bands, several hundred men from the villages in the immediate vicinity poured in to join the uprising. Before long, other T'ung-meng Hui agitators brought in one revolutionary band after another: a band of over six hundred came from the community centered at Shui-k'o *hsü*, another band of some five hundred came from Pai-mang-hua, a third came from Ma-chuang, and so on. Since Shui-k'o, Pai-mang-hua, and Ma-chuang were all market towns, and since the bands are often referred to by the names of these towns, it seems not unlikely that the towns were the natural rallying centers for the local bands. In the earlier Triad uprising (of 1900) and in the later campaigns of Ch'en Chiung-ming (1920 and 1923), both taking place in the same Waichow area, we again find such towns as Tan-shui and Pai-mang-hua mentioned as the centers of local military operations.

The pattern that emerges from all this is a series of centripetal movements: local volunteers first gathered at small towns like Ma-chuang and Pai-mang-hua, which were the centers of their local communities, then came together at central market towns like Tan-shui, and finally joined forces with troops from other central market towns for the siege of Waichow. In the successful uprising of 1911, the revo-

lutionary forces ultimately converged on the great regional center of
Canton.

A clearer picture of this centripetal movement may be gathered
from a brief discussion of Tan-shui as a central market town. In this
capacity Tan-shui was both (a) the heart of a local community, serving
the villages in its immediate vicinity, and (b) the node of a much
larger marketing system, surrounded by a number of smaller market
towns that were in turn the nodes of their own local marketing systems. An attack on Tan-shui affected both the immediate local community and the broader marketing system. The distinctness of the
two systems centered at Tan-shui can be seen in the pattern observable in the mobilization of revolutionary forces: after the takeover of
Tan-shui, volunteers from the villages in the local system appeared
in the town first, followed after a few days by bands from the communities centered around the smaller market towns on the rim of the
central marketing system.

This centripetal movement, also observable during many other uprisings of 1911, contrasts sharply with another common type of revolutionary mobilization, which started in major cities and then spread
to their hinterlands: the military rebellions and coups d'etat staged
by regular government troops in administrative centers. In contrast
to the locally based uprisings led by secret societies, military coups
were arbitrarily imposed on local residents and rarely had their spontaneous support. Feng Yü-hsiang's coup in Peking on October 23,
1924, for instance, completely surprised the city residents. They
simply woke up one morning to find that the city had been occupied
by soldiers wearing white armbands printed with Feng's famous slogans. Nor was the March 29th Uprising popularly based; instead of
helping the revolutionaries, many local people were scared away by
the bombs, and some even actively aided the police.

Another way of viewing the development of secret society rebellions
is in terms of the hierarchy of economic centers. From this angle the
movements of Triad forces are not so much centripetal as linear,
climbing a hierarchy of economic centers from smaller market towns
to greater towns to local cities and, in a successful uprising like that of
1911, even to the regional capital. In other words, the stage of the
drama of Triad rebellion was not an undifferentiated platform on
which the actors moved randomly, but rather a hierarchical structure
of nested local systems of economic life. In the case of the Waichow
Revolution, for instance, we find local troops first gathered at small

towns like Pai-mang-hua and Ma-chuang, then congregated at the central market town of Tan-shui, and finally concentrated at the siege of Waichow.

In the context of this economic hierarchy, another feature of local uprisings commands attention, namely, the emergence of different types of local forces at different levels of the hierarchy. In contrast to the uprisings organized by the secret societies at middle-level marketing centers, the militia forces, clan-feud bands, and the like usually operated at the bottom levels of the marketing hierarchy: villages and market towns. In ordinary times, they resisted, ambushed, and sometimes routed the government troops that invaded their territorial communities. These bands would attack higher-level urban centers only after they had been aroused and had temporarily changed their character. As soon as the revolutionary tide ebbed, these forces would return to their quiet life at the bottom of the hierarchy.[28]

In order to mobilize such forces for goals beyond local towns and markets, a broad network of communication, organization, and coordination was necessary. Secret societies—in the Waichow region, the Triads—often provided this network. The finding that the Triad forces became increasingly prominent as the revolutionary movement ascended the hierarchy of economic centers[29] suggests that in the larger marketing systems, where the lineage considerations they had relied on for a sense of solidarity became less and less important, sworn brotherhood and blood oaths filled the void left by the absence of real brotherhood.

This distinction between lineage-based and secret-society-sponsored forces is comparable in many respects to the distinction between the "communal" and the "associational" forces that Charles Tilly found during his investigation of collective violence in European history.[30] The troops organized for clan wars fit well his category of "communal" forces, which were based on localized, inherited, and slowly changing membership. On the other hand, the forces organized by secret societies, although not the same as modern trade unions, resemble them to some extent. Triad organizations, for instance, were formed to serve well-defined interests—whether to protect the smuggling business or to police a market town. Moreover, they definitely enjoyed a capacity for informing, mobilizing, and deploying large numbers of men rapidly and efficiently in times of insurrection. Thus in many senses the Triad bands may be viewed as a pre-industrial counterpart of modern associational dissident forces.

Salt Smuggling

The finding that Triad uprisings tended to take place in commercial centers hints at the sphere of Triad activities in this region in ordinary peaceful times. In order to have some idea of the possibilities for their involvement in local trade and commerce, let us have a quick look at economic conditions in the Waichow region. Relatively poor in rice yields, this region had developed commerce and manufacturing long before many of the major rice-producing regions in China began to feel the impact of commercialization. The region was not only a great salt-producing center but also a major domestic supplier of cane sugar. In addition, there was a steady flow of exports: tea, paper, silk, dried fruits, salt fish, and many handicraft products. Although there is plenty of evidence that the Triads did not confine their activities to the salt trade and salt smuggling, they certainly were heavily involved in both.* I shall concentrate the following discussion on the government salt monopoly, and in particular the squeeze for salt revenue in the years approaching 1911, because the wealth of information on the subject provides an opportunity for systematic investigation into the immediate background of the Waichow Revolution.

In any case, the huge volume of the salt trade had left definite marks on the economic, social, and political landscape of this region. The town of Tan-shui, where the Revolution was ignited and where many other Triad-sponsored uprisings had been staged, was the largest center of salt trade in Waichow.[31] Its salt market was a thousand years old. Following the shifts of the sandy coastline, the office that directly supervised the local salt works had moved from Tan-shui southward to the small walled garrison town of P'ing-hai, but it was still officially called Tan-shui Post. Meanwhile, the old market town of Tan-shui remained both a great salt-trading center and the seat of the central office in charge of salt distribution and transactions in the East River monopoly system. Parallel to the legitimate trade under the monopoly

* One need only leaf through the voluminous memorials and regulations produced by Ch'ing officials regarding the salt administration in Kwangtung to see the extent of their smuggling operations. For such documents, see Ho Chao-yin, et al., comps., *Liang Kuang yen-fa chih* (Materials on the salt administration in Kwangtung and Kwangsi, 1804); Juan Yüan, et al., comps., *Kuang-tung t'ung-chih* (Gazetteer of Kwangtung province, 1822); and *Ts'ai-cheng shuo-ming shu: Kuang-tung sheng* (Compilation on financial administration: Kwangtung province, 1915, hereafter TCSMS). In particular, see Ch'en Hung-mou's "Eleven Instructions on the Salt Administration," in Ho, ch. 29: 8a–12a. This document is also included in Chou Ch'ing-yün, comp., *Yen-fa t'ung-chih* (A comprehensive anthology on salt administration, 1928), ch. 85: 15b–18a.

system, the illicit smuggling business also centered around Tan-shui. Moreover, other market towns in the region (Pai-mang-hua, Heng-li, Ma-an, etc.) that played a prominent role in the Revolution were also key points of salt trade and inspection.

Kwangtung, with its salt going to markets throughout the provinces of Kwangtung and Kwangsi and parts of Fukien, Kiangsi, Hunan, and Kweichow, was the third largest salt-supplying region in China, surpassed only by Kiangsu (with its Liang-huai salt) and Hopei (with its Ch'ang-lu salt). In particular, seven of the major salt-manufacturing centers in Kwangtung were located in the coastal hsien of Kuei-shan, Hai-feng, and Lu-feng, all within Waichow prefecture. One might expect salt smuggling to be prevalent in a region of such extensive salt production. However, salt smuggling was so notoriously rampant in the Waichow region that a brief explanation seems to be called for. Unlike the areas in western, northern, and central Kwangtung—where the prevention of smuggling required merely (a) inspection of the salt imported through the Bogue, or Boca Tigris, and a few other major points around the mouth of the Pearl River and (b) the control of sales at local markets, the Waichow region had the additional responsibility of controlling salt-production centers. It was apparently much more difficult to suppress smuggling in places that had salterns nearby. This was certainly found to be true at Liang-huai in Kiangsu, another notorious location of salt smuggling in China.

Among the salt-producing centers in China, those of the Waichow region offer even greater than usual difficulties in official control, by virtue of the region's geography. Spread along the coastline of Waichow prefecture with its innumerable harbors, inlets, cliffs, and islands where smugglers' boats could hide, the production areas in Waichow could not be policed so easily as areas in Szechwan where salt wells were conveniently concentrated in isolated places. Kiangsu and Hopei had coastal saltworks, but the straight coastlines of those provinces, formed by sandy alluvial plains, were easier to patrol than the Waichow coast.

Moreover, the markets assigned to Waichow salt were confined to the narrow zone extending northward to the distant and relatively inaccessible mountainous areas along the Kiangsi-Kwangtung border. In order to prevent Waichow salt from trespassing upon the areas of the neighboring Canton Delta and the Han River valley, dozens of checkpoints were set up along both the east and west sides of the Waichow region. Geographic proximity and water traffic, however, attracted large amounts of the Waichow salt to these forbidden areas.[32]

All this goes far toward explaining the perpetuation of smuggling organizations in Waichow, but does very little to explain the Triads' sudden burst of energy to challenge the administrative authorities during the fall of 1911. According to the previously mentioned "Eleven Instructions on the Salt Administration" by Governor-General Ch'en Hung-mou, salt smuggling existed long before the mid-eighteenth century, the Triad involvement in smuggling was taken for granted as early as 1758, when the "Instructions" appeared, and, most significantly, the salt administration and the underground smuggling network had apparently managed to co-exist, if not actually to cooperate, for a long time. Even under pressure from their superiors to wipe out the illicit trade, officials had accommodated the powerful, large-scale smuggling organizations by confining their arrests to a few smugglers who were involved in the illicit trade on a small scale and at the local level. Such sporadic arrests and confiscations were part of the normal "cost" of the trade; as long as such a cost was kept within bearable limits, it would not become the cause of open revolt. The general laxity that prevailed in the eighteenth and early nineteenth centuries is also evidenced by the large amount of arrears, back taxes, and overdue loans that were never paid by the salt merchants. The amount was so large that reforms were carried out in 1789 and 1802, but the illicit trade continued to thrive.

In the years approaching 1911, however, the growing demands of the administrative authorities for salt revenues led to a most radical tightening of controls over the trade, and particularly the illicit part of the trade in which the Triads were so much involved. For an understanding of the immediate background of the massive uprisings in the fall of 1911, therefore, we must focus our attention on the late Ch'ing government's squeeze for salt revenues.

Tightening of Government Control: The Squeeze for Salt Revenues

Ever since the Opium War, the Ch'ing government had been increasingly burdened by expenses. War with foreign powers, great rebellions at home, foreign indemnities, and interest on foreign loans had placed demands on the Imperial treasury that could not be met by existing revenues. The burden was radically increased during the decade following 1900 not only by the Boxer indemnities but also by numerous reform programs: the New Army, new schools, sending students abroad, railways and other modern construction, administrative reforms, experiments in popular assemblies, etc. For the massive increases in revenues that it needed, the government looked primarily and immediately to the commercial sector, for a number of reasons: (a) taxes on trade and commerce would arouse less ideological controversy than burdening the peasants with increased land taxes, (b) various new urban taxes could bypass many of the time-honored, inefficient, and corrupt bureaucratic procedures involved in collecting the old land tax, and (c) at the demand of foreign powers, the payment of foreign loans was guaranteed by likin, salt taxes, and other newly created urban taxes, interest on these loans being paid from such taxes as well.

The trend toward rapid tax increases is illustrated not only by the long lists of new taxes recorded in many local gazetteers[33] but also by such disturbances as the Triad uprising of 1907 in Ch'ing-chou, which was the immediate response to the new sugar tax,[34] and by the Hsiang-shan mob's assault upon tax collectors and the salt monopoly office in 1910.[35] One can cite an endless list of such new taxes and ensuing disturbances in the years before 1911. Many riots arose from resistance to the census surveys of 1909–10, which were seen as a device for increasing taxes; the census surveyors were sometimes simply regarded as tax collectors and beaten up by local mobs.[36]

Although officials were looking in many directions for increased revenues, they were particularly attracted to the salt trade for these additional reasons: (a) there were large arrears to be collected from the licensed merchants; (b) between the legitimate and the illegitimate trade there obviously lay a broad ambiguous area into which government authority could expand; and (c) the salt market, which far exceeded that of sugar or silk, seemed to provide an inexhaustible source of revenue. Thus, new taxes, surcharges, fees, liquidations of old debts, and every other form of exaction fell upon the trade.

The specific finding that administrative tightening-up measures and tax increases provided the immediate cause for the massive uprisings in 1911, however, should be carefully distinguished from the general thesis that links the downfall of the Ch'ing dynasty to the oppressive tax burden on the peasantry, a thesis that has recently been challenged by Wang Yeh-chien.[37] It is not yet clear whether the general standard of living among the Chinese peasantry declined on the eve of the Revolution, although my finding that the revolutionary potential appeared to be concentrated selectively at certain commercial centers rather than spread evenly in the countryside seems to support Wang's argument. Moreover, even for the commercial sector, an increased tax burden means lower profits only if it can be shown that before the tax squeeze started there had been no commensurate rise in merchants' gross income as a result of higher retail prices or higher total sales due to population increases or market adjustments. With all these qualifications considered, however, the provincial authorities' policy of squeezing revenue from the salt trade in Kwangtung and particularly in Waichow during the late Ch'ing period has all the earmarks of severity.

To the basic salt tax there were added 55 others; and the names of these various new taxes suggest that every possible excuse, no matter how trivial or ridiculous, was used to squeeze more money from the salt merchants.[38] When, in 1905, there was no longer any available excuse, a new tax was simply imposed upon the merchants' legal profits.

More important to our study than the mere number of new taxes is the extreme rapidity with which they fell upon the trade. The precipitate trend toward the creation of new taxes during the late Ch'ing can be brought into bold relief by a list of the new salt taxes arranged chronologically according to the date of establishment or last adjustment.* There were only 5 new items in the whole eighteenth century, but 8 in the early nineteenth century (1800–1840). It was after the Opium War and especially after the great rebellions broke out that major taxes were introduced. Thus, in the next four decades (1841–80) 11 more taxes were created or readjusted, and these included such major items as the salt likin and a regular military tax. The great majority of the new taxes, however, were concentrated in the last three decades of the dynasty (1881–1911): 26 items whose dates have been ascertained and 5 whose dates are less certain. Of the 26 items whose dates are known, 20 were created in the years following the Boxer uprising of 1900. In other words, about 75 percent of the entries on the table of salt revenues were created after the Opium War, 50 percent in the last three decades of the Ch'ing dynasty, and 40 percent in the decade immediately preceding the Revolution.

* The two volumes of TCSMS covering Kwangtung contain specific information on salt taxes—the nature and the fixed quota of these taxes as well as totals collected in 1908 and 1909. From lengthy discussions about the historical background of the taxes, it is possible in most cases to ascertain the date when the taxes were originally established or when the major adjustments in them were made. Such data enabled me to compile a list of all taxes levied either exclusively on the Waichow salt trade or on the whole Pearl River monopoly system, including Waichow. This list, too long to be included here, but available in Hsieh, Dissertation, chap. 6, immediately impresses one with the extraordinary burden of taxes on the salt trade during the late Ch'ing.

Such tax increases would not have mattered so much if they had merely been on paper—if there had not been at the same time such systematic and concerted efforts on the part of the administration to tighten up on the salt monopoly. For one thing, the salaries of officials involved in salt administration and in the suppression of smuggling were increased; more important, most of these salaries were now paid regularly and directly from the government treasury, the various *lou-kuei* and other traditional forms of hidden taxation used as substitutes for regular salaries being abolished in 1909. For another, more and more efforts were made to reclaim century-old debts and arrears. Special allowances for salt sales were added to regular quotas so as to help merchants catch up on unpaid military taxes, overdue payments of "salt prices," and interest on these debts. During the late Ch'ing, levies and taxes were established specifically for liquidating arrears and loans and paying interest. A case of particular interest is that of Teng K'eng's clansman Teng Shih-i, who was the head merchant of Tan-shui. Because of his arrears, he was forced to turn the wholesale markets at Tan-shui over to official management, and to lease the office building, storage space, and other facilities to the government. A certain portion of the office rent was then withheld by the government as one way to liquidate Teng's debts within a limited period.

As a result of concerted efforts such as these, salt revenue in Kwangtung increased spectacularly in the late Ch'ing years. A comparison of the 1908 figures with those of 1909, for instance, shows increases in revenues for 33 of the 55 new taxes and levies (the other 22 belonged to such categories as fixed quota, residual debts, and clearance of stored salt). Although we have no reliable figures from years immediately prior to 1908–9, it is reported that salt revenue for 1909 was 3 million taels, twice the average annual figure for the nineteenth century.

The administrative authorities, however, still desperate for revenue, were impatient with these piecemeal reforms, and a much more drastic reform was proposed in 1910 and carried out in 1911. Yüan Shu-hsün, governor-general of Kwangtung and Kwangsi (1909–10), proposed to farm out the whole salt monopoly system in Kwangtung and Kwangsi to a single commercial corporation, estimating the total revenue that could be collected at 10.2 million taels a year. The Court rejected this proposal on the suspicion of favoritism toward one merchant group and also in the belief that 10.2 million taels was an unrealistic figure. Eventually the policy was slightly revised in this way:

the salt monopoly was to be farmed out to a number of head merchants through open competition, and the annual revenues were to be increased in substantial but gradual steps—5.8 million for the first year (1911), 6.2 million for the second year, and 7.8 million from the third year on.

The new management started in late May of 1911, and under rigorous official supervision the monthly revenues were duly collected. By the time the Revolution broke out in October, over two million taels had been paid into the provincial treasury of Kwangtung.[39] One can imagine the rigorous control of the whole process of salt transit that supported this phenomenal accomplishment, from the gates of the salt factories right through to sales at the markets. Modern bookkeeping was introduced when the graduates of the newly established Institute for Salt Management joined the staff of the administration.[40]

One can only speculate about the extent to which this revenue squeeze had cut into the profits of the otherwise untaxed illicit trade, i.e., into the area where the legitimate and the illegitimate trade were so intimately tied together that the roles of licensed merchant and smuggler were scarcely distinguishable. There is ample evidence, though, that salt smuggling was rigorously suppressed: payments to the government forces charged with the task were increased; steamboats were purchased to patrol the waters frequented by smuggling boats; and a large sum of additional revenue was raised at the annual sales of confiscated illicit salt and confiscated boats.

Whether or not the tax increase actually cut the merchants' profits to the bone and deprived the smugglers of their livelihood, however, is far less important than whether or not they thought it did. On the eve of the Waichow Revolution of 1911, what really mattered was their subjective perception of the oppressiveness of the government squeeze for salt revenue. And there is no lack of incidents showing a general resentment against the tax squeeze. We have already mentioned the episode of 1910 in which the Hsiang-shan mob assaulted the salt monopoly office. During the Revolution, salt factories and salt management offices were destroyed in a number of places in the Waichow region.[41] In short, the many people who were involved in the selling, shipping, and smuggling of Waichow salt saw themselves as having a common interest in opposing the government; they listened to the T'ung-meng Hui agitators with great sympathy. Under these circumstances, the Triads readily provided the mechanism for revolutionary mobilization.

Secret Societies, Popular Movements, and the 1911 Revolution

JOHN LUST

Preliminaries—Revolutionary moment and popular unrest—
Iconoclasm and Nationalist myth—Doubts and necessities—
Popular societies and the republicanism of the early 1900's—
Popular movements and the events of 1911–12—Conclusions

Preliminaries

There was scarcely a single episode in the republican movement, from the Canton raid of 1895 to the provincial risings of 1911–12, says Li Wen-hai, from which the secret societies were completely absent.[1] When the old dynastic system vanished, enormous forces were released that expressed themselves as much in social unrest—riots or popular insurgence—as in the conscious activities of republicans or constitutionalists. If the popular societies were an ambiguous element in the republican movement, it was because they themselves were a symptom of the breakdown of the old agrarian society under extreme pressure from a dynamic imperialism. Social banditry, as E. J. Hobsbawm remarks, became a major feature of peasant societies in the grip of such crises in the nineteenth and early twentieth centuries. China was no exception.

It is worthwhile making a broad survey, if a very tentative one, of the relationship between these "movements from below" and the modern republican movement. It is no simple task. Regional monographs are scarce. The popular societies were outsiders and often illegal; hence their documents were destroyed except when they were needed for evidence. The documents of their adversaries were biased or formulistic in their recording of events. However, for better or worse, the societies were an essential element in the fabric of modern Chinese society. To ignore them is to run the risk of impoverishing or distorting one's understanding of the 1911 revolution.[2]

By the late nineteenth century, the extraordinary expansion of the Ko-lao Hui had spread their organization throughout vast areas of

China.[3] They dominated the Yangtze valley, apart from the lower reaches, which were the territory of the Green and Red Gangs. They had moved up into Honan and Shensi, and Hunanese garrison troops had taken their lodges with them to Fukien, Sinkiang, and the far northern border regions. The Triads kept to the three southernmost provinces and the Nanyang area, whereas the sects, thoroughly wrecked in the campaigns of the Taiping period, were predominant only in Shantung and Chihli, if still very strong in Szechwan and Kweichow, side by side with the *hui-t'ang*. The Ko-lao Hui form of organization had become remarkably tough and adaptable, and was to be borrowed by the sects. *Hui-t'ang* were, in principle, open to all. Depending on local conditions, vagrants, discharged soldiers, or salt smugglers joined them, whereas in some regions they were rooted in villages or handicraft industries.[4] But their influence extended also to local political factions, and their role even to the control of banditry where official policing failed. Hence, members from the higher strata of society were not uncommon among them: such people quite naturally bought offices in the societies or ran their own lodges to protect themselves. Society chiefs included merchants, military officials, *sheng-yüan* (students qualified to enter the official examinations), landowners, and the like. The exigencies of radical and republican movements brought in a variety of people with more or less modern educations and outlooks—students, teachers, journalists, army cadets.[5]

Apart from these elaborate organizations, simple forms of social banditry existed among bands in mountainous regions. They had become a familiar feature of China's progressive decline from the late eighteenth century onward.

Revolutionary Moment and Popular Unrest

The 1911 revolution has often enough been seen as a purely military and political event. However, contemporary observers were in no doubt about the profound social and eonomic crisis in which the old regime was plunged. The precarious situations of huge rural populations living at or below subsistence levels were aggravated by the abuse of supplementary taxes and ad hoc levies, by the neglect of irrigation systems, canals, and the like, by the running down of communal granaries intended to alleviate local food shortages, and by the flight of gentry to the towns, leading to the deterioration of their mediatory role between officials and people.[6] Respect for authority was becoming fragile at the very moment when the implementation of the New Policy of modernization was demanding large sums of money that ultimately had to come from the rural and urban lower classes.

Widespread rioting and local outbreaks became a commonplace after the Boxer Protocol. In Kwangsi, a rising that had begun in 1898 with a brief flare-up of Triad activity revived in 1900 on a larger scale and by 1903 was threatening to spread to neighboring provinces.[7] Vast forces were posted in to suppress it, but even so it lingered on until 1906. In Szechwan, the Red Lantern Sect mounted formidable outbreaks and took part in anti-tax riots. In Chihli in the spring of 1902, some 160,000 peasants organized in *lien-chuang hui* (village leagues) were led by Ching T'ing-pin in a vast riot against missionary indemnities. The old Boxer slogan had now been replaced by "Sweep away the Ch'ing, destroy the foreigner; when officials oppress, the people rebel."[8] In Lo-p'ing, Kiangsi, in July 1904, violence flared up in a way that was to become typical of the later wave of New Policy riots. Extra taxes for the new schools, levied on the local staple crop, catalyzed an explosion of old grievances. A riot led by *hui-t'ang* brought in 3,000 participants within a few days. Landowners, too, raised forces to resist the tax,[9] and the outbreak spread to the *hui-t'ang* of Anhwei.

In 1909–11 riots swept through the lower Yangtze region (here defined as including Kiangsu and Hunan), Manchuria, Kwangtung, Szechwan, and Shensi. The main causes of these riots were increased taxes to pay for the new schools, police, etc., the census, preparations for local self-government, rice prices, and the opium poppy ban.[10] The drive for modernization took place during a period of inflation. No nationwide figures exist, but prices of commodities, rents, and services went up by 80–200 percent in local areas throughout eastern China during the first decade of the 1900's, while wages clearly lagged behind.[11] One observer remarked that the margin between a bare livelihood and absolute poverty was never so narrow as it was at that time.

It may be worthwhile to analyze these catalytic grievances in some detail in order to understand the themes of the various uprisings. The running of the New Policy institutions had been handed over to gentry managers (*tung*) who were intended to act as a support for local officials. The gentry seized the opportunity everywhere to advance their administrative and economic positions. New levies were imposed right and left, on the grounds of financing the census, the self-government bureaus, and the other reforms. The "surplus" money raised went into the pockets of the gentry.[12] This intensified exploitation became a major theme of the riots, and the houses of gentry managers became targets for destruction as often as the foreign-type schools, police stations, or self-government offices.[13]

The census was never seen as a straightforward head-count—much less as the necessary foundation for efficient government. Instead, the peasants saw it as a device for increasing taxes, as somehow connected with railway construction, or as part of a looming foreign menace. The new schools, too, could be seen as a hateful sign of foreign influence as well as a symbol of exploitation.

Critical local shortages of grain, another cause of the riots, were brought about not only by crop failures due to drought or floods, but by the growth of speculative grain markets in Shanghai and Manchuria. Hunger riots were therefore directed both against local hoarding and speculation and against the movement of grain to urban centers or out of a province—in particular to foreign firms speculating in, for example, the Shanghai market.

The drive against poppy crops affected poor provinces like Shensi most of all. Troops were often simply sent in to uproot the poppies, with no plan for anything to replace them. If the economy of the region was to survive, an equally profitable crop had to be found on short notice. This was clearly difficult where the soil was poor. The poppy ban could also be seen as a foreign maneuver; hence, the antiforeign theme in the frequent riots in Shansi and Kansu.

The precise mechanism of the riots is difficult to document and must be inferred largely from newspaper reports and the like, but it does seem clear that many of the formal characteristics George Rudé discovered in eighteenth-century riots in Western Europe can be found here as well. The movement of rioters was generally from rural areas to the administrative or market towns. Sheer hunger might be the driving force, or economic or political aims might emerge and be set forth in simple programs. Itinerant bands of rioters intent primarily on punishing hoarders might move from one town to another.[14] Hoarders might be punished by having their stocks destroyed—grain pitched into canals and the like. Since no looting had taken place, such an action might even be approved by a local official.[15] *Taxation populaire* (popular fixing of "fair" prices) also occurred. During famines and other periods of extremely high grain prices, public pressure always made itself felt. Gentry and other middle-class elements petitioned district or provincial officials to institute *p'ing-t'iao*, price-leveling whereby grain was to be sold at pre-famine rates. Officials who were in grain rings might refuse, whereupon peasants and other lower-class elements might attempt to impose leveling or fair prices. If this did not work, riots usually ensued.

The organization of riots frequently drew on the repertory of traditional forms. The action in each *hsiang* (district) of a hsien was usually organized independently of that in the others, although communication probably took place over wide areas between districts that were ripe for rioting. A circular (*ch'uan-tan*), with a chicken feather attached to indicate urgency, was often sent by messenger, as tradition dictated. In some areas, women hunger-rioters commandeered food from gentry houses. Their men stood by, and troops found themselves at a loss.[16] The Red Lantern Sect in Szechwan occasionally acted as cadres for riots, and secret societies in the lower Yangtze region probably did likewise, although the evidence for this is rarely conclusive.[17] The riots were highly localized; hence, in the North the *lien-chuang hui* (essentially a defense against banditry, but often turned against extortionate taxation) could serve as a framework for them.

In tense situations, riots might move to a higher stage on the continuum between resistance to taxes and full-scale rebellion. The outstanding example of such a development in the early 1900's occurred in the Lai-yang district of Shantung in 1910. Here, an alliance of "bad gentry" and the local official had developed a monopoly (*pao-lan*) to channel the proceeds of New Policy taxes through money shops. This intensified exploitation was coupled with a grain shortage. Stocks in the communal granaries had been lent out at usurious rates or sold for private gain by the gentry in the monopoly so that no relief was available. The riot that broke out in response to these conditions was organized by the *lien-chuang hui* of the *hsiang*. Modern artillery was sent in to quell it, and whole villages were destroyed. Shantung notables living outside the province estimated casualties at some forty thousand. It seems that the peasants were held back from actual rebellion only by the devastating power of the explosives used by the government forces and by the restraint imposed by the leader of the *lien-chuang hui*, Ch'ü Shih-wen. The Japanese historian Hazama may have gone too far in placing the incident in the evolution toward the theory of New Democracy,[18] but Lai-yang was certainly prophetic of the sort of situation that arose the following year in western Szechwan, and of the violence inherent in the polarization of classes. The logical outcome in Lai-yang would have been a war without quarter against the "bad gentry."

Can this dangerous social unrest be considered to have influenced political developments in the late Ch'ing period? If so, it must be noted that republican influence can only have been indirect. Republican contacts with the riots were rare and largely military when they did occur.[19] However, the unrest was sapping the morale of the authorities, both central and provincial. In particular, the combination of widespread riots and the one great rising of late 1906, when an alliance of republicans and *hui-t'ang* added to official troubles, panicked local government in the lower Yangtze valley. Ultimately, both the authority and the self-confidence of the establishment were undermined.

Iconoclasm and Nationalist Myth

The ground for a rapprochement between radicalism and the popular societies was prepared by a number of factors delicate to analyze but psychologically important. One of them was anti-Confucianism, a main aspect of which was the *jen-hsia* (knight-errantry) tradition. *Jen-hsia* was a gentry affair, implying not only impulsive chivalry and a spirit of self-sacrifice, but also an outdoor atmosphere of military sports. Among the reform generation of the 1890's, men like T'an Ssu-t'ung and Liang Ch'i-ch'ao, it became associated with a fresh radical patriotism.[20] A parallel movement existed among the lower strata of society, where it might be called Robin-Hoodism. The popular culture associated with *jen-hsia*, scorned by Confucianists, could provide the middle classes with relief from stiff Confucian attitudes and with forms for drawing the lower classes into republicanism. Thus *jen-hsia* could help to bridge the gap between radicals and popular societies.

Here were old themes undergoing transformations. But the growing crisis of Ch'ing society engendered more fundamental forms of iconoclasm as well. The attack on paternalistic relationships such as the Three Bonds (prince to subject, etc.) arose not only from foreign undermining but from internal tensions. Such an attack opened the way to new attitudes toward the lower strata of society and new concepts of history in which the old ruling dynasties would be dislodged from the center of the world. In certain circumstances, they could lead to a Chinese form of populism,[21] a limited osmosis between radicalism and old-style insurgence. The forms that appeared in Chekiang, Kweichow, Hunan, and Honan were transitory ones, unable to survive the break-up of the radical–popular movement alliances of 1911–12. The final flourish of the old Ta-t'ung utopianism was the 1908 manifesto of the Revolutionary Alliance (Ko-ming Hsieh-hui).

The solidest basis for a rapprochement between republicans and popular societies lay in their common hostility toward the Manchus.[22] The republican variety of anti-Manchuism by no means coincided with popular forms often found in oral tradition, but both led ultimately to a theory of the nation—a myth in the Sorelian sense, a guide to action.

Popular anti-Manchuism was a semi-mythical evocation of the mission to destroy the Manchu invaders and restore a good Ming prince. With it went pre-Manchu dress, old official titles, the removal of the queue, and so on. A great deal of this popular symbolism was inherited by the republicans, and it strengthened the impact of their patriotic ideology. It could also create solidarity among the masses depicted by Sun Yat-sen as a loose sheet of sand. The societies took this symbolism very literally. Their dropping the queue was not their only act of defiance toward the Manchus; in 1911–12 they also strutted about the streets in the historical costumes of opera while their chiefs projected themselves into the roles of old magistrates and generals, just as the chiefs of the Small Knife Society had done sixty years before.

The earliest surviving example of characteristic republican anti-Manchuism appears in the deposition given by Lu Hao-tung after his capture in the Hsing-Chung Hui (Society for the Revival of China) raid of November 1895.[23] Lu stated that Sun Yat-sen had turned him from an exclusive concern with the foreign threat toward anti-Manchuism. He attacked the parasitic rule of the Manchus and the perfidy of their Chinese (Han) supporters. Where did all this come from? Sun's contacts were with Triads, not with literati. Triad oral traditions reinforced by the reading of history may have provided the basis for it, but Lu's ideas were more consciously thought out than those of the Triads, and far more so than those of the sects. Were they essentially a reflection of the crisis of summer 1895, or did they draw on oral traditions that may have existed among the educated? Striking similarities to Lu's statement may be noticed in such key documents as the Taiping anti-Manchu proclamation[24] and the violent passage in T'an Ssu-t'ung's *Jen-hsüeh* (Science of humanity; ch. 2). There are ironic echoes of the flattering phrases in Han official documents, and slogans such as "China for the Chinese."

Radical anti-Manchuism became a very complex affair. T'an Ssu-

t'ung had evolved rapidly by 1896, by which time early Ch'ing resistance sources were being republished, and perhaps also versions of
Taiping documents. T'an's sympathy for the troops who found their
haven in *hui-t'ang* solidarity was obvious in his unpublished work.
He was not alone in this attitude, which can be seen as a stage in the
development of the populism of the radicals of the early 1900's.

The new anti-Manchuism drew not only on Triad abuse of Manchus but on gentry history. An early Ch'ing resistance movement, the
seizure of Han lands, and the enslavement of the Han people remained its basis, but it changed as new themes were added. The old
theory of despotism, intended to account for the decline of the Ming,
was re-interpreted in the late 1890's as a justification for anti-dynasticism. However, it could just as well be an argument for republicanism, and so it appeared in the early 1900's.

Analyzing the implications of anti-Manchuism for the lower classes
requires caution, partly because, in spite of such correctives as the
case of Yü Tung-ch'en (Yü the Wild),* it is all too easy to under-
estimate the ability of the illiterate or semi-literate Chinese to size
up political situations. Here, too, however, the implications must
have evolved. Take the word *ko-ming*, the keyword of anti-dynasticism as manifested in the anti-Manchuism that flared up in summer
1895. Its old sense was "change of mandate," but during the 1890's it
was applied to the ideas of the Hsing-Chung Hui, that is, to the notion
of a social revolution.[25] It became a disturbing word, like *Communism* in mid-nineteenth-century Europe. When one finds *ko-ming*
used as an adjective in slogans and elsewhere by one of the two *hui-
t'ang* forces that participated in the P'ing-Liu-Li rising of late 1906,
can one conclude that this *hui-t'ang* saw it in a new light? The word
could not have been so used previously. Such a usage must have
implied at least that a new form of alliance existed. The other *hui-
t'ang* force in the rising resisted such innovations, and even issued
a traditionalist manifesto as a challenge. One may observe that in
alliances of this sort, insurgence was being given new directions. Anti-
foreignism and anti-missionary attacks no longer occurred.

The importance of anti-Manchuism in such alliances was reflected
in early Nationalist historiography. Sun Yat-sen's version describes a

---

* Yü, a coal miner, had become involved in anti-missionary movements in
Szechwan in the 1880's. By the late 1890's he had set up an autonomous patriotic
regime in Ta-tsu hsien that attracted the open sympathy of gentry and officials.
No doubt he had a good deal of contact with local literati who joined his movement, but it seems clear from his manifestos that he was able to think for himself
on the question of the international situation of China.

handful of Ming loyalists who, seeing that the situation was irretriev-
ably lost, formed secret groups to hand down the "seeds" of national
feeling with the slogan "Overturn the Ch'ing, restore the Ming."[26]
T'ao Ch'eng-chang, who was steeped in secret society activity, set out
an equally impassioned historical justification for anti-Manchuism.[27]
However, T'ao's version took a new turn. He seems to have been
disillusioned by experiences in the North in 1900. The "barbaric
revolution" of the Boxers was to him inferior to the great movements
of the South. He rationalized his feelings in a scheme that distinguished the modes of popular movements clearly, but in a way that
brought his scheme under heavy fire from historians.[28] The societies
of the Yangtze and the South were predominantly *hui-t'ang*. Their
members, he said, were rational and political animals, with codes
deriving from the *Shui-hu chuan* and similar literature. Northern
societies, by contrast, were basically sects. Their members, according
to T'ao, were superstitious, stupid, and warlike. T'ao oversimplified
his case, but one cannot dismiss the intuitions of an old revolutionary
even if he backs them up with the wrong arguments. There is no
doubt that the northern sects, politically speaking, had declined
spectacularly since the 1860's, with the exception of the Boxer flare-
up of the late 1890's. Hence the White Lotus and the Hung Hu-tzu[29]
were far less important in the republican movement than the *hui-
t'ang*.

On the question of the popular societies' role in the revolution,
there was certainly a gap between Nationalist myth and reality. The
question was only rarely even posed realistically in 1912. The societies
were not merely a repository of national feeling, or a problem to be
swept under the carpet. In the theory of nationalism their historical
mission had worked itself out, and the old united front that originated in the Yangtze riots of 1891 had come to an end.

The gap between myth and reality increased, if anything, in the
later writings of historians of the Nationalist movement. In Kuomintang history, the role of the secret societies became stereotyped.
Shortly before his death, Sun Yat-sen refused a proposal that he include the history of the secret societies in the official Nationalist history,[30] on the grounds that although the societies had national feelings, their structure was paternalistic and they had little knowledge
of republican principles or popular rights; thus their connections
with republicanism could only be slight. A separate monograph
should be written, he said. This reply seems to have set the tone for
historians of the republican period. However, in the 1930's new

source material appeared in articles of the *Chien-kuo yüeh-k'an* (National construction monthly), for example on the P'ing-Liu-Li rising,[31] and in the later 1940's some loosening of the rigid attitudes of Kuomintang historians could be seen. But it did not go very far.

Since 1949 the historians of the People's Republic have placed emphasis on popular movements, reversing the approach of traditional Nationalist historiography.[32] They have returned in a new way to the earliest dreams of modern historians: to produce a history of the people, rather than the family histories of emperors.[33] Before Liberation, however, Marxist historiography, too, was prone to dismiss the societies, as can be seen in a special number on the 1911 revolution published in 1927 by *Hsiang-tao* (The guide), the leading Marxist journal. The analysis in this number ignored the old united front of republicans and secret societies, along with the unrelenting hostility of the secret societies toward foreigners.

Doubts and Necessities

There were strategic reasons as well as ideological ones for a rapprochement between the republicans and the societies. By about 1905 a central revolution no longer seemed possible, and the republican foothold in the official sphere, apart from connections with influential gentry, was largely restricted to the New Army. The societies could extend republican influence inside provincial armies or among minor yamen officials, and even provide the republican cause with something of a mass basis in rural areas. Local notables who were society chiefs, or were close to societies, might become important allies.

There was also the hold of the environment. In a vast subcontinent like China, where capitalist development had not yet undermined localism or evolved efficient networks of communication, the dialectic of province and whole resembled a fluid international situation. Radicalism emerged from the reform movement of the 1890's in a number of provincial centers. The dominance of Tokyo and Shanghai has tended to overshadow them, and the centralizing function of the T'ung-meng Hui has been grossly exaggerated.[34] Often the centers spread what might be called a climate of radicalism, which gave rise to new initiatives and unexpected developments. The societies, too, were subject to this play of the environment. But their role was not purely passive. The crisis of the 1890's had produced a very loose united front in the South, from which the radicals inherited the role of the old reform or insurgent middle strata. The radical centers

often emerged in schools in Hunan, Chekiang, Szechwan, and elsewhere. Their numbers increased after 1905, when they appeared in
the North, too. Although often short-lived, they provided a base from
which contacts could be built up with secret societies and social
bandits as readily as with local armies, intellectuals, and gentry.

The republicans drew heavily on the rituals and the rich conspiratorial technology of the secret societies, both for their own use and in
order to consolidate alliances with the societies. Whether individual
republicans took their society memberships seriously or regarded
them as a mere tactic probably depended on how far they had gone
in rejecting traditional ways or gentry origins. There were regional
variations in such attitudes: the essentially Westernized republicans
of Kwangtung and the Nanyang region despised secret societies more
than those from Hunan, Szechwan, or Kweichow. A Triad lodge was
set up for republicans in Yokohama,[35] and abridged private ceremonies of the unavoidable rituals were arranged for the squeamish.
Secret society rites, gestures, passwords, and even the elaborate oath-
taking ceremony to establish pseudo-kinship, all were adapted to republican use. Shops, hostels, and teahouses were used as fronts for
headquarters where society members and republicans could meet and
be lodged.[36]

What was the relationship between *hui-t'ang* and republicans? The
great debate on this question that took place in People's China before
the Cultural Revolution turned on a number of questions: for example, whether the societies were junior partners or full partners in
their alliances with the republicans. Wang I-sun, among others, suggests one of the most interesting answers: that, since the republicans
were not fully clear about their social relationship to the peasants,
they found it very difficult to communicate with them and consequently used the societies as intermediaries.

In proposing this interpretation, Wang emphasizes that the relationship was probably not a fully conscious one on the republicans'
part.[37] There is no doubt that the radicals were inhibited by the
habits and social arrangements of the old regime in making direct
approaches to the peasantry.

No discussion of the relationship can ignore the basic conflicts that
were always near the surface and ready to break out. Middle-class
respectability clashed with lower-class vulgarity and superstition; the
traditional sector clashed with the emerging one in social or military
forms, or both. Moreover, there was conflict among the republicans
themselves as to what part the societies should play in their cause.

The young radicals, because of their sense of urgency and their populism, refused to accept cautious attitudes toward the societies. They admired them for their relentless hostility toward the Manchus, for their spartan discipline, and for their equanimity in the face of death.[38] They could see the Hung Hu-tzu and the Kwangsi insurgents as patriots and representatives of China. Sun Yat-sen, however, had strong reservations about them. In July 1905, he criticized the societies of Kwangsi for not producing an outstanding leader. Their internecine feuds reminded him of the infighting that hastened the collapse of the Taipings.[39]

The *hui-t'ang* were accepted in the T'ung-meng Hui constitution of May 1906, provided they agreed to basic principles.[40] But there were those in the central T'ung-meng Hui whose populism was not so strong as Sun's and who went even further than he did in opposing the secret societies. Hu Han-min complained in March 1908 about the heedlessness and indiscipline of the Triads and their tendency to loot and run wild. They could easily bring the revolution into disrepute.[41] In July he further accused them of undependability. Hu's attitude was a measure of the alienation of the bourgeoisie from the old system, and with it the old popular movements. After the abortive mutiny of February 1910 in Canton, and particularly after the failure of the Kwangsi and P'ing-Liu-Li risings, Huang Hsing and Sun himself had come more or less to agree with Hu. Henceforth the societies were to serve as mere diversionary forces for the New Army.[42]

The disillusionment that underlay this new emphasis on the New Army was genuine enough. However, it must be noted that the T'ung-meng Hui somewhat exaggerated their ability to gain control over the New Army forces, even though republicanism itself got a hold in them; thus for practical reasons the retreat from the popular societies, as will be seen, was more apparent than real.

The shift of an important section of the central T'ung-meng Hui to the South and a feeling of frustration among republicans in Tokyo led in summer 1907 to the establishment of the Kung-chin Hui (Society for Common Progress). It was affiliated with, or at least not in opposition to, the T'ung-meng Hui, but it took a new tack. Radicals and secret societies—the Triads, the Ko-lao Hui, the Hung-chiang Hui (Hung River Society), and the Szechwanese Hsiao-i Hui (Society of Filial Piety and Righteousness)—were to be united in a grand Yangtze alliance. The lodge titles were significant: Chung-hua Shan (China Mountain), Hsing-Han Shui (Up-with-Han Water), Kuang-fu T'ang (Restoration Hall), and Pao-kuo Hsiang (Defend-the-Country

Fragrance).[43] For Chang Pai-hsiang, it was a question of braving the interior, not hiding oneself in Tokyo and relying on students. The intellectuals, thought Wu Yü-chang, had got a monopoly in the T'ung-meng Hui and were alienating themselves from the *hui-t'ang*. The program of the new society closely followed T'ung-meng Hui policy, especially on anti-Manchuism, but it changed Sun's principle of equalization of land rights to equalization of human rights. This may have reflected *hui-t'ang* utopianism, but some see the influence of the predominant landowners in it. In practice, the outlooks of Kung-chin Hui leaders ranged from radical to traditionalist. The new society is thought to have made a real impact in the lower Yangtze and in northern Szechwan. As was always the case with grand alliances of societies, in the long run it worked efficiently only on a provincial—or at best an interprovincial—basis, as for Hupeh and Hunan.

Popular Societies and the Republicanism of the Early 1900's

A map of contacts between republican movements and popular societies would have undergone considerable changes during the first decade of the twentieth century, as the movements went through certain stages of development: an upsurge of radicalism, followed by the consolidation of organizations under the stimulus of the T'ung-meng Hui (1905), and a final period of rapid spread and growth.

The reform movement of the 1890's had already within it the seeds of anti-dynasticism: parallel with it was the tremendous flare-up of secret society activity of 1898–1900. Chinese and Japanese historians have seen a turning point toward republicanism in the big abortive rising mounted in the lower Yangtze in 1900 by reformers and secret societies; its leader, T'ang Ts'ai-ch'ang, was claimed as one of their own by republicans in Tokyo in 1905–6.[44] This militancy fused with Western radical thought to produce the ferment of the very early 1900's in Japan and in Shanghai, which in its turn led in 1904 to the conspiratorial experiments in the lower Yangtze.

The climate of radicalism was not confined to this area; it spread to Kweichow, where it gave rise to developments to be mentioned later, and to Kwangsi, where weaker radical centers developed. The continuity between the republican movement and earlier forms of radicalism in Hunan was always broken by conservative-party violence, but a classic case of unbroken development occurs in Chen-feng hsien, Kweichow. A society called the Jen-hsüeh Hui (Humanism Society) was run by a prefect who had probably met T'an Ssu-t'ung in

Changsha and borrowed the name of his famous book while it was still in manuscript.[45] This society typically acted as a forcing ground for radicalism in the early 1900's, and many of its members later joined in the radical alliance with the Ko-lao Hui. In the North, little radicalism existed before 1906–7, and this lack is consonant with the very weak position of the reform movement there.

It can be deduced that the essential ingredient for the emergence of republicanism was the existence of a solid nucleus of radicals whose members were relatively free agents, both because of their social position and because they had freed themselves from rigid neo-Confucianism. Not surprisingly, then, such nuclei were more likely to form in schools than in army units. Secret societies, too, could give rise to such a nucleus. During the late Ch'ing, the societies tended to become more like pressure groups. After 1901, those interested in modernization got official approval. Among the New Armies in Hupeh and Hunan they became the underground arm of republicanism, drawing in troops, intellectuals, and Ko-lao Hui members.

For purposes of analysis, Chinese radicalism before 1908 can be divided into two categories—one strong enough to operate powerful centers and mount large-scale outbreaks, and the other limited to weaker centers and guerrilla-type military activity. Let us examine the two in turn.

One area in which radicalism was quite strong was the lower Yangtze. The movement of radicals from the foci of intellectual ferment in Shanghai and Japan into this area gave rise to two independent organizations in the year immediately before the T'ung-meng Hui was set up—the Kuang-fu Hui (Restoration Society) and the Hua-hsing Hui (Society for the Revival of China). The first, active in Chekiang, Kiangsu, and Kiangsi, was remarkable for its strong populist tendencies. In a drive to find forms in which the rich variety of secret societies in the region could work side by side with the radicals, it established a school in the management of which society chiefs were eventually involved, and where both radicals and society members underwent military training. The ultimate aim was to seize Nanking and its neighboring provinces. In Hunan, the radicalism developing in old reform centers in Changsha and in districts like Liu-yang, with connections to the students in Japan, flowered in the Hua-hsing Hui, set up in late 1903 by Huang Hsing and other radicals. Leaders of this society approached Ma Fu-i, chief of the P'u-chi Tsung-hui (Alliance for Universal Welfare), a vast, very loose confederation of *hui-t'ang* societies centered in the Hunan-Kiangsi border area, to join them in a plan to seize Changsha and parts of Hunan. Ma, it was reckoned, could call on 100,000 *hui-t'ang* members. Here, the problem of relations between intellectuals and rude *hui-t'ang* was tackled by setting up an intermediary society, the T'ung-ch'ou Hui, (Society Against the Common Enemy, i.e. the Manchus), in which society members could be fitted into a military structure based on Japanese models.[46]

The Hunanese strategy involved rather more modern thinking than the Chekiang one, but both failed to establish autonomous regimes. In Hunan the radical nucleus dispersed either out of disappointment or as a consequence of the savage reaction of the authorities. However, a somewhat unexpected shift of the conspiratorial center from Changsha to areas of *hui-t'ang* turbulence led to the most remarkable rising of its kind before the 1911 revolution, the P'ing-Liu-Li rising of 1906–7.[47] Two local radicals, members of the T'ung-meng Hui, had gone to the area during the summer of 1906 when the whole region was in a state of dangerous restlessness. Ma Fu-i had been captured and executed, and floods and famine made an already bad year worse. The two radicals made themselves felt, and when the rising took place, as mentioned above, one of the *hui-t'ang* armies in the field accepted an alliance with republicanism. This force has been pointed out as noteworthy for using *ko-ming* (revolution) on its recognition badges and *Ko-ming chün* (Revolutionary Army) on its banners. Moreover, a radical manifesto, issued in the name of a society chief involved in the rising, incorporated much of the T'ung-meng Hui program. Pottery workmen, coal miners, and vagrants enrolled, and were joined by deserting troops. But the area was a vulnerable one, near major garrison centers. Massive forces with modern artillery were brought in to crush the rising, and ruthless reprisals were ordered against the local population. The fighting, eventually concentrated on one front, lasted for a week. The area was so effectively sealed off that rebel forces could establish no direct liaison either with the T'ung-meng Hui or with outside *hui-t'ang*.

In the discouragement of this defeat, the radicals decided that the *hui-t'ang* were not capable of being taught modern military methods and that in the future, republicanism should look for support in the New Army instead.[48] But P'ing-Liu-Li had seen an alliance of republicans with traditional insurgence, an alliance whose efforts were bolstered by parallel actions of purely traditional forces. Thus it was a forerunner of, for example, the situation in western Szechwan in the autumn of 1911. Thinking of it in this way—and especially in conjunction with the battle on the Chengtu plain, where *hui-t'ang* forces also took over the countryside, but so effectively that they neutralized the garrison forces—allows one to see it in a somewhat more hopeful light than the radicals did at the time.

A second example of a situation in which the radicals were strong occurred in Kweichow.[49] Here, radical populism acquired something of a mass basis through radical societies, Ko-lao Hui lodges, and the societies and organizations set up under the New Policy. Struggles took place not in the military sphere, but in journalism, education, and other intellectual fields. The characteristic radical figure here recalls the Stendhalian hero. The Self-Government Society, set up at the end of 1907 on the basis of a precedent in Tientsin, underwent an unusual evolution to emerge as a broad political grouping with a current of clandestine republicanism and a link, though not a strong one, with the T'ung-meng Hui. Members included, on the one hand, progressive upper-class intellectuals, fairly high officials, landowners, and gentry and, on the other, Ko-lao Hui members, soldiers, students, handicraft workmen, peasants, small traders, and vagrants. Their numbers had risen by 1911 to about a hundred thousand in fifty-odd branches. Radicalism in this province continued to evolve independently until it was destroyed in 1912.

In marked contrast to the situations just described were those in Kwangtung and Szechwan, which would fall into the second, weaker, category of radical development. In neither of these provinces did dominant radical centers emerge, nor did the armies or the nexuses of military academies in either provincial capital take on the role of those in Wuchang.

The shift of the intellectual center of republicanism to Japan in the early 1900's left Kwangtung lagging behind in revolutionary development. Sporadic Triad activities were varied only by a rising launched in the Canton area by an alliance of the Hsing Chung Hui and the Triads and led by a descendant of a Taiping prince.[50] Sun Yat-sen himself was away at the time and did not take part. A curious mixture of old and new can be seen in the documents of the rising, dated according to a Ming dynasty reign period devised by the Triads and advocating a limited monarchy of a Western type.

Although republicanism eventually developed in the Canton–Hong Kong axis, it did not dominate the scene as in Shanghai or even in Changsha. More important were the connections of Kwangtung with the Nanyang region, for the far South was very much outward oriented. Trade with the islands and Southeast Asia and emigration were essential parts of Kwangtung life. Remittances from emigrants were a big item in a Kwangtung budget—and in the republican budget as well. Republicans and Triads alike traveled freely between Kwangtung and Hanoi, Kwangtung and Singapore. The most active center before 1907 was in eastern Kwangtung, where a group consisting mostly of traders and influential Triad chiefs, closely associated with Fukienese and Ch'ao-chou communities in Singapore, launched a series of somewhat archaic outbreaks culminating in the Huang-kang rising of 1907.[51] The nucleus of the rising, which could boast of a very short-lived military government, was probably modern enough, although it seems to have occurred in the midst of a whole spate of traditionalist Triad risings.

The Kwangtung scene was transformed in 1907, when the high-powered group from the central T'ung-meng Hui moved there from Japan at the time of the crisis in Tokyo. The next year or so saw a remarkable series of attempts to launch a northern expedition to the Yangtze valley. During the course of a half dozen risings, the republicans wavered between a number of possible reservoirs of support— New Army officers, outlaws, and discharged troops (*yu-yung*)—and between the poles of modern and archaic.[52] Their failure in all these ventures would seem to show that only a very consolidated locally based alliance of republicans and popular forces would have had much chance of success. They had arrived abruptly in the region, hoping to develop an efficient modern force yet largely lacking the populist feeling of the Chekiang radicals. Probably the main achievement of the Kwangtung radicals in 1907–8 was the recruitment of important Triad and brigand forces to republicanism, and the idea, which will be brought up later, of the brigand reserve.[53]

A similar series of guerrilla-like actions took place in Szechwan, but these were generated internally. The province was comparatively isolated from treaty-port influences, and lagged behind in both economic development[54] and radicalism. One gets the strong impression that Szechwanese republicans were alienated from popular movements. Thus the powerful anti-foreign movement of the miner Yü Tung-ch'en, which for a time in the late 1890's had been backed by an unofficial united front, had broken up without leaving any local organization behind it. And the extremely widespread Red Lantern (Boxer) Sects led an existence detached from the radicals, except for one series of risings northeast of Chengtu (1906), where cooperation took place. The allies of the republicans were the *hui-t'ang*. Republican centers were widely dispersed, in Chungking, in Chengtu, and in

southern towns where schools acted as centers. Hence, risings occurred mostly in areas where republican nuclei existed and *hui-t'ang*
were strong.[55] As in Kwangtung, the series of risings appear to have
been inconclusive. However, they cannot really be dismissed as a
psychological weapon intended merely to shake the government. The
rules of the game were still very archaic; the protagonists lived a
picaresque life and adapted themselves to the ritualistic gestures of
the popular movements; but their intention was certainly to seize the
province.

It will be seen that elements of continuity with earlier forms of
radicalism existed in many areas of the South during the late 1800's
that could provide a basis for the expansion of republicanism. These
elements could be very strong, as in the lower Yangtze, or weak and
apparently dependent on small groups of radicals or a few Triad
bands, as in Kwangsi or Kwangtung. In either case, in especially tense
situations both the professional revolutionaries and their *hui-t'ang*
allies certainly received popular support. There are no election figures
or other such conventional data to indicate trends, but one can point
to the undeniable support aroused by certain boycotts and the widespread resistance to New Policy taxation, railway loans, and threats
of partition. Such obvious hostility toward the central government
was not confined to gentry, merchants, and students, but could be
aroused in craft guilds[56] or peasant organizations under certain circumstances.

Four trends in the relationship between republicans and secret
societies can be singled out in the last years of the old regime. First,
the gentry by virtue of their role in the New Policy had acquired a
strong hold on the lower Yangtze areas. Popular movements were
losing the importance and the functions they once had had there.
As already mentioned, their last fling was the Ko-ming Hsieh-hui
(Revolutionary Alliance), set up in the winter of 1908 by a group of
leading radicals and secret society chiefs from eastern Chekiang.
Their aim was to establish a military government for Kiangsu, Fukien, Anhwei, and Kiangsi, backed by a secret society army.[57] The
proposed government diverged from the T'ung-meng Hui model, in
that *hui-t'ang* modes were taken into account. Details of a conference
to be held in Shanghai were betrayed to the authorities, and the
Alliance foundered. The old associates of Hsü Hsi-lin and Ch'iu Chin
were to emerge in 1911 as commanders of conventional units.

The second trend can be seen in areas with established traditions of contacts between radicals and secret societies, such as Kweichow and Hunan. By 1911 their alliances were spreading to the army and imposing rapprochements on constitutionalist gentry.

Third, from about 1909 onward, new forms of alliances between republicans and Ko-lao Hui—and especially with social brigands— were being formed. The most effective of the latter developed in Kwangtung, beginning about the end of 1907, when a brigand reserve was proposed for a revolutionary rising in the Canton area.[58] There were sound reasons for the proposal. The Pearl River basin was a closely built-up region, with important handicraft industries and big marketing towns. Lineage ties were important when it came to raising troops or consolidating republican influence.[59] Large forces could be mobilized rapidly, once government troops were neutralized. The brigand chiefs, whose names appear on republican lists of 1910 and 1911, were engaged in such enterprises as protection rackets on the West River. In Szechwan two major groups of *hui-t'ang* societies, one in the west, the other in the northwest, emerged in the summer in a loose alliance with republicanism, to be joined by other groups along the Yangtze and in the southwest.

The fourth trend is the development of new bases in the North, generally after 1906. Radicalism was sparse in the North, fewer students than in the South went abroad for study, and Yüan Shih-k'ai kept out new influences by training his cadets at home. A leading radical in northern Shansi even had to join the T'ung-meng Hui by mail.

In Shensi, the main group of republicans formed when the old forces were reorganized as a New Army in spring 1909, and local T'ung-meng Hui members joined.[60] They made contact with Ko-lao Hui members in the ranks, and in July 1910 a Ko-lao Hui ritual established an alliance between the two. Tao-k'o (Swordsmen) chiefs were approached the same year. T'ung-meng Hui members were mostly from the upper strata of society; hence their connections with popular forces were largely an army affair. A vigorous radical center operated in a school in Kuo-hsien in northern Shansi, sending men farther north as early as 1907 to get in touch with brigands.[61] The membership of the T'ung-meng Hui in that area consisted of boxers, cobblers, police chiefs, and the like. They were very active in the border areas and in Mongolia. In Loyang, Honan, radicals in a republican group active from about 1909 onward were in touch with powerful local Tao-k'o bands, among whom some of them had a certain prestige.

Very little possibility of far-reaching alliances with brigands existed in Chihli, for the republicans were very isolated. But one remarkable case should be mentioned. Ting K'ai-chang,[62] a student at Peking who had been strongly influenced by the campaign of 1904 against Russian colonization, conceived the radical idea of a federation of brigand commando forces, to be called the T'ieh-hsüeh Hui (Blood and Iron Society; possibly echoing Bismarck's slogan), that would bring in mounted brigands and Hung Hu-tzu. His scheme seems to have remained a paper one, but he apparently exerted some influence on irregular organization in northern Shansi, and units of the type he proposed appeared for a time in Manchuria. In Manchuria, both reform and radical movements were slow to develop, massive popular movements characterizing unrest in this region up to about 1906. T'ung-meng Hui activity dated from about 1906–7. The leaders were largely against allying themselves with the Hung Hu-tzu, because of the society's record of kidnapping, racketeering, and mercenary service with the Japanese.[63] Nevertheless, local approaches were sometimes made. The T'ung-meng Hui lacked a strong center; hence, republican activity tended to be scattered and limited to education, journalism, and like fields. The main place where radicals and people from the lower strata of society could meet were the *lien-chuang hui*.[64] Strongly armed by spring 1910 because of the partial breakdown of policing against brigandage, these village leagues could and sometimes did act on behalf of republican goals.

Popular Movements and the Events of 1911–12

It might be an overstatement to say that the popular societies played an essential military role in the campaigns that forever destroyed the Confucian state with emperor and court at its center. The situation in 1911 was a peculiar one in which upper-class maneuvers carried out within the forms of the old regime or pressures from the emergent gentry could exert as much influence as military factors. Military superiority was on the side of the republicans, or would be the moment they developed a center to unify their forces and control the gentry who sometimes went along with them and sometimes stole the lead from them. This potential superiority over Yüan Shih-k'ai, evident to foreign observers, lay in the combination of the New Armies (at Wuchang, in Yunnan, in Kwangtung) and the vast reservoir of irregulars. But the irregulars, although determined, were badly armed and archaically trained, and the threat they might have posed never materialized. As their insurgent ferment subsided (their own goals were inconsistent with a permanent insurgence), they were disbanded either voluntarily by the republicans or on the orders of Yüan Shih-k'ai.

However, it is no overstatement to say that the People's Armies played an important role in defeating the idea of a puppet emperor. Combined with the strength of the South in its universal resistance to foreign offers, the role of the People's Armies in preventing Pei-yang troops from reaching the Yangtze front ruled out any such proposal. In a military analysis of the affair, the modern sector would be balanced against the alliances of republicans and irregulars; the colossal demonstration of civil disobedience in Szechwan that broke the fragile structure of central control, against the forces of the Wu-chang front. But the last two might most profitably be viewed together as an effective barrier against the central government in Central China, helping to make possible the rebel successes in Kwang-tung and Kweichow, and imposing the secessions of so many local areas.

In no two provinces did the People's Armies play exactly the same role in the revolution. The geography of the country, with long valleys separating huge land blocks and slowing communications between them, had led to such large differences in local histories that coordination of any movement above the local level was a problem. Remarkable divergences persisted even in the modernized zones. In the lower Yangtze region, as mentioned above, the old popular movements had already receded into the background by about 1909, giving way to gentry and merchant control. In Kwangtung, by contrast, armies of social brigands under loose republican control played a deciding role. However, common elements did exist. Take, for example, the opposition to "despotism," that is, to the Confucian center, which had willy-nilly been transformed into a symbol of the drift toward semi-colonization. An anti-despotic or leftward trend can be seen both among the popular movements, who could no longer be identified solely with the old types of struggle against local officials and the central government, and among many of the gentry, who had gained new ground through their role in the New Policy. These "reformist" gentry had different attitudes toward and different relationships with the lower classes than did those who accepted the republic because they could supplant the old centers of local control.

In order to give as clear an idea as possible of the role of People's Armies in the Revolution, I propose to limit discussion to the classic form of insurgence (Szechwan) and two major emergent forms—alliances between radicals and popular forces and campaigns where brigands provided essential backing for the republican effort. First let us examine the makeup of the Armies.

Leaving aside the New Army and similar modern forces, most of the People's Armies were made up of irregulars—recruited largely from secret societies and brigand bands. When a situation became tense enough, townsfolk, peasants, and local militia joined them, or organized themselves as irregular forces. The uses of secret societies are clear enough: they, and especially the Ko-lao Hui, possessed military structures, or ones that could easily be adapted to military ends. The brigand forces need some explanation. Although their organization was simpler than that of the *hui-t'ang*, they, too, held to social bandit codes, and were knit together by ceremonies establishing pseudo-kinship. Politically they were vaguer than the *hui-t'ang*, but they, too, had histories of insurgence. Their social composition was similar to that of the *hui-t'ang*, although they were likely to contain more men on the run because of revenge killings or outlawed for other reasons (*lu-lin*), and therefore had a lower social standing than, for instance, the Ko-lao Hui. From the republican point of view, the most important areas for brigands by 1911 were Kwangtung and Kwangsi, the Wei valley (Shensi), the Yellow River valley in Honan, the border areas north of Shansi, and Manchuria. In drawing on them as they did for the assault on the court and the central government, the republicans were not so much innovating as following precedent, for government officials had long recruited brigands to their forces at times of special need. New goals and old insurgence found common ground; new allegiances formed that were not just pseudo-filial connections to a commander but genuine attachments to a cause—the republic, however superficially this might be understood.

The idea of a National Army (*kuo-min chün*) had already appeared in the T'ung-meng Hui constitution of 1906. (*Min-chün* or People's Army, the most popular term for a republican unit, appeared about 1909.) It had no doubt been inspired by the armies of the great nationalist revolutions of the West. Concepts of the National Army in radical writings ranged in scale from a great citizen army—an entire people embattled, like the Spartans—to guerrilla units operating illegally in the interior. These diverse concepts prevailed in practice as well as on paper, and by 1911 both *min-chün* and the smaller *t'ieh-hsüeh tui* (Blood and Iron squads) and *kan-ssu tui* (Dare-to-Die squads) existed in many areas. These forms were necessarily imposed on pre-existing types of recruitment, and indeed the *kan-ssu tui* was a traditional commando unit. Like the insurgent armies that had preceded them, they accepted *hui-t'ang* and other such solidarities within their organization, and sometimes even recruited men on society bases.

In Szechwan, the tensions that had been mounting since about 1906 reached their breaking point, and the relative inaccessibility of the province gave the rebels free play. The vast Railway Protection Movement began as a wave of resistance to paying taxes (*k'ang-liang*),[65] advanced to town strikes, then to officially recognized rebellion, and ultimately, under the aegis of the T'ung-meng Hui, to republicanism. In the southwest, Wu Yü-chang, together with certain commanders of irregulars, proclaimed Jung-hsien's independence from Peking a fortnight before Wuchang.[66]

The organizations of the Railway Protection Movement were called Pao-lu T'ung-chih Hui or Hsieh-hui (Societies or Leagues of Comrades for Railway Protection), T'ung-chih Hui for short. In the summer of 1911 negotiations took place between the T'ung-meng Hui and influential *hui-t'ang* chiefs (landowners, merchants, army men, and peasants) of western Szechwan on a strategy for taking over the province. On August 4 the Ko-lao Hui lodges were called on to convert the Societies of Comrades to Armies of Comrades,[67] which became the usual term for Szechwanese People's Armies.

The September 7th incident, when railway shareholders' representatives were arrested, and the later massacres turned the war on paper into a war with weapons.[68] Over 500,000 irregulars, recruited largely from the Ko-lao Hui, peasants, students, handicraft workmen, and banditti, converged on Chengtu, the provincial capital, and in the south over 100,000 were estimated to have joined the Armies of Comrades. In a sense, the logic of the Lai-yang riot had been carried to its conclusion here. On the one hand, Chao Erh-feng ("The Butcher"), the viceroy, made no distinction between ordinary people and brigands. On the other, townsfolk and peasants in the Armies had gone beyond the intentions of gentry and notables, and beyond the cautious plans of the Chungking T'ung-meng Hui. Chengtu was paralyzed. Town after town fell to the Armies, either by internal risings or from the outside. Peasant guerrilla tactics such as land mines, booby traps, and the like were much used in this fighting, and proved highly effective.[69] Gentry now joined the Armies, taking over leadership, or raised their own militia. Since government troops were unable to make their way into the province, the rebellion was free to pursue its own path.

Of the mass of manifestos, posters, and the like that came out during the course of the Szechwan rebellion, little has been available to me;[70] thus I can make only tentative generalizations about the regimes of the "People's Party." It was war to the knife with the official establishment in Chengtu and with its armies, whom the rebels beseiged with appeals to give up the slaughter and desert. Radicalism was not evident: conciliatory attitudes existed side by side with insurgency and the anti-imperialism that had been very strong in Szechwan since the 1880's. There is not enough evidence to allow one to delineate the evolution in attitudes that may have been taking place.

In southern Szechwan, the rather backward state of the region decided the movement of events. In the east, the influence of Hupeh speeded up the moves toward independence. In the north, the Kung-chin Hui (Society for Common Progress) headed actions backed by *hui-t'ang*, carrying local gentry and landowners in its wake.[71] It was strongly influenced by *hui-t'ang* modes, but it set up a Ta-Han Shu-pei Chün-cheng Fu (Great Han Military Government of North Szechwan) in Kuang-an town, which exerted a very loose control over its area. To the east of this area, a powerful movement of the Hsiao-i Hui (Society of Filial Piety and Righteousness) and insurgent peasantry operated under Li Shao-i. Li set up an independent regime, which appears to have broken away from the Kung-chin Hui government. Li's regime, a very archaic one, became a problem for the T'ung-meng Hui leaders in Chungking, and eventually had to be broken up. In folk myth, Li was carried away by a cloud when he was about to be shot. The Kung-chin Hui regime, in which the unruly modes of the *hui-t'ang* were a nuisance, was also dissolved in June 1912.

The weakness of republicanism was the deciding factor throughout the course of the Revolution in Szechwan, our example of classic insurgency. In spite of the enormous strength of insurgency in the West, neither the T'ung-meng Hui nor the radicals could establish a dominating center comparable to the ones in Hunan and Kweichow. Hence, political groups of the old type, made up of gentry, merchants, or the military, tended to assert themselves. Also, the socially undifferentiated nature of the Ko-lao Hui allowed their organization to be adapted to the ends of cliques. The most serious case of this occurred in Chengtu itself. A caretaker government of the old regime had been dislodged, and the viceroy executed. It was replaced by a new regime set up by an ambitious constitutionalist, Lo Lun, and an apolitical militarist, Yin Ch'ang-heng, who was a republican sympathizer. Lo and Yin introduced Ko-lao Hui forms into the administration, presumably in order to strengthen themselves, with the result that a Mafia-like parallel government grew up alongside the regular one. The hold of this parallel structure on the regular government may have been exaggerated, since 60 percent of the officials in the latter were T'ung-meng Hui members.[72] However, complaints of disorder in Chengtu were very bitter.

The Yunnanese republican regime reacted fiercely both to the Chengtu situation and to the dominance of popular regimes in southern Szechwan in general, and pressured Chungking to get them broken up. Ultimately, a "northern expedition," officially supposed to help the Shensi front, was sent into Szechwan. The expedition busied itself with answering calls from local gentry to suppress military governments in which radicals and Armies of Comrades participated. Formally speaking, the Yunnanese were modernist enough, and they were passionately nationalist and localist. But their ideologies were impregnated with neo-Confucianism and elitism.[73] Many people thought they were out to dominate the southwest of China. Chungking saw the *hui-t'ang* threat as a lesser evil than Yunnanese intervention, yet felt that the rule of law had to be imposed. The Chengtu regime was brought to heel, the Ko-lao Hui departments and lodges dissolved, and the irregulars disbanded without compensation or reorganized as regular units.[74]

The control of affairs eventually moved to Chungking, but with a weakened T'ung-meng Hui representation dominated by constitutionalists. The failure of the alliance of the T'ung-meng Hui and popular forces led to a political decline, and to the degeneration of *hui-t'ang* into Mafia-like organizations.

Opposed to this classical kind of insurgence were the situations in Hunan and Kweichow, where far more controlled alliances of radicals and popular movements developed. The two provinces had quite different histories of radicalism. In Hunan radical centers tended to be short-lived, breaking up in violent collisions with conservative landowning gentry and literati and being succeeded in time by new centers. This was the case with the reform circle of 1896–98 and again with the group of Huang Hsing, centered in the Ming-te (Bright Virtue) Academy of 1904–6. Hunan also had considerable permanent reservoirs of *hui-t'ang* in turbulent districts like Liu-yang, where periodic large-scale outbreaks were commonplace. In Kweichow, by contrast, radicalism had emerged from leftist reform trends at the turn of the century. The conservative landowners and literati had not been in a position to maintain complete control. Hence, as has been said, close connections between radicals and secret societies had existed unbroken for a decade.

In Hunan by the summer of 1911, republicans, Ko-lao Hui members, and students were participating in a common front. Republican strength was built up through the Kung-chin Hui and a Ko-lao Hui lodge, the Ssu-cheng Hui (Four Corrections Society), set up by Chiao Ta-feng. Chiao had won the complete confidence of the New Army and was active among the *hui-t'ang* on the eastern border. In late September the republicans decided on a rising,[75] and in mid-October they held talks with constitutionalists.

As soon as Ch'ing power was broken, in a hurried but bloodless operation by the New Army, the alliance of radicals, army, and *hui-t'ang* became a public affair.[76] Against it were posed the great land-owners and gentry and the more moderate constitutionalists. Against their maneuvers, the radical regime held out for only ten days. Thirteen years had passed since the collapse of the first experimental government in Hunan.

The outstanding feature of Chiao's regime was a temporary fusion of radical modes with secret society informality, and an iconoclastic disregard of the dignities of both officials and gentry. Work was done in a mixture of old and new styles, with the help of young people who took their food to work with them. Ko-lao Hui members came and went as they liked. Such a populist atmosphere seemed positively indecent to people from the upper strata of the old society, who complained scornfully that the yamen, once so impressive, was no better than a den of thieves. Chiao did not take adequate measures to fend off counterrevolutionary intrigues, and the scandalmongering in the press ruined the atmosphere of the yamen.[77] The young people withdrew while Chiao stayed aloof. When Chiao's party moved to retrieve republican control by centralizing power in the hands of the military governor, Chiao and his right-hand man were both assassinated in rigged military riots. It seems likely that the plot was widely coordinated and had been mounted by conservative gentry and former officials.[78] After this incident, Chiao's "ragged army" of Ko-lao Hui members outside Changsha and the student force were disbanded. A campaign was launched to suppress radicalism and popular movements in Hunan, and a constitutionalist regime took over.

What Hunan probably lacked was a long period of consolidation of the republican alliance. Kweichow had this advantage, and it bore fruit in 1911.[79] What happened in Kweichow was not just "a handful of revolutionaries stirring up New Armies," but in its way perhaps the most impressive demonstration of the Chinese form of radical populism in the early 1900's. Early in 1911 an elaborate paper scheme for a revolutionary army had been drafted. Under the direction of members of the Self-Government Society, forces were to be recruited along traditional lines from the Ko-lao Hui, banditti, and militia. The rising of November 3, launched in an impatient move by cadets, ended a series of moves by the governor and by constitutionalists to take control of the situation. Chang Pai-lin, conscious of the enormous popular strength behind him, had held back. Now he emerged as a Self-Government Society prime minister under a military governor from the New Army. The governor, elected for diplomatic reasons, seems to have remained a figurehead. The New Army had remained neutral during the preparatory period.

A provisional government was set up, with representatives from the Self-Government Society, the T'ung-meng Hui, and the constitutionalist party. As always, the Ko-lao Hui presence in the regime tended to provoke an uncritical hostility. As a corrective to this attitude, we have the views of one Chou P'ei-i, a Self-Government Society member who held a post in the Privy Council. Maintaining a fairly neutral attitude toward the Ko-lao Hui, Chou insisted that the new government made a determined effort to develop democratic forms.

A number of Ko-lao Hui chiefs were appointed to posts both in Kweiyang and outside the town. It was not just a question of recognizing their contribution to the rising, but of giving them cohesion, settling their ways of life and thought, persuading them to put down roots. A central lodge, into which a leading figure of the Self-Government Society was inducted as chief, was set up in Kweiyang to take responsibility for this, and to send out commissioners to tackle the rehabilitation program.[80]

The big landowners and gentry, and evidently the merchant guilds as well, reacted quickly to this situation. They got one of their supporters to introduce new legislation authorizing anyone to form a secret society lodge. This allowed the conservatives to set up their own lodge, but all the trades began to set up societies, too. Thus the maneuver, directed against the Self-Government Society, succeeded in upsetting normal life in the town altogether. At the same time, the extremists among the conservative party organized a Society of Elders

(Ch'i-lao Hui). A correspondent of the *North-China Herald* stated that its membership was a very respectable one. Republican sources, on the other hand, described it as a sort of parallel government, with its own militia.[81]

The regime lasted until March 1912, the longest-lived of the radical experiments. It followed its own peculiar evolution rather than fusing with the T'ung-meng Hui, with which its contacts were never very intimate. A constitution based on Swiss and Swedish models was drawn up, in the hope that the people would come to accept a non-paternalistic form of government.[82]

The regime was brought to an abrupt end by the intervention of Yunnanese troops under T'ang Chi-yao. The Society of Elders, not strong enough to destroy the Self-Government Society but hostile to attempts to rehabilitate the Ko-lao Hui, had flooded Yunnan with lurid accounts of disorder in Kweichow. Reacting to these accounts, the troops carried out mass executions of Self-Government Society and Ko-lao Hui members, and proscribed the organizations.[83] Chou P'ei-i, in an illuminating comment on these half-forgotten regimes, remarks that if the Yunnanese had had their way, the People's Parties of three provinces (Szechwan, Kweichow, and Hunan) would have been driven out.

The second major emergent form of insurgence to be discussed—campaigns supported by brigands—can profitably be seen as a struggle for survival. The republicans were faced with the problem of breaking up the old centers of power, neutralizing the Peiyang forces, and fending off declarations of independence that threatened to perpetuate the old regime—all at the same time. Behind the apparent disorder in their response to this three-pronged problem a series of determined campaigns can be seen, sometimes using conventional tactics and sometimes using guerrilla warfare. These campaigns must be distinguished from the isolated activities of local banditti and sporadic outbreaks led by *hui-t'ang* or sects.

During a period of indecision in the autumn of 1911 in Kwangtung, when pressures were coming from all sides on the provincial government and the republicans, enormous forces of irregulars emerged. The evolution was from a traditionalist declaration of independence to a republican one. The People's Armies that responded to the T'ung-meng Hui call included at least six forces of over 2,000 each. They were recruited largely from among hired agricultural laborers, handicraft workmen, discharged troops, local banditti, and militia. Their nuclei were made up of a merger of outlaws, Triads, and peasants,[84] and they were led by T'ung-meng Hui members, by bandit chiefs who had previously adopted the republican cause, and by veteran Triad leaders. Canton was solidly republican, but it was outside Canton that a general climate of insurgence prevailed, as one can see from the diary of an army officer in the Hsin-an area.[85] Revolutionary and insurgent impetuses carried all before them, despite the break-up of the central command by a serious defeat. Thus the outlying districts, and not Canton itself, rose first.[86] (It may be that a purely urban rising was not in the cards: even at Wuchang the action originated in the outskirts.)

In Canton, as the result of pressures from the bourgeoisie, and probably also from chiefs of People's Armies, an administration with a strong T'ung-meng Hui representation replaced the compromise regime. In the pungent if patronizing *mot* of the old consul-general, Jamieson, bandit armies had put a compradore government into power.[87] The following months were dominated by Ch'en Chiung-ming's maneuvers to get the upper hand and disband the irregulars, whom he regarded as rabble. No doubt they were difficult to handle. However, Ch'en may well have been "more expert than red," and this eventually told against him in such a difficult transitional situation. Not only were major Ch'ing military commanders allowed to remain in the field, but People's Armies were forcibly disbanded. In the opinion of some historians, the disbanding of these irregulars was an important factor in the ultimate isolation of the Canton government from a mass basis.[88] Moreover, the disbanded men had no money and no land to return to, and banditry increased. Hu Han-min remarked in his autobiography that merchants looked back almost fondly on People's Armies after they had had some experience with warlord forces.[89]

The weakness of both the T'ung-meng Hui and popular forces was important in Kwangsi. Situated between Kwangtung and Hunan, on which it depended for food, and threatened by violence from the popular forces, Kweilin could only declare independence. The military campaigns of the Taiping era had broken the great insurgent armies into numerous small bands, leaving an enormous standing regular army to dominate the province. Hence, although the T'ung-meng Hui could ally itself with brigand bands and outlaws to the east of the Wu-chou area, and in Liu-chou hsien in the north, their strength was inadequate. The brigand bands with which they had been in touch for a year could act as a lever to bring over or chase out recalcitrant officials, but no more.

In this confused situation, Lu Jung-t'ing, an ex-outlaw and a local commander of government forces, began to dominate the provincial government. He had the approval of Sun Yat-sen,[90] but was opposed by the local T'ung-meng Hui and by the brigands.[91] Like so many other ex-brigands of his era, he was politically shallow and inclined to revert to Confucian trappings. He had toyed with the T'ung-meng Hui, but turned away from it.[92] Lu's attitude toward the irregulars resembled that of Ch'en Chiung-ming in Kwangtung. His actual handling of them differed from Ch'en's, however, for he absorbed part of them into his army and settled part of them on land. As Lu's military megalomania developed, he disbanded the old brigand forces, and with them the revolutionary organization.[93]

The second area in which movements of resistance to the old regime took the form of alliances of republicans, secret societies, and brigands was the enormous region to the west of Chihli, stretching over Shensi, Shansi, Honan, and the border areas to the north of them. The campaigns turned on the T'ung-kuan Pass bottleneck in southeastern Shensi, and on occupying the main urban centers, Sian, Kaifeng, and Taiyuan.

The brunt of the fighting was borne by the Shensi republican armies.[94] In the New Army at Sian, the T'ung-meng Hui members were mostly officers, whereas Ko-lao Hui members filled the ranks, only a very few of them serving as breveted officers. This meant that neither republicans nor society members were fully in control during the fighting, and the Ko-lao Hui chiefs naturally expected parity with the T'ung-meng Hui after Sian was taken. However, the rising was a rushed affair, in which it would appear that the Ko-lao Hui did most of the fighting while the T'ung-meng Hui organized the new order of things. A fortnight later the regime found its very survival threatened—from the west by Kansu troops and from the east by a mounting concentration of Peiyang forces. Clearly, a modus vivendi between republicans and *hui-t'ang* had to be worked out. The T'ung-meng Hui provided the bulk of the cadres and a powerful new ideology, whereas the Ko-lao Hui provided the mass basis. The society men were also able to extend this basis outside the army to their membership at large and to the Tao-k'o, and impose discipline on them. (The Tao-k'o, or Swordsmen, were social brigands with reputations as incomparable fighters against the excesses of officialdom. Their bands were spread out north of the Wei River.)[95] At first it was difficult to get the Ko-lao Hui to take the idea of an alliance seriously:[96] in the early days of the regime their participation took

the form of a parallel government rather than of genuine cooperation in the Sian regime. But the Ko-lao Hui leaders were rapidly
absorbed into the military operations—at first because they were essential for controlling irregulars, but eventually in recognition of
their considerable military talents. In the countryside, a drive brought
under control a serious trend toward Mafia-like forms.

The People's Armies were undermanned and run on a shoestring,
but they managed through a hard winter to hold off troops on two
fronts, and even at one moment to bring Peiyang forces to the verge
of capitulation. News of the abdication arrived late, and fighting
went on after it had stopped on other fronts. The peace negotiations
roused feelings of frustration, strong opposition, and even near-panic
in Sian. It was not only that the republican or anti-dynastic mission
was unfinished, but that, because the Peiyang administration remained intact, the republicans might expect savage reprisals.

In Honan a more mobile kind of warfare was used by the republican irregulars against the Peiyang forces. An alliance of radicals,
junior officers, and the widespread popular movements took form
during the summer and fall of 1911. Swordsmen bands,[97] *hui-t'ang*
such as the Jen-i Hui (Society of Humanity and Righteousness), and
sects such as the Tsai-yüan Hui (In-the-Garden Society, that is, the
Peach Garden of the old oath-taking), all with histories of insurgence
and anti-tax and anti-missionary activity, existed in rich profusion
along the Yellow River valley and in the north. As in western Szechwan, the chiefs of such bands took a positive part in organizing the
People's Armies, whose total strength was estimated at some 100,000
in thirty areas as of January 1912.[98] Thus the revolution from above
so often depicted in sources is an exaggeration, growing out of the
elitism of New Army officers and literati.

The projected central command of the alliance of republicans
and popular forces was never established. This may have been because
the alliance failed to get Kaifeng to declare for the republic and because an attempted coup involving 10–20,000 Jen-i Hui irregulars
failed. In one opinion, a certain hesitation to use these irregulars was
a factor in the failure of the coup. The irregulars were energetic
enough. In western Honan, a large insurgent force of peasants belonging to the Tsai-yüan Hui combined with Swordsmen and local
radicals in an attempt to seize Loyang.[99] They failed, but the Yellow
River valley appears to have remained in their hands after the incident.

The political situation hampered the drive against the old regime in Honan. Not only did no break, even of a constitutionalist type, take place with Peking, but the rise to power of Yüan Shih-k'ai, a Honanese by origin, led New Army officers in the province to turn from republicanism to traditional avenues for advancing their careers. The republicans were therefore compelled to fall back on localized cooperative activity with popular forces. By springtime, a curious ambivalence could be seen in the attitudes of the Honanese revolutionary forces. Both the left-wing T'ung-meng Hui and the politically more literate brigand chiefs were opposed to the cease-fire.[100] In radical terms, they did not want to settle for a republic in the South only, while despotism reigned in the North under Yüan. However, after the peace talks ended, most of the leading figures in the People's Armies of western Honan were drawn in by Yüan to staff a new force. One leader who could not be bought over was the powerful Wang T'ien-tsung, a Swordsman by origin. He survived to fight in the Yangtze campaign against Yüan's monarchist adventures.

The looming presence of Yüan was even more strongly felt in Shansi. Powerful forces loyal to Yüan easily reached the military key points of Taiyuan and Niang-tzu-kuan, neutralizing or dispersing concentrations of republican troops there.[101] In the political realm, Yüan's influence acted as a brake on the consolidation of radicalism or even middle-of-the-road republicanism. The situation was epitomized in the person of Yen Hsi-shan, a veteran T'ung-meng Hui member from an influential family of gentry bankers. Yen rode both the republican and Yüan horses as long as he could, but his republican principles soon weakened and he eventually showed a tendency to lean on Yüan's patronage. With the loss of the provincial center of Taiyuan, both republican and popular forces withdrew to the four corners of the province.

In southwestern Shansi, a strong alliance of T'ung-meng Hui, local gentry, merchants, and secret societies was set up.[102] Its fighting forces were made up of defeated republican units from the north and large militia units recruited locally. It was reinforced for a time by an expeditionary army of Ko-lao Hui members and possibly Swordsmen sent from Shensi under overall T'ung-meng Hui command.[103] The republican administration in this area, protected by the defenses centered on T'ung-kuan, set up a Honan-Shensi-Shansi-Kansu Allied Army. Although this force was probably more symbolic than actual, in some opinions the front had the effect of holding up large forces of Kansu troops and the main Peiyang armies that were moving south toward the Yangtze valley.[104] To the east of this republican center,

popular outbreaks continued to follow archaic patterns, except for a
series of risings organized by a Ko-lao Hui chief of peasant stock in
alliance with local T'ung-meng Hui members and gentry radicals.
By the summer of 1912, he came under pressure from the Yen Hsi-
shan regime and reverted to traditional insurgent risings.[105]

The northern areas of this vast region were full of brigand and
outlaw bands, with which radicals and T'ung-meng Hui militants
arranged alliances from small but intensive centers. Much of the
north had been settled fairly recently by soldiers from the old Anhwei
and Hunan armies. The Ko-lao Hui organization they had brought
with them now permeated local administration and affected the development of republicanism. The most effective of the radical centers remained the school in Kuo-hsien, northern Shansi, which had
long promoted republicanism among the lower classes in its area.
By autumn 1911, brigand chiefs and Ko-lao Hui members in small
yamen jobs were directing some 10,000 irregulars and breaking up
local town administrations.[106] The *Min-li pao* of December 30 edi-
torialized that if these irregulars ever combined with defeated government troops, they could present a threat to the Ch'ing rear. However, such an alliance depended on Yen Hsi-shan, who had taken
refuge farther north. He was very reluctant to associate himself with
these popular forces; hence, such ambitious projects as the plan to
attack Peking fell through.[107] The atmosphere of an irregular unit
was described in 1931 by a man who may have been an official.[108] His
description conjures up the feel of a maquis. The outlaws, he thought,
may have been ruffians, but their *Shui-hu chuan* codes were something
the government troops could not possess. Eventually the irregulars
both here and in southern Shansi were forcibly broken up, or in some
cases joined Yen, becoming his retainers when he became a warlord.
These were supposedly the instructions of Yüan Shih-k'ai.[109]

The mounted brigands of Shantung and Chihli were largely outsiders to the events of 1911–12. This was understandable in Chihli.
In Shantung, the apparently complete rift between republicans and
their allies in the modern sector and the old insurgent movements
is worthy of note. The revolutionary excitement of 1911 affected turbulent districts like Ts'ao-chou, which had already been disturbed
by the savage suppression of the Lai-yang riot. But the republicans
appear never to have contacted any forces from these districts.

In Manchuria, radical foci had sprung up during the early 1900's,
often showing populist trends of a rather traditional type. No strongly organized networks of secret societies like that of the Ko-lao Hui

existed here, either among civilians or in the armies. The Hung Hu-
tzu remained numerous and could be drawn on despite their apolitical tendencies. However, their full military potentialities were never
tapped: out of an estimated 35,000 of them,[110] it is unlikely that
more than 5,000 were ever in action. In fact, no large-scale alliances
of republicans and popular forces emerged, although they might well
have been expected to do so. The characteristic form within which
the lower classes could participate in republican activity was the *lien-
chuang hui.*

Conditions for the development of republicanism were certainly
unfavorable in Manchuria. Apart from imperialist threats and strong
royalist currents, there was a certain lag in the political climate in
general that affected even the republican leadership. This, combined
with fear of foreign intervention, made republican moves indecisive.
The republicans had at least been trying to consolidate themselves
in the main urban centers, but they were frustrated by the rapprochement between Chang Tso-lin and the viceroy.[111] (In this agreement,
an archaic official structure was rescued by a reformed Hung Hu-tzu
member.) Once the republicans lost their political foothold in the
towns, their military efforts, too, tended to fall apart.

In the last analysis, the solidest achievement of republicanism in
this northern region must be credited to the drive of the old insurgency. In Chuang-ho and Fu-chou hsien of Fengtien province, both
with histories of tax-resistance riots, an enormous anti-tax outbreak
in the summer of 1911 had developed into a miniature Szechwan
situation.[112] The rebels were eventually defeated, but a republican
center was established there in the autumn on the basis of the village
leagues. Its forces presumably consisted mostly of local peasants and
fishermen, and perhaps Hung Hu-tzu, joined by 600 local militia
and 500 police. Their numbers rose to several thousand. Nevertheless,
officials negotiated with this powerful base in the same old way, trying
to attract them back to legality by alternate threats and promises—a
treatment not altogether undeserved, for the republicanism of these
insurgents came to an end once the negotiations between North and
South had been concluded.

Conclusions

The popular societies were all things to all men; hence the difficulty
of placing them in a historical framework. They have not yet been
defined as a purely socialist or a purely laborite movement could be.
They performed a whole series of functions that have become spe-

cialized ones in capitalist society. They provided some economic benefits and a degree of protection against intolerable pressures from the official system, but they did so in an anarchic manner. They might take their living from the wealthy, but if their uncontrolled exploitation of trade damaged the local economy, the poor were hurt as well. Politically speaking, as has been remarked, they could serve the needs of the higher strata of society as well as those of the oppressed. They reflected the old social structures yet lived outside them, unacknowledged as forms of popular representation.

Thus it is perhaps less surprising than it might otherwise be that Nationalist definitions of the societies' role in the republican movement bear little relation to reality. Whatever the official Nationalist histories may say, it seems clear that the secret societies cannot be dismissed as "mercenaries" or "handfuls of volunteers" in Nationalist exploits. The republicans might aim at purely modern operations, but in the event they had to adapt, to one degree or another, to the insurgent traditions of their allies.

In trying to get a clear picture of the popular role in the revolution, one must avoid being mesmerized by the term *secret society*. It is more accurate to think of a multitude of shifting forms drawing on those of officialdom, of sects (with a long history of improvised forms), and possibly, although this has not been proved, of old artisan *compagnonnages*. Ko-lai Hui forms became more complex than Triad ones, except in Szechwan, where Ko-lao Hui forms apparently remained rather close to their sect origins. Then there were the simpler social brigand forms that had developed since the late eighteenth century. All these associations were part of the republican movement's insurgent backing.

Can the People's Armies be seen as neutral, like mercenaries? It seems unlikely. Such reformed brigands as Tung Fu-hsiang and Chang Tso-lin were no doubt aiming at wealth and careers, but theirs was also a tendency of the old social structure. Members of the lower strata of society, subject to intense social strains, could look for a way out in a pact with the establishment or in the ill-defined insurgent goals they set themselves. When insurgent ferment had subsided, they would revert to the life dictated by an urge for security and for an honored niche in society—unless their programs, like those of the Taipings or of the sects, drove them on to press for more fundamental changes. Anti-Manchuism and the simplified T'ung-meng Hui program acted in a very limited sense as a catalyst for this continued agitation. It should be noted that causes lying outside official T'ung-meng Hui aims, some of them even actively discouraged by the T'ung-meng Hui, could also serve such a catalytic function. Anti-foreignism and anti-missionary activity, strengthened by the growth of national feeling, remained powerful, as was demonstrated in certain boycott campaigns and in the anti-imperialist phraseology that appeared on popular posters in Szechwan.

How far republicanism and nationalism had influenced the rank and file of the popular movements is a matter for conjecture. The available evidence concerns trends among Ko-lao Hui, Triad, or brigand chiefs.[113] When the republican-society alliances broke up in 1911–12 and the radicals disappeared to the big cities or were chased out, the irregulars were disbanded or re-formed as regulars. Some of the chiefs were drawn into warlord service; but many of them had identified themselves so strongly with republicanism that it remained among them as a "Good Old Cause." Hence, opposition to the peace talks of 1912 could be found among society chiefs in Kwangsi, Szechwan, Shensi, and elsewhere, and a number of them fought against Yüan Shih-k'ai. A case is quoted of one family in which leftist tendencies were carried into the 1920's, when a member joined the Communist Party, just as Triad or Ko-lao Hui insurgence could be carried into the radical movements of the early 1900's.

As a social form, the secret societies no doubt continued to fulfill a function for peasants and vagrants in rural areas. But they also degenerated into Mafia-like forms in vast areas of the country. The 1910's saw the growth of the Ch'ing Pang (Green Gang), ultimately a rival of the Triads and the Ko-lao Hui in influence behind the scenes. Can one say that the forms were simply unsuitable for settled society—that they were incapable of taking their place within the framework of a local government more democratic than the old one could be? It is certainly true that the experimental regimes of the radicals all ended in disaster without managing to gain a stable backing from the modern sector (New Armies and bourgeoisie). However, the destruction of these regimes was largely the work of the conservative landowners and great gentry. With the disappearance of the Kweichow regime, the only one that might have had a future, the question must remain in the air.

The Red Spears in the Late 1920's

ROMAN SLAWINSKI

*Sources for the study of the Red Spears—Problems of village
self-defense—Civil and military organization of the Red Spears;
their superstitions—Resistance of the Red Spears to wars
among warlords—Cooperation between the Red Spears and the
Communist Party—Hypotheses on the origins of the Red Spears*

At the time of the first revolutionary civil war in China (1924–1927),
the Society of Red Spears (Hung-ch'iang Hui) played a rather important role among the secret societies active in political and social
life. This peasant association of a mixed religious and military character, which was very powerful in several provinces—Shantung, Honan, Shansi, Shensi, southern Chihli (Hopei), and northern Anhwei
and Kiangsu—carried on a genuine peasant war, first in Shantung
in 1926, and then on a greater scale in Honan and neighboring provinces in 1926 and 1927.

The writings of the members of this association are very rare. Only
an appeal addressed to the inhabitants of Kaifeng and a copy of the
statutes have been found.[1] It is primarily through outside Chinese and
foreign testimony that it is possible to trace the history of the Red
Spears when they were at the head of the peasant movement in North
China. We owe much to Alexander Ivin, a Soviet sinologist who
was convinced that the Chinese Revolution was to profit from this
movement, as well as to an attempt at Marxist analysis of the secret
societies written by Li Ta-chao when he was head of the Chinese
Communist Party for North China. Among twenty or so other documents, the richest in detail are the articles published in *Hsiang-tao*
(The guide), which throw a great deal of light on the situation in
North China and show the interest of the Chinese Communist Party
in the Red Spears and other secret societies. The journal *Materialy
po kitaiskomu voprosu* (Materials on the Chinese question), published by the Institute for Scientific Research on China of the Workers' University in the USSR, contains some translations of Chinese
sources, the chronology of the peasant movement, etc., as do *Novyi*

vostok (New Orient), *Chung-yang fu-k'an* (Central bulletin; published in Wuhan), and other journals of the time. Let us add finally a text by Hsiang Yün-lung written at the High School of Agriculture in Peking in August 1927, which includes an analysis of the Red Spears and lists eighteen secret societies in North China.[2]

These sources show that the Society of Red Spears had as its base certain organizations for village self-defense created to protect peasants and their property from bandit attacks at a time when the *min-t'uan* or village militia directed by rural notables were insufficient to the task. The bandits (ruined peasants, vagabond soldiers, and the like) had become more and more numerous, in particular because of the incessant wars between provincial governors. At the same time, the general economic situation of the majority of the peasants—the exploitation and economic polarization—was getting worse from year to year. Data on Honan indicate that in 1920–1921 there was a famine in the north and west; in 1921 floods caused famine in 45 eastern districts; in 1923 drought struck 93 districts; and in 1925 the flooding of the Yellow River led to famine in 30 eastern districts. In 1926, only one year after this string of natural disasters, taxes were demanded in advance for 1928 and 1929, and even for 1930 in certain regions.[3] The official land tax in the environs of Chengchow in Honan was .60 *chiao* per *mou*, payable in the spring, plus .30 *chiao* on cereals, payable after the harvest.[4] In another district of Honan, at Wei-shih, the tax per *mou* was set at 2 *chiao*, although the maximum income per *mou* in that area was only 4–5 *chiao*. We must also add the likin, an internal tax on commodities, such as salt and textiles. Moreover, the peasants were obliged to pay "military rates" that, under various names, were much greater than the official state tax. Peasants questioned in the environs of Hsi-ma-yin were convinced that the taxes were heavier in the late 1920's than during the reign of the last Empress.[5] Obviously, the economic situation was different for the several strata of the peasantry. The 2,556,679 Honanese households who owned less than 10 *mou* of land, for example, were much worse off than the 359,267 who cultivated more than 100 *mou*.[6] But the totality of the situation presented above shows that it was not only the poor peasants but also those who owned tracts of middling size — indeed, 70 percent of the peasantry of Honan — who found themselves on the verge of bankruptcy.[7] The peasants were on the point of forming a movement of opposition to the taxes and levies of various sorts instituted by the "warlords," and thus they constituted the basis of a movement of armed resistance against the repression of the latter and equally against the district chiefs, who were, in their role as officials responsible to the warlords and the real masters of the land for the collection of taxes, the highest representatives of the established order the peasants had to deal with. The Red Spears will be found among the leading spirits and principal participants in this movement.

The Red Spears were to set up a real organization only in 1921. Very scattered before that date, they had become famous by the beginning of 1925.[8] The name of this organization comes from the members' custom of decorating their sturdy spears with small red flags (*ying*).[9] Offshoots of the society adopted other colors, becoming White, Green, Yellow, and Black Spears. But the Red Spears remained the most numerous and the most powerful. The existing descriptions of the Red Spears sometimes contradict one another in certain respects (armies, organizations), because the several sources describe stages of a movement that was developing rapidly.

What seems certain is that the society had a military structure, more advanced in matters of organization than the simple alliances among villages that were called united village associations (*lien-ts'un hui* or *lien-chuang hui*).[10] (The latter continued to exist when the Red Spears became powerful in 1926–1927,[11] and, although outsiders often confused them with the various secret societies, continued to call themselves *lien-ts'un hui*.) The Red Spears' organizational hierarchy as it existed in at least one region of Honan in 1927 was as follows: principal detachments made up of 10 to 50 detachments, which were made up of 5 to 30 groups, which in turn contained 10 to 40 members.

Perhaps more interesting is the Red Spears' dual system of organization: there were civil departments (*wen-t'uan-pu*) that took care of documents, finances, and local judicial procedures and military departments (*wu-t'uan-pu*) that took care of training troops. For each region made up of several villages or several districts, there were a chief called a *t'ung-ling* and several staff officers. In southern Honan one finds several *t'ung-ling* and a commander-in-chief (*tsung-t'ung-ling*). It is not certain that a central organization existed at the interprovincial or even at the provincial level; more likely, there were several parallel organizations, each covering a part of a single province.[12]

There were several factors making for unity among the Red Spears, first among them being the common struggle. Troops could be sent

to help other Spears in case of necessity. Thus, the chief of the Red
Spears in Chi-hsien was able to concentrate more than 300,000 Red
Spears from three or four neighboring districts despite their pro-
foundly parochial sentiments.[13]

A second unifying factor was a method of training new recruits
that blended superstition and physical conditioning, combined with
a strict system of rules for all members. For a period of 128 days, new
members observed a daily regimen of kneeling naked, praying, drinking cold water in which written incantations had been soaked, and
enduring sharp blows to harden the muscles, at the end of which
time they had to pass an examination. An oath obligated the members to keep secret everything concerning the society and its ideas,
to respect women, not to waste, etc. They were forbidden to have
relations with women for the duration of the elementary training
and, if they were married, for a period of 120 days after the wife's
confinement. Opium, card games, and all acts of violence were strictly
forbidden, and severe punishments were provided for violators.[14]

A third unifying factor was the origin of the chiefs. Most of the
"masters" of the Red Spears—those at least whom we find at the heart
of the movement in Honan—were natives of Shantung.

Finally, there was the conviction of invulnerability. The masters
who trained the troops preached that, by virtue of certain prayers
addressed to the "High Master" living in the K'un-lun Mountains,
of possessing certain talismans, of practicing deep breathing *(shen-
hu-hsi)*, and of drinking water containing the ashes of paper on which
magic formulas had been written, the bodies of the members would
become invulnerable. This indoctrination was so successful that Red
Spears members calmly presented their chests to rifle fire, convinced
that the bullets would bounce off. Even the death of their comrades
before their very eyes did not disillusion them. The masters explained everything very simply: the dead had perished because they
had not believed in the spirits or because they had not pronounced
the incantations properly.[15]

Obviously, many other superstitions existed among the Red Spears.
A long article by Li Ta-chao shows that they considered several of
the best-known divinities of ancient China, as well as certain heroes
of famous novels, to be auxiliary forces for their primitive arms. But,
as Li has also noted, as soon as they had machine guns and rifles,
they no longer needed Chu Pa-chieh, or Sun Wu-k'ung, or talismans,
and their belief in the Five Elements and the Eight Diagrams progres-
sively lost its force.[16] Let us add that the only superstition to have

survived even after the Red Spears had either bought modern weapons or taken them from the warlords' troops, and despite their unfortunate experience, was the conviction of their immunity to rifle bullets. This superstition, too, would begin to disappear, however, when the lesser gentry paid two hundred dollars to the family of each member of the Red Spears who was killed while serving with the National Revolutionary Army as it entered Honan in 1927.[17]

The principal points in Red Spears history as regards their opposition to the warlords are as follows. In 1925, only four years after setting up their formal organization, the Red Spears took up arms against the troops of General Chang Tsung-ch'ang, the governor of Shantung. Chang, in order to increase the number of his troops from sixty to a hundred thousand men and to outfit them for the war against Sun Ch'uan-fang, had levied several special taxes on the peasants. The Red Spears rose throughout Shantung, although the center of the movement was in the region of T'ai-an. The Red Spears resisted for more than six months, attacking cities, railroads, and other prime targets. Profiting from their numerical superiority, they even managed to occupy several cities. But after Chang attacked the center of the movement and began to enroll Red Spears in his army by the thousand, the revolt was doomed. Tens of thousands of men were killed and hundreds of villages destroyed by cannon fire.[18]

That same year (1925), Yüeh Wei-chün succeeded Hu Ching-i as governor of Honan. The forces of the Second Kuo-min-chün (National Army), of which he was the head, stood at more than 200,000 men; it was the largest provincial army after that of Szechwan. In order to feed this enormous army and to prepare for war against Wu P'ei-fu of the Chihli clique, taxes and various levies were increased by 300 percent. Until the summer, the Red Spears had led the fight against bandit troops (in order to do so they had even obtained a thousand silver dollars from Yüeh); but when they began to oppose the collection of various tax levies in October and November, Yüeh tried to crush them. This situation was favorable to Wu P'ei-fu, who made contact with one of the leaders of the Red Spears, Lou Pai-hsün. He promised to make Lou his troop commander and to abolish special taxes for three years if the Red Spears would help him occupy all of Honan. In mid-January of 1926, after the defeats of the Second Kuo-min-chün in battles against Wu P'ei-fu and Chang Tso-lin on the southern and eastern fronts, the Red Spears rose against the National Army in Honan. The revolt centered in the districts of Hsin-yang and Loyang. The slogan "Death to the people of Shensi" arose because most of Yüeh's soldiers were natives of Shensi. The troops of the Second Kuo-min-chün were crushed, and soldiers fleeing from Kaifeng toward Shensi were hunted down like animals.[19]

After Wu P'ei-fu and the Red Spears had won, Wu did not keep his promises. Lou Pai-hsün then ordered the peasants to oppose all taxes. The surprise attack of May 7, 1926, against Pai-ta-chai, Lou's native town, signaled the beginning of Wu's repression of the Red Spears. Pai-ta-chai was completely burned, killing five thousand of its inhabitants. Lou counterattacked and later waged guerrilla warfare against Wu's army.[20]

The Red Spears would once again take up the struggle in 1927, against the army of Fengtien (the Mukden clique) in the north of Honan and against the forces of Chang Fa-k'uei in the south of the province, as well as against the troops of Feng Yü-hsiang. In Shensi, the Red Spears were able to crush the troops of an ally of Wu P'ei-fu, Liu Chen-hua, who had come down from Honan. In the south of Chihli, on the border of Honan, the Red Spears (joined from 1927 on by the members of the T'ien-men Hui, or Society of the Heavenly Gate) carried out several attacks and occupied twenty hsien for a certain period of time. Also in 1927 several risings took place in northern Kiangsu and northern Anhwei.[21]

There was, then, a whole series of risings of the Red Spears against the warlords' troops. Although the Red Spears were not the only organization of the peasantry to resist, they were the largest. Several sources give figures that vary from two to four hundred thousand men in Honan. The most detailed source (as to the number of Red Spears) counts the troops and the names of their chiefs and shows that in Honan this society had at least 398,000 members; in Chihli, 105,000; in Shantung, 20,000 (no doubt after the failure of the great revolt); and in Shansi, 7,000—a total of 530,000 men.[22] In the region that interests us, the second most numerous organization in 1927 was the Society of the Heavenly Gate (T'ien-men Hui) with its 300,000 members in Honan and southern Chihli. Created in the district of Lin-hsien in Chihli and more centralized than the Spears, it was directed by a man of peasant origin, Han Ku-ming, who bore the title of chief general (tsung-t'uan-shih) or veteran chief (lao-t'uan-shih). Han was aided by masters (ch'uan-shih), who were divided into military masters and civil masters, the latter alone authorized to set up the altar (she-t'an).[23] This organization rivaled the Red Spears in the resistance against the Mukden troops, especially at the local level, but the Spears remained at the head of the movement in both numbers and activity.

The Red Spears did not form a unified body, but, as noted above, had several offshoots—White Spears, Yellow Spears, Black Spears, etc. These societies had arisen as much because of rivalry among chiefs as because of divergent superstitions and objectives. The Red Spears themselves were divided into two big sects, the "Red Instruction" and the "Middle Instruction." In the region of Loyang, the split was a matter of differences in religious formulas, oaths, ritual, and training methods. In the region of Chengchow and of Hsin-yang, there was yet another opposition, that between the "Great Red Instruction" and the "Little Red Instruction." The former, following a defensive tactic, grouped together landed proprietors and rich peasants; the latter, following an offensive tactic, grouped together poor and middling peasants. Both groups hoped for an "Empire of Justice" and a "good sovereign."[24] They also nourished monarchical dreams, easily explainable at a time when the Republic had brought them only abusive taxes and interprovincial wars.

Interestingly enough, one finds no trace of opposition to land rent, which in Honan could approach 70 percent of the harvest—at least not before political parties began to propagandize. By that time, the movement of the Red Spears was already known throughout China. Perhaps the absence of such opposition can be explained (leaving aside the power of the landed proprietors) by the fact that, although poor peasants were numerous in the Red Spears and several of the society's chiefs were of peasant origin, the lesser gentry and rural notables tried (usually successfully) to corrupt the chiefs or directly to take power in the society.

The Red Spears, sometimes using the name of *min-t'uan*, already had a certain legal existence at the time when relations between Yüeh Wei-chün and the Red Spears still remained proper: they were authorized to try bandits.[25] Later certain detachments were designated "Red Spears of the system of the rural militia" (*min-t'uan-hsi Hung-ch'iang Hui*). The efforts of the lesser gentry were perhaps crowned by the changes to be seen in the statutes of the Red Spears. For example, after a certain time, there is no longer any trace of feminism to be found, whereas filial piety is the first point of the second paragraph. The first paragraph underlines the principal goals, autonomy and self-defense; later paragraphs set up directorial posts and honorific titles for those who have paid an extraordinary subscription of more than ten dollars.[26]

These factors may explain the enormous difficulties encountered by the political parties that tried to orient the movement in the direction of class struggle, or at least to secure for themselves the favorable attitude of the Red Spears during the Northern Expedition. Moreover, the centralism, the discipline, the secrecy, and the parochial sentiments of the Red Spears made it impossible to put members to work without the authorization of their chiefs, who were practically inaccessible. Here are three examples. In the district of Loyang, of the seven Communists sent in to cooperate in the organization of a rising, two were killed outright, a third died in hospital, and the others were gravely wounded. In Chi-hsien, the Communists did not succeed in their efforts to place themselves at the head of the movement. A secretary of the peasant committee of the Kuomintang sent to make contact with the chief of the T'ien-men Hui succeeded in seeing him only in the course of his fifth trip. The *tsung-t'uan-shih* decided to cooperate with the Kuomintang against the Mukden troops and sent two delegates to Hankow.[27]

These contacts and the possibility of cooperation with the Communist Party and the left wing of the Kuomintang were very precious for three reasons: the real strength of the Red Spears in the war against the warlords in Honan, the social base offered by the Red Spears for the peasant unions (*nung-min hsieh-hui*) the Party hoped to create, and the Spears' army of self-defense (*nung-min tzu-wei-chün*).[28]

The modern peasant movement organized by the parties of the Left began in Honan in August 1925, at first along the railroad lines. It was only in April 1926 that it was possible to call a peasant congress (57 delegates from 15 districts), which set up the Peasant Union of Honan.[29]

The data on the size of the peasant unions in 1926 in Honan (the center of the Red Spears movement) in relation to other provinces are as follows: Kwangtung, 647,766 members; Honan, 270,000; Hunan, 38,400. For all of China, there were 981,442 members in 1926 and 9,153,093 in 1927.[30] If we find Honan in second place, just after Kwangtung, where P'eng P'ai had launched the modern peasant movement as early as 1923, it is because in this province the creation of peasant unions had benefited from the existence of the Red Spears.

The failure of the "first revolution" in 1927 stopped the development of the peasant movement in the north of the country. The Red

Spears were also the object of pitiless repression by warlords and the Nationalists; but they continued the struggle and at the end of 1927 even occupied three hsien to the west of Peking. Successive waves of revolt arose in Shantung in 1929 and 1932. In Shantung, they would participate in the guerrilla fighting against the Japanese, in cooperation with the Sixty-ninth Chinese Army.[31]

Before concluding, there is one more problem, no doubt the most obscure: the origin of the Red Spears. As in the case of many other secret societies, the Red Spears represent the continuation of a tradition. It would thus be of interest to know what elements of superstition are common to the Red Spears of the twentieth century and to the other secret societies that preceded them.

Most of our sources leave aside the problem of the origin of the Red Spears. One finds a few indications in Ivin,[32] and in the articles mentioned above by Li Ta-chao and Hsiang Yün-lung. Ivin traces their history and reveals the existence of a sect called (in Russian) Zheleznye Broni (in Chinese, no doubt the T'ieh-pu Shan, or Armor Mountain), which even before 1911 was spreading superstitions regarding invulnerability. Li says that the Red Spears were the heirs of the Boxers and of the White Lotus, and that members practiced sacred boxing and carried amulets of invulnerability. Hsiang Yün-lung declares that under the Manchus there was in Honan a sect called the Chin-chung Chao (the Golden Bells), which preached that the possession of certain talismans allowed one to survive knife blows and rifle bullets.[33] It is perhaps through the intermediary of these sects that the superstition of invulnerability was spread throughout Honan. We know that it was very common among the Boxers.

Other striking things about the Red Spears—their prohibition of gaming and wine and their prescription of sexual continence at certain times — are also found in a sect called the Huang-yai Chiao (Huang-yai Sect), which was widespread in Shantung in the nineteenth century. Now, as Teng Ssu-yü has noted, there were in this province Ch'ang-ch'iang Hui (Long Spears), who penetrated into Honan about 1920.[34] Several elements show that the Red Spears, as Li Ta-chao has also said, were natives of Shantung. For example, as noted above, the "masters" of the Red Spears were for the most part natives of that province. Furthermore, in the ritual enacted when members of the society met, to the question "Where do you come from?" one had to answer, "I come from Shantung."[35] Obviously elements similar to those found in the statutes and practice of the

Red Spears (for instance, abstinence from certain pleasures, including wine) can be found in the Tsai-li Chiao (Observance Sect), which derived from the White Lotus, but the Tsai-li Chiao was active in the cities of the North, whereas the other sects just mentioned were active among the peasants.

Even if one can base no firm conclusions about origins on these similarities, it seems likely that the superstitions of the various sects existing in the countryside of the North contributed to the formation of the Red Spears' beliefs and were useful to the society in organizing the self-defense of the peasants.

In addition, it is perhaps not impossible that the Huang Chiao-men, the Hung Chiao-men, and the Hei Chiao-men, which as late as 1924 were still integral parts of the Red Spears,[36] originated in the South in the nineteenth century. According to Wang T'ien-chiang there existed about 1860 in the region of the middle Yangtze a sect called the Chai Chiao (Abstinence Sect, or Vegetarians), which was divided into the Hung Chiao (Red Sect) or Tung-shan Chiao (Eastern Mountain Sect), the Pai Chiao (White Sect) or Hsi-shan Chiao (Western Mountain Sect), and the Chin-tan Chiao (Golden Elixir Sect). Of course a sect sometimes changed its name in order to hide itself. Moreover, other sects might have existed under the same name at the other end of China merely by chance. If we are indeed dealing with the same society, however, this would indicate at least that the limits of the zones of influence of the two great secret society systems (the White Lotus in the North and the Society of Heaven and Earth in the South) were not so strict as has usually been imagined.[37]

Finally, at least in the case of the Red Spears, after the "fusion" of the sects and the village leagues (lien-chuang hui), it is no longer possible to make a clear distinction between the sects (chiao-men) and the associations (hui-t'ang), as Wang T'ien-chiang could still do for the secret societies of the nineteenth century. The characteristic traits that allowed such distinctions to be made have disappeared.[38]

The Red Spears remained in the tradition of Chinese secret societies, with their superstitions, their oath and their rituals, their monarchical dreams. In the history of the Chinese peasant movement, they were not the first example of a merger between esoteric organizations and village self-defense alliances or peasant militia. Such had been the case with the Nien, and to a certain extent with the Boxers.[39] At the same time, the Red Spears already belonged to the twentieth-century revolutionary movement. With their resistance to the payment of taxes, their struggle against warlords, their autonomism, they are related to modern peasant unions. That evolution allowed the Communist Party to consider a strategy aimed at incorporating the Red Spears into peasant unions, particularly in Honan at a time when the Party supported the "National Armies" of Feng Yü-hsiang. An analysis of this Communist strategy, however, is beyond the scope of this paper.

The Red Spears were an organization of a mixed intermediary character, reflecting the passage in North China from one epoch to another, a passage which began with the peasantry, the major element of the Chinese population. The Society of the Red Spears was one of the last secret societies to take part in the Chinese revolutionary movement of the twentieth century. Because of its resistance to the warlords from 1925 to 1927, it is worthy of a place in the contemporary history of China.

Secret Societies and Peasant Self-Defense, 1921-1933

LUCIEN BIANCO

*The effectiveness of secret societies' defense against bandits and
the military—The limits and ambiguity of secret society activity—
The role of group defense*

At the time the Chinese Communists were making their first experiments with rural revolutionary base areas, spontaneous peasant agitation (i.e. agitation not guided by professional revolutionaries) continued to be a fundamentally defensive response to a *specific* and
local aggravation of the peasants' condition. The peasants did not
rebel against an exploitative established order, but against some new
development posing a threat to that order. Had the status quo not
been altered by the arrival of soldiers, bandits, or locusts, the impo-
sition of a new tax, or whatever, the peasants would not have rebelled. The essential difference between chronic peasant agitation
and revolutionary action is that the latter is deliberately offensive in
nature, whereas the former resembles the defensive reaction of a be-
leaguered organism. If peasant agitation was chronic (and thus a constant source of worry, not to say alarm, to officials), it was because
the occasions for such conduct were endemic in rural China.[1]

Like spontaneous peasant agitation, as opposed to revolutionary
action, the activities of rural secret societies were fundamentally defensive. The role of traditional secret societies in the countryside and
their persistent success well into the twentieth century can best be
understood in terms of the peasantry's need to defend itself. In ordinary times, obviously, the peasantry would not rely on secret societies for protection and assistance. But when all other means had
proved unavailing, the peasantry might turn to secret societies for
help. In certain rare cases and against certain adversaries, secret societies were better adapted to the peasants' needs than other traditional
forms of resistance.

It was particularly against incursions by bandits and by the military that secret societies demonstrated their effectiveness—or at least

their relative effectiveness when compared with the available alternatives. Apart from the forces of order (it was precisely their defaulting that forced rural Chinese to take matters into their own hands)[2] and the common practice of buying peace by paying the bandits whatever they asked for, the peasants' main recourse was to village corps or self-defense groups (*tzu-wei t'uan, pao-wei t'uan*). The self-defense groups were of two sorts: those composed of mercenaries (*ku tzu-wei t'uan*) and those composed exclusively of villagers (*tzu-wei t'uan*, or "self-defense militia").[3] The second category was apparently the more common. It was not uncommon for the village militia to rout small groups of bandits, capturing or killing some of them,[4] or for the mere fact of their existence to persuade the bandits to prey on villages not similarly endowed with a militia.

Still, no matter how determined the village militia, it could not stand up against a large gang of bandits. For this purpose several neighboring village militias would form "associations," "federations," "alliances," or "leagues" (*lien-chuang hui, lien-ts'un hui*). Such alliances were rare and usually short-lived, since peasants were seldom eager to defend a neighboring village. Furthermore, even though the authorities often encouraged the creation of village militias, they soon became alarmed if a militia grew too large or strong; indeed, a self-defense organization strong enough to provide effective protection against bandits, especially a village federation, ran the risk of being disbanded by the regular army. Thus there was an inherent limit on the growth of these self-defense organizations and also on their life-span. When encounters with the bandits were too costly to life and limb, the militiamen tended to get discouraged and give up. On the other hand, as soon as the immediate pressure from the bandits was relaxed, the other villagers lost interest in contributing to the militia's equipment and training.[5]

It was here that, in a sense, secret societies took up the slack. In fact, they were frequently already involved at the "lower" levels of self-defense, and sometimes even controlled a village federation.* More important, with memberships generally much larger than those of the self-defense organizations described above, secret societies were

---

* See C. C. Geoffrey, "The Red Spears in China," *China Weekly Review*, 40 (March 19, 1927): 68; and U.S. Dept. of State, 893 43/3 (Oct. 24, 1928). Although the distinction between the *lien-chuang hui* and secret societies is made difficult by their occasional overlapping, it must be insisted upon, since a great many "village associations" simply gathered together the strongest and most determined young men in a village without a secret society's entering the picture at all.

in a position to drive off any bandit bands that ventured into a region where they were firmly established. Their myriad branches, the close ties of their members, the sworn oath, the discipline and feeling of invulnerability—all these characteristics made them staunch, effective opponents of bandit bands. On at least one occasion the contrast between their intrepidity and effectiveness and the timidity or indifference of the regular army made the army lose face so badly that jealous soldiers attacked the Red Spears (Hung-ch'iang Hui) when they returned to the village.[6]

This was one of the paths—there were many others—that led secret societies from the fight against bandits to the fight against the forces of order. In fact, defense against bandits did not always precede conflicts with the authorities; it sometimes happened that the original call to action was directed against looting soldiers,* or, more often, against increased taxation. Still, protection against bandits remained, at the local level, the most frequent motive behind the creation or reactivation of a secret society. In 1920–21, it was altogether natural that the Red Spears should appear and enjoy their first successes in the provinces (Shantung, Honan) in which banditry was most prevalent.[7] As late as 1925, the most common reason for the population to turn to the Red Spears was for protection against bandits.[8] At this stage it was common for soldiers and Red Spears to join forces against the bandits.

In the following years, however, conflicts between the military and the Red Spears multiplied. Taken separately, most of the incidents I have isolated beginning in 1927 involved representatives of order as well as bandits. To illustrate the relationship between the two types of protection† and the extent to which secret societies could sometimes succeed, albeit briefly, in instigating rebellion, I shall describe in some detail the 1929 Red Spears uprising in eastern Shantung.

This uprising continued a tradition of several years' standing. But the large uprising of 1926, aimed at the warlord Chang Tsung-ch'ang,

---

* We must not be too quick to impute political significance to such cases. More often than not, the soldiers involved were *k'uei-chün*: soldiers separated from service by defeat, discharge, or default of pay, and forced to wrest their subsistence from the countryside. The authorities as well as the peasant masses were inclined to regard *k'uei-chün* as bandits (*Ko-ming chou-pao*, Sept. 1, 1929, pp. 306, 320).

† The link, I cannot emphasize too strongly, was the defensive and hence circumscribed nature of the secret societies' activities. They defended themselves against authorities and bandits alike. It was a big step from such a defensive posture to a deliberate attack on the established order or on property, and a step that was rarely taken.

was centered farther west,[9] with the eastern portion of the province remaining relatively quiet. Only in one eastern hsien, Lai-yang (in Teng-chou prefecture), do we find a strong concentration of Red Spears.[10] In 1928, Lai-yang was suddenly crisscrossed by village federations, formed to halt a new wave of banditry; battles were constant and several villages were destroyed.[11] The uprising of 1929 can be said to have grown out of this agitation in the fall of 1928; in January 1929 the American consul in Chefoo reported that because of the Red Spears, not a single tax collector had ventured into Chao-yüan hsien (near Lai-yang, and also in Teng-chou prefecture) "for several months."[12] The magistrate of Chao-yüan had resigned, and his successor was unable to enter the hsien to take up his post. The upheaval thus lasted altogether nearly a year, until the fall of 1929.

   The causes of the movement were the upsurge of banditry already mentioned and, more important, the actions of the local military. General Liu Chen-nien, a former officer of Chang Tsung-ch'ang, installed himself at Chefoo in October 1928, and established his au-

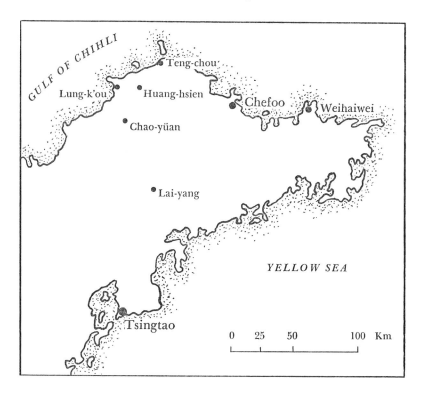

thority over the eastern part of the Shantung Peninsula. In early 1929 a well-organized insurrection, intended to pave the way for Chang Tsung-ch'ang's return, broke out at Lung-k'ou and Huang-hsien; Liu's units immediately jumped into the fray on the rebels' side.[13] What followed was a private war, the cost of which was borne by the peasantry. Looting, burning, and the razing of entire villages were commonplace; women and young girls captured during "military" raids were sold at the market of Huang-hsien for 10 to 20 Mexican dollars apiece. When the population tried to defend itself, it suffered pitiless reprisals: a village razed for the murder of an officer, eight villages destroyed and their inhabitants massacred for an attempt on Chang Tsung-ch'ang's life.[14] It was in these circumstances that the Red Spears extended their control over the rural population.

Sometimes membership in the Red Spears was compulsory, or at least the society set a quota of recruits to be furnished by a given village. By late summer, every family in the villages controlled by the society had to have at least one person in the Red Spears, and those who sent their men to work in Chefoo had to pay a special tax, which was used to buy arms and ammunition. Estimates of Red Spears membership in August 1929 ranged from 50,000 to 60,000.[15] In Teng-chou prefecture (some fifty miles west of Chefoo), the administration was practically run by the Red Spears, who had set up their headquarters in a village there, named a magistrate, and begun to collect a land tax. The Red Spears had also introduced a head tax,[16] while at the same time, at least in Chao-yüan hsien and several other districts, they prevented the payment of any tax whatever to the legal administration. And it was out of the question for the legally designated military officials in the region to take up their duties: the Red Spears shot on sight anyone in a uniform. Even civilians dared not venture into the area held by the Red Spears unless they spoke the local dialect.[17]

Finally, when the Red Spears had grown so strong in Teng-chou that they could no longer be ignored, Liu began his oft-postponed campaign to regain control of the area. On September 23 he launched a large encirclement campaign between Huang-hsien and Teng-chou, burning and looting houses and killing the inhabitants or driving them away. Eighteen villages were totally destroyed, more than sixty others partly or wholly burned: men, women, and children were hunted down in the fields, and even mothers with babes in arms were slaughtered.[18] The campaign lasted two months: by the end of November, the Red Spears had practically ceased to function in

Teng-chou prefecture. To win over those Red Spears who had escaped the slaughter—or were unable to get away—the magistrate of
Chao-yüan gave their defeated leaders jobs and formed a local militia of the rank-and-file members.[19]

No matter how great the Red Spears' strength was at a given time
in the Teng-chou area, it was still destroyed with relative ease and
(once the decision had been made, at any rate) rapidity. The situation was a familiar one. Competition among warlords for control;
official failure to grasp the seriousness of the revolt (civil and military
bureaucrats were so accustomed to the recurrence of minor troubles
that they tended to go on applying routine measures even when a
disturbance had reached dangerous proportions); localization of the
dissidence in a confined area (the agitation in western Shantung in
1928–29 was considerably west of Liu's power base, and eight different petty warlords were fighting over the neighboring region to the
west)[20]—all these factors often delayed punitive action against the
rebels. Once a punitive expedition was sent out, however, it usually
had little difficulty suppressing the rebellion. (Destroying the secret
society itself, of course, was a totally different matter.)

T'ung-hua hsien, between Mukden and Kirin, provides another
example. During late 1927 and early 1928, T'ung-hua was the scene
of a rather large uprising instigated by the Big Knife Society (Ta-tao
Hui). Banditry and oppressive taxation were as usual the underlying
causes of the revolt, though the immediate cause was an act of treach-
ery by the authorities, who, after using the Big Knives against the
bandits, suddenly, on December 12, 1927, arrested several members
of the society and seized the loot (money, horses, and arms) that they
had just taken from the thieves. Indignation at this double-cross un-
leashed an uprising, which the first punitive expedition (January 12,
1928), composed exclusively of local forces, was unable to put down.
But a second expedition, in which the local troops were reinforced
by a contingent of cavalry and foot soldiers from the Heilungkiang
troops garrisoned along the Peking-Mukden Railroad, crushed the
rebellion in a matter of days (January 25–28). The first weeks of February were taken up with reprisals (just over two thousand peasants
were killed, including everyone above twelve years of age in certain
places) and the liquidation of the revolt. Inequality of firepower and
terror of the cavalry certainly help explain the ease with which the
insurrection was quelled. But one must also take into account the
rebels' lack of unity, which was aggravated by their lack of funds

(the small amounts available became the subject of disputes), by the inclination of a good number of Big Knives to join the forces of order once they were offered amnesty and other incentives, and finally by the approach of the Chinese New Year, which brought with it a marked diminution of the rebels' fighting spirit.[21]

The normal upshot of any revolt instigated by a secret society, then, was suppression and a period of recuperation. Though capable of more sustained activity than the simple village self-defense associations, the secret society was nonetheless foredoomed to periods of inaction and eclipse. It continued, of course, to exist as an organization, but most of the men who were active members at a given time sooner or later quit, and its membership had to be rebuilt almost from scratch; it hibernated until the next occasion, which is to say the next emergency. Therefore it is not contradictory to say that peasant agitation led by secret societies was both chronic and sporadic—chronic because the underlying causes were chronic features of rural life, sporadic because each isolated episode lasted only a short time. Defeat or the disappearance of the immediate grounds for revolt (and in most cases both at once, since military defeat was generally accompanied by concessions to the population)[22] cost the society the massive popular support that had temporarily made it an effective force. This extreme vulnerability to the play of circumstance, this lack of staying power, is one major difference between the activity of secret societies and true revolutionary activity.

Many other such characteristics (archaic customs, superstitions, etc.) persisted into the 1920's and 1930's.[23] Rather than demonstrating once again the persistence of a well-documented tradition, I should like to point out that in some ways these ancient practices continued to serve the peasants' needs. Initiation rites and magic potions might not confer the anticipated invulnerability, but they could provide the courage to confront modern weapons with primitive arms. This strange courage in turn terrified bandits and soldiers, to the point where they would refuse to engage in so "unequal" a battle, for example, a battle against the appropriately named *shen-ping* ("supernatural soldiers"), members of a secret society dedicated to freeing the region of Wan-hsien (in eastern Szechwan) of the military scourge.[24] Given the mental attitudes and technical capabilities of both sides, in other words, archaic customs and beliefs were not wholly lacking in effectiveness as tools of peasant defense. On the whole, of course, they vitiated the secret societies' capacity for revolutionary struggle far more often than they buttressed it. One example will suffice to illustrate the difference between the secret societies' "supernatural fighters" and modern China's eminently terrestrial revolutionaries. In early 1928, the well-known warlord Yang Shen (Sen) evacuated I-ch'ang (in western Hupeh) and his troops returned back up the Yangtze through the gorges, looting and burning villages along the way. The members of a "Buddhist Fraternity of Sacred Soldiers of the Virtuous Way" ambushed some eight hundred stragglers from Yang Shen's army, killing every one of them, whereupon they gathered up the dead soldiers' rifles, smashed them to bits, and threw the pieces in the river. "Foreign arms and ammunition," their leader explained, "have been the scourge of China for more than fifteen years. We were much better off during the Empire, when we had never seen a single rifle. In the Sacred Army we use only swords and lances, except for a few rifles that we use to give warning signals."[25] Picture, if you will, the Red Army conscientiously destroying all arms captured from the Kuomintang marked *Made in America*!

Without listing all the traits that distinguished traditional secret society activities in the Chinese countryside in the 1920's and 1930's from contemporary revolutionary action in rural areas, I must at least mention three other characteristics peculiar to secret societies: their chronic tendency to degenerate into gangs, their ambiguous social role, and their particularism. The movement in Teng-chou during the summer of 1929 was as quick to degenerate as previous Red Spears activities in the province.[26] Looting, rape, kidnappings for ransom, robbery pure and simple, became the rule, and the city of Teng-chou was flooded with refugees fleeing the Red Spears, as it had been a few weeks earlier with refugees fleeing the soldiers of Chang Tsung-ch'ang.[27] Naturally, the second wave of refugees belonged to the upper classes, since looting and kidnapping were often selective (their preferred targets were the Christians and the rich), and my source, which sometimes reports hearsay, is quick to call unavoidable emergency measures (such as forced requisitions) acts of brigandage.[28] There can be no question, however, that at times the society rather resembled the Mafia and exacted a heavy toll from the rural population. In the peasants' eyes, the society was alternately the elite and the dregs of the population—or both at once. Heroes or hooligans: thus are the adventurous and those without a fixed place in society regarded by the stay-at-homes. The dual appellation is appropriate to an institution that for the village was both a mainstay and a threat.

Obviously "degeneracy" could take other forms; a secret society might, for example, become a defender of the established order.

Apart from the commonplace practice, already mentioned, of individual or group enlistments in the police force or army, the transformation of a secret society into an upholder of the status quo could come about when self-interest or ambition led the leaders to turn their groups into private militias in the service of the *ti-chu* (landowners). There were even cases in which a secret society was organized at the behest of the *ti-chu* or the rich peasants; one such group was the *fa-ping* ("soldiers of the law") of northern Fukien, to which the majority of villagers belonged but which acted only to defend the interests of the privileged classes.[29]

But how much sense does it make to speak of degeneration when the landed classes set up and controlled a secret society from the start? We must be clear about the social role of rural secret societies: it was protection of the interests of peasant society taken as a whole, and more specifically, as a general rule, the interests of the landed peasantry and gentry, since the defense of peasant society meant the defense of property against theft and excessive taxation. This was true to the point that membership in the Red Spears was sometimes expressly barred to "those without property"[30] to defend—the group became, as it were, a clandestine equivalent of the July Monarchy's Garde Nationale! To be sure, the unmarried men (poor by definition) in the villages of northern Hupeh where the Red Spears practiced this policy of excluding the poor, got their own back by creating the Shiny Egg Society (Kuang-tan Hui), from which the well-to-do were barred.[31] This association of men who were as "bare as eggs" was not unique, but it was extremely unusual. It was much more common for members of the gentry either personally to run or indirectly to control rural secret societies.[32]

If the social role of most rural secret societies can be debated at length, their particularism is beyond dispute. This characteristic cannot be attributed to any falling away from an original purpose; it was inherent in the very nature of the institution. On September 10–11, 1928, six villages in Tan-t'u hsien (near Chen-chiang, in Kiangsu) were suddenly attacked and burned, and two hundred inhabitants killed. Who were the assailants? Two thousand peasants from neighboring villages, members of the Small Knife Society (Hsiao-tao Hui). The villagers they set upon were guilty of organizing sections of the rival Big Knife Society.

Needless to say, the causes of this conflict cannot be reduced to competition between the two secret societies, for questions of economic interests and geographic origins were involved, but involved in a way that nicely illustrates the essentially particularist nature of both "brotherhoods." The Small Knives recruited their membership among immigrants from north of the Yangtze, whereas the Big Knives were all natives of Tan-t'u. The "northerners," who were poorer than the established residents of the area, were from the first looked down upon by their new neighbors. Contact between the two groups was rare, intermarriage even rarer. Later on, when by dint of greater frugality and harder work at least some of the new settlers began to rise in the world, the old-timers' contempt gave way to jealousy and even hatred (an overall pattern that resembles the circumstances in which anti-Semitism spread in other societies).

This latent hostility between two communities who worked the same land side by side suddenly became explosive in 1927 with the change in the political situation and the appearance of bandits. The bandits' raids consistently spared the newcomers (the bandits we can assume were also "northerners" and, like Small and Big Knives, respectful of group identity), and several immigrants were even convicted of hiding bandits. In Tan-t'u hsien and three neighboring districts the old residents retaliated by setting fire to several thousand huts occupied by "northerners." The new settlers immediately founded Small Knife societies (following the classic pattern, the secret society was created, or at any rate revived, for purposes of self-defense), and once they were well organized they paraded their strength in the streets. These armed parades, which took place in February 1928, as well as the actions of certain uncontrollable elements who under cover of revenge indulged in pure and simple banditry, naturally provoked feverish efforts by the natives to organize the Big Knife societies. And since the Big Knives were by far the more numerous, the Small Knives took fright and launched a preventive attack in September 1928.[33]

This episode, Ta-tao Hui against Hsiao-tao Hui, is instructive. On both sides the organization was the same;[34] we are dealing with two sister societies, as it were, and not only in name.[35] And yet they fought each other. There were rich (insofar as a Chinese peasant can ever be described as rich) and poor in each of the two communities, but the conflict was not one of rich against poor. It set one socially heterogeneous group against a neighboring group that was of similar social composition but was considered an intruder. Each of the antagonistic secret societies fulfilled the same role: group defense.

Group defense: ultimately, was this not the essential role of rural secret societies in twentieth-century China? A group may be defined by its social role, just as it may be defined along professional or geographic lines. More often, members of the group were united by several kinds of ties at the same time. But if group identity varied, its nature remained closer to that of a multi-class clan or lineage than to that of a homogeneous social class.

Once we define the role of secret societies as group defense, we are in a position to account for some of the apparent contradictions that we find in their behavior, notably the ambivalence of which several examples have been given above and in the writings of other historians.[36] Is it not the case, however, that ambivalence lies in the eyes of the beholder? Wittingly or not, we tend to evaluate secret societies in terms of a norm or orientation that we bring with us to the study of their history (progress, justice, the established order, modern revolutionary movement, etc.): in brief, with our eye on historical trends. My own distinction between fighting bandits and fighting soldiers was nonexistent for the peasants involved; it may be useful for analytical purposes, but the peasants did not ordinarily see things in these terms. Whether the threat to them came from bandits or from soldiers, they were defending themselves against attack. If, then, in refusing to enumerate and contrast lights and shadows (lights and shadows with respect to what, exactly?) we appraise secret societies in terms of the needs to which the institution was a response, we find ourselves back at our starting point: peasant self-defense, an absolute necessity in a society where order was always precarious, and exploitative when it existed.

To say that the role of the secret society was group defense is also to take a stand on the oft-debated question of the secret society's capacity for revolution.* Secret societies and revolutionaries at times worked toward the same ends—and even, on occasion, joined

---

* Today we tend automatically to discuss secret societies, which harass rather than threaten the established order, almost exclusively in terms of their capacity for revolution. If we tried instead to understand secret societies in relation to the prevailing philosophy of another period, we would discover that these heterodox organizations were nonetheless imbued with Confucian ideals: as restrictive fraternities, for instance, they routinely practiced *pieh-ai* (the love that makes distinctions) and were hardly aware of the *chien-ai* (universal love) of Mo-tzu. Again, if we considered rural secret societies in the light of their role in the modern anti-imperialist and nationalist movement, we would find ourselves evoking the well-known tradition that links the anti-Christian riots of the latter half of the nineteenth century to the Boxers and to the anti-Japanese resistance in Manchuria and China proper. Moreover, we would also inevitably be led to acknowledge that xenophobia and mistrust of "outsiders" lay behind much of this patriotic struggle; indeed, the Red Spears in Honan seem to have been less interested in guerrilla warfare against the Japanese than in protecting their village and its property from the refugees from Chengchow and even, on occasion, exploiting and robbing these

forces[37]—just as, in other circumstances, secret societies and the police or secret societies and bandits worked together. Still, just as bandits who kill policemen who are defending the established order, or police who kill bandits who are oppressing the population, do not automatically qualify as revolutionaries, secret societies cannot be regarded as revolutionary movements simply because the goals of the two sometimes coincide. Group defense: each element in the term expresses the opposite of what one ordinarily means by revolutionary action, which implies both a totalistic goal (the revolution will resolve everyone's problems) and an offensive strategy (the revolutionaries must take power). Group defense or protection is inherently limited, both in scope and in the kinds of things it will attempt. It can react vigorously, but it rarely takes the initiative. In a way, it is at the mercy of its adversary, whose incursion triggers the defensive action and often puts an end to it.

---

compatriots from the city (Graham Peck, *Two Kinds of Time* [Boston: Houghton Mifflin, 1967], pp. 329, 341). Here again, recognition of the real role of rural secret societies—group defense—clears up the contradiction, which exists only in connection with a notion that we have imposed from the outside on a reality that bears no relation to it.

The I-kuan Tao Society

LEV DELIUSIN

The disbanding of the I-kuan Tao Society by the authorities of the People's Republic of China—Origins of the sect; its religious syncretism—Practices designed to deceive the believers—Reasons for joining—Collaboration with the Japanese—Collusion with the Kuomintang after 1945

As Communist power increased in China in the years immediately following World War II, measures were taken by Communist authorities to dissolve and disband all sects, unions, and societies of a "feudal" character, whose activities were seen as opposed to the interests of the people and advantageous to the enemies of the new government. The campaign to disband secret societies started even before the official proclamation of the People's Republic, and lasted for several years. One of the first decrees calling for a ban on secret societies, the compulsory registration of their members, and the dissolution of their organizations was adopted by the government of North China on January 4, 1949.[1] Other city and provincial administrations took similar action as Communist forces pushed south. Finally, in May 1950, Kwangtung province adopted anti-secret-society measures.[2]

The governmental directives concerning secret societies particularly stressed the necessity of disbanding the largest of them, the I-kuan Tao (Way of Basic Unity), together with societies affiliated with it under other names. This society had a widespread organization with active branches in numerous provinces, and many of its members enjoyed great influence among the lower orders. The decrees banning and dissolving the I-kuan Tao were designed to eliminate an important source of strength of feudal and counterrevolutionary elements, thus safeguarding the interests of the masses of the people and reinforcing the people's democratic dictatorship.[3] The society was described as "a counterrevolutionary instrument, in the pay of and controlled by the imperialists and the Kuomintang bandit clique," and as "a reactionary mystical organization of feudal character that leads the backward masses astray and does them harm."[4] At the same time, the Chinese press explained that although the government was disbanding the reactionary sects, it would not prohibit worshiping God and/or praying to Buddha; its measures were strictly ideological and in no sense directed against the freedom of religious belief guaranteed to the people by the government's program.[5]

The history of the I-kuan Tao casts considerable light on certain traits of Chinese society, notably the way of life, turn of mind, and social characteristics of the urban and rural poor. The clandestine character of the group's activities of course makes research difficult; nevertheless, a number of books and articles giving an account of this secret society were published at the time attention began to focus on its operations, including a description of the sect by a former member, Li Shih-yü,[6] and a series of articles by a European missionary, Wilhelm Grootaers.[7] The newspapers and periodicals of early 1950, containing statements by members of the society and declarations by its propagandists, are even more useful, since they contain concrete accounts of its organization and its methods of working among the population. The present article draws mainly on these sources.[8]

Like other secret societies, the I-kuan Tao had known periods of growth and periods of decline throughout its history. At times its activities went unnoticed, attracting no attention from the authorities; at other times the society attained great influence. In such periods its membership expanded rapidly, and it became well known despite the aura of secrecy surrounding its activities. The Chinese press does not furnish precise details concerning the date of the society's first appearance. According to one source it appeared in Tientsin about 1932.[9] Others locate its birthplace in Shantung province at about the same time.[10] In either case, it seems likely that the society was founded by a certain Chang Kuang-pi (alias Chang T'ien-jan), a vagabond from Shantung who claimed to be Maitreya, the future Buddha. Announcing that he had come from heaven to save mankind, Chang created a secret society and named it the I-kuan Tao.[11]

According to Li Shih-yü, however, the first I-kuan Tao sects made their appearance in 1911. They did not form a single organization until 1928, by his account, and it was only after 1936 that the organization became an influential mass secret society. Li Shih-yü divides the society's history into four periods: 1911–28, limited, clandestine activity; 1928–36, leadership of Chang T'ien-jan; 1936–45, expansion in the Japanese-occupied regions; after 1945, decline.[12]

Just as there is disagreement on the society's origins, so there are various interpretations of its name; the likeliest derivation is from the famous quotation of Confucius in the *Analects*: "Wu tao i i kuan chih" ("My teaching is universal").[13] The implication is that the society was universal in the sense of not being bound by any particular religious or ethical doctrine.

The society's religious doctrine, like that of other secret societies, did not constitute a fully developed, logically formulated system. Some aspects of it were borrowed from medieval secret societies. The White Lotus Society, in particular, furnished the idea that during the course of its development humanity passes through "Three Suns": the era of the "Blue Sun" (*ch'ing yang*), or the past; the era of the "Red Sun" (*hung yang*), or the present, related to the action of Sakyamuni; and the era of the "White Sun" (*pai yang*), or the future, tied to the coming of Maitreya.[14] The aim of this teaching seems to have been to draw the attention and hopes of the society's members to the promise of a better future; it encouraged them to believe that their suffering would not be eternal. But another interpretation of the three eras was also taught, according to which the era of the Blue Sun was the time of the legendary Fu Hsi, the era of the Red Sun was the time of King Chao of the Chou dynasty, and the era of the White Sun was the present.[15]

Chang T'ien-jan and his followers preached that membership in their society would enable poor people to put an end to the difficulties and misfortunes of life, to overcome the consequences of natural calamities, to cure sickness, to perfect themselves, and ultimately to attain celestial beatitude after death. Their sermons preached the necessity of observing the three kinship ties (*san-kang*) and the five moral principles (*wu-ch'ang*). The society's propagandists also called for the application of traditional moral principles such as loyalty (*chung*), filial piety (*hsiao*), and justice (*i*).[16] The literature of the society often made use of Chinese folk legends, particularly the legend about the good monk Chi-kung, who was said to have returned to earth to dwell among men in order to save them, the implication being once again that those who joined the society would be delivered from the sufferings and afflictions of life.[17]

The society's rituals incorporated numerous elements from the prayer rituals of Taoist sects, as well as Taoist mystical conceptions of the origins of the universe. Li Shih-yü holds that the society's religious dogma borrowed from the Confucians their ethical rules of conduct, from the Taoists their notions of cosmogony, and from the Buddhists some sacred texts as well as numerous names of saints and various special terminology. Many traditional superstitions were added to the doctrine; the "Eternal Mother" (wu-sheng lao-mu), for example, was proclaimed the supreme head of the sect.[18]

Li Shih-yü tells us that the society's leaders were guided by a single principle, "Let none who comes be sent away," and that they accordingly worked out a system by which "the Three Doctrines fuse into One." In fact, they did not limit themselves to the Three Doctrines but made constant use also of Christian and Islamic teachings.[19] This liberal attitude toward the various religious doctrines is reflected in the society's officially accepted history. According to these sanctioned traditions, the society originated with the mythical figures P'an-ku and Huang-ti, the legendary emperors Yao and Shun, and the philosophers Confucius and Mencius; later the society emigrated westward and linked its destiny with that of Sakyamuni. When Boddhikharma came from India to China in the first century A.D., the doctrine came to life again on Chinese soil.[20]

This mixture of varied ideas and notions drawn from the three principal religious and ethical doctrines of China, compounded with extensive borrowing from local superstitions, lent a particularly hazy and diffuse character to the society's teachings. At the same time, it had the advantage of offering each new member something that corresponded to notions already familiar to him.

The society's leaders and propagandists used every possible means to convince its members that the hierarchy had supernatural powers and could evoke spirits, predict the future, and cure illnesses and sterility.[21] (The last claim attracted many barren women.) All sorts of mysterious performances and séances took place in the society's temples with the aim of impressing and frightening the uninstructed. In Chungking, for example, demonstrations of a so-called "divine whip" were staged. By means of a pistol mounted inside this "whip," the officiating leader could strike down a previously designated person during a prayer session, usually someone who had openly questioned the veracity of the sermons.

After the I-kuan Tao was disbanded, many of its former members (commonly young men and girls) told of the stratagems used by its leaders to deceive their unwitting flocks. One woman had had a lot of broken plates, bricks, and dirt thrown through the window into her room one night, to the accompaniment of strange noises. She had been told that it was the work of I-kuan Tao spirits, but later she and her neighbors had caught the culprit, a member of the society who lived in the same house.[22] In Chengtu, a servant girl of the temple told of a preacher who had convinced the faithful of the omnipotence of Buddha by strewing sugar on the sandy floor of the temple before the service; after prayers he would proclaim to his congregation that Buddha, in his mercy, had heard their prayers and transformed the sand into sugar.[23]

Still another device used by I-kuan Tao leaders to deceive the uninitiated, with the help of adepts who were in on the society's secrets, was a sort of automatic writing. A young disciple, who had studied the magic formulas in advance on the orders of his mentor, would draw in the sand certain characters allegedly inspired by the celestial powers, to the astonishment of his ignorant audience.[24] A variation of this device used in the village of Ya-men-ko was described to the Australian journalist Wilfred Burchett. A female medium, sitting in a sand pit and seemingly in a trance, scrawled hieroglyphs convulsively in the sand with a stick. The priests in charge asserted that the characters were supernatural messages, and the poor peasants, after prostrating themselves several times, returned to their wretched huts firmly convinced that they had heard the gods speak. Burchett writes:

A few months previously there had been a mass meeting at Ya Men Ko where the local priests and the girl medium demonstrated before all the villagers how they worked. The girl told of how she had been sold from childhood to the priests and after months and years of beatings and being locked up in cellars without food, she had painfully learned to write characters in the sand in the complicated way demanded by the priests. Her eyes were never really closed and the priests always indicated to her which characters should be written.[25]

Tricks like this designed to fool the populace were by no means uncommon; they were practiced in all the temples of the society.[26]

Members of the society had to swear never to divulge its secrets, on pain of being struck by lightning and losing all their blood. In addition, members were urged to recruit new members. A member who recruited one new member was promised deliverance from all suffering; if he recruited ten new members, his whole family would be delivered from misfortune. It was made clear that the society's protection and magical powers covered members only.[27] The society's policy of recruiting entire families was seemingly designed to help preserve its secret character.

In some cases, new recruits were forced to pay exorbitant dues and had other money extorted from them. After 1949, many people were ruined by the society's exactions. In Tientsin, for example, several hundred small tradesmen, most of them ignorant and many of them terrorized, gave up their savings to buy the society's protection, and some even sold their land.[28]

In the countryside, the society's members were mostly poor peasants and agricultural laborers. According to a survey taken after the founding of the People's Republic in the Shansi village of Shang-hua-chuang, approximately 74 percent of the poor and middle peasants were members of the society. In one hsien of Liaosi province, 41 percent of the society's local leaders were poor peasants and 30 percent were middle peasants.

Motives for joining the I-kuan Tao varied. Some joined to protect themselves and their families, others to improve their lot, still others to cure illness or overcome some misfortune. The society's agents were quick to learn of people's misfortunes and turn them to the society's advantage. "You are ailing; join our society and be healed." "You have no children; join our society and you will have children." "You grieve because your loved ones have died; join our society and you will speak with them, and when you are dead you will rejoin them in heaven."

That these crude appeals were often effective is evident from the Shang-hua-chuang survey. Of the 502 members of the society in Shang-hua-chuang 230 men had joined to insure themselves and their families against natural calamities and the vicissitudes of life; 72 persons in the hope of getting rich; 45 to cure their children's diseases, and 15 their own diseases; 42 to obtain the gods' protection for a son in the army; 38 to assure an afterlife with their deceased husbands, wives, and parents; 23 to obtain help in having children; 21 to rid themselves of bad habits; and 11 women because they were worried about husbands who had left home for various reasons.[29] Another survey, conducted in a section of Chengtu, found that of 1,108 members of the society, 341 had joined to insure themselves and their families against natural calamities and the vicissitudes of life, 325 to be healed, 165 to obtain material blessings, 136 to enjoy a blessed afterlife, 80 to become saints or immortals, and 61 to have children.[30]

The society was divided into two "threads": the "dark thread" (an-hsien) or secret structure, and the "bright thread" (ming-hsien) or open structure. The society's leaders, branch directors, and preachers and the guardians of its temples all belonged to the "dark thread."

The ordinary members belonged to the "bright thread." They were not in on the society's internal secrets; their function was merely to pray, listen to sermons, and contribute to the society's treasury.

The dignitaries of the I-kuan Tao were classed hierarchically. At the top stood the patriarch, descended from P'an-ku himself. At the local level were the "guardians of the altar" (*t'an-chu*), the "guardians of the Three Forces of Heaven, Earth, and Man" (*san-ts'ai t'an-chu*), "ancients" (*ch'ien-jen*), "preachers" (*tien-ch'uan-shih*), and "local deans" (*tao-chang*). The preachers represented the patriarch himself and alone possessed the authority to initiate new members into the society.[31] All these dignitaries belonged to the "dark thread" and lived on the offerings of their congregation.

The I-kuan Tao did not enjoy particularly great influence until the outbreak of the Sino-Japanese War in 1937. Its rapid increase in influence among both the urban and the rural populace after 1937 seems to have had two causes. First, the war aggravated the already difficult situation of China's urban and rural poor to the point where they saw no solution to their problems short of the intervention of a miraculous, supernatural force. Ready to grasp at anything that was offered, they took the dim torch of the I-kuan Tao for a beacon of hope.

Second, there was the fact of the society's ties with the Japanese occupation forces. Its founder, Chang T'ien-jan, held a high post in the Ministry of Foreign Affairs of Wang Ching-wei's puppet government in Nanking, and some of its branch leaders held positions at the provincial and hsien levels. Through his army of propagandists, Chang spread the Japanese theory that "the Chinese and Japanese have a single culture and belong to one race," that "China and Japan are united by a time-honored friendship," and that "the Chinese should not resist, but should participate with the Japanese in the building of the Greater East Asian Co-Prosperity Sphere."[32] Japan's invasion of China was explained as follows: "The Japanese are the descendants of the five hundred young men and girls whom Ch'in Shih Huang-ti sent eastward from Ch'ang-an in search of the elixir of immortality. They belong to the same race as the Chinese and now want to come back to their country; but the Chinese government is opposing them, so they are compelled to clear a path by force to return home. Only when they reach Ch'ang-an [Sian] will peace be restored." Though the crudeness of these assertions is striking, they were well adapted to the unsophistication of Chang's audience.[33]

According to reports in the Chinese press, after the defeat of Japan the society's leaders made contact with the secret police of the Kuo-mintang and worked under its supervision and protection. At the end of the war the society had branches in the north, the northeast, the northwest, the southwest, and other regions of the country. No reliable membership figures exist, though incomplete data for Shansi put the membership there at about 810,000. In Szechwan, if the society's leaders can be believed, their members constituted 30 percent of the population in 1950. "If atomic war breaks out, 70 percent of the population of Szechwan will be destroyed, but 30 percent will survive thanks to their membership in the society."[34] In a campaign to attract members, the Szechwan leaders even used the famous revolutionary song "The East Is Red, the Sun Is Rising," interpreting the verses to mean that Japan would return to China in the future since a rising sun appears on the Japanese flag.[35]

When the People's Republic was founded, the leaders of the I-kuan Tao actively opposed it. They spread reports to the effect that the government of Chiang Kai-shek would soon be restored and terrorized the rural population with slanderous rumors, for example that the new government would castrate all men and sterilize all women without exception. In several regions they tried to incite peasants to oppose the distribution of land belonging to landlords.[36] They forbade their followers to join peasant associations or the Sino-Soviet Friendship Association; and in Manchuria, Honan, Szechwan, and elsewhere they tried to foment opposition to the people's government.[37]

Camouflage was necessary if the society was to keep operating under the new conditions. To this end, its branches carried on under new names, among them "the Heavenly Way Sect" (T'ien-tao Chiao), "the Way of Confucius and Mencius" (K'ung-Meng Tao), "the Way of Chu-ko Liang" (K'ung-ming Tao), "the Society of the Great Secret" (Mi-mi Hui), "the Way of the Basic Duality" (Erh-kuan Tao), "the Lodge of the Eastern Flower" (Tung-hua T'ang), "the Way of the Long-haired Ones" (Ch'ang-mao Tao), "the Way of the Old Mother" (Lao-mu Tao), "the Perfect Security Sect" (Wan-ch'üan Chiao), and "the Way Without End" (Wu-chi Tao). The leaders put pressure on the members to remain loyal, saying that anyone who left the society or revealed its secrets would be a marked man and that the "Five Thunders would annihilate him" (*wu lei hung shen*). Under the conditions established by the new government, however, these threats had little force, and members left en masse.

Between 1949 and 1953, the I-kuan Tao, one of the last and largest of China's secret societies, was officially and finally dissolved.

The wide influence of the I-kuan Tao and similar secret organizations proves that reactionary elements were very much alive in the China of the 1930's and 1940's. In both the city and the country, the society worked chiefly among the most oppressed and politically backward social orders, people who were unaware of the causes of their poverty and whose discontent with the existing order was unconscious and ill-defined. The prominence among them of all sorts of mystical and superstitious notions made them receptive to the blandishments of the I-kuan Tao and similar groups. Their illiteracy and ignorance, coupled with their age-old habit of submission, made them easy marks for clever adventurers, men who paradoxically were made rich by these nearly destitute people.

The society's rise in influence was also favored by the powerlessness of China's urban and rural populace before 1949. The masses were for the most part denied the most elementary rights; the poor were protected neither by administrative bodies nor by the law. In the circumstances, people frequently saw no choice but to entrust their fate to a sect having mysterious magical powers.

Notes

Secret Societies in China's Historical Evolution

1. B. Porchnev, *Les Soulèvements populaires en France de 1623 à 1648* (Paris, 1963); V. Lanternari, *Religions of the Oppressed: A Study of Modern Messianic Cults* (New York, 1963); P. Worsley, *The Trumpet Shall Sound* (London, 1957); W. Mühlmann, *Messianismes révolutionnaires du Tiers Monde* (Paris, 1968); S. Thrupp, *Millennial Dreams in Action* (The Hague, 1962); N. Cohn, *The Pursuit of the Millennium* (Paris, 1962); J. Le Goff, *Hérésies et sociétés dans l'Europe préindustrielle* (Paris, 1968); O. Lutaud, *Les Niveleurs* (Paris, 1967); E. Hobsbawm (in collaboration with G. Rudé), *Captain Swing* (London, 1969) and *Primitive Rebels in Modern Europe* (Paris, 1966).

2. Here, for example, is Fang Chao-ying's comment on the Boxers, as cited in Arthur W. Hummel, ed., *Eminent Chinese of the Ch'ing Period* (Washington, D.C., 1943–44), p. 407: "Led by shrewd and opportunistic rascals, these destitute and ignorant farmers began to stage riots and commit robberies."

3. There exists no good overall study of the place of secret societies in the political and social evolution of imperial China. See Vincent Shih's chapter "Some Rebel Ideologies Prior to the Taiping" in his book *The Taiping Ideology* (Seattle, 1967), pp. 329–90.

4. For the works of these and other writers mentioned in this paper, see the Bibliography, pp. 279–88.

5. Since organizations thus defined are, as it were, consubstantial with the social machine, it is not surprising to find secret societies in Chinese communities overseas. (There is a vast literature on this subject; see especially the works of L. F. Comber, S. M. Lyman, M. Topley, M. L. Wynne, and W. P. Morgan cited in the Bibliography.) Although these overseas secret societies are extremely interesting to anthropologists and sociologists, who can study them in the field in the mid-twentieth century, they are outside the bounds of this volume.

6. At a missionary conference in Shanghai in 1890, the Reverend F. H. James presented a report on secret societies in Shantung based on information supplied by one of his converts, who (as was frequently the case) was himself a former secret society member. James reported that "a large number of the Christians of that province come from these sects." He rejected the description of the secret societies as idolatrous, and concluded that *"their religious expressions indicate some advance on the three prevalent religions"* (underlined in the original). *Records of the 1890 Missionary Conference* (Shanghai, 1890), pp. 196ff.

7. Alexander Wylie, "Secret Societies in China," in *Shanghai Almanac for 1854* (Shanghai, 1854), p. 323.

8. Here I am following the table in T'ao Ch'eng-chang, "Chiao-hui yüan-liu k'ao" (Origins of the societies and sects), in Ch'ai Te-keng et al., comps., *Hsin-hai ko-ming* (The Revolution of 1911; Shanghai, 1957), vol. 3.

9. On this point, see Vincent Shih's study cited above and Yuji Muramatsu, "Some Themes in Chinese Rebel Ideologies," in Arthur F. Wright, ed., *The Confucian Persuasion* (Stanford, 1960), pp. 241–67.

10. See G. G. Dunstheimer's paper in this volume.

11. See Boris Novikov's paper in this volume.

12. See, for example, the Reverend E. H. Rottger's brochure *Geschichte der Bruderschaft des Himmels und der Erden, der kommunistischen Propaganda China's* (Berlin, 1852). Before Rottger, the well-known Gützlaff had made the same point, drawing a severe reply from Marx in *Neue rheinische Zeitung*, January 31, 1850. Marx expresses his joy at this "Chinese socialism," which, though "as different from European socialism as Chinese philosophy from the philosophy of Hegel," nonetheless "denounces the difference between rich and poor." These lines concern the Triads, and not the Taipings as some have believed: see "Ma-k'o-ssu yü T'ien-ti Hui," *Li-shih yen-chiu*, 1960, no. 5, p. 40.

13. See C. A. Curwen's paper in this volume.

14. On the continuity in ideological tradition between the secret societies and the Taiping, see Shih, chap. 11.

15. G. W. Cooke, *China, . . . 1857–1858* (London, 1859), pp. 436–41, reproduces a report to this effect by a Hanlin academician.

16. See Wakeman's paper below and the paper by J. Fass in the French edition of this volume.

17. *Ch'in-fei chi-lüeh* (Dossier on the "gold bandits"), reproduced in *Chin-tai shih tzu-liao*, 3 (1955): 147.

18. See Fass, *loc. cit.*

19. On the Nien, see the works of Chiang Siang-tseh and Teng Ssu-yü cited in the Bibliography.

20. Wang T'ien-chiang, "Shih-chiu shih-chi hsia-pan chih Chung-kuo ti mi-mi hui-she" (Secret societies in China during the second half of the nineteenth century), *Li-shih yen-chiu*, no. 2, 1963.

21. See Ho Ping-ti, *Studies on the Population of China* (Cambridge, Mass., 1959), pp. 240–46; and Mary Backus Rankin, "The Revolutionary Movement in Chekiang: A Study in the Tenacity of Tradition," in Mary Clabaugh Wright, ed., *China in Revolution: The First Phase, 1900–1913* (New Haven, Conn., 1968), pp. 321–28.

22. Fass, *loc. cit.*, points out the presence of urban workers among the Small Knives of Shanghai as early as 1853. The trend accelerated in the second half of the century; see Jean Chesneaux, *The Chinese Labor Movement, 1919–1927* (Stanford, 1968), p. 123.

23. See Ma Ch'ao-chün, "Pang-hui chih" (Origins of the *pang-hui*), in *Chung-kuo lao-tung yün-tung shih* (History of the Chinese labor movement; Chungking, 1942), pp. 74–77, on the crisis of the barge industry on the Grand Canal; and Wang T'ien-chiang, *loc. cit.*

24. Wang, *loc. cit.*; see also T'an Ssu-t'ung's denunciation of the massacring of discharged soldiers that the government wanted to get rid of in *T'an Ssu-t'ung ch'üan-chi* (Collected works of T'an Ssu-t'ung; Peking, 1954), pp. 63–64.

25. See Charlton Lewis's paper in this volume.

26. Rankin, pp. 322–25.

27. Wang, *loc. cit.*

28. Account of Père Palâtre in *Missions catholiques,* September 1878, nos. 13, 20, 21.

29. *Anti-foreign Riots in China* (Shanghai, 1892), pp. 74–75.

30. Cited in Wang, *loc. cit.*

31. These aspects were emphasized for the first time, to our knowledge, in G. G. H. Dunstheimer, "Le Mouvement des Boxeurs: Documents et études publiés depuis la deuxième guerre mondiale," *Revue historique,* 470 (April–June 1964): 387–416. Other recent works on the Boxers, notably those of Purcell, Ch'en, and Muramatsu (see Bibliography), insist as Dunstheimer does on the proto-nationalist character of the movement.

32. See, for example, Chester Tan, *The Boxer Catastrophe* (New York, 1955). Chinese intellectuals' disdain for the Boxers, as evidenced in the quotation from Fang Shao-ying in note 2 above, is also characteristic of Communist intellectuals of the early period: see Ch'en Tu-hsiu's article of 1918 cited in Hélène Carrère d'Encausse and Stuart Schram, *Le Marxisme et l'Asie* (Paris, 1965), p. 290.

33. See the articles on this strike in *Revue historique* for October 1956 and in *Li-shih yen-chiu,* 1958, no. 3.

34. Henry McAleavy, *Black Flags in Vietnam* (London, 1968), pp. 208–9, 225.

35. See Guy Puyraimond's paper in this volume.

36. L. Borodovskii, "Khungkhuzy," *Entsiklopedicheskii slovar'* (St. Petersburg, 1903), vol. 37a, book 74: 778.

37. See the volumes of *Hsin-hai ko-ming hui-i-lu* (Recollections of the Revolution of 1911), published in Peking beginning in 1961, and the memoirs of Wu Yü-chang in his *The 1911 Revolution* (Peking: Foreign Languages Press, 1964) and of Chu Teh in Agnes Smedley, *The Great Road: The Life and Times of Chu Teh* (New York, 1956).

38. See Lilia Borokh's paper in this volume and Teng Ssu-yü, "Dr. Sun Yat-sen and the Chinese Secret Societies," in Robert K. Sakai, ed., *Studies on Asia,* 4 (Lincoln, Neb., 1963).

39. The case of Chekiang is analyzed in Rankin, *loc. cit.*

40. See John Lust's paper in this volume.

41. Mary Clabaugh Wright, for example, refuses to analyze the revolution in terms of the "dynastic cycle"; see her Introduction to *China in Revolution,* p. 58.

42. As Mary Wright has shown (*ibid.,* pp. 30–44), the revolution did indeed involve "a new society in the making": newspapers, youth, women, a new kind of soldier, overseas communities, bourgeoisie, working class.

43. Lyon Sharman, *Sun Yat-Sen: His Life and Its Meaning* (New York, 1934), p. 141.

44. L. Favre, "Les Sociétés de frères jurés en Chine," *T'oung pao,* 19 (1920): 1–40.

45. *Shih-shih hsin-pao,* May 14, 1918. For other cases of strikes led by secret societies, see Chesneaux, *Chinese Labor Movement,* p. 127.

46. See Chen Po-ta, *A Study of Land Rent in Pre-Liberation China* (Peking, 1962).

47. See E. A. Belov's study in *Voprosy istorii*, 2 (1960). Belov shows that the term "White Wolf" is a misinterpretation; in fact, the leader of the revolt bore the surname Pai (white), a very common name in the northwest.

48. *China Weekly Review*, March 18, 1922; see also, in the British archives, FO 228/3273 (information kindly communicated to me by Professor Robert Kapp of Rice University).

49. *North-China Herald*, April 26, 1924.

50. See Roman Slawinski's paper in this volume.

51. See Lucien Bianco's paper in this volume.

52. On the Hsien-t'ien Ta-tao, see Marjorie Topley, "The Great Way of Former Heaven: A Group of Chinese Religious Sects," *Bulletin of the S.O.A.S.*, 26.2 (1963). On the I-kuan Tao, see Lev Deliusin's paper in this volume. On the Ta-t'ung Hui, see *Politique de Pékin*, Sept. 9 and 23, Oct. 7 and 14, 1923. The Ta-t'ung Hui preached an imminent cosmic catastrophe followed by a "great harmony" (*ta-t'ung*); in this connection it made much of the Tokyo earthquake of 1923, which provoked great uneasiness throughout the Far East. Topley mentions other sects in the general region of the Hsien-t'ien Ta-tao, notably the T'ung-shan She (Society of the Common Good). According to Wang T'ien-chiang, *loc. cit.*, the Tsai-li Hui of North China in the twentieth century "degenerated into a religious association whose sole object was to keep its members from smoking opium and drinking alcohol, and to see that they recited Buddhist prayers."

53. Information furnished by my colleague Stuart Schram.

54. See Stuart Schram, "Mao Tse-tung and the Secret Societies," *China Quarterly*, 3 (July–Sept. 1960).

55. Li Ta-chao, "Lu Yü Shan teng sheng ti Hung-ch'iang Hui" (The Red Spears in Shantung, Honan, Shensi, and other provinces), in *Li Ta-chao hsüan-chi* (Selected works of Li Ta-chao; Peking, 1959).

56. On Chu Teh's links with the Ko-lao Hui, see Smedley, *The Great Road*. On Ho Lung and Liu Chih-tan, see Edgar Snow, *Red Star Over China*, rev. ed. (New York, 1968), pp. 77, 210–13.

57. Hsi-wu Lao-jen, *Erh-ch'i hui-i-lu* (Memories of February 7; Peking, 1957), p. 32.

58. Snow, p. 332.

59. Long extracts from this appeal are reproduced in Schram's *China Quarterly* article.

60. In the former category are Sun Wu (see Wu Yü-chang, *The 1911 Revolution*, p. 58); Chü Cheng, president of the Judicial Yuan during World War II (*ibid.*); and Ch'en Ch'i-mei (Teng Ssu-yü, "Dr. Sun Yat-sen and the Secret Societies," p. 91). In the latter category the most notable member is Chiang Kai-shek; see Howard L. Boorman and Richard C. Howard, eds., *Biographical Dictionary of Republican China*, 1 (New York, 1967): 321.

61. Harold Isaacs, *The Tragedy of the Chinese Revolution*, 2d rev. ed. (Stanford, 1961), pp. 142–43.

62. Harold Isaacs, "Gang Rule in Shanghai," in *Five Years of Kuomintang Reaction* (Shanghai, 1932).

63. See Y. C. Wang, "Tu Yüeh-sheng (1888–1951): A Tentative Political Biography," *Journal of Asian Studies*, 26.3 (May 1967).

64. See W. P. Morgan, *Triad Societies in Hong Kong* (Hong Kong, 1960), p. 72, and Tadao Sakai's paper in the French edition of this volume.

65. Wang Yu-chuang, "The Organization of a Typical Guerrilla Area in South Shantung," in Evans F. Carlson, *The Chinese Army* (New York, 1940), pp. 104–6.

66. Extracts from this manual are included in Chalmers A. Johnson, *Peasant Nationalism and Communist Power* (Stanford, 1962), pp. 88–89.

67. Han Suyin, *Un Eté sans oiseaux* (Paris, 1968), p. 132. The author's family, which had links both with the local banks and with the gentry, seems to have been in close contact with the Ko-lao Hui.

68. Liao T'ai Ch'u, "The Ko-lao Hui in Szechwan," *Pacific Affairs* (June 1947).

69. This was true of some of the most influential persons in Chiang Kai-shek's entourage, among them T'ai Li, one of the chiefs of the secret service (Han Suyin, p. 94).

70. Han Suyin, p. 240.

71. Topley, p. 380.

72. The *hui* is from *hui-t'ang* or *hui-tang*, the *men* from *chiao-men*; the addition of *tao* reflects the increasing influence of new sects such as the I-kuan Tao and the Hsien-t'ien Ta-tao.

73. Report on public security reproduced in *Jen-min shou-ts'e*, 1957, pp. 81–84.

74. On the campaign against the I-kuan Tao, see Lev Deliusin's paper in this volume. Other campaigns were launched in Shenyang against the Hou-t'ien Tao (Way of Latter Heaven) and in Hankow against the Tou-mu T'an (Altar of the Bushel-Mother). The leader of the Tou-mu T'an proclaimed "emperor" an eight-year-old boy named Chu, allegedly a descendant of the Ming. *Jen-min jih-pao*, May 12, 1951, and *Ch'ang-chiang pao*, March 12, 1952.

75. This new surge of secret society activity prompted an article on the subject by Teng Hsiao-p'ing in *Jen-min jih-pao*, July 7, 1955. Once again I-kuan Tao members were hunted down all over China (Topley, *loc. cit.*). The Pai-yün Tsung-tui (White Cloud Battalion) was active in Fukien, the Ho-p'ing chih Kuang (Light of Peace) in Szechwan, the Ta Ming-Ch'ing Chün (Great Army of the Ming and Ch'ing) in Shansi; see *Fu-chien jih-pao*, July 3, 1955, *Hsin-wen jih-pao*, August 18, 1955, and *Kuang-ming jih-pao*, July 13, 1955.

76. Mary Rankin's pages on the secret societies in Chekiang (in Wright, ed., *China in Revolution*, pp. 321–28) show what is to be gained by studying secret societies in the economic and sociological context of a particular province.

77. See her paper in the French edition of this volume.

78. *Loc. cit.* (n. 19).

79. *Li-shih chiao-hsüeh*, 1957, no. 1.

80. See his paper on the Nien and the Lao-niu Hui (Old Buffalo Society) in the French edition of this volume, which draws on Li Tung-shan, *Nien-chün ko-yao* (Songs and tales of the Nien Army; Shanghai, 1960).

81. *Nien-chün ko-yao*, p. 16.

82. *Ibid.*, p. 33.

83. *Ibid.*, p. 113.

84. Quoted in Chiang Siang-tseh, *The Nien Rebellion* (Seattle, 1954), p. 15.

85. See George T. Yü, *Party Politics in Republican China: The Kuomintang, 1912–1924* (Berkeley, Calif., 1966); Yü's Chapter 5, "The Secret Society Model," is devoted to the Chung-hua Ko-ming-tang. For Chu Teh's remarks, see Smedley, *The Great Road*, p. 87: "Foreign and Chinese reactionaries charged that the cell system of the Chinese Communist Party was an alien idea imported by the Russian Bolsheviks. When I mentioned this, General Chu dismissed it as stupid if not a deliberate fabrication. . . . The cell system, he said, was as old as Chinese secret societies, and the Tung Meng Hui had taken it over from the ancient Ko Lao Hui."

Some Religious Aspects of Secret Societies

1. The term "secret society," probably arising from certain putative resemblances to Freemasonry, seems to have been of British invention. We find it, for example, in a communication delivered in 1827 by a Dr. Milne at the Royal Asiatic Society. This term appeared subsequently in numerous Western publications and was adopted by the Japanese, e.g., Hirayama Amane (Shū) in his *Chung-kuo pi-mi she-hui shih* (History of secret societies in China; Shanghai, 1912).

2. Terminology applied to secret societies is listed in Li Shih-yü, *Hsientai Hua-pei mi-mi tsung-chiao* (Contemporary secret religions in the north of China; Chengtu, 1948), p. 1. See also J. de Groot, *Sectarianism and Religious Persecution in China* (Amsterdam, 1903–4), pp. 8, 15; and Jean Chesneaux, *Les Sociétés secrètes en Chine aux XIXᵉ et XXᵉ Siècles* (Paris, 1965), p. 83. It seems that the Chinese literati were above all impressed by the heretical character of the sects, whereas it was their clandestine character that particularly interested the Westerners.

3. It has been estimated that in the nineteenth century there was one bureaucrat for every ten thousand inhabitants; see F. Michael, "State and Society in Nineteenth-Century China," in *World Politics*, 7.3 (April, 1955): 420; C. K. Yang, *Religion in Chinese Society* (Berkeley, 1961), p. 138.

4. I use the term "sect" without any of the pejorative connotations that are often associated with this term. I give it the sense of "an organized group of people who have the same doctrine inside one religion."

5. Huang Yü-pien, *P'o-hsieh hsiang-pien* (A detailed refutation of heresies; 1834). The preface discusses those sections of the *Ta-Ch'ing lü-li* dealing with heresies and illegal religions. R. A. Stein has made a thorough study of this preface and of most of Huang's first chapter; see the résumés in the *Annuaire de l'Ecole Pratique des Hautes Etudes, Section des Sciences Religieuses*, 1958–59, pp. 60–62; 1959–60, pp. 51–52.

6. J. R. Levenson, "Confucian and T'ai-p'ing Heaven," in *Comparative Studies in Society and History*, 4.4 (July 1962): 447.

7. The importance of Maitreya was not confined to northern Chinese *chiao-men*. For an account of this cult south of the Yangtze, see Marjorie Topley, "The Great Way of Former Heaven: A Group of Chinese Secret Religious Sects," in *Bulletin of the School of Oriental and African Studies*, 26.2 (1963): 362–92.

8. Yuji Muramatsu, "Some Themes in Chinese Rebel Ideologies," in *The Confucian Persuasion*, ed. A. F. Wright (Stanford, 1960), p. 247.

9. Tai Hsüan-chih, "Pai-lien-chiao ti pen-chih" (The nature of the White Lotus Society), *Shih ta-hsüeh pao* (Bulletin of the University of the Capital), 24. 1 (1962): 119.

10. *Ibid.*

11. J. Ch'en, "The Nature and Characteristics of the Boxer Movement: A Morphological Study," *Bulletin of the School of Oriental and African Studies*, 23.2 (1960): 292, n. 1.

12. W. A. Grootaers, "Une Séance de spiritisme dans une religion secrète à Péking en 1948," *Mélanges chinois et bouddhiques*, 9 (1948–51): 96, n. 1.

13. Liu I-t'ung, "Min-chiao hsiang-ch'ou tu-men wen-chien-lu" (Collected observations on the hostilities between the Chinese and the converts), in *I-ho T'uan* (The Boxers; Shanghai, 1951), 2: 188.

14. Yuji Muramatsu, p. 268.

15. *Ibid.*

16. Tai Hsüan-chih, p. 119. Tai's article begins with a brief résumé of the different religious groups that helped form the doctrine of the White Lotus Society.

17. *Ibid.*

18. That adherence did not prevent him from outlawing the White Lotus Society, any more than it prevented the latter from revolting against the mandarinate of the new dynasty.

19. Kenneth Ch'en, *Buddhism in China* (Princeton, 1964), pp. 297–300.

20. Edouard Chavannes and Paul Pelliot, "Un traité manichéen retrouvé en Chine," *Journal Asiatique*, 1913, pp. 138–40.

21. *Ku-fo t'ien-chen k'ao-cheng Lung-hua pao-ching* (Precious sutra of Lung-hua, revised by the Ancient Buddha of Heavenly Reality), abridged to *Lung-hua pao-ching*. Cf. Huang Yü-pien, 1: 1a–15a. The sutra is cited in Fu Hsi-hua, *Catalogue des baojuan* (Centre d'études sinologiques de Pékin, 1951), p. 19. A re-edition of the sutra appeared in Peking in 1918. Sitting at the foot of the tree of Lung-hua, Mi-le-fo obtained illumination. According to the sutra mentioned, it is under this tree that the assemblies for the salvation of humanity are held.

22. Li Shih-yü, p. 46; cf. Topley, pp. 371–74.

23. Topley, p. 374.

24. Huang Yü-pien, 1: 2a.

25. "The Unexcelled *wu-chi*! And yet the Supreme *t'ai-chi*!" says Chou Tun-i.

26. Huang Yü-pien, 1: 2a.

27. *Ibid.*, p. 13b.

28. *Tao-tö king*, trans. and ed. J. J. L. Duyvendak (Paris, 1953), 6: 3.

29. "Original elements," according to Topley, p. 373. In the vocabulary of modern chemistry, *yüan-tzu* designates "atom." A semantic slip seems to have occurred that led these sects to attach a great importance to the H-bomb.

30. Li Shih-yü (p. 47) and Topley (p. 373) mention only nine million of these beings: "They became corrupted by men and could not return to the Void."

31. Li Shih-yü, p. 47.

32. *Ibid.*, p. 48.

33. *Ibid.*, p. 47.

34. Huang Yü-pien, 1: 2b–3a. The I-kuan Tao also employed the designation *huang t'ai*. Cf. Li Shih-yü, p. 47.

35. Huang Yü-pien, 1: 12a–12b. According to De Groot (pp. 351 and 353), a certain Chen Chin-yü proclaimed that Maitreya would be reborn in the Wu-ying mountains. In 1791 the Emperor ordered that measures be taken against the sects, especially in the region of the sub-prefecture of Teng-feng in Honan, "where the Wu-ying mountains lie."

36. Li Shih-yü, p. 91.

37. *Ibid.*, pp. 91–93.

38. Grootaers (p. 94) contains an account of a soothsayer's séance held in 1948: "The better part of his discourse," says the author, "was devoted to contemporary events, precursors of the final cataclysm; one felt that it would have not taken much to turn this séance into a political meeting."

39. Other religious aspects of the sects, which included meditative concentration, prophecy, and syncretism, will be treated in later studies.

The Secret Societies of Kwangtung, 1800–1856

1. Sasaki Masaya, *"Hsien-feng shinen Kuang-tung T'ien Ti-hui no han-ran"* (The Cantonese Triad insurrection of the fourth year of Hsien-feng), *Kindai Chūgoku kenkyū Sentā ihō*, 2 (Apr. 1963): 1–2.

2. Charles Gützlaff, *China Opened; or, A Display of the Topography, etc., of the Chinese Empire* (London, 1838), 1: 137; *Chinese Repository*, 4 (May 1835–Apr. 1836): 193. Here, and later in this paper, I have not bothered to document background material that is covered in my book *Strangers at the Gate: Social Disorder in South China, 1839–1861* (Berkeley, Calif., 1966).

3. FO 17/227, Desp. 86, Feb. 14, 1855; FO 17/228, Desp. 108, Feb. 28, 1855 ("FO" numbers refer to British Foreign Office archives on file in the Public Record Office, London); Yen-yu Huang, "Viceroy Yeh Ming-ch'en and the Canton Episode (1858–1861)," *Harvard Journal of Asiatic Studies*, 6 (Mar. 1941): 53, nn. 36 and 54.

4. "In the districts where such heads of heresies live, their followers fill the functions of yamen-servants, and act as their spies about what is going on." Imperial decree of March 1851, cited in J. J. M. de Groot, *Sectarianism and Religious Persecution in China: A Page in the History of Religions* (Amsterdam, 1904), 2: 548. Minor bureaucrats are also singled out as Triads in an important memorial by Tseng Wang-yen, at the time of the writing in his seventies and a prestigious member of the Hanlin Academy with Cantonese origins (Hsiang-shan hsien). Tseng, of course, was mayor of Peking during the Opium War, and severely anti-foreign. I have used a translation of his memorial prepared by Wade, Chinese Secretary at Canton in 1855 (FO 17/234, Incl. 1 in Desp. 331, Oct. 12, 1855). The Chinese original can be found in Peking University, Wen-k'o Yen-chiu-so, comp., *T'ai-p'ing t'ien-kuo shih-liao* (Historical materials of the Taiping Heavenly Kingdom; Peking, 1950), pp. 523–27.

5. Ch'en Po-t'ao, ed., *Tung-kuan hsien-chih* (Gazetteer of Tung-kuan hsien; 1919), ch. 35: 13a (hereafter cited as TKHC); FO 228/270, Incl. 2 in Desp. 4, Nov. 8, 1859.

6. Shih Ch'eng, ed., *Kuang-chou fu-chih* (Gazetteer of Kuang-chou prefecture; 1879), 81: 14a–21a (hereafter cited as KCFC); TKHC, 33: 25a; Cheng Meng-yü, ed., *Hsü hsiu nan-hai hsien chih* (Revised gazetteer of Nan-hai hsien; 1872), ch. 14: 19b, 38a, ch. 15: 8a, 10a (hereafter cited as NHHC); T'ien Ming-yüeh, ed., *Hsiang-shan hsien-chih* (Gazetteer of Hsiang-shan hsien; 1879), ch. 14: 44a, ch. 19: 19b, ch. 20:5b (hereafter cited as HSHC); Miyazaki Ichisada, "The Nature of Taiping Rebellion," *Acta Asiatica*, 8 (Mar. 1965): 1–39.

7. See Laai Yi-faai's carefully researched study, "The Part Played by the Pirates of Kwangtung and Kwangsi Provinces in the T'ai-p'ing Insurrection" (Ph.D. diss., University of California, Berkeley, 1950), pp. 13–15. Also Chou Ch'ao-huai, ed., *Shun-te hsien-chih* (Gazetteer of Shun-te hsien; 1929), ch. 23: 8a (hereafter cited as STHC); Grace Fox, *British Admirals and Chinese Pirates, 1832–1869* (London, 1940), pp. 102–26; HSHC, ch. 15: 35a.

8. Hsiao I-shan, *Ch'ing-tai t'ung-shih* (A complete history of the Ch'ing dynasty; Taipei, 1963), 3: 4–5.

9. Sasaki Masaya, "*Hsien-feng shinen*," pp. 1–2; TKHC, ch. 33: 20a–20b; STHC, ch. 23: 3b.

10. Henri Cordier, *Les Sociétés secrètes chinoises* (Paris, 1888), p. 4.

11. For a full account of this, see Wei Yüan, *Sheng-wu chi* (A record of imperial military exploits; photolithographic reprint, Taipei, 1963), ch. 7: 41a–45a.

12. *Chinese Repository* (May 1832–Apr. 1833): 80; KCFC, ch. 81: 30a.

13. Hsia Hsieh, *Yüeh-fen chi-shih* (A record of the miasma in Kwangtung; 1869), ch. 1: 2a.

14. TKHC, ch. 34: 22a–b.

15. KCFC, ch. 81: 42b; HSHC, ch. 15: 33a; Tseng Wang-yen's memorial (see note 4). For a description of the Hong Kong Triads' officers and initiation (which corresponds precisely to Tseng Wang-yen's insofar as he mentions such details), see W. P. Morgan, *Triad Societies in Hong Kong* (Hong Kong, 1960), pp. 99–104, 190–278. On July 22, 1845, the Emperor noted the Shun-te feud and commented on the unwillingness of local officials to investigate the matter. See *Tung-hua ch'üan-lu* (Complete records of the Tung-hua [gate]; photolithographic reprint, Taipei, 1963), Tao-kuang, ch. 12: 4b–5a.

16. Gunther Barth, *Bitter Strength: A History of the Chinese in the United States, 1850–1870* (Cambridge, Mass., 1964); Maurice Freedman, "Immigrants and Associations: Chinese in Nineteenth-Century Singapore," *Comparative Studies in Society and History*, 3.1 (Oct. 1960): 25–48; Stanford M. Lyman, "Chinese Secret Societies in the Occident: Notes and Suggestions for Research in the Sociology of Secrecy," *Canadian Review of Sociology and Anthropology*, 1.2 (1964): 79–102, and "Rules of a Chinese Secret Society in British Columbia," *Bulletin of the School of Oriental and African Studies*, 27.3 (1964): 530–39; Morgan, *Triad Societies in Hong Kong*; G. William Skinner, *Chinese Society in Thailand: An Analytical History* (Ithaca, N.Y.,

1957), and *Leadership and Power in the Chinese Community of Thailand* (Ithaca, N.Y., 1958); Victor Purcell, *The Chinese in Malaya* (London, 1948), p. 143.

17. Daniel Kulp, *Country Life in South China: The Sociology of Familism*, vol. 1, *Phenix Village, Kwangtung, China* (New York, 1925), pp. 114–15.

18. NHHC, ch. 17: 10a; STHC, ch. 22: 18b.

19. Marion J. Levy, Jr., *The Family Revolution in Modern China* (Cambridge, Mass., 1949), pp. 82–83.

20. See Simmel's discussion of secrecy in Kurt H. Wolff, trans. and ed., *The Sociology of Georg Simmel* (Glencoe, Ill., 1950).

21. Li Tsun-i, *Hsing-i wu-hsing ch'üan* (The five boxing styles of Hsing-i; Taipei, 1963), p. 1.

22. In Macao even today, the town's largest temple to Kuan-yin, the P'u-chi Chuan-yüan, has an especially large and airy room reserved for the temple boxers' workouts.

23. HSHC, ch. 15: 36a.

24. FO 228/158, Desp. 141, Parkes–Bonham, Oct. 8, 1853.

25. FO 17/214, Desp. 67, Bowring–Clarendon, June 27, 1854.

26. Tseng Wang-yen's memorial (see note 4); HSHC, ch. 15: 31a, 33a.

27. Tseng's memorial; KCFC, ch. 81: 42b; HSHC, ch. 15: 33a; *Tung-hua ch'üan-lu*, Tao-kuang, ch. 12: 4b–5a.

28. *Tung-hua ch'üan-lu*, Tao-kuang, ch. 12: 20ab.

29. NHHC, ch. 17: 6a.

30. TKHC, ch. 70: 7a.

31. Ch'en K'un, *Yüeh-tung chiao-fei lüeh* (An outline of the pacification of the bandits of eastern Kwangtung; 1871), 1: 1a–18a; Li Wen-chih et al., comps., *Chung-kuo chin-tai nung-yeh shih tzu-liao* (Historical materials on modern Chinese agriculture; Peking, 1957), 1: 451, 506; Hatano Yoshihiro, "Taihei Tengoku ni kansuru nisan no mondai ni tsuite" (On some questions concerning the Taiping Heavenly Kingdom), *Rekishigaku kenkyū*, 150 (Mar. 1951): 34.

32. Laai Yi-faai, "Pirates of Kwangtung and Kwangsi," pp. 209–19.

33. Ch'en K'un, *Yüeh-tung chiao-fei lüeh*, ch. 1: 1a–18a; FO 228/113, Incl. 1 in Desp. 97, Aug. 16, 1850, Desp. 112, Sept. 3, 1850; FO 228/126, inclosures in Desp. 9, Jan. 7, 1851; FO 228/127, Incl. 1 in Desp. 114, July 12, 1851, Desp. 97, June 14, 1851, Desp. 117, July 14, 1851, Desp. 143, Aug. 26, 1851, Desp. 152, Sept. 26, 1851, Desp. 174, Oct. 25, 1851, Desp. 192, Nov. 27, 1851.

34. FO 17/188, Incl. 1 in Desp. 42, Mar. 29, 1842; FO 228/143, Incl. 1 in Desp. 111, July 21, 1852, Desp. 116, Aug. 10, 1852.

35. FO 17/191, Incl. 1 in Desp. 84, July 22, 1852.

36. Liang Ting-fen, ed., *P'an-yü hsien hsü-chih* (Revised gazetteer of P'an-yü hsien; 1931), ch. 19: 23b (hereafter cited as PYHC); Liang Chia-pin, *Kuang-tung shih-san-hang k'ao* (The hong merchants of Canton; 2d ed., Taipei, 1960), p. 263.

37. FO 17/190, Incl. 2 in Desp. 57, June 19, 1852; FO 17/191, Incl. 1 in Desp. 84, July 22, 1852; FO 17/199, Desp. 16, Jan. 27, 1853; FO 228/156, Desp. 44, Apr. 14, 1853.

38. FO 228/126, Incl. 1 in Desp. 57, Mar. 17, 1851, Desp. 64, Apr. 19, 1851; FO 17/193, Desp. 157, Nov. 11, 1852.

39. FO 17/153, Incl. 1 in Desp. 6, Jan. 12, 1849; FO 17/154, undated inclosures in Desp. 50; FO 17/191, Incl. 1 in Desp. 84, July 22, 1852; FO 17/203, Desp. 63, July 6, 1853.

40. NHHC, 17: 16a; FO 17/154, Incl. 1 in Desp. 149, June 19, 1849; FO 17/193, Desp. 157, Nov. 11, 1852, Desp. 166, Nov. 27, 1852.

41. Unless otherwise noted, my basic sources for the account of the Red Turban revolt are KCFC, ch. 82: 3b–24a, and Ch'en K'un, *Yüeh-tung chiao-fei lüeh*, ch. 1: 17b to ch. 2: 1a. The two basically agree, although there are occasional discrepancies (e.g., KCFC gives July 4 as the date Fatshan was captured, Ch'en K'un July 5). Ch'en K'un's account is much more detailed when it comes to listing military contingents. Both, however, are rather dry and uninspired chronicles.

42. FO 228/156, Desp. 54, Apr. 20, 1853; FO 17/202, Incl. 2 in Desp. 47, May 27, 1853; FO 228/157, Incl. 1 in Desp. 85, June 17, 1853; FO 228/158, Desp. 141, Oct. 8, 1853, Desp. 160, Nov. 9, 1853, Desp. 170, Nov. 25, 1853, Desp. 180, Dec. 24, 1853; FO 228/172, Incl. 1 in Desp. 5, Jan. 9, 1854, Incl. 1 in Desp. 16, Jan. 25, 1854; Sasaki Masaya, "Hsien-feng shinen," p. 8; J. Scarth, *Twelve Years in China: The People, the Rebels and the Mandarins* (Edinburgh, 1860), pp. 235–40.

43. Sasaki Masaya, "*Hsien-feng* shinen," p. 9. For a chronicle of each local revolt, see the appendix to Wakeman, *Strangers at the Gate*.

44. Ch'en K'un, *Yüeh-tung chiao-fei lüeh*, ch. 1: 20b–21a.

45. NHHC, ch. 17: 10a.

46. PYHC, ch. 21: 6a; NHHC, ch. 19: 10a; TKHC, ch. 72: 8b; STHC, ch. 20: 12b, ch. 23: 6a.

47. FO 17/215, Incl. 1 in Desp. 112, Aug. 5, 1854; FO 17/216, Incl. 1 in Desp. 135, Aug. 31, 1854, Incl. 1 in Desp. 142, Sept. 8, 1854.

48. STHC, ch. 18: 11b, ch. 23: 6b.

49. NHHC, ch. 13: 40a, ch. 17: 13a–15b; FO 17/215, Incl. 1 in Desp. 112, July 20, 1854; FO 17/226, Incl. 1 in Desp. 33, Jan. 15, 1855, Desp. 36, Jan. 19, 1855, Desp. 39, Jan. 20, 1855; FO 17/225, Incl. 1 in Desp. 87, Feb. 14, 1855.

50. STHC, ch. 23: 6a.

51. Rebel proclamation, translated by Caldwell, in FO 17/215, Incl. 1 in Desp. 123, Aug. 26, 1854.

52. FO 17/215, Incl. 1 in Desp. 112, Aug. 5, 1854.

53. HSHC, ch. 15: 16b.

54. STHC, ch. 20: 14a, ch. 21: 6a, ch. 23: 6a; PYHC, ch. 24: 18b.

55. NHHC, ch. 15: 12a; Chien Yu-wen, *T'ai-p'ing t'ien-kuo ch'üan-shih* (A complete history of the Taiping Heavenly Kingdom; Hong Kong, 1962), 2: 824.

56. TKHC, ch. 35: 5a, 6b, ch. 72: 7b; NHHC, ch. 14: 12a, ch. 17: 7a, 14, 17a; STHC, ch. 15: 15b, ch. 18: 10a, 13b, ch. 19: 3a; HSHC, ch. 15: 21, 24a–b, 39b; PYHC, ch. 19: 9a, ch. 20: 19a, ch. 22: 10b, 19a–b, 21b, ch. 24: 13b, 16b, ch. 26: 15a.

57. NHHC, ch. 21: 4b; Sasaki Masaya. "*Shun-te hsien* kyoshin to tokai

jurokusa" (The gentry of Shun-te hsien and the sixteen delta lands of the Eastern Sea), *Kindai Chūgoku kenkyū*, 3 (1963): 173.

58. NHHC, ch. 19: 21a.

59. There were many cases of this. See, for example, NHHC, ch. 17: 14a, 15a; STHC, ch. 17: 3a.

60. Ch'en K'un, *Yüeh-tung chiao-fei lüeh*, ch. 2: 1a. For Yeh Ming-ch'en's memorials to the Emperor reporting these successive victories, see *Ta-Ch'ing li-ch'ao shih-lu* (Veritable records of successive reigns of the Ch'ing dynasty; photolithographic edition of the Manchukuo Council of State Affairs, 1937), Hsien-feng, ch. 167: 1b–2b, 12b–16a, ch. 169: 20b–21a.

61. STHC, ch. 23: 7a; FO 17/235, Incl. 1 in Desp. 368, Nov. 13, 1855; FO 17/250, Incl. 1 in Desp. 282, Sept. 11, 1856. Ch'en K'un devotes the last three *chüan* of his book to the final suppression of the hill bands.

62. NHHC, ch. 17: 13a, ch. 19: 20a; STHC, ch. 3: 5a–6b, ch. 17: 9b, ch. 18: 6ab, 13a, 14b; PYHC, ch. 22: 20a, ch. 25: 2a; *Tung-hua ch'üan-lu*, Hsien-feng, ch. 35: 13b; Sasaki Masaya, "Shun-te hsien," p. 174.

63. George Wingrove Cooke, *China: Being the Times' Special Correspondence from China in the Years 1857–1858* (London, 1858), pp. 406–7; FO 17/231, Incl. in Desp. 208, June 8, 1855; FO 17/233, Desp. 297, Sept. 13, 1855; FO 17/235, Incl. 1 in Desp. 368, Nov. 13, 1855; FO 17/249, Incl. 1 in Desp. 251, Aug. 8, 1856.

64. Sun Yat-sen is cited in Hsiao I-shan, ed., *Chin-tai pi-mi she-hui shih-liao* (Historical materials on modern secret societies; Peking, 1935), p. 3a (Preface).

65. A recent study of the 1911 revolution in Kwangtung shows the lack of continuity in terms of both organization and ideology between the Triad leaders of the Waichow Rebellion of 1900 and the T'ung-meng Hui revolutionaries of 1911. See Winston Hsieh, "The Revolution of 1911 in Kwangtung" (Ph.D. diss., Harvard University, 1969), chap. 2, and Professor Hsieh's paper in this volume.

The Anti-Manchu Propaganda of the Triads, ca. 1800–1860

1. Notable among these documents are those contained in Hsiao I-shan's *Chin-tai pi-mi she-hui shih-liao* (Historical materials on modern secret societies; Peking, 1935), hereafter cited as CTSL. Most of these documents were written in Fukien and concern especially the first half of the nineteenth century. Certain manuscripts of the T'ien-ti Hui in Kwangtung were found in 1863 in the house of a Chinese settler of Padang, Sumatra, and were published by the Dutch Sinologist G. Schlegel in his *Thian-Ti-Hwui* (Batavia, 1866). The documents collected by Lo Erh-kang in his *T'ien-ti Hui wen-hsien lu* (Documents of the Heaven and Earth Society; Shanghai, 1947), hereafter TTH, deal with the period of the Taiping Rebellion. One of these texts survives to us from the rebel state of Ta-ch'eng Kuo (Kingdom of Great Achievement) founded in Kwangsi by supporters of the T'ien-ti Hui. This collection also includes a long manuscript originating in Canton. Documents originating in various regions (Kiangsu, Yunnan, Szechwan) are contained in Chu Lin's *Hung Men chih* (An account of the Hung Men; Shanghai, 1947), hereafter HMC.

2. Sun Yat-sen, *Selected Works* (Moscow, 1964), p. 261. In the Chinese edition, *Sun Chung-shan hsüan-chi* (Peking, 1956), see p. 171.

3. CTSL, ch. 2, appendix: 2b.

4. See *ibid.*, ch. 1: 3b, 7b, 10a–18a, 26a, 29a, 31b, 35b, 36b; TTH, pp. 4–5; HMC, pp. 44–48, 51–59, 122; Schlegel, *Thian-Ti-Hwui*, pp. 34– 36, 39, 41, 42, 44, 45, and Illustrations II, VII, IX, XI, XIII, XV.

5. TTH, p. 47.

6. Another version has "Fu-te."

7. CTSL, ch. 4: 29a.

8. *Ibid.*, ch. 5: 30a; TTH, p. 5; Schlegel, p. 149.

9. CTSL, ch. 6: 126; Schlegel, p. 215.

10. CTSL, ch. 4: 3a, 15b; Schlegel, p. 60.

11. CTSL, ch. 5: 20a. The same motivation can be found in other texts; for instance, CTSL, ch. 1: 13b, ch. 4: 3b, 7b, 15a, ch. 5: 21b, 28a; TTH, pp. 25, 47, 52; Schlegel, p. 208.

12. See CTSL, ch. 1: 9b, ch. 4: 3ab, 13b, 15a, 25a, 27b, 29b, ch. 5: 20a, 22a, 22b, 24b, 26b, 27a, 32a; TTH, pp. 13, 33, 49; Schlegel, pp. 73, 76, 227.

13. CTSL, ch. 6: 15a; Schlegel, p. 176.

14. See CTSL, ch. 1: 8b, 9a, 11b, 12a, 14b, 15b, 16b, 18a, 22a, 22b, 23a, 31b, ch. 4: 2b, 3a, 9b, 10b, 13b, 14a, 21b, 25b, 29b, 32a, ch. 5: 1b, 2b, 3a, 3b, 10b, 14a, 16b, 18a, 20a, 22b, 24a, 28a, 30b, 35a, ch. 6: 7b, 8a, 10a, 15a; TTH, pp. 7, 8, 17, 46, 48, 50; Schlegel, pp. 39, 42, 67, 70, 80, 82, 99, 113, 174–76, 214, 218, etc.

15. CTSL, ch. 4: 156, ch. 6: 14a; Schlegel, p. 60.

16. CTSL, ch. 5: 31b.

17. This document was found in Macao in 1828 and is published in R. Morrison, "A Transcript in Roman Characters, with Translation, of a Manifesto in the Chinese Language, Issued by the Triad Society," *The Journal of the Royal Asiatic Society of Great Britain and Ireland*, 1 (London, 1834): 94–95.

18. Schlegel, p. 99.

19. CTSL, ch. 4: 20b.

20. HMC, p. 200.

21. *Chung-kuo chin-tai shih ts'an-k'ao t'u-p'ien chi*; (Illustrations for the study of modern Chinese history; Peking, 1953), p. 16.

22. CTSL, ch. 4: 16a.

23. Schlegel, p. 174.

24. *Ibid.*, pp. 108, 185.

25. CTSL, ch. 5: 39a.

26. TTH, p. 54.

27. Karl Marx, *Le 18 brumaire de Louis Bonaparte* (Paris, 1969), p. 15.

28. Schlegel, p. 190.

29. CTSL, ch. 5: 18a.

Taiping Relations with Secret Societies and with Other Rebels

1. Chung Wen-tien, *T'ai-p'ing-chün tsai Yung-an* (The Taipings at Yung-an; Peking, 1962), p. 162.

2. Liang Jen-pao, "Chin-t'ien ch'i-i ch'ien Kuang-hsi-ti nung-min ch'i-i"

(Peasant risings in Kwangsi prior to the Chin-t'ien rising), *Li-shih chiao-hsüeh*, 1957, no. 1, pp. 14–18.

3. *P'ing-Kuei chi-lüeh* (Account of the pacification of Kwangsi), *T'ang-fei tsung-lu* (A complete record of "T'ang" Bandits), *Ku-fei tsung lu* (A complete record of "Ku" Bandits), and *Kuang-hsi chao-chung lu* (Record of loyal luminaries of Kwangsi). Hsieh Hsing-yao's work (see note 6 below) is based mainly on these.

4. Vincent Y. C. Shih, *The Taiping Ideology, Its Sources, Interpretations, and Influences* (Seattle and London, 1967), p. 296: "One might even assume that their [popular novels'] influence reached the Taipings directly through the secret societies."

5. Jen Yu-wen, *T'ai-p'ing T'ien-kuo tien-chih t'ung-k'ao* (A study of Taiping institutions; Hong Kong, 1962), 2: 1190–91.

6. On the social characteristics of Hakka women, see Lo Hsiang-lin, *K'o-chia yen-chiu tao-lun* (Introductory studies on the Hakka; Hsin-ning, 1933), pp. 241–43. There were several women at the head of secret society risings in Kwangsi and Hunan in this period; see Hsieh Hsing-yao, *T'ai-p'ing T'ien-kuo ko-ming ch'ien-hou Kuang-hsi fan-Ch'ing yün-tung* (The anti-Ch'ing movement in Kwangsi before and after the Taiping Rebellion; Peking, 1950), *passim*.

7. Hsieh Hsing-yao, p. 32.

8. Shih (pp. 296–303) has a brief discussion of this topic.

9. Theodore Hamberg, *The Visions of Hung Siu-tshuen and the Origin of the Kwang-si Insurrection* (Hong Kong, 1854). Hamberg was a missionary who got his information from Hsiu-ch'üan's cousin Hung Jen-kan.

10. *T'ai-p'ing T'ien-kuo ch'i-i tiao-ch'a pao-kao* (Report of investigations into the Taiping rising; Peking, 1956), pp. 84–85.

11. See Hamberg. Li Hsiu-ch'eng, in the deposition he wrote after his capture in 1860, has a slightly different account, suggesting that the bandit leaders refused to join the Taipings because "they were not very strong and unlikely to come to anything." See *Li Hsiu-ch'eng ch'in-kung shou-chi* (Facsimile of Li Hsiu-ch'eng's autographic deposition; Taipei, 1962), p. 5, translated in my unpublished thesis "The Deposition of Li Hsiu-ch'eng" (London University, 1968), 1: 134.

12. Chung Wen-tien, p. 166.

13. *Kuei-p'ing hsien-chih* (Gazetteer of Kuei-ping hsien), quoted in Jen Yu-wen, *T'ai-p'ing T'ien-kuo ch'üan-shih* (A complete history of the Taiping Heavenly Kingdom), 1: 135. See also *T'ai-p'ing T'ien-kuo ch'i-i tiao-ch'a pao-kao*, p. 39.

14. For a survey of opinions on this subject see Teng Ssu-yü, *New Light on the History of the Taiping Rebellion* (Cambridge, Mass., 1950), pp. 20–24. The most detailed discussions are: Lo Erh-kang, "Hung Ta-ch'üan k'ao" (Study of Hung Ta-ch'üan), *T'ai-p'ing T'ien-kuo shih-shih k'ao* (Historical studies on the Taipings; hereafter TPTKSSK; Peking, 1955), pp. 75–185; Jung Meng-yüan, "T'ien-ti Hui ling-hsiu Hung Ta-ch'üan" (The Heaven and Earth Society leader Hung Ta-ch'üan), in *T'ai-p'ing T'ien-kuo ko-ming yün-tung lun-wen chi* (Essays on the Taiping revolutionary movement; Peking, 1950), pp. 77–119; Hsieh Hsing-yao, "T'ien-te Wang Hung Ta-ch'üan chuan" (Biography of the T'ien-te Wang Hung Ta-ch'üan), in his *T'ai-p'ing*

T'ien-kuo shih-shih lun-ts'ung (Collection of essays on Taiping history; Shanghai, 1935), pp. 125–36.

15. Ming-hsin tao-jen (pseud.), *Fa-ni ch'u-chi* (A preliminary record of the long-haired rebels), in Chung-kuo chin-tai-shih tzu-liao ts'ung-k'an (Materials on modern Chinese history), *T'ai-p'ing T'ien-kuo* (hereafter, TPTK; Shanghai, 1952), 4: 455.

16. This is Lo Erh-kang's view (see below); he believes that an unimportant prisoner was taken and the evidence forged in order to win merit.

17. See Lo Erh-kang, pp. 180–81.

18. P'eng Tse-i, "Kuan-yü Hung Ta-ch'üan ti li-shih wen-t'i" (On the problem of Hung Ta-ch'üan), *Li-shih yen-chiu*, 1957, no. 9, pp. 49–54.

19. In *Ch'in-ting chiao-p'ing Yüeh-fei fang lüeh* (Strategy in suppressing the Yüeh rebels; 1872), ch. 4.

20. See TPTK, 4: 431–49. The authenticity of this work was strongly challenged by Lo Erh-kang; see his *T'ai-p'ing T'ien-kuo shih-liao pien-wei chi* (Collection of studies on the authenticity of Taiping materials), pp. 5–37.

21. In the *Shih-lu* (Veritable records) and the *Tung-hua hsü-lu* (Supplementary transcriptions of archives from the Tung-hua Gate), for instance.

22. T. T. Meadows, *The Chinese and Their Rebellions* (London, 1856), p. 157.

23. See the revealing memorial of Tseng Wang-yen in Chin Yü-fu et al., eds., *T'ai-p'ing T'ien-kuo shih-liao* (Historical materials on the Taipings; Peking, 1959), pp. 500–504. There is an English translation of the memorial in G. Wingrove Cooke, *China in 1857–1858* (London, 1858), pp. 434–45.

24. T'ao Ch'eng-chang, *Chiao-hui yüan-liu k'ao* (Origins of the societies and sects), in Ch'ai Te-keng et al., comps., *Hsin-hai ko-ming* (Shanghai, 1957), 3: 99–100.

25. F.O.682/137/6, Public Record Office, London.

26. Hua Kang, *T'ai-p'ing T'ien-kuo ko-ming chan-cheng shih* (History of the Taiping Revolutionary War; Shanghai, 1949), p. 80 n.

27. See, for instance, Teng Ssu-yü, *New Light on the Taiping Rebellion*.

28. See F.O.682/1968/4, Public Record Office, London.

29. Teng Ssu-yü, p. 26.

30. In the *Chinese Repository, North-China Herald, China Mail*, and *Friend of China*, for instance; particularly the articles by "Enquirer" (A. P. Happer) in the *Overland China Mail*, No. 76 (Aug. 23, 1853) and No. 84 (Dec. 27, 1853).

31. TPTK, 1: 160, 167 note 3.

32. See Mao I-heng, "T'ai-p'ing T'ien-kuo yü T'ien-ti Hui" (The Taipings and the Heaven and Earth Society), in *Shen-pao yüeh-k'an* (Shen-pao monthly), 4.1 (Jan. 1953): 169–73; and Jung Meng-yüan, "T'ien-ti Hui ling-hsiu Hung Ta-ch'üan."

33. *Li Hsiu-ch'eng ch'in-kung shou-chi*, p. 8.

34. See several documents in the F.O.682 series in the Public Record Office, London.

35. Both Lo Erh-kang and Jen Yu-wen tend to do this.

36. F.O.682/253/A3, Public Record Office, London.

37. F.O.682/340B/12, Public Record Office, London.

38. *Overland Friend of China*, Supplement, July 7, 1853.
39. *Tung-kuan hsien-chih* (Tung-kuan hsien gazetteer; 1921), ch. 35: 4a.
40. F.O.682/378B1, Public Record Office, London.
41. Jen Yu-wen, 2: 962b.
42. *Ibid.*, p. 950a.
43. This is clear from their proclamations, some of which are in the F.O.682 series, Public Record Office, London.
44. The Taiping ban on alcohol does not seem to have been applied strictly in Shih Ta-k'ai's army: "some of his officers, Canton men, drink a little at meals." From an account given by an Irishman in Taiping service, *Friend of China*, Supplement, Jan. 30, 1857.
45. The painting is reproduced in *T'ai-p'ing T'ien-kuo wen-wu t'u-lu pu-pien* (Supplementary collection of Taiping cultural relics; Shanghai, 1955) and discussed in Lo Erh-kang, *T'ai-p'ing T'ien-kuo shih-chi tiao-ch'a chi* (Record of investigation into historical traces of the Taipings; Peking, 1958), pp. 89–104.
46. *Li Hsiu-ch'eng ch'in-kung shou-chi*, p. 40.
47. According to an article by I. J. Roberts in the *North-China Herald*, October 1, 1853.
48. Lin-le (A. F. Lindley), *Ti-Ping Tien-Kwoh, the History of the Ti-Ping Revolution* (London, 1866), p. 169.
49. F.O.17/414, quoted in full in J. S. Gregory, *Great Britain and the Taipings*, London, 1969, pp. 177–89.
50. Lin-le, p. 169.
51. Jen Yu-wen, 1: 685–95 and Lo Erh-kang, "T'ai-p'ing T'ien-kuo yü T'ien-ti Hui kuan-hsi k'ao-shih" (Study of Taiping relations with the T'ien-ti Hui), in TPTKSSK, pp. 34–74.
52. *Ibid.*
53. F.O.682/378/B1.
54. See Chiang Ti's *Ch'u-ch'i Nien-chün shih lun-ts'ung* (Historical essays on the early stage of the Nien Army; Peking, 1956, 1959), pp. 1–38, and his "Lun T'ai-p'ing T'ien-kuo yü Nien-chün ti kuan-hsi" (On relations between the Taipings and the Nien Army), *Li-shih yen-chiu*, 1963, no. 3, pp. 65–86; and Teng Ssu-yü, *The Nien Army and Their Guerilla Warfare, 1858–1868* (Paris, 1961), p. 46.
55. Chiang Ti, "Lun T'ai-p'ing," p. 73.
56. *Li Hsiu-ch'eng ch'in-kung shou-chi*, p. 17.
57. *Ibid.*, p. 40, and *Li Hsiu-ch'eng chih Chang Lo-hsing shu* (Letter from Li Hsiu-ch'eng to Chang Lo-hsing), in TPTK, 2: 721–22.
58. Chang Lo-hsing's deposition was printed in *Kuang-ming jih-pao*, Oct. 10, 1962.
59. *Li Hsiu-ch'eng ch'in-kung shou-chi*, p. 40.
60. Tao k'ou yü-sheng (pseud.), *Pei-lu chi-lüeh* (A record of capture), in *T'ai-p'ing T'ien-kuo tzu-liao* (Historical materials on the Taipings; Peking, 1959), p. 214.
61. Quoted in Teng Ssu-yü, *The Nien Army*, p. 98.
62. Whether this army should be considered a continuation of the Taiping movement or of the Nien has been the subject of some controversy; see Lo Erh-kang, *T'ai-p'ing T'ien-kuo hsin-chün ti yün-tung chan* (The

mobile warfare of the New Taiping Army; Shanghai, 1955), and **Chiang Ti**'s article in *Li-shih yen-chiu.*

63. Hsü Yao-kuang, *T'an Che* (On Chekiang), in TPTK, 6: 602.

64. Chao Chih-lien, "Chin-ch'ien Hui so-chi" (Brief notes on the Golden Coin Society), in *Chin-ch'ien Hui tzu-liao* (Materials on the Golden Coin Society; Shanghai, 1958), p. 45.

65. *Li Hsiu-ch'eng ch'in-kung shou-chi,* p. 70.

66. *Ch'in-ting chiao-p'ing Yüeh-fei fang-lüeh,* ch. 266: 32a.

The Making of a Rebel: Liu Yung-fu and the Formation of the Black Flag Army

1. More information survives on the leaders of the Taiping Rebellion than on any other single group, though the reliability of surviving Taiping documents varies considerably. For a discussion of some of the Taiping leaders' confessions, see Franz Michael, in collaboration with Chung-li Chang, *The Taiping Rebellion* (Seattle, 1966), 1, *History:* 182–88.

2. Several versions of Liu's autobiography exist. The one I have used most extensively is based on the original manuscript dictated to Huang Hai-an, to which useful notes by Lo Hsiang-lin have been added: Huang Hai-an, *Liu Yung-fu li-shih ts'ao* (Draft biography of Liu Yung-fu; Taipei, 1957; reissue of 1936 ed.). (Hereafter cited as LST.) A slightly revised version, without Lo Hsiang-lin's notes, appears in Shao Hsün-cheng et al., eds., *Chung-Fa chan-cheng* (The Sino-French War), Modern Chinese Historical Material Series, No. 6 (Shanghai, 1955), 1: 169–316. Li Chien-erh, *Liu Yung-fu chuan* (Biography of Liu Yung-fu; Taipei 1966; reissue of 1938 ed.), though a biographical study, incorporates verbatim large sections of Liu's own account. Li's emphasis is on colorful anecdotes; unlike Lo Hsiang-lin, he does not clearly distinguish his comments from the text of the original autobiography. (Hereafter cited as *Chuan.*) The most recent work on Liu Yung-fu in a Western language is Henry McAleavy, *Black Flags in Vietnam: The Story of a Chinese Intervention* (London, 1968), a book whose scope is much wider than the title indicates. Occasionally, the demands of Mr. McAleavy's highly readable style lead him to gloss over details of some importance. The extermination campaign against the Yellow Flags in 1875, for example, was in a sense a continuation of the 1869 campaign as Mr. McAleavy says (p. 167); but more important was the fact that in the interim the Yellow Flags had allied themselves with the French and then had joined with the Miao tribes in an uprising that not only threw northern Tonkin into turmoil, but threatened to involve tribes in Yunnan and Kwangsi as well. For the involvement of the Yao tribes of Yunnan in 1874–75, see the memorial of Ts'en Yü-ying, governor of Yunnan, to the Tsungli Yamen, dated 18 April 1875 (KH 1/3/13), in Kuo T'ing-i et al., eds., *Chung-Fa Yüeh-nan chiao-she tang* (Tsungli Yamen Archives concerning relations between China, France, and Vietnam; Peking, 1962; hereafter cited as YNT).

3. The autobiography benefits in some ways and suffers in others from having been composed in Liu's old age, long after the events it describes. On the one hand, Liu could speak fairly bluntly on certain subjects. On the other hand, having achieved respectability, Liu glossed over the more disreputable aspects of his past. A cross-check of Liu's account of military ac-

tions against other sources indicates that Liu Yung-fu, like many illiterate persons, could recall the specific details of past events with a high degree of accuracy. The information on his earlier career in Vietnam is more detailed than that on later periods of his life. The early part of the autobiography provides considerable insight not only into the conditions that preceded the Taiping Rebellion, but also into the social anarchy and lawlessness that followed in its wake even after the rebellion had established its major center in the Yangtze Valley.

4. According to Lo Hsiang-lin, Liu Yung-fu's original name was Liu I, and it was only after he went to Vietnam that he was called Yung-fu (LST, p. 30). *Chuan*, p. 2, says his original name was Liu Chien-yeh, and that later he adopted the *hao* of Yüan-t'ing (LST, p. 27). Lo Hsiang-lin also notes that because he regarded himself as a younger brother to his mother's son by her first marriage, he was known in Kwangtung as "Liu the second" (Liu Erh).

5. He is often called a Shang-ssu man because he was very young when (as noted below) his family migrated to Kwangsi, and he grew up in Shang-ssu. The biography of Liu Yung-fu in the *Ch'ing shih*, for instance, calls him a Shang-ssu man. See *Ch'ing shih* (Official history of the Ch'ing Dynasty), ed. Military History Bureau, Ministry of National Defense, Republic of China (Taipei, 1961), 7: 5049.

6. LST, p. 27.

7. Present-day Mei-hsien, in an almost exclusively Hakka area. The family of Hung Hsiu-ch'üan moved from here four generations before the Taiping leader was born (Michael, p. 21). A descendant of the branch of the family that had remained in Chia-ying-chou told Lo Hsiang-lin the family records contained the names of Liu Pang-pao and his ancestors (LST, p. 30). Unless otherwise indicated, my account of the Liu family history and Liu Yung-fu's youth is drawn from LST, pp. 27–30, and to a lesser extent from *Chuan*, pp. 2–4.

8. It is difficult to tell from any of the versions of this conversation in the autobiography whether Liu I-lai was being offered the status of dependent relative, tenant, or resident laborer (LST, p. 28; *Chuan*, pp. 2–3). The land offered could not have been of very good quality, since it is consistently referred to as *p'o*, which means "slope" or "embankment," and since the crop Liu I-lai grew there was some variety of tuberous vegetable, a crop usually grown on land unsuitable for rice cultivation, which in Kwangtung and Kwangsi usually meant the poorer land on the upper slopes of the hills.

9. LST, p. 28; *Chuan*, pp. 3, 4.

10. LST, p. 31. Although the Taipings were known as "long-haired bandits," this reference is not necessarily to them. Since the queue and shaved forehead were symbols of Chinese submission to the Manchus, long hair as a symbol of opposition to the Ch'ing was not exclusive to the Taipings. It is, in fact, unlikely that Liu meant specifically Taipings. In both versions of the LST the slogan is given as *Fan Ch'ing, fu Han* ("Overthrow the Ch'ing, restore the Han"; LST, p. 31, and *Chung-Fa chan-cheng*, 1: 171). The version in the *Chuan* is mixed in with the compiler's later interpolations, and Liu Yung-fu is described as joining the "Hung army" (*Chuan*, p. 10). If Liu's recollection is correct, the slogan "Overthrow the Ch'ing, restore the Ming,"

the usual secret society slogan, may have been interchangeable with "Overthrow the Ch'ing, restore the Han" as early as the mid-nineteenth century. Both slogans called for the expulsion of alien Manchus and the restoration of native Chinese rule, but Liu's version suggests a dilution of Ming loyalist traditions in the south to the point where the appeal was already ethnic rather than political.

11. Lloyd E. Eastman, *Throne and Mandarins: China's Search for a Policy During the Sino-French Controversy, 1880–1885* (Cambridge, Mass., 1967), p. 48. The translation of the passage from LST, p. 31, is Professor Eastman's.

12. LST, p. 31; *Chuan*, p. 10.

13. It is quite possible that any one of the six might already have joined a secret society, but the autobiography is silent on this point.

14. For a discussion of the rebel groups in Kwangsi in the late 1850's see Hsieh Hsing-yao, *T'ai-p'ing t'ien-kuo ch'ien-hou Kuang-hsi ti fan-Ch'ing yün-tung* (The anti-Ch'ing movement in Kwangsi before and after the Taiping Rebellion; Peking, 1950), pp. 215–22.

15. LST, pp. 32–33. The name Wu Ling-yün is given in a note by Lo Hsiang-lin on p. 33, and also in *P'ing-Kuei chi-lüeh* (A chronological account of pacifying the Kwangsi rebellion), an anonymous book included in the *Kuang-hsi t'ung-chih chi-yao* (Essential materials on all of Kwangsi; blockprint edition, Kweilin, 1899), ch. 3: 11a.

16. Hsieh, p. 216.

17. *P'ing-Kuei chi-lüeh*, ch. 2, p. 14a.

18. *Ibid.*, ch. 3, p. 11b.

19. According to Liu Yung-fu's account, Wu began styling himself *wang* in 1858, when he occupied Lien-lo (a town in Hsüan-hua, a metropolitan hsien of Nan-ning prefecture), although his exact title was the less exalted *Yen-ling kuo-chu*. Liu's account stipulates that the latter title was bestowed on Wu by the Taiping ruler (LST, p. 32). If Liu is correct, this may reflect the Taiping practice of reserving the title *wang* for the top leadership. According to a loyalist account of the suppression of the rebellion in Kwangsi, however, Wu Yüan-ch'ing first referred to himself as *wang* in 1860. According to this account, Wu Yüan-ch'ing's elder son, Ya-chung, directed the assault on T'ai-p'ing, and his younger son, Chu-yüan, the attack on Yang-li-chou. (The elder son's name is given as Wu Ya-chung in *P'ing-Kuei chi-lüeh*, ch. 4, p. 7b; ch. 3: 11a of the same work gives his name simply as Wu Chung. LST, p. 32, gives his name as Wu Ya-chung, with a different character for "chung." *Chuan*, p. 11, has Wu A-chung, with the same character for "chung" as LST. The younger son's name is given in *P'ing-Kuei chi-lüeh*, ch. 3: 11a.) While these operations were still under way, in late September or early October of 1860, Wu Yüan-ch'ing had a state seal carved and the construction of a palace begun, and awarded appropriate titles to his chief followers (*P'ing-Kuei chi-lüeh*, ch. 3: 11a). He did not, however, take the final step of adopting the title *wang* until he captured T'ai-p'ing several months later. (The full title was *Yen-ling kuo-wang*; *P'ing-Kuei chi-lüeh*, ch. 4: 1a.) Wu Yüan-ch'ing's association with the Taiping Rebellion seems less direct in this account than in Liu Yung-fu's version. Kuo T'ing-i, a modern specialist on the Taiping Rebellion, refers to Wu as "Wu Ling-yün, Prince of Yen-ling, and a member of the Triad" in *T'ai-p'ing t'ien-kuo shih-shih jih-chih* (A

daily record of the history of the Heavenly Kingdom of Great Peace; Taipei, 1965, p. 869). This identification of Wu Yüan-ch'ing with the Triad Society rather than the Taipings is more congruent with the account in the *P'ing-Kuei chi-lüeh*, where Wu's claims to royal status are of his own making. It would not have been unnatural, however, for Wu to seek to associate himself with the larger rebellion; certainly the Imperial forces that later pacified Kwangsi made few distinctions between actual Taipings and local rebels who appropriated the symbols of legitimate rule.

20. LST, p. 32. *Chuan*, p. 12. Several of Wu Erh's subordinates seem to have come from western Kwangtung—for example, Ling Kuo-chin.

21. LST, p. 43.

22. LST, pp. 43–44.

23. *P'ing-Kuei chih-lüeh*, ch. 4: 4b.

24. *Ibid.*, ch. 4: 7b.

25. LST, p. 48.

26. *Ta-Ch'ing li-ch'ao shih-lu* (Veritable records of successive reigns of the Ch'ing dynasty), series for the T'ung-chih period (Taipei, 1964; continuous pagination edition, p. 4650), ch. 204: 12a.

27. Feng, too, was a Ch'in-chou man. See his biography in A. W. Hummel, *Eminent Chinese of the Ch'ing Period* (Washington, D.C., 1943), pp. 244–47.

28. Hsieh, pp. 220–21.

29. LST, p. 52.

30. LST, p. 54. The Black Flag Army still lacked one important prerequisite for an "established" group—a permanent base. Liu's followers did not acquire this until they settled in the Vietnamese village of Luc-an. Even after he had his own banner, Liu referred to his followers only as his "men" (*jen*) or "band" (*chung*) until they arrived at Luc-an, after which he consistently referred to them as the "Black Flag Army" (LST, p. 47).

31. For this concept I am indebted to G. William Skinner's articles "Marketing and Social Structure in Rural China," *Journal of Asian Studies*, 24 (1964–65): 3–43, 195–228, 363–99.

Some Notes on the Ko-lao Hui in Late Ch'ing China

1. T'ao Ch'eng-chang, "Chiao-hui yüan-liu k'ao" (Origins of the societies and sects), in Hsiao I-shan, ed., *Chin-tai pi-mi she-hui shih-liao* (Historical materials on modern secret societies; Taipei, 1965), p. 5. T'ao states that members of the Triad Society (San-ho Hui, a Hung Men branch) infiltrated the Hunan Army on orders of Taiping leaders, and adopted the name Ko-lao Hui as an alias.

2. See "Le Hongbang (Bande rouge) aux XIXᵉ et XXᵉ siècles" in the French edition of this volume, pp. 318–19.

3. Jerome Ch'en, "Rebels Between Rebellions—Secret Societies in the Novel *P'eng Kung An*," *Journal of Asian Studies*, 29.4 (August 1970): 815.

4. *Pi-hsieh chi-shih* (1871 ed., first preface dated 1861), Appendix, "Ko-lao Hui shuo" (On the Ko-lao Hui), pp. 13a, 15a.

5. *Hu-nan chin-pai-nien ta-shih chi-shu* (Chronological record of the main events in Hunan during the last hundred years; Changsha, 1959), pp. 94–95.

6. *Liu-yang hsien-chih* (1873 ed.), 13: 15b.

7. Ch'en, "Rebels," p. 814.

8. Paul A. Cohen, *China and Christianity* (Cambridge, Mass., 1963), p. 279.

9. *Pi-hsieh chi-shih*, Appendix, pp. 15a–b.

10. On the Ch'ing Men, see Jerome Ch'en, "The Origin of the Boxers," in Jerome Ch'en and Nicholas Tarling, eds., *Studies in the Social History of China and Southeast Asia* (Cambridge, Eng., 1970), pp. 65–70. On the division of the Ch'ing Men into the Ch'ing Pang and the Hung Pang, see Ch'en, "Rebels," pp. 816–17.

11. Lo Erh-kang, *Hsiang-chün hsin-chih* (A new account of the Hunan Army; Changsha, 1939), pp. 201–2.

12. Wang Wen-chieh, *Chung-kuo chin-shih shih shang ti chiao-an* (Missionary cases in recent Chinese history; Foochow, 1947), p. 110.

13. Tai Wei-kuang, *Hung Men shih* (History of the Hung Men; Shanghai, 1947), p. 98.

14. *Hu-nan chin-pai-nien*, p. 95. Parts of this memorial have been translated by Jerome Ch'en, "Rebels," p. 814.

15. *Hu-nan chin-pai-nien*, pp. 101–4.

16. *Ibid.*, pp. 104–5.

17. This story, which may be an invention of revolutionary propagandists, tells how Tso was obliged to join the Ko-lao Hui himself to prevent a mutiny of his troops. It thus implies that the Moslem rebellion was suppressed not by Ch'ing power but by the anti-Ch'ing heirs of the Ming dynasty. See *Ko-ming chih ch'ang-tao yü fa-chan* (The advocacy and development of the revolution; first series of *Chung-hua min-kuo k'ai-kuo wu-shih nien wen-hsien* [Documents on the first fifty years of the Chinese Republic], vol. 10, Taipei, 1963), p. 473. An English version appears in T'ang Leang-li, *The Inner History of the Chinese Revolution* (New York, 1930), pp. 6–7.

18. Victor Purcell, *The Boxer Uprising: A Background Study* (Cambridge, Eng., 1963), p. 168.

19. Mason was tried in the Shanghai Supreme Court, imprisoned for nine months, and deported. For documents relating to the case, see *Further Correspondence Respecting Anti-Foreign Riots in China* (London, 1892), pp. 96–115, 135–39.

20. One of several Japanese pan-Asian activists who worked with Chinese revolutionaries before 1911. See his biography in *Zoku taishi kaiko roku* (Supplement to recollections of China; Tokyo, 1931), 2: 1207–17.

21. Appendix to *Nihon oyobi Nihonjin* (Japan and the Japanese), no. 569 (Oct. 28, 1911). Pp. 48–67 concern the Ko-lao Hui.

22. For example, Hsü K'o, comp., *Ch'ing pai lei ch'ao* (Minor documents of the Ch'ing; Shanghai, 1917), 27: 50–91; *Ko-ming chih ch'ang-tao*, pp. 477–98.

23. Lo Erh-kang, *T'ien-ti Hui wen-hsien lu* (Documents on the Heaven and Earth Society; Shanghai, 1947), p. 95.

24. Hirayama wrote in a revolutionary era, and appears to have given too much credit to Ko-lao Hui unity in support of the revolutionary movement. On this point see also Ch'en, "Rebels," p. 816, n. 34, and note 51 below.

25. See pp. 274–88 on the Ko-lao Hui. Matsuzaki traveled extensively in China and resided as a student in Hunan before and after the Revolution of 1911. His account combines selections from Hirayama and other writers with his own observations.

26. This example is from Hirayama, p. 51. A similar example for another lodge is given in *Ch'ing pai lei ch'ao,* 27: 61.

27. The next two paragraphs are drawn from Hirayama, p. 52, and Matsuzaki, pp. 277–78.

28. Translations of organizational terms are more or less literal and do not pretend to capture the original connotation.

29. Matsuzaki, p. 277.

30. Hirayama, p. 53; Matsuzaki, pp. 278–79. *Tou-hai* is described as a term for punishments, and therefore was used for an oath-taking ceremony of the utmost sincerity.

31. *Chung* and *i,* Confucian virtues prominent in the *Shui-hu chuan.* Other versions have as the reply here "To unite with the Hung."

32. The number 108 may be derived from the 108 delusions that Buddhists believe man is heir to. See W. E. Soothill and Lewis Hodus, comps., *A Dictionary of Chinese Buddhist Terms* (London, 1937), p. 8. The *Shui-hu chuan* also identifies by name 108 heroes of Liang-shan po.

33. Matsuzaki, p. 281. For the very different initiation procedure of the Hung Men in South China, see J. S. M. Ward and W. G. Stirling, *The Hung Society or The Society of Heaven and Earth* (London, 1925–26), 1: 53–76.

34. Matsuzaki, p. 275. Another version of the precepts is given in *Ch'ing pai lei ch'ao,* 27: 66.

35. Hirayama, pp. 63–65, illustrates this procedure with diagrams.

36. From Matsuzaki, pp. 283–84. Many additional terms are listed.

37. Chang Kuo-t'ao, "Wo-ti hui-i" (My recollections), *Ming-pao yüeh-k'an,* 1.6 (March 1966): 6.

38. Chang P'ing-tzu, "Wo so chih-tao ti Ma Fu-i" (The Ma Fu-i that I knew), in *Hsin-hai ko-ming hui-i lu* (Recollections of the Revolution of 1911; Peking, 1961–63), 2: 240.

39. G. W. Skinner, "Marketing and Social Structure in Rural China," Part I, *Journal of Asian Studies,* 24.1 (November 1964): 37.

40. Liu K'uei-i, *Huang Hsing chuan-chi* (Biography of Huang Hsing; Taipei, 1952), p. 4.

41. Matsuzaki, p. 282.

42. *Ibid.*

43. Hirayama, p. 48. Li Hung-tsao (1820–97) never served in Kwangtung, and Hirayama erroneously describes him as the younger brother of Li Hung-chang. Li Hung-chang's *older* brother, Li Han-chang, served six years as governor-general at Canton (1889–95) and was known for his wealth.

44. Lo, *T'ien-ti Hui,* pp. 81–82.

45. C. T. Hsia, *The Classic Chinese Novel* (New York, 1968), p. 93.

46. See the Puyraimond chapter in this book, pp. 113–24.

47. *Liu K'un-i i-chi* (The works of Liu K'un-i; Shanghai, 1959), 2: 685–86.

48. See the Puyraimond chapter in this book, p. 116.

49. *The Anti-Foreign Riots in China in 1891* (Shanghai: *North-China Herald,* 1892), pp. 30–34.

50. *Chang-wen-hsiang-kung ch'üan-chi* (The complete works of Chang Chih-tung; Taipei, 1963), 136: 5b–6a; *Anti-Foreign Riots,* p. 50.

51. For example, Hirayama, p. 49, or Liu Lien-k'o, *Pang-hui san-pai-nien ko-ming shih* (Three hundred years' revolutionary history of the secret soci-

eties; Macao, 1940), p. 97. Both these sources reverse chronology and state that the Yangtze valley riots were the Ko-lao Hui's revenge for the Chinese government's handling of the Mason conspiracy.

52. See Ch'en, "Rebels," p. 816.

53. On the distribution of tracts in central China, see Marshall Broomhall, *The Chinese Empire* (London, Preface dated 1907), p. 183.

54. For a summary of foreign expansion in central China, see Wang Wenchieh, pp. 111–12. For the influence of the opening of Chungking on the riots of 1891, see *Anti-Foreign Riots*, p. 188.

55. For a discussion of the literature circulated in 1891, see Charlton M. Lewis, "The Opening of Hunan," Ph.D. dissertation, University of California, Berkeley, 1965, pp. 30–39.

56. See John's letter in *North-China Herald*, Nov. 6, 1891, pp. 641–42.

57. Great Britain, Foreign Office, FO 17/1146.

58. Edmund S. Wehrle, *Britain, China, and the Antimissionary Riots, 1891–1900* (Minneapolis, 1966), p. 27.

59. Liu K'un-i, *Works*, 2: 714.

60. On Li Shih-chung and his son's plan for revenge, see Hirayama, p. 49, Liu Lien-k'o, pp. 96–97, and Liu K'un-i, *Works*, 2: 715.

61. Liu K'un-i describes in detail how the leaders of the plot were tracked down. Liu K'un-i, *Works*, 2: 713–15, 768–71.

62. Harold Z. Schiffrin, *Sun Yat-sen and the Origins of the Chinese Revolution* (Berkeley, 1968), pp. 176–77.

63. Feng Tzu-yu, *Ko-ming i-shih* (Reminiscences of the revolution; reprinted Taipei, 1953), 1: 75.

64. Lewis, p. 104.

65. On this point, see Mary Backus Rankin, "The Revolutionary Movement in Chekiang: A Study in the Tenacity of Tradition," in Mary C. Wright, ed., *China in Revolution: The First Phase, 1900–1913* (New Haven, 1968), pp. 334–35, 340.

66. Lewis, p. 103.

67. No source explains how the T'ung-ch'ou Hui functioned. We can conjecture that it served as a secret society arm of the Hua-hsing Hui, much as the Fu-yu Shan was an arm of the Tzu-li Hui in 1900. The name, of course, suggests the anti-Manchu aims that revolutionaries were now fostering in the Ko-lao Hui.

68. The revenge motive is mentioned in several sources, e.g. Ch'ai Te-keng et al., comps., *Hsin-hai ko-ming* (The Revolution of 1911; Shanghai, 1957), 2: 463.

69. The manifestos are printed in *Hsin-hai ko-ming*, 2: 475–80.

70. Vidya Prakash Dutt, "The First Week of Revolution: The Wuchang Uprising," in Wright, pp. 415–16.

The Ko-lao Hui and the Anti-Foreign Incidents of 1891

1. This pamphlet literature has been presented and its main themes analyzed by J. K. Fairbank, "Patterns Behind the Tientsin Massacre," *Harvard Journal of Asiatic Studies*, 20 (1957): 499–504. Griffith John of the London Missionary Society was the first to discover that the center for the diffusion of these pamphlets was at Changsha. See the article by G. John in the *Chi-*

nese Recorder, 1883, p. 361, and his letter to the same journal in 1892, p. 49. According to the English commentator in *A Complete Picture Gallery* (Hankow, 1891), these various writings may have been diffused through the medium of the yamen at least until the Tientsin disturbance. They were often distributed to candidates for the official examinations.

2. Cf. Liu Lien-k'o, *Pang-hui san-pai-nien ko-ming shih* (Three hundred years' revolutionary history of the secret societies; 2d ed., Macao, 1940), pp. 95–98.

3. Yazawa Toshihiko, "Chōkō ryūiki kyōan no kenkyū," (The anti-foreign revolts of 1891), *Kindai Chūgoku kenkyū* (1960), p. 116.

4. Tseng Kuo-fan distributed 50,000 taels monthly. The sum is from Wagner, *Correspondance politique des consuls*, vol. 14, dispatch dated June 19, 1891.

5. Yazawa, p. 141.

6. English translation in the *North China Daily News*, May 20, 1891.

7. Wagner, May 23, 1891.

8. Yazawa, p. 141.

9. *The Anti-foreign Riots in China in 1891* (Shanghai, 1892), pp. 13, 23.

10. H. Havret, "Quelques Notes sur les faits récemment arrivés à la mission catholique de Wu-hu," *Correspondance politique*, vol. 14, folio 60.

11. Wagner, May 23, 1891.

12. Wagner, May 29, 1891. It is a noteworthy sidelight that in this particular episode only the American (Protestant) establishment suffered, whereas the Catholic facilities were undamaged; J. Dautremer, *La Grande Artère de la Chine, le Yangzi* (Paris, 1911), p. 216. Dautremer, an eyewitness, reports that "the Muslims of Nanking, who had good relations with the Jesuit fathers, came armed to the mission en masse to protect it. It was thanks to them that the Catholic mission was saved in 1891."

13. Wagner, *loc. cit.*, May 29, 1891.

14. Wu-hsüeh, present-day Kuang-chi, was not open to foreign trade, but there was a customs bureau there for the collection of likin. Wu-hsüeh was in Hupeh, i.e., outside the governor-generalship of Liu K'un-i but within that of Chang Chih-tung.

15. See the article by G. John in the *North China Daily News*, Oct. 14, 1891. This latter belief is not completely justified. The Tsungli Yamen did react to these disturbances. See, in particular, "Lettres des ministres du *Tsungli Yamen* à M. Ristelhueber," May 22 and July 5, 1891, in *Correspondance politique (Chine)*, vol. 78. See also the imperial decree of June 13.

16. Wagner, June 19, 1891.

17. F. H. Balfour, "Secret Societies in China," in *Journal of the Manchester Geographical Society*, 7 (1891): 40–56.

18. *Tung-hua hsü-lu* (Tung-hua supplementary records), ch. 104, report of Liu K'un-i, dated July 1891.

19. *Ching-chi wai-chiao shih-liao* (Historical materials on diplomatic relations in the late Ch'ing), ch. 84, June 1891.

20. "Correspondence Respecting Anti-foreign Riots in China," in *Blue Book*, p. 16 (The Marquess of Salisbury to Sir John Walsham), Foreign Office, July 10, 1891.

21. *Chang Wen-hsiang kung ch'üan-chi* (The complete works of Chang Chih-tung; Peking, 1928), ch. 98, official document 13.

22. Balfour, pp. 40–56.

23. *Annales de la Propagation de la Foi*, vol. 63: 380; H. Havret, *La Mission du Kiang-nan* (Paris, 1900), p. 131.

24. "Correspondence Respecting Anti-foreign Riots," p. 36.

25. Yazawa, p. 128.

26. *Ibid.*, p. 132.

27. "Further Correspondence Respecting Anti-foreign Riots," in *Blue Book* (Consul Everard to the Marquess of Salisbury), I-ch'ang, Sept. 1, 1891.

28. Liu Lien-k'o, p. 96; "Correspondence Respecting Anti-foreign Riots," pp. 61–65.

29. For the responsibility of Chou Han in this, see the summary in Edmund S. Wehrle, *Britain, China, and the Antimissionary Riots, 1891–1900* (Minneapolis, 1966), p. 66.

30. The orphanage in Yangchow was held responsible on May 2 as was the one in An-ch'ing, where on May 16 a crowd attempted to force its doors. In Wu-hu on Sunday, May 10, two days before the riot, two young Chinese Catholics were arrested and accused of having rendered two children deaf and dumb. They were released when, in the meantime, it became apparent that the children were able to speak after all. The missionaries were nonetheless accused of having expanded their activities by paying a bribe of 600 taels to the district magistrate. In Wu-hsüeh the Wesleyan Methodist Missionary Society was attacked because it had been taking in a large number of very young children.

31. On June 8 in Wu-hsi the bodies of certain children were exhumed for the purpose of examining them for mutilations alleged to have been inflicted by the missionaries. In I-ch'ang on August 23, bands of Chinese pushed their way inside the church of the Scottish mission in search of the place where, rumor had it, children had their eyes cut out. See "Correspondence Respecting Anti-foreign Riots," pp. 38–52.

32. J. K. Fairbank, pp. 500–501; cf. the lurid accounts contained in *Mingshih*, ch. 325; *T'ien-hsia chun-kuo li-ping-shu*, ch. 119; and *Hai-kuo t'u-chih*. Such rumors were the more easily spread because the rites of confession and extreme unction left the penitent and the dying face to face alone with a priest, who reputedly took advantage of the situation by tearing out people's eyes, etc.

33. Obed. S. Johnson, *A Study of Chinese Alchemy* (Shanghai, 1929).

34. Taken on the whole, however, the literati rarely acted in this manner. Chang Chih-tung, for example, in his *Ch'üan-hsüeh p'ien* (Exhortation to study) mercilessly exposed the absurdity of such accusations.

35. The opinion of the prefect Wen Chao-lan, given in N. N. Harfeld, *Opinions chinoises sur les barbares d'Occident* (Brussels and Paris, 1909), p. 94.

36. See Li Wen-chih, "T'ai-p'ing t'ien-kuo tui pien-ko feng-chien sheng-ch'an kuan-hsi ti tso-yung" (The function of the Taiping insurrection in altering feudal production relationships), in *Kuang-ming jih-pao*, January 16, 1961.

37. Ugo Ojetti, "La Cina e gli Stranieri," *Bolletino della Società Geografica Italiana*, 1892, p. 167.

38. For more on Yü Tung-ch'en, alias Yü Man-tzu ("Yü the Wild"), see A. Flachère, *Msgr. de Guebriant* (Paris, 1946), p. 415.

39. *Lettre commune des missions étrangères de Paris*, 1891; communications from M. Blettery (p. 77), from M. Palissier, and from Msgr. Chausse.

40. J. Dautremer, p. 179.

41. F. H. Balfour.

42. Liu Lien-k'o, p. 97.

43. Flachère, p. 404.

44. This is of course an extremely simplified view. Assuming that there was an overall plan conceived by the secret societies in which the Ko-lao Hui participated, it concerned at the very most an action organized at the level of the local chiefs. There was no real unity of command.

45. Liu Lien-k'o, p. 95.

46. *Ta-Ch'ing lü-li* (Paris, 1812), tr. by R. de Sainte-Croix, p. 457.

47. For the *Pi-hsieh chi-shih* and its author, see P. A. Cohen, *China and Christianity* (Cambridge, Mass., 1963), appendix 2, p. 277. Although originally published in 1861, the text of this work was updated in editions of 1871 and, particularly, 1866, and remained topical as late as 1891.

48. C. K. Yang, *Religion in Chinese Society* (Berkeley, 1967), p. 222.

49. *Essai sur les associations en Chine* (Paris, 1925), p. 173.

50. See P. Vincent Lebbe, *Essai sans titre*, p. 27, cited in Leopold Levaux, *Le Père Lebbe* (Brussels and Paris, 1948).

51. The Taiping wars had led to unimaginable destruction. The Western intrusion was in the process of destroying the old socioeconomic order. A tense and troubled mood had become general, translating itself into such things as the irresolution of the central government, attempts at a kind of *aggiornamento* undertaken by certain high officials, and the endeavors of another literati faction, comprising in part the Hunanese pamphleteers, to return to a strict interpretation of orthodoxy. These all were aimed at preserving, by different means, the old order. By contrast, the population was, without being fully conscious of the fact, searching for a new order. The Ko-lao Hui was one of the instruments used in this quest, which in this period was still expressed in the symbol of restoring the Ming.

The Hung Hu-tzu of Northeast China

1. Colonel Sokovnin, "Khunkhuzy Manchzhurii" (The Hung Hu-tzu of Manchuria), *Voennyi sbornik*, 12 (1903), 195.

2. On the Hung Hu-tzu in this region, see I. Nadarov, "Khunkhuzy v Iuzhno-Ussuriiskom krae" (The Hung Hu-tzu on the South Ussurian border), *Voennyi sbornik*, 9 (1896): 183–204.

3. Sokovnin, p. 196; Jean Chesneaux, *Secret Societies in China in the Nineteenth and Twentieth Centuries* (Ann Arbor, Mich., 1971), p. 43.

4. Francis Mury, "Un Mois en Mandchourie avec les Houngouses," *Le Tour du monde*, 18 (April 1912): 183.

5. V. N. Rudokopov, "Khunkhuzy" (The Hung Hu-tzu), *Istoricheskii vestnik*, June 1910, pp. 923–54, esp. 933–41.

6. Chesneaux, pp. 132–34.

7. Ku Hang, "Hung Hu-tzu ti sheng-huo kuan," *Tung-fang tsa-chih*, 24.13 (July 1927): 73–77. For an English translation, see Chesneaux, pp. 61–63.

8. See, for example, H. J. Howard, *Ten Weeks with Chinese Bandits* (London, 1927).

9. "Pai-ma" Chang's regulations were published in summary form for the first time in 1927. They were probably formulated after the destruction of the Zheltuga Republic.

10. Alexandre Ular, "L'Epopée communiste des proscrits mandchouriens," *Revue blanche*, 1901, p. 202.

11. Mury, p. 186.

12. According to Mury, the Zheltuga Republic was founded in 1865, at which time it had three or four thousand inhabitants. He says that by 1880 its population was over 20,000 (see Ular, p. 203), but that it never passed 25,000.

13. Mury, pp. 189–90.

14. Ular, p. 202.

15. *Ibid.*, p. 203. Mury, p. 188, says 25.

16. Ular, p. 204.

17. Mury, p. 189.

18. Ular, pp. 204–5.

19. *Ibid.*, p. 205.

20. Mury, p. 186.

21. *Ibid.*

22. Ular, pp. 203, 205.

23. Mury, p. 186.

24. The exact date of the destruction of the Zheltuga Republic cannot be determined. The account given here is from Mury, pp. 201–2.

Notes on the Early Role of Secret Societies in
Sun Yat-sen's Republican Movement

1. Cf. Teng Ssu-yü, "Dr. Sun Yat-sen and the Chinese Secret Societies," in Robert K. Sakai, ed., *Studies on Asia*, 4 (Lincoln, Neb., 1963), pp. 81–99. In the works of Sun Yat-sen and in the various memoirs of HCH members, the term generally used for secret societies was San-ho Hui (Triads), Hung Men, or *hui-t'ang*.

2. The documents of the HCH were partially destroyed when the Canton uprising of 1895 was crushed. The oath—never written down—and certain kinds of missing information from the membership lists were reconstructed after the Revolution of 1911 by Feng Tzu-yu, who had taken the oath himself in 1895. See Feng Tzu-yu, *Ko-ming i-shih* (Reminiscences of the revolution; Chungking, Shanghai, 1945–47, 5 vols.), 4: 25–65 (hereafter cited as KMIS). The imperial edicts are reproduced in Ch'ai Te-keng et al., comps., *Hsin-hai ko-ming* (The Revolution of 1911; Shanghai, 1957, 8 vols.), 1: 230–32, 274 (hereafter cited as HHKM).

3. "China's Present and Future," *Fortnightly Review* (London), 61 (1897): 424–40, as reproduced in *Russkoe bogatstvo*, no. 5 (1897), p. 44; *Kidnapped in London* (Bristol and London, 1897); "Incredible Stories, Told by the Chinese Dr. Sun Yat-sen of His Escape from Detention in London," *Russkoe bogatstvo*, no. 12 (1897), pp. 28–31.

4. *Sun Chung-shan hsüan-chi* (Selected works of Sun Yat-sen; Peking, 1956), 1: 168–85 (hereafter cited as SCSHC); *Kuo-fu ch'üan-chi* (Complete works of Sun Yat-sen; Taipei, 1961), p. 6 (hereafter cited as KFCC).

5. Tsou Lu, *Chung-kuo Kuo-min-tang shih-kao* (A draft history of the

Kuomintang; Shanghai, 1929). In the chapter entitled "The Defeat at Canton in the Year I-Wei," there are archival texts (Ch'ing decrees) indicating that secret societies participated in the 1895 uprising.

6. Ch'en Shao-pai, "Hsing-Chung-hui ko-ming shih-yao" (The essential history of the 1911 revolution), in HHKM, 1: 21–76; Ch'en Ch'un-sheng, "Keng-tzu Hui-chou ch'i-i chi" (The Waichow uprising of 1900), in HHKM, 1: 235–44; Miyazaki Torazō, "A Dream of Thirty-Three Years," translated by Huang Chung-huang, in HHKM, 1: 90–132.

7. Sun Yat-sen reportedly told the Russian translator of *Kidnapped in London* that the southeastern provinces teemed with secret organizations. *Russkoe bogatstvo*, no. 12 (1897), p. 29.

8. KMIS, 1: 8.

9. Teng, p. 83.

10. KMIS, 1: 24 (in Ch'en Shao-pai's memoirs it is mentioned that Cheng Shih-liang belonged to the San-tien Hui); HHKM, 1: 23; Sun Yat-sen, *Kuo-fu Sun Chung-shan hsien-sheng nien-p'u ch'u-kao* (A preliminary draft for a chronological biography of Sun Yat-sen, the founding father; hereafter cited as KF; Taipei, 1958), 1: 35; and SCSHC, 1: 168.

11. On such evidence, Lu Hao-tung, Ch'eng K'uei-kuang, Yang Hao-ling, and others have been connected with secret societies; Teng, p. 82.

12. The inhabitants of his native district ordinarily joined the T'ien-ti Hui: Ch'en Hsi-ch'i, *T'ung-meng Hui ch'eng-li ch'ien ti Sun Chung-shan* (Sun Yat-sen before the founding of the T'ung-meng Hui; Canton, 1957), p. 16.

13. SCSHC, 1: 168.

14. HHKM, 1: 23.

15. According to Sun Yat-sen (KF, 1: 39), this episode was recounted by a *hui-t'ang* leader from one of the Pacific islands. Sun himself and Ch'en Shao-pai do not mention it in their memoirs. Feng Tzu-yu attributes great importance to this event: "The advice of Cheng An had consequences for what happened thereafter"; cf. Teng, p. 82.

16. SCSHC, 1: 172.

17. KMIS, 1: 24.

18. KFCC, 6: 152.

19. KMIS, 1: 43. Teng Yin-nan, having become an active member of the HCH, donated a large sum of money to the organization's treasury, and left for China to take part in the uprising.

20. KMIS, 4: 40–42.

21. SCSHC, 1: 170.

22. KMIS, 4: 53–56.

23. HHKM, 1: 67.

24. KMIS, 4: 54.

25. HHKM, 1: 67.

26. KMIS, 4: 53–56.

27. W. Theodore de Bary, *Sources of Chinese Tradition* (New York, 1964), 2: 307.

28. KMIS, 2: 23.

29. The HCH manifesto put the blame for domestic failures on the Man-

chus, holding them responsible for the situation in the country. "The vile enslavers have brought such misfortune upon the country, they have done so much harm to the people that, having stumbled, we cannot get up again." There are even more brutal anti-Manchu accusations than this in the Confession of Lu Hao-tung. After the failure of the 1895 conspiracy, Lu Hao-tung openly declared that for him and his political companions the idea of an anti-Manchu struggle was fundamental, and that for many years they had been preparing vengeance against the Manchu enemy.

30. "T'ien-ti Hui wen-shu," *T'ai-p'ing t'ien-kuo*, 2: 891; 1: 161–62.

31. HCH members established links with the *hui-t'ang* of the hsien of Sun-te, Hsiang-shan, Hui-chou, Pei-chiang, and Ch'ao-chou. Dozens of command posts were established in the north and south of Hsi-chiang. KMIS, 1: 11.

32. *Kidnapped*, p. 24.

33. HHKM, 1: 31, 232.

34. Sun Yat-sen, *Kidnapped*, p. 24.

35. Accounts of preparations for the uprising are not the only mention of the insurgents' red turbans. In a decree published after the discovery of the plot, the local authorities called upon the population to take off the red turbans and have nothing to do with bandits. The existence of a system of passwords was one of the proofs exhibited by the Ch'ing authorities against the organizers of the uprising. HHKM, 1: 227, 232.

36. HHKM, 1: 60.

37. *Ibid.*, pp. 60–61. Ch'en Shao-pai's memoirs contain a detailed description of the San-ho Hui initiation rite, which the members called *k'ai-t'ai*, "set the stage" or "open the table." The ceremony was not completely traditional when Ch'en entered the society: it took place at Ch'en's home, and the only people present were Ch'en himself, his sponsor Ch'en Nan, and the Triad elder who welcomed him into the society. As was customary, after the ceremony the new member offered a meal to his brothers in the society. Ch'en spent nearly 100 *yüan* to arrange this banquet in honor of the members of local *hui-t'ang*.

Incidentally, Ch'en gives some information on the special hierarchy of the Triads. He explains that those who receive and transmit information are called *ts'ao-hsieh* (straw sandals) and that people having the rank of *hung-kün* (red pole) have very extensive powers, including the punishment of delinquent society members.

38. HHKM, 1: 61.

39. *Ibid.*, pp. 61, 110. The arrival of this group is described in the memoirs of Ch'en Shao-pai and Miyazaki, who welcomed them in Hong Kong. According to Ch'en, the group was composed of several tens of people.

40. Miyazaki, in HHKM, 1: 110.

41. The initiation ceremony was not complicated. The Ko-lao Hui leaders lit the ritual candles and pronounced the words of the oath. After having cut a rooster's throat and mixed the blood with wine, they invited Ch'en to drink this mixture. To complete the ceremony, they made him raise his hand above his head. HHKM, 1: 61.

42. KF, 1: 87; HHKM, 1: 112. From Miyazaki's memoirs it is possible to

reconstruct the titles of the Ko-lao Hui leaders who took part in this meeting. Four of them were *shan-chu* (masters of the mountain), and three were *ku-kung* (pillars).

43. HHKM, 1: 112.

44. *Ibid.*, pp. 67–68, 242, 235–36, 239–40, 241. *Lü-lin* groups from Hsinan district whose leaders had entered the organization also took part in the uprising (*ibid.*, p. 67). There were 600 insurgents in the *avant-garde* detachment. According to Hong Kong newspapers, when the revolutionary upsurge was at its peak, this number reached 20,000 (*ibid.*, p. 239).

45. Cheng Shih-liang had barely 300 rifles. HCH members hoped to receive some of their arsenal from Japan and buy some from a local military garrison (HHKM, 1: 236); KMIS, 4: 54.

46. KF, 1: 87.

47. HHKM, 1: 241.

48. *Ibid.*

49. *Ibid.*, pp. 243, 239, 242.

50. Teng, p. 96.

51. Letter to Ts'ai Yüan-p'ei and Chang Hsiang-wen on the preparation of the *History of the Republic* (1919); KFCC, 5: 321–22.

52. *Ibid.*, p. 321.

Triads, Salt Smugglers, and Local Uprisings

1. An analysis of the relationship of the two hierarchical systems can be found in the introduction of my dissertation, "The Revolution of 1911 in Kwangtung" (Harvard, 1970; hereafter cited as Hsieh, Dissertation) and in a recent paper of mine, "The Economics of Warlordism in Twentieth-Century China," presented at the Western Conference of the Association for Asian Studies, San Diego, Oct. 1971 (copies available). A major forward thrust of this systemic approach is provided in two multi-author volumes on Chinese urban society: G. W. Skinner, ed., *The City in Late Imperial China*, and Mark Elvin and G. W. Skinner, eds., *The Chinese City between Two Worlds* (hereafter Elvin and Skinner), both to be published by the Stanford University Press; particular attention should be directed to Mr. Skinner's introductory essays in both volumes.

2. See Charles Tilly's "Collective Violence in European Perspective," in *The History of Violence in America*, ed. by T. R. Gurr and H. Graham, rev. ed. (Bantam Books, 1970), pp. 4–44, and his "Does Modernization Breed Revolution?" (paper presented at Pennsylvania State University, 1971).

3. See H. Z. Schiffrin, *Sun Yat-sen and the Origins of the Chinese Revolution* (Berkeley, 1968); M. B. Jansen's *The Japanese and Sun Yat-sen* (Harvard, 1954); and Lilia Borokh's paper in the present volume, pp. 135–44.

4. Feng Tzu-yu, *Chung-hua-min-kuo k'ai-kuo ch'ien ko-ming shih* (A history of the revolutionary movement prior to the founding of the Republic; Taipei reprint, 1954; hereafter *K'ai-kuo shih*), 2: 166–70; and Tsou Lu, *Chung-kuo kuo-min-tang shih-kao* (A draft history of the Kuomintang; Shanghai, 1929; hereafter *Shih-kao*), pp. 663–66.

5. Winston Hsieh, "The Ideas and Ideals of a Warlord: Ch'en Chiung-

ming (1878–1933)," *Papers on China*, 16 (Dec. 1962): 198–251. Also see *Ch'en Ching-ts'un hsien-sheng nien-p'u* (A biographical chronicle of Ch'en Chiung-ming; Hong Kong, n.d.; hereafter Ch'en, *nien-p'u*), for incidents occurring before 1912.

6. See Tsou Lu, *Kuang-chou san-yüeh erh-shih-chiu ko-ming shih* (A history of the March 29th Uprising in Canton; Shanghai, 1926), p. 104, and Ch'en, *nien-p'u*, p. 14.

7. For a major account of the March 29th Uprising, see Tsou Lu's work cited above.

8. The account of the Tan-shui uprising in this and later pages is mainly based on (a) Miao Chih-hsin's article in Chung-kuo jen-min cheng-chih hsieh-shang hui-i, wen-shih tzu-liao yen-chiu wei-yüan-hui, ed., *Hsin-hai ko-ming hui-i lu* (Recollections of the Revolution of 1911; Peking, 1961; hereafter HHKMHIL), 2: 343–47; (b) Wang Ying-lou's reminiscences, *ibid.*, pp. 348–51; and (c) Ch'en, *nien-p'u*, pp. 16–17.

9. Kuomintang Archives, comp., *Chung-hua-min-kuo k'ai-kuo wu-shih-nien wen-hsien* (Documents in celebration of the fiftieth anniversary of the founding of the Republic of China; Taipei, 1966; hereafter KKWH), part 2, vol. 4, p. 439.

10. HHKMHIL, 2: 314–17.

11. The preceding account is based on Kan Shan-chai's article, *ibid.*, pp. 352–57.

12. The account of Wang's career is based on (a) interviews with K. P. Mok (Mo Chi-p'eng), a T'ung-meng Hui comrade of Wang, and (b) Feng Tzu-yu's accounts as found in *K'ai-kuo shih*, 2: 174–80, 191–200, 205–20; and in his *Ko-ming i-shih* (Reminiscences of the revolution; Chungking and Shanghai, 1939–47; hereafter KMIS), 2: 216–21.

13. KMIS, 2: 216.

14. For Liu and the Black Flags, there are two well edited primary sources in Chinese: Lo Hsiang-lin, ed., *Liu Yung-fu li-shih ts'ao* (A draft of the life history of Liu Yung-fu; Taipei, 1957) and Li Chien-erh, *Liu Yung-fu chuan* (A biography of Liu Yung-fu; Changsha, 1940).

15. For Kuan's biography, see *K'ai-kuo shih*, 2: 191–200.

16. KKWH, part 2, vol. 4, pp. 475–77. For the participation of Wang's forces in the Tan-shui uprising see the section on the Kuan-lan case in Winston Hsieh, "Peasant Insurrection and the Urban Hierarchy," in Elvin and Skinner.

17. Shang Ping-ho, *Hsin-jen ch'un-ch'iu* (Annals of 1911–12; Peking [?], 1924; Taipei reprint, 1962; hereafter HJCC), ch. 18: 3a.

18. Ch'en, *nien-p'u*, pp. 19–20; Wu Hsiang-hsiang, ed., *Chung-kuo chin-tai shih ts'ung-k'an* (Collected works on modern Chinese history; Taipei, 1960; hereafter Ts'ung-k'an), 2: 429–30.

19. Ch'en, *nien-p'u*, p. 16.

20. HHKMHIL, 2: 385–91.

21. For a broader perspective on secret society rebellions in Kwangtung province, see Frederic Wakeman's paper in the present volume, pp. 29–47.

22. Teng Lun-pin et al., eds., *Hui-chou fu chih* (Gazetteer of Waichow prefecture, 1879; hereinafter HCFC), ch. 18: 16b–17a.

23. Ch'en Po-t'ao et al., eds., *Tung-kuan hsien chih* (Gazetteer of Tung-kuan hsien, 1919; hereafter TKHC), ch. 33: 20a–b.

24. HCFC, ch. 18: 17a–b; TKHC, ch. 33: 20b.

25. TKHC, ch. 33: 20b–21a.

26. Such Triad incidents as are recorded in the archival materials are listed in Kuo T'ing-i, *Chin-tai Chung-kuo shih-shih jih-chih* (Daily chronicle on modern Chinese history; Taipei, 1963; hereafter *Chronicle*), 1: 41–43, 47, 104, 133, 135, 142, 151, and 219.

27. The following account of the Red Turban revolt is taken from TKHC, ch. 35: 3b–9b; HCFC, ch. 18: 23a–72a.

28. The local-defense character of such forces is explored in W. Hsieh, "Peasant-Bandits in Towns and Cities: People's Armies in Kwangtung, 1911–24" (which I presented at the Conference on Urban Society and Political Development in Modern China, St. Croix, Virgin Islands, Dec. 1968) and in Hsieh, Dissertation, chap. 2. Also, see Lucien Bianco's paper in the present volume, pp. 213–24.

29. See Hsieh, "Peasant Insurrection and the Urban Hierarchy," especially the sections on the Shih-ch'i and Kuan-lan uprisings.

30. Tilly, "Revolution and Collective Violence," in F. I. Greenstein and N. W. Polsby, *Handbook of Political Science* (Reading, Mass., 1972).

31. According to a nationwide survey of local products conducted in 1936 by the China Postal Service, one of the more reliable sources of quantitative data for this region, the salterns supervised by the monopoly office at Tan-shui produced an annual average of 200,000 piculs, a figure far exceeding that given for salt production in other towns and cities of Kwangtung. (The figure actually given is 20 million *tan* [piculs], but since only 4 million piculs were reported from all of Kwangtung province, this is presumably a typographical error for 20 million *chin* [catties].) The illegal export of salt from Tan-shui likely amounted to another 200,000 piculs, if we accept the view of Ch'ing and Republican officials that legal and illegal salt exports were roughly equal. See also Tsou Lin, *Yüeh-ts'o chi-shih* (An account of the salt administration in Kwangtung; Canton, 1927), rev. ed., part 3, p. 3.

32. For an official account of the system during the late Ch'ing, see *Ts'ai cheng shuo ming shu: Kuang-tung sheng* (Reports on fiscal administration: Kwangtung; hereafter TCSMS. Govt. survey, 1915). "Yen k'o shui li" (Taxes and revenues on the salt trade), 44–50 [separately paged].

33. For example, see Chou Ch'ao-huai, ed., *Shun-te hsien hsü-chih* (The gazetteer of Shun-te hsien; 1929), which lists such taxes for the late Ch'ing in ch. 6: 1a–5b.

34. For a full account of the uprising, read Lo Shou-chang, "Ch'in-hsien san Na fan-k'ang t'ang-chuan tou-cheng yü Ch'in Fang chih i" (The struggles in opposition to the sugar taxes at the "Three Na" area in Ch'in-chou and the battles at Ch'in-chou and Fang-ch'eng), in HHKMHIL, 2: 392–95; also see *K'ai-kuo shih*, 2: 174–80, and *Shih-kao*, pp. 674–79.

35. Discussed against the background of the town of Shih-ch'i in Hsieh, "Peasant Insurrection and the Urban Hierarchy."

36. A readily available source on such cases in 1909–11 is the "Chronicle" section appended to *Tung-fang tsa-chih*, a leading Chinese periodical in those years.

37. Wang Yeh-chien, "The Fiscal Importance of the Land Tax during the Ch'ing Period," *Journal of Asian Studies*, 30.4 (Aug. 1971): 829–42. For details, see his dissertation, "China's Land Taxation in the Late Ch'ing" (Harvard, 1969).

38. All the data about the salt revenue squeeze, whenever without bibliographic citation, are based on TCSMS, 1: 1–44. (For specific references, see Hsieh, Dissertation, especially table 10 and the bibliographic notes to chap. 6.)

39. Tsou Lin, rev. ed., part 1, p. 5.

40. TCSMS, 2, "Ts'ai-cheng fei," pp. 38–40.

41. Hu Hsiang-yün, ed., *Chung-kuo tsui-chin yen-ch'ang lu* (A nationwide survey of salt factories in China; Peking, 1915), p. 25.

Secret Societies, Popular Movements, and the 1911 Revolution

1. *Hsin-hai ko-ming wu-shih chou-ch'i chi-nien lun-wen chi* (Symposium for the fiftieth anniversary of the 1911 revolution; Peking, 1962), 1: 178. This work is hereafter cited as HHKM-50-CC.

2. Teng Ssu-yü, "Dr. Sun Yat-sen and the Chinese Secret Societies," in Robert K. Sakai, ed., *Studies on Asia*, 4 (Lincoln, Neb., 1963), pp. 81–99. This point is also made clear throughout the papers included in Mary Clabaugh Wright, ed., *China in Revolution: The First Phase, 1900–1913* (New Haven, 1968), especially in Mary Backus Rankin's paper on Chekiang.

3. On Ko-lao Hui expansion during the 1860's through the 1880's, see Wang T'ien-chiang, "Shih-chiu shih-chi hsia-pan chih Chung-kuo ti mi-mi hui-she" (Secret societies in China during the second half of the nineteenth century), *Li-shih yen-chiu* (Historical studies), no. 2, 1963. References to this journal are hereafter abbreviated LSYC. The fundamental sources are those of Hirayama Shū and T'ao Ch'eng-chang. T'ao's book shows an incomparable understanding of the societies he knew, and Hirayama's contains some unique documents. An article by Kung Shu-to and Ch'en Kuei-yang (HHKM-50-CC, 1: 222–23) contains interesting material gathered during a hurried survey of archival material. See also *ibid.*, 2: 540–44 on Chekiang and *Hsin-hai ko-ming hui-i-lu* (Recollections of the 1911 revolution; Peking, 1961–63; hereafter HHKMHIL), 5: 104–5 on Shensi.

4. See Wang, and the discussion at the Wuhan conference on the 1911 revolution, summarized in LSYC, 1961, no. 6.

5. This is a point stressed by Rankin regarding Chekiang (Wright, pp. 323–25).

6. For an overview see Hsiao Kung-chuan, *Rural China: Imperial Control in the Nineteenth Century* (Seattle, 1960), *passim*.

7. LSYC, 1957, no. 11, pp. 57–76.

8. Chia I-chün in *Li-shih chiao-hsüeh*, 1960, no. 6, pp. 37–38. Reports of the outbreak can be found in the *North-China Herald* (hereafter NCH).

9. Chang Chen-hao, in *Chung-kuo k'o-hsüeh-yüan li-shih yen-chiu-so ti-san-so chi-k'an* (Journal of the Institute of Modern History of Academia Sinica), 1 (1954): 188–97.

10. Hatano Yoshihiro, "Shingai kakumei chokuzen ni okeru nōmin ikki" (The peasant riots immediately preceding the 1911 revolution), *Tōyōshi kenkyū*, 13 (1954), nos. 1–2. A map of riot areas in Manchuria appears in

Kirin Academica Sinica, comp., *Chin-tai Tung-pei jen-min ko-ming yün-tung shih* (Modern revolutionary history of the Northeast; Ch'ang-ch'un, 1960), p. 180. Yanashita Komeko's article in *Tōyō Bunka Kenkyūjo kiyō*, no. 37, 1965, p. 148, contains maps of the riot areas in Chekiang and Kiangsu.

11. Data on local conditions are plentiful in the Decennial Reports of the Maritime Customs, consular reports, etc. Local histories, for example those of Szechwan, are eloquent on the long-term growth of the tax structure.

12. Cf. a memorial of 1907, *Kuang-hsü-ch'ao Tung-hua hsü-lu* (Selected documents of the Kuang-hsü period), 5: 5803–5.

13. Item on the causes of the riots in the financial section of *Tung-fang tsa-chih* (Eastern miscellany), 1905, no. 4, pp. 59ff.

14. Based on reports in NCH, *Tung-fang tsa-chih*, the *Chinese Recorder*, official sources such as the *Kuang-hsü Tung-hua hsü-lu*, and the like.

15. NCH, July 13, 1906, p. 117 (Kiangsu); March 22, 1906, p. 611 (Shao-hsing area); May 2, 1910, p. 379 (Yangchow area).

16. NCH, March 16, 1907, p. 645.

17. FO 228/1660 (Chengtu 35/07).

18. *Tōyōshi kenkyū*, 22.2 (1963). On the riot, see also Chang and the report of the notables in *Chin-tai shih tzu-liao* (Material on modern history; hereafter, CTSTL), no. 1 (1954), pp. 26–47.

19. As for example in the Ch'in-chou riot in western Kwangtung in the spring of 1908 and the Changsha rice riots in the spring of 1910.

20. T'an had a passion for riding horses. Liang's self-bestowed name (*hao*) was Jen-kung, an allusion to the *Mo-tzu*, reflecting the literary side of the movement.

21. Cf. Rankin in Wright, p. 338. Her view is that Chekiang populism cannot be equated with the attitudes of the young Russian *narodniki* of the 1870's and 1880's, who advocated "going to the people" in their fight against Tsarism (*ibid.*, p. 340). However, it is probably not by chance that Lenin, familiar as he was with the *narodniki* at home, saw in the political ideas of Sun Yat-sen a Chinese version of Russian populism. See *Polnoe sobranie sochinenii* (Collected works), 21 (1961): 400–406. Lenin might have been even more impressed if he had known that Sun was probably the only one in the southern T'ung-meng Hui in 1907–8 not to worry about the earthy smell of the Triad chiefs.

22. See the paper of Boris Novikov in this volume.

23. The deposition was apparently published first in Feng Tzu-yu, *Chung-hua-min-kuo k'ai-kuo ch'ien ko-ming shih* (Chinese revolutionary history before the Republic; Shanghai, 1928), 1: 19–20.

24. Lo Erh-kang, *T'ai-p'ing t'ien-kuo wen-hsüan* (Taiping anthology; Shanghai, 1956), pp. 77–79.

25. Feng Tzu-yu, *Ko-ming i-shih* (Reminiscences of the revolution; Chungking and Shanghai, 1939–47; hereafter KMIS), 1: 1.

26. See his "Chien-kuo fang-lüeh" (Strategy for national reconstruction), in *Sun Chung-shan hsüan-chi* (Selected works), 1 (1956): 171.

27. See Rankin in Wright, pp. 319ff.

28. Jerome Ch'en's critique is summarized in *Ch'ing-shih wen-t'i* (Problems in Ch'ing history; New Haven, 1966), 1.3.

29. On the Red Beards, see the paper by Mark Mancall and Georges Jidkoff in this volume.

30. *Tsung-li ch'üan-chi* (Collected works of Sun Yat-sen), 3: 329.

31. Some of the important articles are reprinted in Ch'ai Te-keng et al., comps., *Hsin-hai ko-ming* (The Revolution of 1911; Shanghai, 1957; hereafter HHKM).

32. This reversal is very striking in the rich materials based on oral testimony that have been collected in HHKMHIL.

33. An idea of Liang Ch'i-ch'ao's. Cf. Chang P'eng-yüan, *Liang Ch'i-ch'ao yü Ch'ing-chi ko-ming* (Liang Ch'i-ch'ao and the Ch'ing revolution; Taipei, 1964), p. 93, and *T'an Ssu-t'ung ch'üan-chi* (Collected works of T'an Ssu-t'ung; Peking, 1954), p. 139.

34. Compare the complaint of Chou K'ai-ch'ing in *Ssu-ch'uan yü hsin-hai ko-ming* (Szechwan and the 1911 revolution; Taipei, 1964), p. 139: "Many people know about what happened at Wuhan, but not about the rich revolutionary history of Szechwan."

35. HHKMHIL, 4: 226.

36. Such was the secret headquarters established by Ch'en Ch'i-mei as a gathering place for the revolutionaries of Chekiang and Kiangsu, which got the reputation of a Liang-shan-po (the famous bandit lair in the novel *Shui-hu chuan*).

37. HHKM-50-CC, 2: 124–25.

38. See Huang Hsing's biography in HHKM, 4: 284.

39. HHKM, 2: 210.

40. *Ibid.*, p. 8, clause no. 5.

41. See Hsiang Yung-ching's biography of Hu Han-min in *Chung-kuo hsien-tai shih ts'ung-k'an* (Miscellany on modern Chinese history; Taipei, 1960), 3: 109.

42. Hsüeh Chün-tu, *Huang Hsing and the Chinese Revolution* (Stanford, 1960), pp. 79–81.

43. Yang Yu-ju, *Hsin-hai ko-ming hsien-chu chi* (First steps of the 1911 revolution; Peking, 1958), p. 14.

44. Cf. E. S. K. Fung, "The T'ang Ts'ai-ch'ang Revolt," in *Papers on Far Eastern History*, 1 (1970): 75; and *Min-li pao* (Taipei facsimile), no. 1 (1905), no. 10 (1906).

45. HHKMHIL, 1: 226–27; 3: 407.

46. Hsüeh, pp. 15ff.

47. The name is compounded of the abbreviations for three districts on the Hunan-Kiangsi border. On the rising see Ch'en Ch'un-sheng's account in HHKM, 2: 463–98; the biography of Wei Tsung-yüan in vol. 4 of Tsou Lu's *Chung-kuo kuo-min-tang shih-kao* (Draft history of the Kuomintang; Shanghai, 1944); A. S. Kostyaeva, "Lozung 'Doloi Ts'in'" (The slogan "Down with the Ch'ing!"), in *Manchuzhurskoe vladichestvo* (The Manchu domination; Moscow, 1966); *Hu-nan chin-pai-nien ta-shih chi-shu* (Chronology of Hunan for the last century; Changsha, 1959).

48. *Hsin-hai shou-i hui-i-lu* (Recollections of the Wuchang rising; Peking, 1961–63), 2: 465.

49. KMIS, 3: 357–62; 4: *passim*. See also Chou P'ei-i, "Kuei-chou min-

tang t'ung-shih" (The tragic history of the People's Party of Kweichow), in HHKM, 6; and the memoirs of Hu Kang in HHKMHIL, 3, and in CTSTL.

50. HHKM, 1: 315–21. Translations of documents are in the British Colonial Archives, Hong Kong series.

51. The rising was taken in under the umbrella of Sun's attempts, but the connection was rather slight, including an attempt to transport arms from Japan to the Ch'ao-chou area that ended in near farce.

52. For brief accounts, see Hsüeh and standard Nationalist histories.

53. See pp. 192–97 of this article.

54. Wei Ying-t'ao in HHKM-50-CC, 1: 491. Wei has also written an interesting series of articles on the Boxer movement in Szechwan.

55. Summarized in the memoirs of Hsiung K'o-wu, in HHKMHIL, 3.

56. For example, in 1909 a Chinese workman was alleged to have died in Kiukiang as the result of a blow from a police superintendent. A boycott of British ships lasted for several weeks. Among organizations evidently involved were the Hu-k'ou local association and Kiukiang guilds (FO 228/1768, Sept. 13; FO 228/1709, May 8, 21, June 15; Sept. 28).

57. HHKMHIL 3: 21; KMIS, 5: 60; Hirayama mistakenly attributed it to T'ao Ch'eng-chang.

58. Deduced from Tsou Lu, *Kuang-chou san-yüeh erh-shih-chiu ko-ming shih* (History of the March 29th Uprising in Canton; Shanghai, 1926); and KMIS, 2: 238–39.

59. There were a number of chiefs of the same name in each district. For lists see Li Yü-ch'i and Chang Lei in *Li-shih chiao-hsüeh*, 1962, no. 5; HHKMHIL, 2: 410–16. CTSTL, no. 2, 1958, p. 52, is interesting on the problem of handling one's kin.

60. Kuo Hsi-jen, "Ts'ung-jung chi-lüeh" (Life in the field), in HHKM, 6; sources are also in *Chung-hua-min-kuo k'ai-kuo wu-shih nien wen-hsien* (Documents on the fiftieth anniversary of the founding of the Republic of China), second series (Taipei, 1963– ; hereafter KKWH/2), 3, and HHK-MHIL, 5 and 6.

61. HHKMHIL, 5: 197–98, 208–9, 253.

62. CTSTL, no. 2, 1955, pp. 21–30; manifesto in *Tung-fang tsa-chih*, no. 1, 1905. He was the author of "The Classic of the Hidden and Open Principles of the Heroes of the Marshes," evidently a military manual for brigand guerrillas.

63. HHKMHIL, 5: 538–41.

64. *Min-li pao*, Dec. 14, 1910; *Chin-tai Tung-pei jen-min ko-ming yün-tung shih*, p. 134.

65. *Min-li pao*, Sept. 21, 1911.

66. *Jung-hsien chih* (Local history of Jung-hsien; Taipei facsimile, 1929), section 15, pp. 43–45.

67. HHKMHIL, 3: 143–44; on the northwestern groups see pp. 218–20.

68. P. 64.

69. HHKMHIL, 2: 68, 107, 219–21; *Min-li pao*, Oct. 14, 1911, p. 28.

70. Manifestos, one by Sun Tse-p'ei, a commander of poor peasant origins, are in *Min-li pao*, Nov. 28, 1911, and *Ssu-ch'uan pao-lu yün-tung shih-liao* (Material on the Railway Protection Movement; Peking, 1959), pp. 485–86.

71. HHKMHIL, 3: 198–201, 292.

72. P. 109.

73. Pp. 33, 95, 285; KKWH/2, 5: 129–33.

74. A certain regret over the shabby treatment of irregulars is apparent among veterans; cf. HHKMHIL, 3:13.

75. KKWH/2, 2: 13.

76. A sympathetic account is in Wen Kung-chih, *Tsui-chin san-shih-nien chün-shih shih* (Military history of the last thirty years; n.p., 1929), 1: 301; a pro–T'an Yen-k'ai view is in Tzu-hsü-tzu, *Hsiang-shih chi* (The events in Hunan; Changsha [?], 1912); whereas aristocratic attitudes prevail in Shang Ping-ho, *Hsin-jen ch'un-ch'iu* (Annals of 1911–12; n.p., 1924).

77. The slanders were printed in full in *Min-li pao*, although many of them were myth. The paper was certainly out of touch with Hunan.

78. FO 228/1798 (Changsha 78/11); HHKMHIL, 2: 151–54, 202–3.

79. See note 49 above for sources.

80. For sources see note 49 above. A list of officers of the lodge, probably taken down from memory, is in Hirayama, pp. 164–69. The name of the lodge is wrong. Hirayama's material evidently came from hostile sources.

81. *Yün-nan Kuei-chou hsin-hai ko-ming tzu-liao* (Material on the 1911 revolution in Yunnan and Kweichow; Peking, 1959), p. 214.

82. HHKM, 6: 456–58.

83. *Ibid.*, pp. 401–5; *Yün-nan Kuei-chou*, p. 169. Li Shih-chieh, in his *Yüan Shih-k'ai chih-huo Ch'ien* (Yüan Shih-k'ai strikes at Kweichow; Tai-pei facsimile, 1912), saw Yüan's machinations at the bottom of the tragedy.

84. See the article by Li Yü-ch'i and Chang Lei in *Li-shih chiao-hsüeh*, 1962, no. 5.

85. KKWH/2, 4: 433–35.

86. KMIS, 3: 255–56. The T'ung-meng Hui command would have preferred Canton to rise first, to lend prestige to the republic.

87. His theory was that it was a revolution of a compradore class as opposed to the revolution of the lawyer class seen in the French Revolution.

88. Cf. Yao Yu-p'ing in HHKMHIL, 1: 419–28.

89. KKWH/2, 4: 424–25. Hu had been suspected by some at the time of using the People's Armies as a bargaining point against Ch'en. The material available to me has not helped to clarify the contradictions that are implicit here.

90. HHKMHIL, 2: 445.

91. *Min-li pao*, Dec. 12, 1911.

92. KKWH/2, 4: 226–27, saw it as a case of the riffraff (*liu-mang*) in Lu, brought out by bad associates.

93. HHKMHIL, 2: 445, 447.

94. The diary of Kuo Hsi-jen, chief of staff in the regime (see note 60 above), remains the main source here. His non-elitist attitude makes his work valuable for clarifying the relations inside the regime. The memoirs and further material in KKWH/2 are also of great interest.

95. See HHKMHIL, 6: 512–28 on the Swordsmen. Kuo's tribute to one of them, who died in action, deserves to be quoted. The man, who came from a poor family and had been a coolie in a pottery kiln, had risen to the rank of a Swordsman chief. "He was a taciturn man, who spoke in measured terms like a scholar. He did not intervene in discussions. He would not smoke

opium. . . . His eyes were full of life, bright like falling stars. He treated his subordinates like a father, and his death came as a blow to the T'ung-meng Hui leader and his army."

96. Lists of officials are in KKWH/2, 3: 50–52; HHKMHIL, 5: 108–9.

97. The *Min-li pao* took an interest in them, as the Dec. 29 number shows.

98. *Ibid.*, Jan. 12, 15, 1912.

99. HHKM, 7: 368; HHKMHIL, 5: 393; *Min-li pao*, Dec. 19.

100. Manifestos produced by both parties were published in *Min-li pao*, Jan. 14, 15.

101. See an article by Chiang Ti, "Shan-hsi hsin-hai ko-ming" (The 1911 revolution in Shansi), *Wen-shih-che*, 1958, no. 11, pp. 30–33; HHKMHIL, 5: 129–30.

102. HHKMHIL, 5: 121–22, 166.

103. *Ibid.*, pp. 174, 176–77.

104. *Ibid.*, pp. 122–24, 140–41.

105. *Ibid.*, p. 179.

106. Lists of brigand commanders appear in *ibid.*, pp. 199, 209.

107. P. 200; *Wen-shih-che*, 1958, no. 12, p. 32.

108. HHKMHIL, 5: 188–99.

109. *Ibid.*, p. 227.

110. Quoted in *Chin-tai Tung-pei jen-min ko-ming yün-tung shih*, p. 219.

111. The general feeling in the memoirs is that if the republican commander Lan T'ien-wei had taken the bull by the horns (he had strong support in the New Army), Chang Tso-lin's move, which was a tentative and rather stealthy affair, would have fallen through (HHKMHIL, 5: 546–47, 597–99). Lan certainly got frosty reception in Shanghai when he arrived there after escaping.

112. *Min-li pao*, Oct. 4; Li Shih-yüeh's article in LSYC, 1959, no. 6.

113. Based on biographical material collected while preparing this paper.

The Red Spears in the Late 1920's

1. *Tung-fang tsa-chih*, 24.21 (Nov. 10, 1927): 35–36; *Materialy po kitaiskomu voprosu* (Materials on the Chinese question; hereafter *Materialy*), no. 13 (1928), pp. 98–100.

2. Alexander Ivin, "Krasnye Piki" (Red Spears), in *Krestianskoe dvizhenie v Kitae* (Chinese peasant movements; Moscow, 1927); Ivin, *Ocherki partizanskogo dvizhenia v Kitae* (Sketches of the guerrilla movement in China, 1927–30; Moscow, 1930); Li Ta-chao, "Lu Yü Shan teng sheng ti Hung-ch'iang Hui" (The Red Spears in Shantung, Honan, Shensi, and other provinces), in *Li Ta-chao hsüan-chi* (Selected works of Li Ta-chao; Peking, 1959), pp. 564–70; Hsiang Yün-lung, "Hung-ch'iang Hui ti ch'i-yüan chi ch'i shan-hou" (Origin and prospects of the Red Spears Society), *Tung-fang tsa-chih*, 24.21 (Nov. 10, 1927): 21–27.

3. G.S. (an anonymous correspondent), "Krestianskoe vosstanie v Khenani, pis'mo iz Kitaia" (The peasant uprising in Honan: A letter from China), *Novyi vostok*, nos. 13–14 (1926), p. 4; *Hsiang-tao chou-pao*, no. 169 (1926), reprinted Tokyo, 1963, p. 1714; "Khenanskie 'Krasnye Piki,' iz dnevnika uchastnika Khenanskogo pokhoda" (The "Red Spears" of Honan, from the diary of a participant in the Honan campaign), *Materialy*, no. 10 (1928), p. 169.

4. The exchange rate was 3.5 *chiao* to one silver dollar; one *mou* equals 1/16 hectare.

5. "Khenanskie 'Krasnye Piki,' " p. 169.

6. Ivin, "Krasnye Piki," p. 12.

7. *Novyi vostok*, nos. 13–14, p. 3.

8. C. C. Geoffrey, "The Red Spears in China," in *China Weekly Review*, March 19, 1927; reprinted from the *Chinese Student Monthly* and translated in *Tung-fang tsa-chih*.

9. *Ibid.*, p. 35; *Li Ta-chao hsüan-chi*, p. 564.

10. Geoffrey, *loc. cit.*

11. Tanaka Tadao lists them beside the other organizations. Cf. text cited in *Chung-kuo chin-tai nung-yeh shih tzu-liao* (Materials on the history of modern Chinese agriculture; Peking, 1957), 2: 659.

12. "Khenanskie 'Krasnye Piki,' " p. 170; Hsiang, *loc. cit.*

13. Hsiao Hsiang, "Ho-nan Hung-ch'iang Hui pei Wu P'ei-fu chün-tui t'u-sha chih ts'an-chuang" (The pitiful state of the Red Spears after the massacre by Wu P'ei-fu's troops in Honan), *Hsiang-tao chou-pao*, June 16, 1926, pp. 1545–46.

14. This information on the regimen and statutes of the Red Spears comes from the *China Weekly Review*, March 19, 1927; Ivin, "Krasnye Piki," p. 24; "Khenanskie 'Krasnye Piki,' " p. 171; *Materialy*, no. 13, pp. 98–100. This scarcely Confucian feminism would later disappear from the statutes. We have no exact date for this disappearance, but it was certainly after the Red Spears fell increasingly under the direction or control of the local lesser gentry.

15. This superstition perhaps bears witness to the continuation of a Boxer tradition among the Red Spears. See "Khenanskie 'Krasnye Piki,' " pp. 171–72, where two examples of Red Spears prayers are given; Hsiang, *loc. cit.*; *Chung-kuo ch'ing-nien*, no. 47, p. 15; Ivin, "Krasnye Piki," pp. 84–85; and V. V. Visniakova-Akimova (Vera Akimova), *Dva goda v vosstavsem Kitae, 1925–27, Vospominania* (Memoirs of two years of insurrection in China, 1925–27; Moscow, n.d.), p. 138.

16. *Li Ta-chao hsüan-chi*, p. 567.

17. "Khenanskie 'Krasnye Piki,' " p. 173.

18. Ivin, "Krasnye Piki," pp. 83, 86–91; Li Chien, "Shan-tung ti Hung-ch'iang Hui" (The Red Spear Society in Shantung), *Chung-yang fu-k'an* (Wuhan), no. 31, 1927.

19. The sources used for this episode are G.S., p. 7; Ivin, "Krasnye Piki," pp. 25, 65ff; Hsiao Hsiang, pp. 1545–46; Hsiang, p. 35; Visniakova-Akimova, pp. 138–39; V. M. Primakov, *Zapiski volontera, grazhdanskaia voina v Kitae* (Notes of a volunteer in the Chinese civil war; Moscow, 1967), pp. 127–28; and *Li Ta-chao hsüan-chi*, p. 565.

20. Hsiao Hsiang, pp. 1545–46.

21. Ivin, *Ocherki*, p. 13; *Li Ta-chao hsüan-chi*, p. 565; Tzu Chen, "Fan Feng chan-cheng chung chih Yu-pei T'ien-men Hui" (The Society of the Heavenly Gate of northern Honan in the war against the Fengtien clique), *Hsiang-tao chou-pao*, no. 197 (June 8, 1927), pp. 2163–64; "Khronika" (Chronicle), in *Materialy*, no. 10 (1928), p. 194.

22. So Huai, "Ho-nan chün-shih chuang-k'uang yü cheng-chih chien-t'u" (The military situation and political future of Honan), *Hsiang-tao chou-*

pao, no. 169 (1926), p. 1713; Hsiang, p. 381. The number of secret society members in all of China may have been greater than two million; see Primakov, p. 126.

23. Tzu Chen, pp. 2163–64.

24. It should be noted here that the Black Spears were less puritanical than the Red Spears. On the differences mentioned in this paragraph, see Ivin, "Krasnye Piki," pp. 24–27; G.S., p. 5; and *Li Ta-chao hsüan-chi,* p. 566.

25. Ivin, "Krasnye Piki," p. 25.

26. *Materialy,* no. 13 (1928), pp. 98–100.

27. Visniakova-Akimova, p. 138.

28. Tzu Chen, pp. 2163–64.

29. "Ti-i-tz'u kuo-nei ko-ming chan-cheng shih-ch'i ti nung-min yün-tung" (The peasant movement during the first revolutionary war), *Chung-kuo hsien-tai shih tzu-liao ts'ung-k'an* (1953), p. 422.

30. Ivin, "Krasnye Piki," pp. 17–18.

31. Ivin, *Ocherki,* p. 13; personal communication from Lucien Bianco (see also his contribution to this volume), who consulted sources in the United States Department of State; E. F. Carlson, *The Chinese Army* (New York, 1940), p. 105.

32. Ivin, "Krasnye Piki," pp. 22–24.

33. Hsiang, p. 35.

34. Teng Ssu-yü, *The Nien Army and Their Guerrilla Warfare, 1851–1868* (The Hague, 1961), pp. 122, 128–29.

35. Gamble notes a "school teacher from Honan" as the organizer of the Red Spears in a village near T'ai-an in Shantung. For us, this would seem to be a special and late case. Cf. Sidney D. Gamble, *North China Villages: Social, Political, and Economic Activities Before 1933* (Berkeley, 1963), pp. 301–2. See also "Khenanskie 'Krasnye Piki,' " pp. 170, 171.

36. Yü Ch'ing, "Ho-nan Chang-te ti nung-min kai-k'uang" (The peasants of Chang-te, Honan), *Chung-kuo ch'ing nien,* no. 47 (1924), pp. 14–15.

37. Wang T'ien-chiang, "Shih-chiu shih-chi hsia pan chih Chung-kuo ti mi-mi hui-she" (Secret societies in China during the second half of the nineteenth century), *Li-shih yen-chiu,* 1963, no. 2, pp. 87, 83–100; see also T'ao Ch'eng-chang, "Chiao-hui yüan-liu k'ao" (Origins of the societies and sects), Ch'ai Te-keng et al., comps., *Hsin-hai ko-ming* (The Revolution of 1911; Shanghai, 1957), 99–100.

38. According to Wang T'ien-chiang, sects and associations are distinguished from one another in the following ways, among others: patriarchal system / equality among the "brothers"; peasant chiefs / non-peasant chiefs; attachment to religions and superstitions / the belief in certain divinities as moral exemplars; no relationship with the armies / influence among the troops.

39. See note 15 above.

Secret Societies and Peasant Self-Defense, 1921–1933

1. Cf. Lucien Bianco, "Les Paysans et la révolution: Chine, 1919–1949," *Politique étrangère,* 2–3 (1968): 117–42. The present study deals only with the 1920's and early 1930's; at the time it was written my most important source (the Diplomatic Archives of the U.S. State Department) was unavailable beyond December 31, 1933.

2. "When the forces of order heard the word *t'u-fei* [bandits], they jumped like a mouse who had heard a cat meow." Liu Po, "O-pei Hung-ch'iang Hui chih chen-hsiang" (The truth about the Red Spears of northern Hupeh), *Ko-ming chou-pao*, Sept. 1, 1929, p. 310 (hereafter cited as KMCP).

3. Akira Nagano, *Shina nōmin undō kan* (The peasant movement in China; Tokyo, 1933), p. 250.

4. Several examples may be found in *ibid.*, pp. 250, 251–53. For further details on all the information given above and in the next paragraph, see *ibid.*, pp. 247–68.

5. An important book on the background and structure of such local defense leagues has appeared since I prepared this article, namely, Philip A. Kuhn, *Rebellion and Its Enemies in Late Imperial China: Militarization and Social Structure, 1796–1864* (Cambridge, Mass.: Harvard University Press, 1970). Kuhn's study adds enormously to our knowledge of these organizations, and his observations suggest some similarities and differences between the nineteenth-century groups he discusses and the twentieth-century groups superficially touched on here. The similarities are obvious and suggest some link between the earlier groups and the later ones. Both the *tzu-wei t'uan* and the *pao-wei t'uan* of the Republican era may be compared to the *t'uan-lien* of the Ch'ing dynasty; the *ku tzu-wei t'uan* to the *yung* (the second-level organization described in Kuhn, p. 168); and the *lien-chuang-hui* or *lien-ts'un-hui* to Kuhn's "multiplex *t'uan*" (Kuhn, pp. 67–68), or, perhaps even better, to the *lang-yüeh* (Kuhn, pp. 127–28). Such similarities involve not only institutional patterns (levels of organization, etc.), but also such important characteristics as the fact that there were definite limits to the size of the defense leagues or confederations (Kuhn, p. 76). There may, however, be an important difference between the self-defense associations of the nineteenth century and their twentieth-century counterparts. The former were led by the gentry or other influential villagers; in fact, they were organized, at least at the time of the White Lotus Rebellion and the first part of the nineteenth century, under state control (Kuhn, pp. 49, 55, 62). During the Republican period, however, the state no longer controlled any of the institutions described in this paper, and the gentry itself apparently did not always play an active part in leading or organizing them. It may be that such groups gradually moved away from gentry control; we will not know until there has been far more research on "orthodox" local defense corps of the twentieth century (as opposed to the "heterodox" secret societies with which this book deals). If such a trend did occur, it would suggest that in the early twentieth century the rivalry between a threatened and degenerating central state and the local elite became a less significant issue on the local scene than the rivalry between a threatened and degenerating local elite and other rural classes.

6. Nagano, pp. 259–60.

7. *Ibid.*, p. 258.

8. *Ibid.*

9. See Roman Slawinski's paper in this volume.

10. Dept. of State, 893 43/1, Sept. 7, 1927. In addition to the series 893 43, which focuses particularly on the Red Spears, the best source on the Teng-chou incident is the monthly reports dispatched by Consul Webber (893 00 PR Chefoo).

276 Notes to Pages 216–22

11. Dept. of State, 893 00 PR Chefoo/8 (Nov. 1, 1928), p. 2, and 893 43/3 (Oct. 24, 1928).

12. Dept. of State, 893 00 PR Chefoo/14 (Feb. 2, 1929), p. 3.

13. *Ibid.*, PR Chefoo/15 (March 2, 1929), pp. 2–3.

14. *Ibid.*, PR Chefoo/16 (April 2, 1929), p. 12.

15. *Ibid.*, PR Chefoo/21 (Sept. 1, 1929), p. 13, and 893 43/2 (Sept. 12, 1929).

16. Two Mexican dollars per male member of each family. The special tax for each absent male was six dollars.

17. Dept. of State, 893 00 PR Chefoo/14 (Feb. 2, 1929), pp. 2–3.

18. At Shih-chia, near Teng-chou (*ibid.*, PR Chefoo/23, Oct. 2, 1929). See also PR Chefoo/22 (Oct. 12, 1929) and PR Chefoo/24 (Nov. 1, 1929). The burning of eighteen villages attracted attention even in the Comintern press (*Inprecorr*, Oct. 15, 1929, p. 2322: "Die Bauernbewegung in China").

19. Dept. of State, 893 00 PR Chefoo/25 (Dec. 3, 1929), pp. 2, 5, 6.

20. *Ibid.*, PR Chefoo/14 (Feb. 2, 1929), p. 3.

21. On the T'ung-hua incident, see *ibid.*, PR Mukden/2–5 (Jan. 2–April 17, 1928), and especially 893 00/9774 (Jan. 26, 1928) and 893 00/9891 (March 29, 1928).

22. In the case of T'ung-hua the concessions included relaxed fiscal measures and better credit arrangements. For details see *ibid.*, PR Mukden/5.

23. See in particular *ibid.*, 893 00/9870 (March 10, 1928), and KMCP, *passim* and conclusion, p. 321.

24. Dept. of State, 893 43 Sh/4 (May 3, 1929).

25. Dept. of State, 893 00/9870 (March 10, 1928).

26. Li Ta-chao, "Lu Yü Shan teng sheng ti Hung-ch'iang Hui" (The Red Spears in Shantung, Honan, Shensi, and other provinces), in *Li Ta-chao hsüan-chi* (Selected works of Li Ta-chao; Peking, 1959), p. 565.

27. Dept. of State, 893 00 PR Chefoo/18 (June, 1929).

28. *Ibid.*, PR Chefoo/21 (Sept. 1, 1929) and .../19 (July 1, 1929).

29. Tung Huan-jan, "Min-pei nung-ts'un ti i-chung shen-mi chieh-she" (A rural secret society in northern Fukien), *Chung-kuo nung-ts'un*, 4.2 (Feb. 1938): 81–86.

30. KMCP, p. 306.

31. *Ibid.*, p. 319.

32. *Ibid.*, p. 321. See also *ibid.*, pp. 307–8, 310, 312, for the close ties between the Red Spears and the district authorities. Compare the "political indeterminacy" of the groupings of the first two levels distinguished by Kuhn (pp. 179–80) and the "social indeterminacy" of the twentieth-century "heterodox hierarchy" described above.

33. Dept. of State, 893 00/10239. The author of this extremely interesting eight-page document, appended to the dispatch, was none other than J. L. Buck. He should have been very well informed, since he mentions an attempt at mediation that originated in the Agriculture and Forestry College of Nanking University, where he was teaching.

34. *Ibid.*, p. 2.

35. Compare a similar local war fought between Red Spears and Yellow Spears (Huang-ch'iang Hui; KMCP, p. 319), and two bloody battles between Red Spears bands from different villages (KMCP, pp. 310–11).

36. See, for example, Jean Chesneaux, *Secret Societies in China in the Nineteenth and Twentieth Centuries* (Ann Arbor: University of Michigan Press, 1971), pp. 187–91.

37. To the already well-known cases (dual membership, Mao's appeal to the Ko-lao Hui, etc.), we can now add several instances of collaboration between the Chinese Communist Party and the Big Knife Society in Fukien and Hupeh (Ho Lung's Army); see Dept. of State, 893 00 PR Foochow/50 (March 7, 1932) and 893 00/11541 (Hankow, June 17, 1931).

The I-kuan Tao Society

1. *Jen-min jih-pao*, Dec. 20, 1950.
2. *Nan-fang jih-pao*, May 20, 1950.
3. *Ibid.*
4. *Jen-min jih-pao*, Dec. 20, 1950.
5. *Nan-fang jih-pao*, May 20, 1953.
6. Li Shih-yü, *Hsien-tai Hua-pei mi-mi tsung-chiao* (Contemporary secret religious sects in North China; Chengtu, 1948). This work contains a brief history of the society and information about its religious teachings, its methods of disseminating propaganda among the people, its secret ceremonies and rites, and the canonical books used by its preachers and leaders. Li Shih-yü was a member of the society for three years, having joined in order to study its workings firsthand.
7. Willem Grootaers, "Une société secrète moderne I-Koan-tao: Bibliographie annotée," *Folklore Studies*, 5 (1946); "La Voie de l'Unité Foncière, Ji-Kouan-Tao," *Folklore Studies*, 6 (1947); "Une Séance de spiritisme dans une religion secrète à Péking en 1948," *Mélanges chinois et bouddhiques* (Brussels), 9 (1948–51).
8. The articles and correspondence published during the campaign to liquidate the I-kuan Tao are concerned exclusively with the negative aspects of the society's activity. In our opinion, this does not detract from the authenticity of these sources, especially since the facts they present coincide for the most part with the information furnished by Li Shih-yü.
9. *Ssu-ch'uan jih-pao*, June 3, 1951.
10. Sha K'o, "I-kuan Tao chen-hsiang" (The truth about the I-kuan Tao), in *Chien-chüeh ch'ü-ti I-kuan Tao* (Sian, 1951).
11. *Ibid.*
12. Li Shih-yü, p. 32.
13. *Lun-yü*, 4: 15. Alternatively, "My doctrine is that of an all-pervading unity."
14. Li Shih-yü, p. 32.
15. *Ibid.*, p. 46.
16. Sha K'o, p. 19.
17. *Ibid.*, p. 35.
18. Li Shih-yü, p. 45.
19. *Ibid.*, p. 48.
20. *Ibid.*, p. 35.
21. *Ssu-ch'uan jih-pao*, May 7, 1951; *Nan-fang jih-pao*, May 20, 1953.
22. Sha K'o, p. 25.
23. *Ssu-ch'uan jih-pao*, June 10, 1951.

24. *Ibid.*, June 3, 1951.

25. Wilfred I. Burchett, *China's Feet Unbound* (London: Lawrence and Wishart, 1952), p. 44.

26. Sha K'o, p. 13.

27. *Ibid.*, p. 12.

28. *Ssu-ch'uan jih-pao*, issues of March–June, 1951.

29. Sha K'o, p. 12. Fifteen members are unaccounted for.

30. *Ssu-ch'uan jih-pao*, June 10, 1951.

31. Li Shih-yü, p. 89.

32. *Nan-fang jih-pao*, May 20, 1953.

33. G. G. H. Dunstheimer (*T'oung pao*, 47.3: 336) writes that in 1943 the Japanese harried I-kuan Tao members in northern Shansi, but on balance the evidence is persuasive that the society as a whole and its top leaders collaborated with the Japanese occupation forces.

34. *Ssu-ch'uan jih-pao*, Feb. 8, 1951.

35. *Ibid.*, June 3, 1951.

36. *Hsin-Hua yüeh-pao*, no. 6 (20), 1951, p. 266; *Jen-min jih-pao*, Dec. 20, 1950.

37. *Hsin-Hua yüeh-pao*, no. 12 (14), 1950, p. 314.

Bibliography of Works Concerning Secret Societies

The following bibliography has been selected and compiled by the editor, with contributions of Japanese sources from Professors Masataka Banno and Yūichi Saeki.

Balfour, F. H. "Secret Societies in China," *Journal of the Manchester Geographical Society*, 7 (1891): 40–56.

Banno Ryokichi, "Shanhai Shōtōkai no hanran" (The Small Knife Society rebellion in Shanghai), *Rekishigaku kenkyū*, no. 353 (Oct. 1969), pp. 1–13.

Blackburn, Fei-ling (Fei-ling Davis). "Role and Organization of Chinese Secret Societies in the Late Ch'ing." Unpublished M.Phil. thesis, University of London, 1968.

Borodovskii, L. "Khunkhuzy" (The Hung Hu-tzu), *Entsiklopedicheskii slovar'*, (St. Petersburg, 1903), vol. 37a, book 74.

Brace, A. J. "Some Secret Societies of Szechwan," *Journal of the West China Border Research Society*, 8 (1936).

Butuzov, V. N. "Khunkhuzy vostochnoy Mongoliy" (The Hung Hu-tzu of Eastern Mongolia), *Kharbinskiy vestnik* (a supplement to the review *Zheleznodorozhnaya zhizn na Dalnem Vostoke*), 1911.

Ch'ai Te-keng et al., comps. *Hsin-hai ko-ming* (The Revolution of 1911). 8 vols. Shanghai, 1957.

Chang P'ing-tzu. "Wo so chih-tao ti Ma Fu-i" (The Ma Fu-i that I knew), in *Hsin-hai ko-ming hui-i-lu*, 2: 240.

Chang Tsu-t'ung. "T'ai-p'ing t'ien-kuo shih-ch'i Che-chiang ti Lien-p'eng t'ang ch'i-i" (The insurrection of the Lien-p'eng Lodge in Chekiang during the period of the Taiping), *Kuang-ming jih-pao*, April 22, 1965.

Chang Wen-ch'ing. *Nien-tang ch'i-i* (Nien insurrection). Shanghai, 1960.

Chao Chih-lien. "Chin-ch'ien Hui so-chi" (Brief notes on the Golden Coin Society), in *Chin-ch'ien Hui tzu-liao* (Materials on the Golden Coin Society). Shanghai, 1958.

[Chao Wei-pang]. "A Chinese Secret Society: The Rise and Growth of the Ch'ing Pang," *China Review* (London), 3.4 (1934).

———. "Secret Religious Societies in North China in the Ming Dynasty," *Folklore Studies*, 7 (1948): 95–115.

Chao Yüan-ying. "Hung-ping chi-shih" (Notes on the "Red Soldiers"), *Chin-tai shih tzu-liao*, no. 3, 1955.

Ch'en Chieh. *I-ho T'uan yün-tung shih* (History of the Boxer movement). Shanghai, 1931.

Ch'en, Jerome. "The Nature and Characteristics of the Boxer Movement, a

Morphological Study," *Bulletin of the School of Oriental and African Studies,* 18.2 (1960).

———. "Secret Societies," *Ch'ing-shih wen-t'i,* 1.3 (Feb. 1966): 13–16.

———. "Rebels Between Rebellions—Secret Societies in the Novel *P'eng Kung An," Journal of Asian Studies,* 29.4 (Aug. 1970): 807–22.

———. "The Origin of the Boxers," in Jerome Ch'en and Nicholas Tarling, eds., *Studies in the Social History of China and Southeast Asia* (Cambridge, Eng., 1970), pp. 57–84.

Ch'en Pai-ch'en. *Sung Ching-shih li-shih tiao-ch'a chi* (Studies of the history of Sung Ching-shih). Peking, 1957.

Ch'en Po-t'ao et al., comps. *Tung-kuan hsien-chih* (Gazetteer of Tung-kuan hsien). N.p., 1919.

Cheng P'ei-hsin. "Ta-ch'eng-kuo ti fan-Ch'ing ch'i-i" (The anti-Manchu uprising of Ta-ch'eng-kuo), *Shih-hsüeh yüeh-k'an,* no. 12, 1958.

Chesneaux, Jean. *Les Sociétés secrètes en Chine aux XIXᵉ et XXᵉ siècles.* Paris, 1965. English edition, *Secret Societies in China in the Nineteenth and Twentieth Centuries,* Ann Arbor, Mich., 1971.

Chiang Siang-tseh. *The Nien Rebellion.* Seattle, 1954.

Chiang Ti. *Nien-chün shih ch'u-t'an* (Preliminary studies of the Nien Army). Peking, 1956.

———. "Fu-chün" (The Army of the Turbans), *Hsin-shih hsüeh t'ung-hsün,* no. 10, 1956.

———. *Ch'u-ch'i Nien-chün shih ts'ung* (Historical essays on the early stage of the Nien Army). Peking, 1956.

———. "Lun T'ai-p'ing t'ien-kuo yü Nien-chün ti kuan-hsi" (On relations between the Taipings and the Nien), *Li-shih yen-chiu,* 1963, no. 3.

Chou P'ei-i (Chou Su-yüan). *Kuei-chou min-tang t'ung-shih* (The tragic history of the People's Party of Kweichow), in Ch'ai Te-keng et al., comps., *Hsin-hai ko-ming,* 6: 405–77. Originally published separately in 1937. The version in *Hsin-hai ko-ming* is a reprint of the 1937 edition collated with the author's manuscript.

Chu Lin. *Hung Men chih* (An account of the Hung Men). Shanghai, 1947.

Chung-hua Hung Men Lien-ho-hui ch'eng-li ta-hui t'e-k'an (Special publication for the inauguration of the Hung Men Federation in China). Shanghai, 1943.

Chung-kuo jen-min cheng-chih hsieh-shang hui-i, wen-shih tzu-liao yen-chiu wei-yüan-hui, ed. *Hsin-hai ko-ming hui-i-lu* (Recollections of the 1911 revolution). 6 vols. Peking, 1961–63.

Chung-kuo nung-min ch'i-i lun-chi (Collected essays on peasant insurrections in China). Peking, 1954.

Cohen, Paul A. *China and Christianity.* Cambridge, Mass., 1963.

Comber, Leon F. *A Chinese Secret Society in Malaya: A Survey of the Triad Society, 1800–1900.* New York, 1959.

Cordier, Henri. "Les Sociétés secrètes chinoises," *Revue d'ethnographie,* 7.1–2 (1888): 52–72. Also published separately (same title; Paris, 1888).

Coulet, G. *Les Sociétés secrètes en terre d'Annam.* Saigon, 1926.

Culin, S. "The I-hing or 'Patriotic Rising,' a Secret Society Among the Chinese in America," *Proceedings of the Numismatic and Antiquarian Society of Philadelphia for the Years 1887–89.*

Dautremer, J. *La Grande Artère de la Chine, le Yangzi*. Paris, 1911.

D'Enjoy, P. "Associations, congrégations, et sociétés secrètes en Chine," *Revue indochinoise*, Apr. 15, 1907.

Dillon, Richard H. *Hatchet Men: The Story of Tong Wars in San Francisco's Chinatown*. New York, 1962.

Dunstheimer, G. G. H. "Le Mouvement des Boxeurs: Documents et études publiés depuis la deuxième guerre mondiale," *Revue historique*, no. 470 (Apr.–June 1964), pp. 387–416.

———. "Religion et magie dans le mouvement des Boxeurs d'après les textes chinois," *T'oung Pao*, 47 (1959): 323–67.

Dusson, H. *Les Sociétés secrètes en Chine et en terre d'Annam*. Saigon, 1911.

Fang Shih-ming. *Shang-hai Hsiao-tao Hui ch'i-i* (Uprisings of the Small Knife Society in Shanghai). Shanghai, 1965.

Favre, B. *Les Sociétés secrètes en Chine*. Paris, 1933.

Favre, L. "Les Sociétés de frères jurés en Chine," *T'oung Pao*, 19 (1920): 1–40.

Fei Lieh. *Hung Men sou-mi* (Investigations of the secrets of the Hung Men). Macao, 1956.

Feng Tzu-yu. *Ko-ming i-shih* (Reminiscences of the revolution). 5 vols. Vols. 1–3 published in Chungking, 1939–43; republished in Shanghai, 1946–47, along with vols. 4–5.

Freedman, Maurice. "Immigrants and Associations: Chinese in Nineteenth-Century Singapore," *Comparative Studies in Society and History*, 3.1 (Oct. 1960).

Fromageot, H. *Mémoire sur l'organisation et le rôle des associations ouvrières et marchandes en Chine*. Paris, 1897.

Fukuda Setsuo. "Shindai himitsu kessha no seikaku to sono yakuwari, tokuni nōson shakai to no kankei ni oite" (Characteristics and role of secret societies during the period of the Ch'ing from the angle of their relations with rural society), *Shigaku kenkyū*, no. 61 (Feb. 1956).

Fung, Edmund S. K. "The T'ang Ts'ai-ch'ang Revolt," in *Papers on Far Eastern History* (Canberra: Australian National University), Mar. 1970.

Gamba, C. "Chinese Associations in Singapore," *Royal Asiatic Society Journal* (Malayan Branch), 39, part 2 (Dec. 1966): 123–263.

Geoffrey, C. C. "The Red Spears in China," *China Weekly Review*, Mar. 19, 1927; reproduced from the *Chinese Student Monthly*, 22.4 (1927): 27–29, published by Chinese students in the United States.

Glick, C., and Hong Sheng-hua. *Swords of Silence: Chinese Secret Societies Past and Present*. New York, 1947.

Groot, J. J. M. de. *Sectarianism and Religious Persecution in China*. 2 vols. Amsterdam, 1903–4.

Grootaers, Willem A. "Une société secrète moderne, I-Koan-tao: Bibliographie annotée," *Folklore Studies*, 5 (1946).

———. "Une Séance de spiritisme dans une religion secrète à Péking," *Mélanges chinois et bouddhiques*, 9 (1948–51).

Gützlaff, C. F. "On the Secret Triad Society of China," *Journal of the Royal Asiatic Society of Great Britain and Ireland*, 8 (1846).

Hamberg, T. *The Visions of Hung Siu-tshuen and the Origin of the Kwang-si Insurrection*. Hong Kong, 1854.

Hatano Yoshihiro. "Shingai kakumei chokuzen ni okeru nōmin ikki" (The peasant riots immediately preceding the 1911 revolution), *Tōyōshi kenkyū*, 13.1–2 (1954).

Hazama Naoki. "Santo Raiyō bōdō ron" (A discussion of the unrest at Laiyang, Shantung Province), *Tōyōshi kenkyū*, 22.2: 1–27.

Hirayama Shū (Hirayama Amane). *Chūgoku himitsu shakai shi* (History of secret societies in China). Shanghai, 1912.

————. "Shina kakumeitō oyobi himitsu kessha" (Secret societies and revolutionary parties in China), *Nippon Oyobi Nipponjin*, no. 569 (Nov. 1911). Chinese translation: *Chung-kuo pi-mi she-hui shih* (History of secret societies in China), Shanghai, 1912.

Hoffmann, J. "Triad Ritual," *Chinese Repository*, 18 (June 1849).

Horikawa Tetsuo. "Giwadan undōshi kenkyū josetsu" (Introduction to the study of the Boxers), *Tōyōshi kenkyū*, 23.3 (Dec. 1964).

Hoshi Ayao. "Shindai no suishu ni tsuite" (Sailors during the period of the Ch'ing), *Tōhōgaku*, June 12, 1956.

Howard, H. J. *Ten Weeks with Chinese Bandits*. London, 1927.

Hsiang Yün-lung. "Hung-ch'iang Hui ti ch'i-yüan chi ch'i shan-hou" (Origin and prospects of the Red Spears Society), *Tung-fang tsa-chih*, 24.21 (Nov. 10, 1927): 35–41.

Hsiao Hsiang. "Ho-nan Hung-ch'iang Hui pei Wu Pei-fu chün-tui t'u-sha chih ts'an-chuang" (The pitiful state of the Red Spears after the massacre by Wu Pei-fu's troops in Honan), *Hsiang-tao chou-pao*, June 16, 1926.

Hsiao I-shan. "T'ien-ti Hui ch'i-yüan k'ao" (A study of the origins of the Heaven and Earth Society), an introductory chapter to the following book.

————, ed. *Chin-tai pi-mi she-hui shih-liao* (Historical materials on modern secret societies). Peking, 1935; reprinted Taipei, 1965.

Hsieh Hsing-yao. *T'ai-p'ing t'ien-kuo ch'ien-hou Kuang-hsi ti fan-Ch'ing yün-tung* (The anti-Ch'ing movement in Kwangsi before and after the Taiping Rebellion). Peking, 1950.

Hsin-hai ko-ming. See Ch'ai Te-keng et al., comps.

Hsin-hai ko-ming hui-i-lu. See Chung-kuo jen-min . . . wei-yuan-hui, ed.

Hsü Huo-tuan. *Min-nan min-chün yen-i* (The epic of the people's army in southern Fukien). Singapore, 1939.

Huang Hai-an. *Liu Yung-fu li-shih ts'ao* (A draft biography of Liu Yung-fu). Taipei, 1936; new edition 1957.

Huang San-te. *Hung Men ko-ming shih* (History of the Hung Men Revolution). N.p., 1936.

Hughes, G. "The Small Knife Rebels: An Unpublished Chapter of Amoy History," *China Review*, 1 (1872–73).

Huston, James. "Chinese Secret Societies," *China Journal of Science and Arts*, vol. 9 (1928), nos. 4, 5, and 6; vol. 10 (1929), no. 1.

I-ho T'uan (The Boxers). 4 vols. Shanghai, 1951.

I-ho T'uan yün-tung chih lun-ts'ung (Collected essays on the Boxer movement). Peking, 1956.

Inaba Seiichi. "Shindai no himitsu kessha" (The secret societies in the Ch'ing period), *Shibun*, no. 5 (Oct. 1952), pp. 12–24.

Inoue Kobai (Inoue Susumu). *Hito* (The robbers). Shanghai, 1923.

Isaacs, Harold R. "Gang Rule in Shanghai," in *Five Years of Kuomintang Reaction* (a reprinting of articles from the *China Forum*), Shanghai, 1932.

Ivin, A. "Krasnye Piki" (Red Spears), in *Krestianskoe dvizhenie v Kitae* (Chinese peasant movements), Moscow, 1927.

James, Rev. F. H. "Secret Societies in Shantung," in *Records of the 1890 Missionary Conference*, Shanghai, 1890.

"Khenanskie 'Krasnye Piki' iz dnevnika uchastnika khenanskogo pokhoda" (The Honan "Red Spears," from the diary of a participant in the Honan campaign), *Materialy po kitaiskomu voprosu* (Material on the Chinese question), no. 1, 1928.

Kirin Academia Sinica. *Chin-tai Tung-pei jen-min ko-ming yün-tung shih* (Modern revolutionary of the Northeast). Ch'ang-ch'un, 1960.

Kitayama Yasuo. "Himitsu kessha to shingai kakumei" (Secret societies and the Revolution of 1911), *Rekishi kenkyū*, no. 1 (Nov. 1963), pp. 1–12.

"Ko-lao Hui shuo" (On the Ko-lao Hui), in T'ien-hsia ti-i shang-hsin jen, *Pi-hsieh chi-shih* (A record of facts to ward off heterodoxy), n.p., 1861.

Ku Hang. "Hung Hu-tzu ti sheng-huo-kuan" (The Red Beards' outlook on life), *Tung-fang tsa-chih*, 24.13 (1927).

Kubo Noritada. "Ikkandō ni tsuite" (On the I-kuan Tao), *Tōyō Bunka Ken-kyūjo kiyō*, no. 4 (March 1953).

———. "Ikkandō hokō" (Supplement to the treatise on the I-kuan Tao), *Tōyō bunka kenkyūjo kiyō*, no. 11 (Nov. 1956).

Kujirai Masako. "1853 nen chōkō karyūiki non nomin kigi" (The peasant revolt of 1853 in the lower Yangtze valley), *Ochanomizu shigaku*, no. 3 (Nov. 1960).

Kuo Hsi-jen. "Ts'ung-jung chi-lüeh" (Life in the field), in *Hsin-hai ko-ming*, 6: 60–103. Originally published separately in 1913.

Kuo T'ing-i, ed. *Chin-tai Chung-kuo shih-shih jih-chih* (A daily chronicle of modern Chinese history). 2 vols. Taipei, 1962.

Kuomintang Archives, comp. *Chung-hua-min-kuo k'ai-kuo wu-shih-nien wen-hsien* (Documents in celebration of the fiftieth anniversary of the founding of the Republic of China). Taipei, 1966.

Laai Yi-faai. "The Part Played by the Pirates of Kwangtung and Kwangsi Provinces in the T'ai-p'ing Insurrection." Unpublished Ph.D. dissertation, University of California, Berkeley, 1950.

Leboucq, P. *Associations de la Chine*. Paris, 1880. A collection of letters.

Li Chien. "Shan-tung ti Hung-ch'iang Hui" (The Red Spear Society in Shantung), *Chung-yang fu-k'an* (Wuhan), no. 31, 1927.

Li Chien-erh. *Liu Yung-fu chuan* (Biography of Liu Yung-fu). Taipei, 1938; new edition 1966.

Li Shih-yü. *Hsien-tai Hua-pei mi-mi tsung-chiao* (Contemporary secret religious sects in North China). Chengtu, 1948.

Li Ta-chao. "Lu Yü Shan teng sheng ti Hung-ch'iang Hui" (The Red Spears in Shantung, Honan, Shensi, and other provinces), in *Li Ta-chao hsüan-chi* (Selected works of Li Ta-chao), Peking, 1959.

Li Tung-shan. *Nien-chün ko-yao* (Songs and tales of the Nien Army). Shanghai, 1960.

Li Wen-chih. "T'ai-p'ing t'ien-kuo ko-ming tui pien-ko feng-chien sheng-ch'an kuan-hsi ti tso-yung" (The role of the Taiping Rebellion in the reform of feudal relationships of production), *Kuang-ming jih-pao*, Jan. 16, 1961, p. 310.

Liao T'ai-ch'u. "The Ko-lao Hui in Szechwan," *Pacific Affairs*, June 1947.

Liu Lien-k'o. *Pang-hui san-pai-nien ko-ming shih* (Three hundred years' revolutionary history of the secret societies). 2d ed., Macao, 1940.

Liu Po. "O-pei Hung-ch'iang Hui chih chen-hsiang" (The truth about the Red Spears of northern Hupeh), *Ko-ming chou-pao*, Sept. 1, 1929, pp. 306–21.

Liu Shih-liang. *Han-liu shih* (History of the Hung Men). Chengtu, 1946.

Lo Erh-kang. "Hung Ta-ch'üan k'ao" (A study of Hung Ta-ch'üan), in *T'ai-p'ing t'ien-kuo shih-shih k'ao* (Notes on the history of the Taiping Rebellion), Peking, 1955.

————. "T'ai-p'ing t'ien-kuo yü T'ien-ti Hui kuan-hsi k'ao-shih" (On relations between the Taipings and the Heaven and Earth Society), in *T'ai-p'ing t'ien-kuo shih-shih k'ao* (Notes on the history of the Taiping Rebellion; Peking, 1955), pp. 34–74.

————. *T'ien-ti Hui wen-hsien lu* (Documents of the Heaven and Earth Society). Shanghai, 1947.

Lo Han. "Documents of the Heaven and Earth Society," *Kwang-tung hsüeh-pao*, Jan. 1, 1937. (Also contained in the preceding work.)

Losza, P. "Khunkhuzy v Manchzhurii: Ocherki iz puteshestviya po Manchzhurii v 1897–1898 gg." (The Hung Hu-tzu in Manchuria: Sketches from travels through Manchuria in 1897–98), *Russkoe bogatstvo*, 6 (1902).

Lung Hsiang-san. *Hung Men chin-hsi kuan* (Observations on the Hung Men of yesterday and today). N.p., n.d.

————. *Hung Men wen-ta* (The catechism of the Hung Men). N.p., n.d.

Lyman, Stanford M. "Rules of a Chinese Secret Society in British Columbia," *Bulletin of the School of Oriental and African Studies*, 27.3 (1964).

————. "Chinese Secret Societies in the Occident: Notes and Suggestions for Research in the Sociology of Secrecy," *Canadian Review of Sociology and Anthropology*, 1.2 (1964).

Ma Ch'ao-chün. "Pang-hui chih" (Origins of the *pang-hui*), in *Chung-kuo lao-tung yün-tung shih* (History of the Chinese labor movement), Chungking, 1942; reprinted in Taipei (5 vols.), 1959.

Mao I-heng. "T'ai-p'ing t'ien-kuo yü T'ien-ti Hui" (The Taipings and the Heaven and Earth Society), *Shen-pao yüeh-k'an*, 4.1 (Jan. 1935).

Mao Tse-tung. "Su-wei-ai chung-yang cheng-fu tui Ko-lao Hui ti hsüan-yen" (Appeal from the Chinese Soviet Government to the Elder Brothers Society), *Tou cheng*, July 12, 1936.

Mason, C. W. *The Chinese Confessions of C. W. Mason (Ko-lao Hui)*. London, 1924.

McAleavy, Henry. *Black Flags in Vietnam: The Story of a Chinese Intervention*. London, 1968.

Milne, W. C. "The Triad Society in China," *Transactions of the Royal Asiatic Society of Great Britain and Ireland*, 1 (1825): 240–50.

Morgan, W. P. *Triad Societies in Hongkong*. Hong Kong, 1960.

Morita Akira. "Shindai suishu kessha no seikaku ni tsuite" (The basis of the sailors' associations during the Ch'ing), *Tōyōshi kenkyū*, 13.5 (Jan. 1955).

Morrison, R. "A Transcript in Roman Characters, with Translation, of a Manifesto in the Chinese Language Issued by the Triad Society," *The Journal of the Royal Asiatic Society of Great Britain and Ireland*, 1 (1834).

Muramatsu Yuji. "The Boxers in 1898–1899," *Annals of the Hitotsubashi Academy*, Apr. 1956.

———. "Some Themes in Chinese Rebel Ideologies," in A. F. Wright, ed., *The Confucian Persuasion*, Stanford, 1960.

Mury, Francis. "En Mandchourie: Les Hongouses," *Le Correspondant*, 214: 78 (Jan.–Mar. 1904).

———. "Un mois en Mandchourie avec les Houngouses," *Le Tour du monde*, 18 (1912).

Nadarov, I. "Khunkhuzy v Iuzhno-Ussuriiskom krae" (The Hung Hu-tzu on the South Ussurian border), *Voennyi sbornik*, 9 (1896).

Napier, S. "Can Mao Overcome the Secret Societies?" *Contemporary Review*, 197 (Jan. 1960): 27–28.

Newbold, T. J., and F. W. Wilson. "The Chinese Secret Triad Society of T'ien-ti-hui," *Journal of the Royal Asiatic Society of Great Britain and Ireland*, 6 (1840).

Nieh Ch'ung-ch'i. *Nien-chün tzu-liao pieh-chi* (Material on the Nien Army). Shanghai, 1958.

———. *Chin-ch'ien Hui tzu-liao* (Material on the Golden Coin Society). Shanghai, 1959.

Nien chün (Nien Army). 6 vols. Shanghai, 1953.

Nien-chün ku-shih chi (Collection of Nien Army stories). Shanghai, 1962.

"La Nouvelle Religion éclectique de la Chine," *Politique de Pékin*, Oct. 14, 1923; see also issues of Sept. 9, Sept. 23, and Oct. 7, 1923.

Ono Shinji. "Nenshi to Nengun: Shinmatsu nōmin sensō no ichi sokumen" (The Nien and the Nien Army: An aspect of the peasant wars at the end of the Ch'ing), *Tōyōshi kenkyū*, 20.1 (June 1961).

Palâtre, Père. "La Magie et le Nénuphar Blanc en Chine," *Missions catholiques*, 1878.

P'ao Ko nei-mu (Inside the P'ao Ko). Chungking, 1946.

Pelliot, Paul. "La Secte du Lotus Blanc et la Secte du Nuage Blanc," *Bulletin de l'Ecole Française d'Extrême-Orient*, 3.2 (Apr.–June 1903): 304–17; 4.1/2 (Jan.–June 1904): 436–40.

P'eng Tse-i. "Kuan-yü Hung Ta-ch'üan ti li-shih wen-ti" (Historical notes on Hung Ta-ch'üan), *Li-shih yen-chiu*, no. 9 (1957).

Pi-hsieh chi-shih (A record of facts to ward off heterodoxy). N.p., 1871 ed. First published in 1861 (see Paul A. Cohen, listed above, pp. 277–81, 365). Contains an appendix on the Ko-lao Hui.

Pickering, W. H. "Chinese Secret Societies and Their Origin," *Journal of the Royal Asiatic Society (Straits Branch)*, 1 (1878).

Playfair, G. M. H. "Chinese Secret Societies," *China Review*, 15 (1886–87).

Political Implications of Chinese Secret Societies. U.S. Office of Strategic Services, Research Analysis Branch, Washington, D.C., 1945.

Porter, D. H. "Secret Societies in Shantung," *Chinese Recorder*, 17 (1886).

Pouvourville, Albert de. "Révolution et sociétés secrètes en Chine," *Revue de Paris*, Mar. 1912.
Purcell, Victor. *The Boxer Uprising: A Background Study.* Cambridge, Eng., 1963.
Reynolds, C. N. "The Chinese Tongs," *American Journal of Sociology*, 40.5 (1935).
Röttger, E. H. *Geschichte der Bruderschaft des Himmels und der Erden, der kommunistischen Propaganda China's.* Berlin, 1852.
Rudokopov, V. N. "Khunkhuzy" (The Hung Hu-tzu), *Istoricheskii vestnik*, June 1910.
Saeki Tomi. *Shindai ensei no kenkyū* (Salt administration under the Ch'ing). Kyoto, 1956.
Sakai Tadao. "Gendai Shina ni okeru shūkyō kessha no kenkyū" (Study of religious organizations in contemporary China), *Tōa Kenkyū*, 1944.
―――. "Gendai Chūgoku ni okeru himitsu kessha" (Secret societies in contemporary China), *Kindai Chūgoku kenkyū*, 1948.
―――. "Minmatsu no Muikyō ni tsuite" (The Non-Action Sect at the end of the Ming), *Tōyō shigaku ronshū*, 4 (1954).
Sasaki Masaya. "Kampō sannen Amoi Shotokai no hanran" (Small Knife Society uprising at Amoy), *Tōyō gakuhō*, 45.4 (Mar. 1963).
―――. "*Hsien-feng* shinen *Kuang-tung T'ien Ti-hui* no hanran." See next entry.
―――. "Kampō yonen Kanton Tenchikai no hanran" (The revolts of the Heaven and Earth Society in Kwangtung during the fourth year of the reign of Hsien-feng), *Kindai Chūgoku Kenkyū Sentā ihō*, 2, 3 (1963).
―――. *Shinmatsu no himitsu kessha; zempen, Tenchikai no seiritsu* (The secret societies in the late Ch'ing period; Part 1, The Origins of the Heaven and Earth Society). Tokyo, 1970.
―――, comp. *Shinmatsu no himitsu kessha shiryō hen* (Collection of documents relating to secret societies in the late Ch'ing period). Tokyo, 1967.
Sawada Mizuho. "Raso no Muikyō" (The Non-Action Sect founded by Lo Tsu), *Tōhō shukō*, 1 (Oct. 1951), 2 (Sept. 1952).
―――. "Dōkō Hakuyōkyō shimatsu" (The White Sun Sect during the era of Tao Kuang), *Tōhōgaku ronshū*, 1 (Feb. 1954).
Sawazaki Kenzō. "Seikai Kōmanchi kai ni tsuite" (On the worldwide Red Beard Society), *Tōa jin bungakuhō*, Dec. 1942.
Schlegel, G. *Thian-Ti-Hwui, The Hung League.* Batavia, 1866.
Schram, Stuart. "Mao Tse-tung and the Secret Societies," *China Quarterly*, 3 (July–Sept. 1966).
Sha K'o. "I-kuan Tao chen-hsiang" (The truth about the I-kuan Tao), in *Chien-chüeh ch'ü-ti I-kuan Tao* (Suppression of the I-kuan Tao), Sian, 1951.
Shang-hai Hsiao-tao Hui ch'i-i shih-liao hui-pien (Collection of materials concerning the Small Knife insurrection in Shanghai). Shanghai, 1958.
Shao Hsün-cheng. "Mi-mi she-hui tsung-chiao ho nung-min chan-cheng" (Peasant wars and the religion of the secret societies), in *Chung-kuo feng-chien she-hui nung-min chan-cheng tao-lun chi* (Discussions on peasant wars in Chinese feudal society), Peking, 1962.

Shen Lan-sheng. "Hung-ch'iang Hui chih li-lun yü shih-chi" (Facts and theory about the Red Spears), *Chung-yang fu-k'an* (Wuhan), June 1927.

Shibuya Takeshi. "Shina no kaizoku oyobi dohi ni kansuru chōsa" (An inquiry concerning pirates and Chinese robbers), *Tōa keizai kenkyū*, Jan. 1928.

Shih, Vincent Y. C. *The Taiping Ideology: Its Sources, Interpretation, and Influences*. Seattle, 1967.

Shuai Hsüeh-fu. *Ch'ing Hung shu-yen: Chung-kuo pang-hui san-pai-nien ko-ming* (Origin of Ch'ing and Hung secret societies: the three-hundred-year revolution of Chinese secret societies). Taipei, 1960.

Skurkin, P. V. *Khunkhuzy, etnograficheskie rasskazy* (Ethnographic narratives of the Hung Hu-tzu). Harbin, 1924.

Sokovnin, Colonel Ts. "Khunkhuzy Manchzhurii" (The Hung Hu-tzu of Manchuria), *Voennyi sbornik*, 12 (1903).

Stanton, W. "The Triad Society," *China Review*, 21 (1894–95).

Suemitsu Takayoshi. *Shina no himitsu kessha to jizen kessha* (Secret societies and philanthropic societies in China). Tokyo, 1932.

Sung Ching-shih shih-liao (Material on the history of Sung Ching-shih), edited by Pei-ching Ta-hsüeh Wen-ke Yen-chiu So-pien (Peking University, Graduate School of Liberal Arts). Peking, 1953.

Sung Ching-shih tang-an shih-liao (Material and archives of Sung Ching-shih). Peking, 1959.

Sung Chung-k'an. "Fu Kuang-lin," in *Ssu-ch'uan Ko-lao Hui kai-shan chih shang-ch'üeh* (Discussions of the reform of the Elder Brothers Society in Szechwan), Chengtu, 1940.

Suzuki Chusei. "Shindai ni okeru shūkyō kessha no kenkyū" (Studies of religious organizations during the Ch'ing), *Tōyō Bunka Kenkyūjo kiyō*, Sept. 9, 1948.

Tai Hsüan-chih. "Pai-lien Chiao ti pen-chih" (The nature of the White Lotus Society), *Shih ta-hsüeh pao*, 24.1 (1967).

Tai Wei-kuang. *Hung Men shih* (History of the Hung Men). Shanghai, 1947.

Tan, Chester. *The Boxer Catastrophe*. New York, 1955.

T'ao Ch'eng-chang. "Che an chi-lüeh" (A brief account of the revolts in Chekiang), in *Hsin-hai ko-ming*, 3: 3–99.

———. "Chiao-hui yüan-liu k'ao" (Origins of the societies and sects), in *Hsin-hai ko-ming*, 3: 99–111; also in Hsiao I-shan, ed., listed above.

Teng Lun-pin et al., comps. *Hui-chou fu chih* (Gazetteer of Waichow prefecture). N.p., 1879.

Teng Ssu-yü. "The Problem of Taiping Connections with Secret Societies," in *New Light on the History of the Taiping Rebellion*, Cambridge, Mass., 1950.

———. "A Political Interpretation of Chinese Rebellions and Revolution," *Tsinghua Journal of Chinese Studies*, N.S. 3 (Sept. 1958).

———. *The Nien Army and Their Guerrilla Warfare*. Paris, 1961.

———. "Dr. Sun Yat-sen and the Chinese Secret Societies," in Robert K. Sakai, ed., *Studies on Asia*, 4 (Lincoln, Neb., 1963), pp. 81–99.

"T'ien-ti Hui wen-chien ch'ao-pen" (Documents and manuscripts of the

Heaven and Earth Society), British Museum, Oriental Section (8207, 2337).

"T'ien-ti Hui wen-shu" (Official Dispatches of the Heaven and Earth Society), in *T'ai-p'ing t'ien-kuo* (Taiping Heavenly Kingdom; Shanghai, 1953), vols. 1 and 2.

Topley, Marjorie. "The Emergence and Social Function of Chinese Religious Associations in Singapore," in *Contemporary Studies in Society and History*, 3 (1961): 289–314.

————. "The Great Way of Former Heaven: A Group of Chinese Secret Religious Sects," *Bulletin of the School of Oriental and African Studies*, 26.2 (1963).

Tso Chih-pai. "Li Yung-ho Lan Ch'ao-ting ch'i-i shih-mo" (The beginning and end of the insurrection of Li Yung-ho and Lan Ch'ao-ting), *Kuang-ming jih-pao*, April 14, 1955.

Tso Shen-ch'eng. "Che-nan Hung-chin Chün shih-liao chi-lu" (Collection of material for the history of the Red Turban Army in southern Chekiang), *Chin-tai shih tzu-liao*, no. 1, 1963.

Tung Huan-jan. "Min-pei nung-ts'un ti i-chung shen-mi chieh-she" (A rural secret society in northern Fukien), *Chung-kuo nung-ts'un*, 4.2 (Feb. 1938): 81–86.

Tzu Chen. "Fan-Feng chan-cheng chung chih Yü-pei T'ien-men Hui" (The Society of the Heavenly Gate in northern Honan during the war against Feng), *Hsiang-tao chou-pao*, no. 197 (June 8, 1927).

Ular, Alexandre. "L'Epopée communiste des proscrits mandchouriens," *Revue blanche*, 1901.

Wang T'ien-chiang. "Shih-chiu shih-chi hsia-pan chih Chung-kuo ti mi-mi hui-she" (Secret societies in China during the second half of the nineteenth century), *Li-shih yen-chiu*, no. 2, 1963.

Wang Yu-chuang. *The Organization of a Typical Guerrilla Area in South Shantung*, reproduced in Evans F. Carlson, *The Chinese Army: Its Organization and Military Efficiency*, New York, 1940.

————. "Tu Yüeh-sheng, 1888–1951," *Journal of Asian Studies*, May 1967.

Ward, J. S. M., and W. G. Stirling. *The Hung Society or the Society of Heaven and Earth*. 3 vols. London, 1925–26.

Wehrle, E. S. *Britain, China, and the Antimissionary Riots, 1891–1900*. Minneapolis, 1966.

Wei Chu-hsien. *Chung-kuo pang-hui* (Secret societies in China). Chungking, 1946.

"What Chinese Fugitive Soldiers and Hung Hu-tzu Are Capable of," *Dairen Chamber of Commerce* [Proceedings], 6 (1933).

Williams, S. Wells. "The Oath Taken by the Triad Society, and Notices of Its Origin," *Chinese Repository*, 17.6 (June 1849): 281–95.

Wylie, Alexander. "Secret Societies in China," in *Shanghai Almanac for 1854*, Shanghai, 1854.

Wynne, M. L. *Triad and Tabut: A Survey of the Origin of Chinese and Mohammedan Secret Societies in the Malay Peninsula, 1800–1935*. Singapore, 1941.

Yazawa Toshihiko. "Chōkō ryūiki kyōan no kenkyū" (The anti-foreign revolts of 1891), *Kindai Chūgoku kenkyū*, 1960.

Glossaries

1. Secret Societies

This and the following two glossaries were prepared by Sheriden Dillon, based largely upon the work of Mme. Flora Blanchon in the French edition. The translations proposed by Mr. Dillon are not to be considered definitive (cf. remarks pertinent to this point in the Introduction). Names and terms from papers that appear only in the French text have been retained.

Chai Chiao	斋教	Abstinence Sect, Vegetarians
Ch'ang-ch'iang Hui	長枪会	Long Spear Society
Ch'ang-mao Tao	長毛道	Way of the Long-Haired Ones
Ch'ang-sheng T'ang	長胜堂	Eternal Victory Lodge
Ch'ao Pang	潮邦	Ch'ao Gang
Chi-i T'ang	吉义堂	Good Fortune and Righteousness Lodge
Ch'i-hsia Shan	栖霞山	Mountain of the Setting Sun
Ch'i-sheng T'ang	起胜堂	Lodge of the Rising Victory
Chia-ying Pang	嘉应邦	Chia-ying Gang
Chiang-hu T'uan	江湖团	River and Lake Group
Chien Pang	連邦	Fukien Gang
Chien-tzu Hui	劍仔会	Fine Swords Society
Chih-kung T'ang	致会堂	Attain Impartiality Lodge
Chih-sung T'ang	智松堂	Wisdom and Pine Lodge
Chih-tao T'ang	至道堂	Achievement-of-the-Way Lodge
Chin-ch'ien Hui	金錢会	Golden Coin Society
Chin-chung Chao	金鈡罩	Golden Bells
Chin-lan Chiao	金兰教	Golden Orchid Sect
Chin-tan Chiao	金丹教	Golden Elixir Sect
Ch'in-sheng T'ang	欽胜堂	Respected Victory Lodge
Ch'ing-chin Hui	青巾会	Green Turban Society
Ch'ing Men	清門	Ch'ing League, lit. "Pure Family"
Ch'ing Pang	青邦	Green Gang
Ch'ing Pang	庆邦	Ch'ing Band
Ch'ing-shui Hui	清水会	Clear Water Society
Ch'ing-shui P'ao-ko	清水袍哥	Sworn Brothers of the Clear Water
Ch'ing-teng Chao	青灯照	Reflection of the Green Lamp
Chü-sheng Ho	聚胜和	Harmony of Assembled Victories
Chü-sheng T'ang	巨胜堂	Great Victory Lodge
Ch'ün-ho	群和	Harmony Within the Multitude

Ch'ün-ying Shan 群英山	Mountain of Assembled Heroes
Chung-hua Shan 中华山	China Mountain
Chung-i T'ang 忠义堂	Fidelity and Justice Lodge
Chung-nan Hui 終南会	Extreme South Society
Chung-nan Shan 終南山	Extreme South Mountain
Erh-kuan Tao 二貫道	Way of the Basic Duality
Fei-lung Shan 飞龙山	Flying Dragon Mountain
Fen-hsiang Chieh-meng 焚香結盟	Incense Burners' League
Fu-hsing She 复兴社	Restoration Society
Fu-hu Hui 伏虎会	Crouching Tiger Society
Fu-hua Shan 复华山	Restore China Mountain
Fu-hua She 复华社	Restore China Society
Fu-i T'ang 福义堂	Happiness and Equality Lodge
Fu Tang 幅党	Association of the Turbans
Fu-yu Shan 福有山	Happiness Mountain
Hai-nei-wai Hung Men Lien-ho Hui 海内外洪門联合会	Hung Men Federation in China and Overseas
Han-liu Hui 汉留会	Society for the Restoration of the Han
Hei-ch'i Chün 黑旗軍	Army of the Black Flags
Hei Chiao-men 黑教門	Black Sect
Hei Pang 黑邦	Black Gang
Ho-p'ing chih Kuang 和平之光	Light of Peace
Hou-t'ien Tao 后天道	Way of Latter Heaven
Hsi-shan Chiao 西山教	Western Mountain Sect
Hsi-wen Chiao 习文教	Literary Sect
Hsia-i She 俠誼社	Sect of the Knights Errant
Hsiao-hung-ch'i Hui 小紅旗会	Small Red Flag Society
Hsiao-i Hui 孝义会	Filial Piety and Righteousness Society
Hsiao-tao Hui 小刀会	Small Knife Society
Hsien-t'ien Ta-tao 先天大道	Great Way of Former Heaven
Hsin-an 新安	New Peace
Hsin-lien T'ang 信廉堂	Truthfulness and Confidence Lodge
Hsin-sheng Ho 新胜和	Harmony of the New Victory
Hsin-sheng T'ang 新胜堂	New Victory Lodge
Hsin-tang T'ang 信党堂	Confidence Association Lodge
Hsing-fu Hui 兴复会	Restoration Society
Hsing-Han Hui 兴汉会	Society for the Restoration of the Han
Hsing-hua Pang 兴化邦	Change and Prosperity Gang
Hua Shan 华山	China Mountain

Huang-ch'iang Hui	黄枪会	Yellow Spear Society
Huang Chiao	黄教	Yellow Sect
Huang Chiao-men	黄教門	Yellow Sect
Huang-han She	黄汉社	Yellow Han Society
Huang-hao Chün	黄号軍	Yellow Signal Army
Huang-yai Chiao	黄崖教	Huang-yai Sect
Hun-shui Pao-ko	渾水袍哥	Sworn Brothers of the Troubled Waters
Hung Chia	洪家	Hung Family
Hung-chiang Hui	洪江会	Hung River Society
Hung-ch'iang Hui	紅枪会	Red Spear Society
Hung Chiao	紅教	Red Sect
Hung Chiao-men	紅教門	Red Sect
Hung-chin Hui	紅巾会	Red Turbans Society
Hung-fu Hui	洪福会	Hung Prosperity Society
Hung-hao Chün	紅号軍	Red Signal Army
Hung-hsing Cheng-i Hui	洪兴正义会	Hung Prosperity and Justice Society
Hung-hsing Hsieh-hui	洪兴协会	Hung Prosperity Society
Hung-hsing T'ang	洪兴堂	Hung Prosperity Lodge
Hung Hu-tzu	紅胡子	Red Beards
Hung-i T'ang	洪义堂	Loyalty to the Hung Lodge
Hung Men	洪門	Hung Men or Hung League, lit. "Vast Gate"
Hung Men Chien-kuo Hui	洪門建国会	Hung Men Association for National Reconstruction
Hung Men Hui	洪門会	Hung Men Society
Hung Men Lien-ho Hui	洪門联合会	Hung Men Federation
Hung Pang	洪邦	Hung Band
Hung Pang	紅邦	Red Gang
Hung-sheng T'ang	洪胜堂	Hung Victory Lodge
Hung-shun T'ang	洪順堂	Hung Faithfulness Lodge
Hung-teng Chao	紅灯照	Reflection of the Red Lamp
Hung-teng Chiao	紅灯教	Red Lantern Sect
Hung-teng Hui	紅灯会	Red Lamp Society
Hung-yang Chiao	紅阳教	Red Sun Sect
I-heng T'ang	义衡堂	Discernment of Justice Lodge
I-ho Ch'üan	义和拳	Fists of Harmony and Justice (Boxers)
I-ho T'uan	义和团	Harmony and Justice Group
I-kuan Tao	一貫道	Way of Basic Unity
I She	益社	Utilitarian Society

I-sheng T'ang 义胜堂	Righteousness and Victory Lodge
Jen-i Hui 仁义会	Society of Humanity and Righteousness
Jen-wen T'ang 仁文堂	Benevolence and Culture Lodge
Kao-hua Hui 告化会	Prophets of Change Society
Ko-lao Hui 哥老会	Elder Brothers Society
Ko-ti Hui 哥弟会	Society of Brothers
Ku-yün Shan 峪云会	Clouds of the Valley Mountain
Kuang-i Kung-she 广益公社	Universal Benefit Society
Kuang-i T'ang 广义堂	Propagation of Equality Lodge
Kuang Pang 广邦	Kwangtung Gang
Kuang-shou T'ang 广寿堂	Longevity Lodge
Kuang-tan Hui 光蛋会	Shiny Egg Society
K'uang She 匡社	Assistance Society
Kuei-ken Men 归根門	Return-to-the-Root Sect
Kung-chin Hui 共进会	Society for Common Progress
K'ung-Meng Tao 孔孟道	Way of Confucius and Mencius
K'ung-ming Tao 孔明道	Way of Chu-ko Liang
Lan-teng Chao 蓝灯照	Reflection of the Blue Lamp
Lao An 老安	Ancient Peace
Lao-chün Hui 老軍君会	Society of the Ancient Masters
Lao-mu Tao 老母道	Way of the Old Mother
Lao-niu Hui 老牛会	Old Buffalo Society
Li-to T'ang 礼德堂	Rites and Virtue Lodge
Lien-ho T'uan 连合团	Community Group
Lien-i T'ang 联义堂	Continued Righteousness Lodge
Lien-p'eng Tang 蓮篷党	Lotus Mat Association
Lien-sheng T'ang 联胜堂	Common Victory Lodge
Lien-sheng T'ang 連胜堂	Successive Victories Lodge
Lin-lien She 邻联社	Union of Neighbors Society
Lo Chiao 罗教	Lo Sect
Lo-han T'ang 罗汉堂	Arhat Lodge
Lung-hua Hui 龍华会	Dragon Flower Society
Ma-ni Chiao 魔尼教	Mani Sect (Manichaeans)
Mi-le Chiao 弥勒教	Maitreya Society
Mi-mi Hui 祕密会	Society of the Great Secret
Miao Pang 庙邦	Temple Gang
Min-hsin She 民新社	Renovation of the People Society
Min-hsing She 民兴社	Restoration of the People Society
Niao T'ang 鸟堂	Bird Lodge
Nien Chün 捻軍	Nien Army
Nien T'ang 捻堂	Nien Lodge

Ning-po Pang	宁波邦	Ningpo Gang
Niu-t'ou Hui	牛头会	Cow's Head Society
Pa-kua Chiao	八卦教	Eight Trigrams Sect
Pa-shang T'ang	拨胜堂	Total Victory Lodge
Pai Chiao	白教	White Sect
Pai-hao Chün	白号軍	White Signal Army
Pai-lien Chiao	白蓮教	White Lotus Sect
Pai-lung Tang	白龍党	White Dragon Association
Pai-lung T'ang	白龍堂	White Dragon Lodge
Pai Pang	白邦	White Gang
Pai-pu Hui	白布会	White Cloth Society
Pai-shan Chiao	白扇教	White Fan Sect
Pai Shang-ti Hui	拜上帝会	God Worshippers' Society
Pai-yang Chiao	白阳教	White Sun Sect
Pai-yün Tsung-tui	白云纵队	White Cloud Regiment
P'an An	潘安	P'an Peace
P'an Chia	潘家	P'an Family
P'an Ch'ing	潘庆	P'an Celebration
P'an Men	潘門	P'an Gate
Pang Hui	棒会	Fraternity Society
P'ao Ko	袍哥	Brothers Wearing Robes of the Same Color
P'i-shou Hui	匕首會	Dagger Society
Pien-ch'ien Hui	編錢会	Strings of Cash Society
Po-tzu Hui	鉢子会	Cymbal Society
P'u-chi Ta-hui	普渡大会	Great Society for Universal Prosperity
P'u-chi Tsung-hui	普济總会	Alliance for Universal Welfare
P'u-tu Chiao	普渡教	Universal Crossing Sect
San-chieh Chiao	三阶教	Three Epochs Sect (Manichaeism)
San-ho Hui	三合会	Three Harmonies Society (Triads)
San-tien Hui	三点会	Three Dots Society (Triads)
Shang-hai Pang	上海邦	Shanghai Gang
Shen-ch'üan Chiao	神拳教	Boxing Sect
Sheng-hsien Chiao	圣賢教	Saints and Sages Sect
Sheng-p'ing T'ien-kuo	昇平天国	Heavenly Kingdom of Ascending Peace
Shih-chai Chiao	食斋教	Abstinence Sect
Shih-lung Shan	十龍山	Mountain of the Ten Dragons
Shuang-lung Hui	雙龍会	Double Dragon Society

Shuang-tao Chiao　双刀教	Double Knife Sect
Shuang-tao Hui　双刀会	Double Knife Society
Shun-t'ien Chiao　順天教	Fidelity to Heaven Sect
Ssu-cheng Hui　四正会	Four Corrections Society (Ko-lao Hui)
Ta-ch'eng Chiao　大乗教	Great Vehicle Sect
Ta-ch'eng Shan　大成山	Mountain of Great Success
Ta-chung-nan Shan　大終南山	Mountain of the Southern Limit
Ta-hua Shan　大华山	Great China Mountain
Ta-lu Shan　大陆山	Mountain of the Great Continent
Ta-lung Shan　大龍山	Great Dragon Mountain
Ta Ming-Ch'ing Chün　大明清軍	Great Army of the Ming and Ch'ing
Ta-sheng T'ang　大胜堂	Great Victory Lodge
Ta-tao Hui　大刀会	Big Knife Society
Ta-t'ung Hui　大同会	Society of the Great Harmony
Ta-t'ung Shan　大同山	Mountain of the Great Harmony
T'ai-hua Shan　泰华山	Tranquil Flower Mountain
T'ang-ch'iao Pang　塘桥邦	Ponds and Bridges Gang
Tao-k'o　刀容	Swordsmen
Tao-yu Hui　道友会	Friends of the Way Society
Te-yüan T'ang　德元堂	Beginning of Virtue Lodge
Teng-hua Chiao　灯花教	Sparks from the Lamp Sect
T'ieh-hsüeh Hui　鉄血会	Blood and Iron Society
T'ieh-pu Shan　鉄布山	Armor Mountain
T'ien-hua Shan　天花山	Heavenly Flower Mountain
T'ien-li Chiao　天理教	Sect of the Celestial Order
T'ien-lung Shan　天龍山	Celestial Dragon Mountain
T'ien-men Hui　天門会	Society of the Heavenly Gate
T'ien-shou Shan　天寿山	Celestial Longevity Mountain
T'ien-shui Chiao　天水教	Milky Way Sect
T'ien-tao Chiao　天道教	Heavenly Way Sect
T'ien-ti Hui　天地会	Heaven and Earth Society (Triads)
Ting-sheng T'ang　定胜堂	Certain Victory Lodge
Tou-mu T'an　斗母坛	Altar of the Bushel-Mother
Tsai-li Chiao　在理教	Observance Sect
Tsai-yüan Hui　在园会	In-the-Garden Society
Ts'ai T'ang　菜堂	Vegetarian Lodge
Ts'an-chün Hui　灿均会	Splendid Equality Society
Tung-hua T'ang　東花堂	Lodge of the Eastern Flower
Tung-shan Chiao　東山教	Eastern Mountain Sect

T'ung-chi Kung	同济公	League of the Common Well-being
T'ung-chi T'ang	同济堂	Common Welfare Lodge
T'ung-ch'ou Hui	同仇会	Society Against the Common Enemy
T'ung-pao She	同胞会	Compatriots Society
T'ung-shan She	同善社	Society of the Common Good
T'ung-sheng T'ang	同胜堂	Common Victory Lodge
T'ung-teng Shan	同登山	Common Ascension Mountain
Tzu-li Hui	自立会	Independence Society
Wan-ch'üan Chiao	万全教	Perfect Security Sect
Wei Pang	围邦	Circle Gang
Wen-hsien Chiao	文賢教	Culture and Wisdom Sect
Wu-chi Hui	無极会	Society of the Way Without End
Wu-chi Tao	無极道	The Way Without End
Wu-chou Hung Men	五洲洪門	Hung Men of the Five Continents
Wu-hang Shan (Wu-hsing Shan)	五行山	Mountain of the Five Elements
Wu-lun T'ang	五伦堂	Five Social Relations Lodge
Wu-sheng Shan	五圣山	Five Saints Mountain
Wu-tai Tang	烏帶党	Black Belt Society
Wu-wei Chiao	無為教	Non-action Sect
Yen Pang	烟邦	Opium Gang
Ying Lien	英联	Union of Heroes
Ying-tu Hui	硬肚会	Strong Stomachs Society
Yu-i Lien-huan She	友誼联欢社	Festival of Friendship Society
Yu-sheng T'ang	友胜堂	Friendship and Victory Lodge
Yün She	云社	Cloud Society
Yung-i Hui	义永会	Eternal Justice Society
Yung-lo Kung-she	永乐公社	Eternal Joy Society
Yung-sheng T'ang	勇胜堂	Heroic Victory Lodge

2. Persons Connected with Secret Societies

Chai Ho-ku 翟火姑	Triad
Chai Ming-chiang 翟明江	Hung Pang
Chang Ch'ang-sheng 張長生	Triad, Shanghai
Chang Chao 張剑 (alias, the Great Ram)	Triad, Canton
Chang Ch'eng-lu 張成陆	Triad, Shanghai
Chang Chih-han 張志汉	Hung Pang
Chang Chu-p'ing 張仵坪	Hung Pang, overseas
Chang Feng-hui 張風翅	Ko-lao Hui
Chang Hsien-tao 張先道	Hung Pang
Chang I-ch'en 張一尘	Triad, Shanghai
Chang Kao-yu 張高友	Triad, Kwangsi
Chang Kuei-ho 張貴和	Mi-fan Chu, Kwangsi
Chang Kung 張公	Ko-lao Hui
Chang Lao-min 張老敏 or Chang Min-hsing 張敏行	Nien
Chang Lo-hsing 張樂行 or Chang Lao-lo 張老樂 or Chang Lo-hsing 張洛行	Nien
Chang Lung 張龍	Triad, Kwangtung
Chang Meng-hu 張猛虎	Red Spears
Chang Pai-hsiang 張百祥	Hsiao-i Hui
Chang Pai-lin 張百麟	Ko-lao Hui
Chang Pai-ma 張白馬	Hung Hu-tzu
Chang Pao-shan 張保山	Shih-chai Chiao, Kweichow
Chang Ping-lin 張炳麟	Ko-lao Hui
Chang Shu-sheng 張树声	Green Gang
Chang T'ien-jan 張天然 or Chang Kuang-pi 張光壁	I-kuan Tao
Chang Tsung-yü 張宗禹	Nien
Chang Tzu-lien 張子廉	Triad, overseas
Chang Tzu-tang 張子党	Triad, Shanghai
Chang Wu-hai 張五孩	Nien
Chen An 奠安	Triad

Ch'en A-lin　陈阿林	Hsiao-tao Hui
Ch'en Chen-fang　陈真芳	Triad, Canton
Ch'en Cheng-ch'eng　陈正成	Hsiao-tao Hui
or Ch'en Ch'ing-chen　陈庆真	
Ch'en Chi　陈吉	Triad
Ch'en Ch'i-mei　陈其美	Green Gang
Ch'en Chiung-ming　陈炯明	Triad
Ch'en Hsing-wan　陈兴晚	Fu-i T'ang
Ch'en K'ai　陈开	Triad, Kwangtung
Ch'en Lan-ssu-chi　陈烂四屐	Triad
Ch'en Li-nan　陈礼南	Triad
Ch'en Nan　陈南	Triad
Ch'en P'ei-te　陈培德	Triad, Shanghai
Ch'en Shao-pai　陈少白	Triad
Ch'en Te-ts'ai　陈德才	Nien
Ch'en Tso-hsin　陈作新	Ko-lao Hui
Ch'en Ya-fu　陈亚夫	Triad, Shanghai
Ch'en Ya-hsiang　陳亜湘	Triad, Pai-shan Chiao
Cheng Shih-liang　郑士良	Triad
Cheng Tzu-liang　郑子良	Hung Pang
Chiang Chieh-shih　蒋介石	Green Gang
(Chiang Kai-shek)	
Chiao Ta-feng　焦达峰	Ko-lao Hui, Kung-chin Hui
Chiao Yü-ching　焦玉晶	Triad
or Chiao San　焦三	
Chien Pao-hsien　蹇宝賢	Ko-lao Hui, Szechwan
Chien Hsi-nung　蹇萘农	Ko-lao Hui, Szechwan
Ching T'ing-pin　景廷兵	I-ho T'uan
Ch'iu Erh　邱二	Triad, Kwangsi
Chou Chen-k'un　周鎮坤	Triad, Shanghai
Chou Fu-ch'en　周拂塵	Triad, Shanghai
Chou Han-ch'ing　周汉鄉	Hung Pang
Chou Hsun-yü　周迅予	Hung Pang, Szechwan
Chou Li-ch'un　周立春	Triad
Chou Po-kan　周伯甘	Triad, Shanghai
Chou Shao-t'ien　周少田	Triad, overseas
Chu Cho-wen　朱卓文	Hung Pang
Chu Hsiu-san　朱秀三	Chin-ch'ien Hui, Chekiang
Chu Hung-ying　朱洪英	Sheng-p'ing T'ien-kuo, Kwang-tung
Chu I-kuei　朱一貴	Triad, Fukien
Chu Lin　朱琳	Triad, Shanghai
Chu Lin-fu　朱林夫	Triad, Shanghai

Chu Te (Chu Teh)　朱德	Ko-lao Hui
Chü Cheng　居正	Ko-lao Hui
Ch'ü Chen-han　翟振汉	Red Turbans, Chekiang
Chung Tzu-t'ing　鍾紫庭	Triad
Fan Shao-tseng　范紹增	Ko-lao Hui, Szechwan
Fan Yün-ch'ing　范云卿	Ko-lao Hui, Szechwan
Fang Mao-shan　方茂山	Hung Pang
Feng Yün-shan　馮云山	Pai Shang-ti Hui
Han Ku-ming　靽谷明	Red Spears
Han Lao-wan　靽老万	Nien
Han Lin-erh　韓林兒	White Lotus
Han Shan-t'ung　韓山童	White Lotus
Ho I-min　何益民	Hung Pang, Hong Kong
Ho Liu　何六	Triad
Ho Lung　賀龍	Ko-lao Hui
Ho Te-sheng　何德胜	Shih-chai Chiao, Kweichow
Ho Wan　何晚	Triad, Kwangsi
Ho Wen-ch'ing　何文庆	Lien-p'eng Tang, Chekiang
Hou Shih-wei　侯士侍	Nien
Hsia Chang　夏昌	Shih-chai Chiao, Kweichow
Hsiang Fo-shih　頊佛時	Triad, Shanghai
Hsiang Hai-ch'ien　向海潜	Hung Pang
Hsiang Sung-p'o　向松坡	Hung Pang, Shanghai
Hsieh Fen-sheng　謝慎生	Hung Pang, Hong Kong
Hsieh Tsuan-t'ai　謝纘泰	Triad
Hsiung K'o-wu　炁克武	Ko-lao Hui
Hsü Feng-hsiang　許風翔	Triad, Shanghai
Hsü Huai-li　徐怀礼	Hung Pang
Hsü I　徐逸	Hung Pang
Hsü Lang-hsi　徐朗西	Hung Pang, Shanghai
Hsü T'ing-chieh　徐廷杰	Shih-chai Chiao, Kweichow
Hsü Wu　徐五	Kwangsi bandit
Hsü Hsi-lin　徐錫麟	Ko-lao Hui, Kuang-fu Hui
Hsü Hsing-kuei　許星桂	Triad
Hsü Yao　徐耀	Lo-han T'ang
Hsü Ying　許英	Kuang-i T'ang
Hsü Yüeh-kuei　許月桂	Triad
Hu Li-min　胡利民	Triad, Shanghai
Hu Yu-lu　胡有禄	Sheng-p'ing Tien-kuo, Kwangtung
Huang Chao-kuan　黃昭观	Mi-fan Chu, Kwangsi
Huang Chin-jung　黃金荣	Green Gang

Huang Chin-liang	黃金亮	Triad, Kwangsi
Huang Fu	黃福	Triad
Huang Hui-lung	黃惠龍	Triad, overseas
Huang Kuang-hua	黃光华	Triad, Kwangtung
Huang Lien-pin	黃联宾	Triad, Shanghai
Huang San-te	黃三德	Triad, overseas
Huang (Tao-shih)	黃道士	Ko-lao Hui, Taoist priest
Huang Wei	黃威	Hsiao-tao Hui, Fukien
Huang Yao-t'ing	黃耀庭	Triad
Huang Yu-lin	黃玉林	Triad
Hung Shao-chih	洪少楨	Triad, overseas
Hung Ta-ch'üan	洪大全	Triad
or T'ien Te	天德	
or Chiao (Ch'iao) Liang 焦(侨)亮		
Jan T'ien-yüan	冉天元	Hung Pang
Jen Chu	任柱	Nien
Jen Han-ch'ing	任汉卿	Hung Pang, Szechwan
Jen Wen-ping	任文炳	Triad, Canton
Kan Hsien	甘先	Triad, Canton
Kao Han-sheng	高汉声	Triad, Shanghai
Kuan Jen-fu	关仁甫	Triad
K'uang Shih-ming	匡世明	Ko-lao Hui, Kiangsu and Fukien
Kung Ch'un-t'ai	龚春台	Triad, Hunan
Kung Te	龚德	Nien
Lai Wen-kuang	賴文光	Nien
Lan Ch'ao-ting	蓝朝鼎	Fen-hsiang Chieh-meng, Yunnan,
or Lan Ta-shun	蓝大顺	Szechwan
Lei Pen-chou	雷本洲	
Lei Tsai-hao	雷再浩	Triad, Hunan
Li Chao-shou	李昭寿	Nien
Li Ch'eng-po	黎澄波	Nien
Li Chi-t'ang	李紀堂	Triad, overseas
Li Fu-lin	李福林	Green Gang
Li Hsien-chih	李咸池	Triad
Li Hsien-yün	李仙云	Hsiao-tao Hui, Shanghai
Li Hung	李洪 (鴻)	Ko-lao Hui
or Li Hsien-mo	李顯謀	
or the Grand Marshal		
Li K'ai-ch'en	李凱臣	Triad, Shanghai
Li Ping-ch'ing	李炳青	Triad, Shanghai

Li Shao-i 李紹裔   Hsiao-i Hui
Li Shih-chin 李式金   Triad
Li Shih-chung 李世忠   Ko-lao Hui
Li Ta-chieh 李大姐   Hung Pang
Li Teng-po 李登波
Li Yüan-fa 李沅发   T'ien-ti Hui, Hunan
Li Yung-ho 李永和   Fen-hsiang Chieh-meng, Yunnan,
                                         Szechwan

Liang Chih-ch'ing 梁之庆   Triad, overseas
Liang Chiu-hsi 梁九喜   Triad
Liang Jui-hua 梁瑞华   Triad, Kwangtung
Liang Ming-ch'ing 梁明青   Mi-fan Chu, Kwangsi
Liang P'ei-yu 梁培友   Triad, Kwangsi
Liang Ta-p'ao 梁大砲   Triad
Liang Ya-chang 梁亞長   Kwangsi pirate
Liao Hai-ch'eng 廖海澄   Hung Pang, Szechwan
Liao Sung-pai 廖松柏   Hung Pang, Szechwan
Lin A-fu 林阿福   Hsiao-tao Hui
Lin Shuang-wen 林爽文   Triad, Taiwan
Lin Tzu-yüan 林則阮   Triad, Shanghai
Lin Yu-min 林有民   Hung Pang
Ling Erh-mei 淩二姝   Mi-fan Chu, Kwangsi
Ling Shih-pa 淩十八   Triad
  or Liu Pa 刘八
Ling Ya-tung 淩亚東   Triad, Kwangsi
Liu Chan-k'ao 刘占考   Ch'ang-ch'iang Hui, Shantung
Liu Chih-tan 刘志丹   Ko-lao Hui
Liu Erh-lao-yüan 刘二老渊   Nien
  or Liu Yü-yüan 刘玉渊
  or Liu Kou 刘狗
Liu Hui-min 刘惠民   Ko-lao Hui
Liu I-shun 刘仪順   Shih-chai Chiao, Kweichow
Liu K'o-p'in 刘克斌   Triad, Shanghai
Liu K'uan-wu 刘冠五   Triad, overseas
Liu Li-ch'üan 刘丽川   Triad, Hsiao-tao Hui, Shanghai
Liu Meng-li 刘梦梨   Hung Pang, Hong Kong
Liu Po-ch'in 刘伯琴   Triad, Hong Kong
Liu San-niang 刘三娘   Nien
Liu Tao-i 刘道一   Triad
Liu Wan-kung 刘皖公   Triad, overseas
Liu Yao-shou 刘耀寿   Triad, Shanghai

Liu Yung-ching 刘永敬	Nien
Liu Yung-fu 刘永福	Black Flags
or Liu I 刘毅	
or Liu Chien-yeh 刘建业	
or Liu Yüan-t'ing 刘渊亭	
or Liu Erh 刘二	
Lo P'ei-san 罗培三	Triad, Shanghai
Lo Ta-kang 罗大細	Triad, Canton
Lou Pai-hsün 娄百循	Red Spears, Honan
Lu Hsin-chiao 陆梓樵	Triad, Shanghai
Lu Jung-t'ing 陆荣廷	Black Flags
Lu Yün-sheng 路云生	Triad, Shanghai
Lung Ch'ing-ch'üan 龍清泉	Triad, Shanghai
Lung Hsiang-san 龍襄三	Hung Pang, Shanghai
Lung Ming-chien 龍鳴劍	Ko-lao Hui
Ma Fu-i 馬福益	Ko-lao Hui, P'u-chi Tsung-hui
Ma I-hua 馬逸华	Hung Pang
Mao Shih-fu 毛士福	Shih-chai Chiao, Kweichow
Mao Ta 毛大	Shih-chai Chiao, Kweichow
Mao Wei-yüan 毛位元	Shih-chai Chiao, Kweichow
Mei Chi-ting 梅济鼎	Shih-chai Chiao, Kweichow
Mei Kuang-p'ei 梅光培	Triad, Shanghai
Miao P'ei-lin 苗沛霖	Nien
Ming Te 明應	Triad, Shanghai
or Ming Jun-shen 明潤身	
Ni Kuang-ho 倪广和	Ch'ang-ch'iang Hui, Shantung
Ou Ch'i 欧启	Triad, Kwangtung
Pai Tzu-hou 白子侯	Hung Pang, Szechwan
Pai Yü-shan 白玉山	Hung Pang, Shanghai
P'an Ch'i-liang 潘起亮	Pai-lung T'ang
P'an Ch'ing 潘庆	Green Gang, mythical founder
P'an Ta 潘达	Triad, Shanghai
P'an Yüeh-heng 潘月恒	Triad, overseas
P'eng Huan-chih 彭焕知	Triad, Shanghai
Pi Yung-nien 畢永年	Ko-lao Hui
She Ying 余英	Ko-lao Hui
or She Ching-ch'eng 余意成	
Su San-niang 苏三娘	Triad, Canton
Su T'ien-fu 蘇添福	Nien
Sun Chung-shan 孫中山	Triad
or Sun Yat-sen 孫逸仙	

Sun K'uei-hsin 孫葵心	Nien
Sun Po-ch'ün 孫伯群	Hung Pang
Sun Wu 孫武	Ko-lao Hui
Sung Chi-p'eng 宋繼鵬	Yen-hsien Chiao
Sung Ching-shih 宋景詩	White Lotus
Szu-t'u Mei-t'ang 司徒美堂	Triad, overseas
T'ai Li 太理	Green Gang
T'an Jen-feng 譚人風	Ko-lao Hui
T'ang Chan-yün 湯展云	Triad, overseas
T'ang Shao-wu 唐紹武	Ko-lao Hui
T'ang Ts'ai-ch'ang 唐才常	Tzu-li Hui, Fu-yu Shan
T'ao Ch'eng-chang 陶武章	Ko-lao Hui, Lung-hua Hui
Teng Hsing-ch'üeh 刄兴雀	Triad, Kwangsi
Teng K'eng 鄧鏗	Triad
Teng Yin-nan 刄荫南	Ts'an-chün Hui
T'ien Fang 田芳	Triad, Canton
or the Great Carp	
T'ien Te-sheng 田德胜	Hung Pang, Szechwan
Ting Chu-ch'ing 丁竹卿	Ko-lao Hui, Szechwan
Ting Tzu-huang 丁子璜	Triad, Shanghai
Ts'ai Hsiao-chieh 蔡小姐	Nien
Ts'ai Yüan-p'ei 蔡元培	Ko-lao Hui
Tso Ya-fu 鄒亚夫	Ko-lao Hui
Tu Yüeh-sheng 杜月笙	Green Gang
Wang Ch'ao-hsiung 王超雄	Ko-lao Hui
Wang Chi-i 王紀益	Triad, overseas
Wang Chih-pen 王知本	Hung Pang, Shanghai
Wang Chin-fa 王金发	Pang Hui, Chekiang
Wang Chung-san 王仲三	Triad, Shanghai
Wang Ho-shun 王和順	Triad, Kwangsi
Wang I-p'ing 王一平	Triad, overseas
Wang Kuang-chi 王广継	Ch'ang-ch'iang Hui, Shantung
Wang Lai-feng 王来風	Ch'ang-ch'iang Hui, Shantung
Wang Shih-lin 王士林	Kwangsi bandit
Wang T'ien-chieh 王天杰	Ko-lao Hui
Wang T'ien-tsung 王天縱	Swordsmen
Wang Yü-ch'eng 王禹丞	Hung Pang, Szechwan
Wei Shih-hsiao 韋世尭	Mi-fan Chu, Kwangsi
Wen Ch'ün-ch'ing 文純鄕	Triad, Shanghai
Wu Chu-yüan 吳朱元	Triad
Wu Erh 吳二	Kwangsi bandit (Triad)
Wu Pi-ling 吳必灵	Kwangsi bandit

Wu Ya-chung 吳亚終	Triad
or Wu Chung 吳忠	
or Wu A-chung 吳阿忠	
Wu Yü-chang 吳玉璋	Ko-lao Hui, Kung-chin Hui
or Wu Yung-shan 吳永珊	
Wu Yüan-ch'ing 吳元清	Triad
or Wu Hsi 吳四	
or Wu Ling-yün 吳淩云	
Yao Keng-pai 姚庚白	Triad, Shanghai
Yeh Sheng 叶声	Hung Pang, Kwangtung
Yeh Ying-liang 叶寅亮	Triad, Shanghai
Yu Lieh 尤列	Triad
Yü Tung-ch'en 余棟臣	Ko-lao Hui (?)
or Yü Man-tzu 余蛮子	
Yüan Hsi-fan 原洗凡	Hung Pang

3. Secret Society Terminology

an-hsien　暗綫　　"Hidden Thread" (I-kuan Tao division)

cheng-lung-t'ou　正龍头　　Chief Dragon Head (Ko-lao Hui dignitary)

ch'eng-hsiung　成兄　　Mature Brother, Introducer (Ko-lao Hui)

ch'i　旗　　banners, rebel units

Ch'i-hsin chiu　齐心酒　　"wine that unites hearts"

chiao-fei　教匪　　bandits who belonged to religious sects

chiao-men　教門　　religious sects

Chieh-fu chi-p'in　却富济貧　　"Rob the rich, help the poor"

chieh-hui shu-tang　結会树党　　formation of illegal leagues (Ch'ing Code)

Chieh-lüeh tien-k'u　却掠典庫　　"Plunder the pawnshops and state treasuries"

chien-min　賤民　　common people

ch'ien-fang　前房　　"Avant-garde," the five principal lodges (Triad)

ch'ien-jen　前人　　the ancients (I-kuan Tao)

chih-t'ang　執堂　　Registrar (Ko-lao Hui office)

ch'ih-shui fang-shui　喫水放水　　"Drink water and let it flow," egoism

ch'ih-ya　吃鴨　　"eat ducks," piracy (Triad)

chin-chih shih-wu hsieh-shu　禁止师巫邪術　　prohibition of heretical practices and witchcraft (Ch'ing Code)

chin-pu-huan　金不换　　"gold not exchanged," secret documents (Ko-lao Hui)

ch'ing-yang　青阳　　Blue Sun (Manichaeans, I-kuan Tao, White Lotus)

ch'iung-kuang-tan　穷光蛋　　"poor shiny eggs," the poor (Nien)

Ch'u-pao an-liang　除暴安良　　"Drive out the tyrants; assure peace to good men"

ch'uai-hsien　踹綫　　"walk on a thread," follow a route (Ko-lao Hui)

ch'uan-shih 傳師	Master Who Transmits the Doctrine (Red Spears, Society of the Heavenly Gate, etc.)
chüan-hsi pi-hsing hsieh-shu 傳習避刑邪術	art of propagating perverse ideas capable of immunizing one against legal punishment (Ch'ing Code)
ch'üan-tzu 圈子	ring : affairs of members (Ko-lao Hui)
chung-i 忠义	loyal and righteous
chung-i t'ang 忠义堂	Hall of Fidelity and Righteousness (Triad)
erh tsung 二宗	the Two Principles (Manichaeism)
fa-ping 法兵	soldier of the law
Fan-Ch'ing fu-Han 反清复汉	"Overthrow the Ch'ing, restore the Han"
Fan-Ch'ing fu-Ming 反清复明	"Overthrow the Ch'ing, restore the Ming"
fei chiao 匪教	rebel sects
Fen-chieh fu-hao 焚却富豪	"Burn and rob the rich and the powerful"
fu-fei 幅匪	bandits with turbans
fu-lung-t'ou 副龍头	Deputy Dragon Head (Ko-lao Hui dignitary)
hai-pi 海皮	"all-out change," universal revolution
hai-ti shu 海地书	Sea and Land Book (Ko-lao Hui documents)
Han liu 汉留	heritage of the Han
hei-ch'i kuan-shih 黑旗管事	Keeper of the Black Flag (Ko-lao Hui office)
hou-fang 后房	"Rear Guard," the five secondary lodges (Triad)
hsiang-chang 香長 hsiang-chu 香主	Incense Master (Ko-lao Hui office)
hsiang-ming 香名	incense name (one of four names of all secret societies in the South)
hsiao-chiu 小九	Small Nine (Ko-lao Hui title)
hsiao-fei 梟匪	"bandits of the night," salt smugglers
hsiao-man 小滿	Lesser Sufficiency (Ko-lao Hui title)
hsiao-ming wang 小明王	Minor Illuminated King (Manichaeism)
hsiao-p'ai 小牌	Small Placard (Triad rank)

hsiao-yao	小幺	Lesser Youngest (Ko-lao Hui title)
hsieh-chiao	邪教	heretical sect
hsien	綫	"thread," route (Ko-lao Hui)
hsien-feng	先鋒	Vanguard (Triad rank)
hsin-fu	心复	Advisor, lit. "mind and belly" (Ko-lao Hui dignitary)
hsin-tsai-hsüan	新在玄	"new to the secret," new member (Ko-lao Hui)
hsing-i	刑意	popular boxing, South China
hsing-t'ang	刑堂	Supervisor of Punishments (Ko-lao Hui dignitary)
hsiung-ti	兄弟	brother (Triad)
hsün-feng	巡風	Lookout, lit. "patroller of the wind" (Ko-lao Hui dignitary)
hsün-lao	熏老	"age from smoke," opium (Ko-lao Hui)
hu-chiang	虎将	Tiger Generals, legendary founders of the Triads
hua-ch'i	花旗	rebels of diverse obedience
huang-lien sheng-mu	黃蓮聖母	Holy Mother of the Yellow Lotus (Boxers)
hui-fei	会匪	bandit, member of secret society
hui-fu Chung-kuo	恢复中國	restoration of China
hui-t'ang	会党	secret society
hui-tao-men	会道門	secret societies and sects (People's China)
hung-ch'i kuan-shih	紅旗管事	Red Flag Leader (Ko-lao Hui office)
Hung-fei	洪匪	bandit who claims to support the Ming
hung-hua	紅花	"red flowers," alcoholic drink (Ko-lao Hui)
hung-kun	紅棍	Red Pole or "Enforcer" (Triad office)
hung-shun t'ang	洪順堂	a lodge name
hung-yang	洪阳	Red Sun
i-chung	义忠	justice and faithfulness
i-hsing jen tan-ch'a hsüeh-ting meng fen-piao chieh-pai ti-hsiung 異姓人但敢血訂盟焚表結拜弟兄		the crime of gathering people of different clans into fraternities through blood sacrifice and ritual oaths (Ch'ing Code)
jen-hsia	任俠	knights errant (also chivalry, "Robin-Hoodism")
k'ai-shan	开山	"open a mountain," gather for a meeting (Ko-lao Hui)

k'ai-t'ai 开枱	"set the stage," initiation rite (Triad)
k'ao-hsün 靠熏	"depend on smoking," opium smoker (Ko-lao Hui)
ko-fei 戈匪	bandit armed with a spear
k'o 客	"strangers," marginal social elements
k'ou-hao 口号	code terms used as passwords (Ko-lao Hui)
ku-kung 股肱	Pillar (Ko-lao Hui title)
ku tzu-wei t'uan 傶自卫团	mercenary self-defense group, village military organization
Kuan-pi min-fan 官逼民反	"When officials exploit, let the people revolt"
kuan-shih-che 管事者	President of the Meeting (Ko-lao Hui initiation ceremony)
kuang-kun 光棍	"bare sticks," single men, secret society members
kuei-shih 柜尪	Treasurer (Ko-lao Hui office)
k'uei-chün 潰军	routed soldiers
kun-fei 棍匪	bandit armed with a club
lao erh 老二	Second Brother (Ko-lao Hui dignitary)
lao san 老三	Third Brother (Ko-lao Hui dignitary)
lao-ta-ko 老大哥	Elder Brothers (Ko-lao Hui chiefs)
lao t'uan shih 老团师	veteran chief (Red Spears group leader)
li-t'ang 理堂	Manager (Ko-lao Hui dignitary)
lien-chuang hui 联莊会	association of united villages, village leagues
lien-ts'ün hui 联村会	association of united villages
ling-ch'i 領旗	banner commander (Nien)
lü-lin 綠林	"green forests," forest bandits, outlaws
lung-t'ou 龍头	Dragon Head (Hung Pang office; chief of a Ko-lao Hui lodge)
lung-t'ou chih lung-t'ou 龍头之龍头	Dragon Head of Dragon Heads (Ko-lao Hui dignitary)
ma-tsei 馬賊	mounted bandit
ma-tzu 馬子	"colt," uninitiated (Ko-lao Hui)
men 門	gate (Triad lodge)
men-sheng 門生	disciples
meng-cheng 盟証	oath-taker (Ko-lao Hui)

mi-fan chu　米飯主 — Rice hosts or masters (Kwangsi rebels)

mi-mi hsieh-hui　秘密协会 — secret society

mi-mi she-hui　秘密社会 — secret society

Mieh-Ch'ing fu-Ming　灭清复明 — "Annihilate the Ch'ing and restore the Ming"

Mieh-Man hsing-Han　灭满兴汉 — Destroy the Manchus and restore the Han

ming-hsien　明綫 — "Visible Thread" (I-kuan Tao division)

ming-wang　明王 — Illustrious King (Manichaeism)

mo-fan　没犯 — treason (Ch'ing Code)

mo-p'an　没叛 — rebellion (Ch'ing Code)

Mu-yang Ch'eng　木楊城 — City of Poplars (City of Willows)

nei-ko ta-ch'en　内閣大臣 — high officers of the inner council (Ko-lao Hui)

nei-kuan shih　内管事 — Director of Internal Affairs (Ko-lao Hui)

nei-lün　内論 — insubordination (Ch'ing Code)

nei-pa t'ang　内八堂 — Lodge of the Inner Eight (Ko-lao Hui)

ni-fei　逆匪 — rebels

nü-kuang kun　女光棍 — "female bare sticks," female members (Ko-lao Hui)

pa-ch'u erh-wa　把出耳挖 — "unstop the ears," pillage the stores (Triad)

pa-p'ai　八牌 — Eight Placards, members from unclean trades (Ko-lao Hui)

pai-chih-shan　白紙扇 — White Paper Fan (Triad dignitary)

pai-shan　白扇 — White Fan (Triad rank)

pai-yang　白阳 — White Sun (Manichaeans, I-kuan Tao, White Lotus)

pang-hsiung　邦兄 — state brother (Ko-lao Hui)

pao　宝 — "treasure" (enrollment card of new Ko-lao Hui member)

pao-chü　抱举 — guarantor (Ko-lao Hui, initiation rite)

pao-wei t'uan　保卫团 — self-defense guards, peasant militia

Pao-yang mieh-Man　保洋灭满 — "Protect the foreigners, destroy the Manchus"

p'ao-ko　袍哥 — brothers, lit. "of the same robe" (Ko-lao Hui)

p'ao-p'i nao　袍皮鬧 — Revolt of the Scorchers

pei 被   passive of *to be*: "to be captured" (Ko-lao Hui)

p'ei-t'ang 陪堂   Deputy-Seating-the-Hall (Ko-lao Hui office)

p'ing-tzu 餅子   "cakes," pieces of silver money (Ko-lao Hui)

san chi 三际   Three Moments (Manichaeism)

san hsin 三辛   Three Plagues (I-kuan Tao)

san tsai 三灾   Three Calamities (Buddhism)

san-ts'ai tan-chu 三才坛主   Guardian of the Three Forces (heaven, earth, men; I-kuan Tao)

sao-ch'ing sheng 扫清生   barbers (Ko-lao Hui code)

Sha-fu chi-p'in 殺富給貧   "Kill the rich, give to the poor"

Shan-chu 山主   Master of the Mountain (Ko-lao Hui title)

Shan-kan jen-min 煽惑人民   stir up the passions of the people (Ch'ing Code)

shan-ming 山名   mountain name, one of the four names of every secret society in the South

shan-t'ang 山堂   mountain lodge

she-t'an 設坛   to build an altar

shen-chia pu ch'ing-pai 身家不清白   man without honor (Ko-lao Hui)

shen-hu-hsi 深呼吸   deep breathing (Red Spears)

shen-ping 神兵   supernatural soldiers (Szechwan peasants, 1920)

sheng-hsien 聖賢   Sage and Worthy (Ko-lao Hui office)

Sheng-p'ing T'ien-kuo 升平天國   Heavenly Kingdom of the Ascending Peace

shih-ch'i 十旗   ten flags: distribution of rebel units

shih-chieh 十戒   ten prohibitions (Ko-lao Hui)

shih-o 十恶   ten capital crimes

shou 首   leaders, chiefs

shou-kuei 收柜   Receptionist (Ko-lao Hui rank)

shu 韦   "book," prison (Ko-lao Hui)

shu-ts'ai chang-i 疏財仗义   to make voluntary contributions based on justice

shui-ming 水名   water name, one of the four names of every secret society in the South

shun-t'ien hsing-tao 順天行道   Follow the will of heaven, put the Way into practice ta che-ku 打鷓鴣   "hunt the partridge," to rob along the major routes (Triad)

Ta-ch'eng Kuo 大成國   Kingdom of Great Achievement

ta-chiu 大九   Great Nine (Ko-lao Hui title)

Ta-fu chi-p'in 打富济貧   "Down with the rich, aid the poor"

Ta-Han Kuo 大汉国   Empire of the Great Han

Ta-Han Meng-chu 大汉盟主   Chief of the Alliance of the Great Han (Nien)

Ta-Han Ming-ming Wang 大汉明命王   King of the Great Han who received the Mandate of Heaven

ta-ko 大哥   Elder Brother (bandits)

Ta-kuan pu ch'in-min 打官不侵民   "Down with bureaucrats, do not harm the people"

ta-man 大滿   Greater Sufficiency (Ko-lao Hui title)

Ta-Ming Kuo 大明國   Empire of the Great Ming (Hung Societies)

ta-ming wang 大明王   Major Illuminated King (Manichaeism)

ta-p'ai 大牌   "great placards," military divisions (Triad)

ta-ta-yu 打大游   "leave on a cruise," attack a village (Triad)

ta-t'ung 大同   great harmony

ta-yao 大么   Greater Youngest (Ko-lao Hui title)

ta yüan-shuai 大元帥   Grand Marshal (Triad)

tai-ma 帶馬   Horse-leaders (founders of the Triad)

tan-chia (Tanka) 蛋家   "egg family," fishermen in the Southeast

t'an-chu 坛主   Guardian of the Altar (I-kuan Tao)

tang-chia 当家   Master of the House (Ko-lao Hui dignitary)

t'ang-k'ou 堂口   to enter the lodge (Triads)

t'ang-ming 堂名   lodge name, one of the four names of every secret society in the South

tao-chang 道長   Dean (I-kuan Tao)

tao-li 道理   reason, principle

Tao-shih 道师   Taoist master

t'ao-yüan chieh-i 挑园結义   to bind oneself by an oath of fraternity in the peach garden

ti-hui 弟会	fraternity (Triad)
t'i-t'ien hsing-jen 替天行仁	to practice humanity in the name of heaven
t'i-t'ien hsing-tao 替天行道	to practice the Way in the name of heaven
t'iao-pan sheng 跳板生	code for *yu-ling*, jugglers, acrobats, etc. (Ko-lao Hui)
t'ieh-pan 鉄板	code for "boots" (Triads)
tien-ch'uan shih 点传师	preacher
t'ien-p'ing sheng 天平生	sedan-chair carriers (Ko-lao Hui)
t'o-pa-tzu 扡把子	Man at the Helm, Pilot (Ko-lao Hui dignitary)
t'ou-hai 抖海	"shaking the seas" (Ko-lao Hui ceremony)
t'ou-mu 头目	leader (Ko-lao Hui)
tsai-li 在理	to obey a prohibition
ts'ao-hsieh 草鞋	"Straw Sandals" (or "Grass Sandal" Officers), those who receive and transmit information (Triads)
tsei-wo 贼窝	robbers' nest
tso-t'ang 坐堂	Judge, lit. "seating-the-hall" (Ko-lao Hui dignitary)
tso-tao i-tuan chih shu 左道異端之術	practice of heresy and false doctrine (Ch'ing Code)
tsu 祖	deceased master
tsung-t'uan shih 总团师	General (Red Spears)
tsung-t'ung-ling 总統領	Commander-in-chief (Red Spears)
t'u 徒	an ordinary member (as opposed to *shou*)
t'u-fei 土匪	local bandits
t'ung-ling 統領	Chief (Red Spears)
tzu-wei t'uan 自卫团	self-defense militia, peasant association
wai-kuan shih 外管事	Director of External Affairs (Ko-lao Hui)
wai-pa t'ang 外八堂	Lodge of the Outer Eight (Ko-lao Hui)
wang 王	King (Black Flags)
wei-wu yao-tzu 威武窑子	"war-threatening brothel," yamen (Ko-lao Hui)
wen-t'uan pu 文团部	civil department (Red Spears)
wu-hu chiang 五虎将	Five Tiger Generals (Triad)
wu-lei hung-shen 五雷裹身	annihilation by the five thunderclaps (I-kuan Tao)

wu-sheng fu-mu 無生父母   Eternal Parents, lit. "parents without birth" (I-kuan Tao)

wu-sheng lao-mu 無生老母   Eternal or Unbegotten Mother, lit. "old mother without birth"

wu-t'uan pu 武团部   military department (Red Spears)

yao-chiao 妖教   witchcraft sect

yao-p'ing 腰凭   sign of recognition

yen-fei 烟匪   bandit who smuggles opium

yen-fei 塩匪   bandit who smuggles salt

Yen-ling kuo-chu 廷齡国主   Prince of Yen-ling (Kwangsi rebels, 1860–70)

yin-chiao 淫教   degenerate or depraved sect

yu-min 游民   vagabond

yu-shih 游士   wandering scholar

yu-yung 游勇   soldier

Yü-huang Ta-ti 玉皇大帝   Great Jade Emperor

yüan-tzu 原子   original son (I-kuan Tao)

4. Chinese and Japanese Authors of Works Listed in the Bibliography

Chinese and Japanese authors whose works are in English may be omitted from this glossary.

Banno Ryōkichi　坂野良吉
Ch'ai Te-keng　柴德賡
Chang P'ing-tzu　張平子
Chang Tsu-t'ung　張祖桐
Chang Wen-ch'ing　張文清
Chao Chih-lien　超之謙
Chao Wei-pang　趙衛邦
Chao Yüan-ying　趙沅英
Ch'en Chieh　陳結
Ch'en Pai-ch'en　陳白尘調查記
Ch'en Po-t'ao　陳伯陶
Cheng P'ei-hsin　郑佩鑫
Chiang Siang-tseh　蔣湘澤
Chiang Ti　江池
Chou P'ei-i (Chou Su-yüan)
　周培藝（周素園）
Chu Lin　朱琳
Fang Shih-ming　方詩銘
Fei Lieh　飞烈
Feng Tzu-yu　馮自由
Fukuda Setsuo　福田節生
Hatano Yoshihiro　波多野善大
Hazama Naoki　狹間直樹
Hirayama Shū (Amane)　平山周
Horikawa Tetsuo　堀川哲男
Hoshi Ayao　星斌夫
Hsiang Yün-lung　向云龍
Hsiao Hsiang　蕭湘
Hsiao I-shan　蕭一山
Hsieh Hsing-yao　謝興堯
Hsü Huo-tuan　許火段
Hu Hsiang-yun　胡翔雲
Huang Hai-an　黃海安

Huang San-te　黃三德
Inaba Seiichi　稻葉誠一
Inoue Kobai (Susumu)
　井上紅梅
Kitayama Yasuo　北山康夫
Ku Hang　孤航
Kubo Noritada　窪德忠
Kujirai Masako　鯨井允子
Kuo T'ing-i　郭廷以
Li Chien　李建
Li Chien-erh　李健兒
Li Shih-yü　李世瑜
Li Ta-chao　李达剑
Li Tung-shan　李東山
Li Wen-chih　李文治
Liu Lien-k'o　刘联珂
Liu Po　六波
Liu Shih-liang　刘师亮
Lo Erh-kang　罗尔细
Lo Hsiang-lin　羅香林
Lung Hsiang-san　龍襄三
Ma Ch'ao-chün　馬超係
Mao I-heng　毛以享
Mao Tse-tung　毛泽东
Morita Akira　森田明
Nieh Ch'ung-ch'i　聶崇岐
Ono Shinji　小野信爾
P'eng Tse-i　彭澤益
Saeki Tomi　佐伯富
Sakai Tadao　酒井忠夫
Sasaki Masaya　佐々木正哉
Sawada Mizuho　澤田瑞穗
Sawazaki Kenzō　澤崎堅造

Sha K'o　沙克

Shao Hsün-cheng　邵循正

Shen Lan-sheng　申蘭生

Shibuya Takeshi　澁谷剛

Shuai Hsüeh-fu　帅学富

Suemitsu Takayoshi　末光高之

Sung Chung-k'an　宋仲堪

Suzuki Chusei　鈴木中正

Tai Hsüan-chih　戴玄之

Tai Wei-kuang　戴魏光

T'ao Ch'eng-chang　陶成章

Teng Lun-pin　鄧掄斌

Tso Chih-pai　鄒知白

Tso Shen-ch'eng　鄒身城

Tung Huan-jan　董煥然

Tzu Chen　子真

Wang T'ien-chiang　王天奬

Wang Ying-lou　王映樓

Wei Chu-hsien　衛聚賢

Wu Hsiang-hsiang　吳湘相

Yazawa Toshihiko　矢澤利彦

Index

Index